Discrete Math in Coding Theory

Discrete Math in Coding Theory

Guest Editor

Patrick Solé

MDPI

Basel • Beijing • Wuhan • Barcelona • Belgrade • Novi Sad • Cluj • Manchester

Guest Editor
Patrick Solé
I2M
Aix-Marseille University
Marseilles
France

Editorial Office
MDPI AG
Grosspeteranlage 5
4052 Basel, Switzerland

This is a reprint of the Special Issue, published open access by the journal *Entropy* (ISSN 1099-4300), freely accessible at: https://www.mdpi.com/journal/entropy/special_issues/DBJG0P13L5.

For citation purposes, cite each article independently as indicated on the article page online and as indicated below:

Lastname, A.A.; Lastname, B.B. Article Title. *Journal Name* **Year**, *Volume Number*, Page Range.

ISBN 978-3-7258-6216-0 (Hbk)
ISBN 978-3-7258-6217-7 (PDF)
https://doi.org/10.3390/books978-3-7258-6217-7

Contents

About the Editor

Patrick Solé

Patrick Solé received the Ingénieur and Dr.-Ing. degrees from Ecole Nationale Supérieure des Télécommunications, Paris, France, in 1984 and 1987, respectively, and the Habilitation á Diriger des Recherches from Université de Nice Sophia Antipolis, Sophia Antipolis, France, in 1993. He has held visiting positions with Syracuse University, Syracuse, NY, USA, from 1987 to 1989; Macquarie University, Sydney, Australia, from 1994 to 1996; and Lille University, Lille, France, from 1999 to 2000. Since 1989, he has been a permanent member of CNRS, with rank of "Directeur de Recherche" since 1996. He is currently a member of the CNRS Lab, I2M, Marseilles, France. His research interests include coding theory (codes over rings and quasi-cyclic codes), interconnection networks (graph spectra and expanders), vector quantization (lattices), and cryptography (Boolean functions and pseudorandom sequences).

Preface

Discrete mathematics, as opposed to continuous mathematics, broadly comprises algebra, combinatorics, geometry, and number theory. From Shannon's counting arguments and Assmus–Mattson's theorem to Goppa's estimates, it is safe to say that all these fields have contributed to coding theory. The Special Issue collected some interesting papers in this field. More specifically, the following areas (the list is not exhaustive):

- Codes and finite geometry: Space–time codes, rank metric codes, AG codes, and Boolean functions;
- Codes and combinatorics: Designs, maximal codes, few-weight codes, and Hadamard matrices;
- Algebraic coding theory: Codes over rings and modules, and codes as ideals and modules over rings;
- Algorithms for effective construction and efficient decoding;
- Character sums: Gauss sums; exponential sums for explicit enumeration.

Patrick Solé
Guest Editor

entropy MDPI

Article

Bounds on the Probability of Undetected Error for q-Ary Codes

Xuan Wang [1], Huizhou Liu [2] and Patrick Solé [3,*]

[1] School of Mathematical Sciences, Anhui University, Hefei 230601, China; wang_xuan_ah@163.com
[2] State Grid Anhui Electric Power Co., Ltd., Hefei 230601, China; 18756027866@163.com
[3] I2M, CNRS, Aix-Marseille Univetsity, Centrale Marseille, 13009 Marseilles, France
* Correspondence: patrick.sole@telecom-paris.fr

Abstract: We study the probability of an undetected error for general q-ary codes. We give upper and lower bounds on this quantity, by the Linear Programming and the Polynomial methods, as a function of the length, size, and minimum distance. Sharper bounds are obtained in the important special case of binary Hamming codes. Finally, several examples are given to illustrate the results of this paper.

Keywords: error correcting codes; probability of undetected error; linear programmming

1. Introduction

Let $A = \{a_1, \ldots, a_q\}$ be an *alphabet* with q distinct symbols, where $q \geqslant 2$ and the alphabet do not have any structure. For instance, A can be $\mathbb{F}_q$, the finite field with q elements, or $\mathbb{Z}_q$, the ring of integers modulo q. Moreover, a linear $[n, k]$ code is a subspace of the vector space $\mathbb{F}_q^n$ and k is the dimension of the subspace. For every two vectors $\boldsymbol{x}$, $\boldsymbol{y} \in A^n$, the (Hamming) distance $d_H(\boldsymbol{x}, \boldsymbol{y})$ between $\boldsymbol{x}$ and $\boldsymbol{y}$ is defined as the number of coordinates where they are different. A nonempty subset C of A^n with cardinality M is called a q-ary (n, M) code, whose elements are called *codewords*. The minimum distance d of the code C is the minimum distance between any two different codewords in C. The distance distribution of C is defined as

$$A_i = \frac{1}{M}|\{(\boldsymbol{x}, \boldsymbol{y}) : \boldsymbol{x}, \boldsymbol{y} \in C, d_H(\boldsymbol{x}, \boldsymbol{y}) = i\}|, \quad i = 0, 1, \ldots, n. \tag{1}$$

Assume that the code C is used for error detection on a discrete memoryless channel with q inputs and q outputs. Each symbol transmitted has a probability $1 - p$ of being received correctly and a probability $p_q = p/(q-1)$ of being transformed into each of the $q - 1$ other symbols. It is natural to let $0 \leqslant p \leqslant (q-1)/q$. Such a channel model is called a q-ary symmetric channel $qSC(p)$. When such a code is used on the symmetric q-ary channel $qSC(p)$, errors occur with a probability $\frac{p}{q-1}$ per symbol.

Let $\boldsymbol{x} \in C$ be the codeword transmitted and $\boldsymbol{y} = \boldsymbol{x} + \boldsymbol{e} \in \mathbb{F}_q^n$ be the vector received, where $\boldsymbol{e} = \boldsymbol{y} - \boldsymbol{x}$ is the error vector from the channel noise. Obviously, $\boldsymbol{e} \in C$ if and only if $\boldsymbol{y} \in C$. Note that the decoder will accept $\boldsymbol{y}$ as error free if $\boldsymbol{y} \in C$. Clearly, this decision is wrong, and such an error is not detected. Thus, when error detection is being used, the decoder will make a mistake and accept a codeword which is not the one transmitted if and only if the error vector is a nonzero codeword [1,2]. In this way, the probability that the decoder fails to detect the existence of an error is called the probability of undetected error and denoted by $P_{ue}(C, p)$, which is defined as

$$P_{ue}(C, p) = \sum_{j=1}^{n} A_j \left(\frac{p}{q-1}\right)^j (1-p)^{n-j}. \tag{2}$$

In general, the smaller the probability of undetected error P_{ue} for some p, the better the code performs in error detection. However, this function is difficult to characterize in general.

As for the code C, comparing its P_{ue} with the average probability $\overline{P_{ue}}$ [3,4] for the ensemble of all q-ary linear $[n,k]$ codes is a natural way to decide whether C is suitable for error detection or not, where

$$\overline{P_{ue}}(p) = q^{-(n-k)}\left(1-(1-p)^k\right).$$

According to [4], there exists a code C such that $P_{ue}(C,p) > q^{-(n-k)}$ and there are many codes, the P_{ue} of each of whom is smaller than $q^{-(n-k)}$. In fact, it was commonly assumed that $P_{ue}(C,p) \leqslant q^{-(n-k)}$ for the linear $[n,k]$ code C in [5], where $q^{-(n-k)} = q^{-r}$ is called the q^{-r} bound. The q^{-r} bound is satisfied for certain specific codes, e.g., Hamming codes and binary perfect codes, when $0 < p < 1/2$.

For the worst channel condition, i.e., when $p = (q-1)/q$,

$$P_{ue}\left(C, \frac{q-1}{q}\right) = q^{-(n-k)}\left(1-\left(1-\frac{q-1}{q}\right)^k\right) = \overline{P_{ue}}\left(\frac{q-1}{q}\right).$$

From the above formula, a code C is called *good* if $P_{ue}(C,p) \leqslant P_{ue}((q-1)/q)$ for all $0 < p < (q-1)/q$. In particular, if $P_{ue}(C,p)$ is an increasing function of p in the interval $[0,(q-1)/q]$, then the code is good, and the code is called *proper*. There are many proper codes [1], for example, perfect codes (and their extended codes and their dual codes), primitive binary 2-error correcting BCH codes, a class of punctured of Simplex codes, MDS codes, and near MDS codes (see [5–9] for details). Moreover, for practical purposes, a *good* binary code C may be defined a bit different, i.e., $P_{ue}(C,p) \leqslant cP_{ue}(C,1/2)$ for every $0 \leqslant p \leqslant 1/2$ and a reasonably small $c \geqslant 1$. Furthermore, an infinite class $\mathcal{C}$ of binary codes is called *uniformly good* if there exists a constant c such that for every $0 \leqslant p \leqslant 1/2$ and $C \in \mathcal{C}$, the inequality $P_{ue}(C,p) \leqslant cP_{ue}(C,1/2)$ holds. Otherwise, it is called *ugly*, for example, some special Reed–Muller codes are ugly (see [10]).

Another way to assess the performance of a code for error detection is to give bounds of the probability of undetected error. In [11], Abdel-Ghaffar defined the *combinatorial invariant* F_j of the code C and proved that

$$P_{ue}(C,p) = \sum_{j=1}^{n} F_j\left(\frac{p}{q-1}\right)^j\left(1-\frac{qp}{q-1}\right)^{n-j},$$

where

$$F_j = \sum_{i=1}^{j} A_i\binom{n-i}{n-j},\ j = 1,2,\ldots,n.$$

Using combinatorial arguments, Abdel-Ghaffar [11] obtained a lower bound on the undetected error probability $P_{ue}(C,p)$. Later, Ashikhmin and Barg called F_j the binomial moments of the distance function and derived more bounds for P_{ue} (see [12,13]).

In particular, constant weight codes are attractive and many bounds are developed, for example, binary constant weight codes (see [14,15]) and q-ary constant weight codes (see [16]). In fact, the probability of an undetected error for binary constant weight codes has been studied and can be given explicitly (see [14,16]).

Note that when $A = \mathbb{F}_q$ and $p \to 0$, according to Equation (2), we have

$$P_{ue}(C,p) \sim A_d p_q{}^d(1-p)^{n-d}, \tag{3}$$

where $p_q = p/(q-1)$, d is the minimum distance of C and A_d is called the *kissing number* of the linear code C. In 2021, Solé et al. [17] studied the kissing number by Linear Programming and the Polynomial Method. They gave bounds for A_d under different conditions and made tables for some special parameters. Motivated by the work, this paper is devoted to studying the function P_{ue} using the same techniques.

The rest of this paper is organized as follows. In Section 2, we briefly give the definition of the (dual) distance distribution of q-ary codes and give some trivial bounds of the probability of an undetected error. In Section 3.1, linear programming bounds are discussed. The applications of Krawtchouk polynomial (Polynomial Method) to error detection are given in Section 3.2. In Section 4, some bounds better than the 2^{-m} bound are given for binary Hamming codes. Finally, we end with some concluding remarks in Section 5.

2. Preliminaries

Recall some basic definitions and notations from [2,18–20]. Throughout this paper, to simplify some formulas, we let $p_q = \frac{p}{q-1}$ and $k = \log_q |C|$ for some real k. Furthermore, in this paper, it is natural to define $p < (q-1)(1-p)$, equivalently, $p_q < 1-p$.

2.1. Dual Distance Distribution

Assume that $A = \mathbb{F}_q$ is the finite field of size q and C is a subspace of $\mathbb{F}_q^n$, i.e., C is a linear code over $\mathbb{F}_q$. Then, the *dual code* $C^\perp$ of C is the orthogonal complement of the subspace C. That is to say,

$$C^\perp = \{\boldsymbol{v} \in \mathbb{F}_q^n : \boldsymbol{v} \cdot \boldsymbol{u} = 0 \text{ for all } \boldsymbol{u} \in C\},$$

where $\boldsymbol{v} \cdot \boldsymbol{u} = \sum_{i=1}^n v_i u_i$, $\boldsymbol{u} = (u_1, \ldots, u_n)$ and $\boldsymbol{v} = (v_1, \ldots, v_n)$. The distance distribution A_i' of $C^\perp$ can be determined similarly. It is well known (see Chapter 5. §2. in [2]) that

$$A_i' = \frac{1}{|C|} \sum_{i=0}^{n} A_j P_i(j), \tag{4}$$

where $P_i(j)$ denotes the Krawtchouk polynomial of degree i. For each integer $q \geqslant 2$, the *Krawtchouk polynomial* $P_k(x;n)$ is defined as

$$P_k(x;n) = \sum_{j=0}^{k} (-1)^j \binom{x}{j} \binom{n-x}{k-j} (q-1)^{k-j}.$$

When there is no ambiguity for n, the function $P_k(x;n)$ is often simplified to $P_k(x)$.

Note that Equation (4) holds when C is linear. When C is nonlinear, the *dual distance distribution* A_i' is defined by Equation (4). Furthermore, by the MacWilliams–Delsarte inequality,

$$A_i' \geqslant 0, \tag{5}$$

holds for all $i = 0, 1, \cdots, n$. Moreover, $A_0 = 1$ and

$$q^k = 1 + \sum_{j=1}^{n} A_j, \quad \text{when} \quad |C| = q^k. \tag{6}$$

2.2. Probability of Undetected Error

The *q-ary symmetric channel* with symbol probability p, where $0 \leqslant p \leqslant (q-1)/q$, is defined as follows: symbols from some alphabet A with q elements are transmitted over the channel, and

$$\mathcal{P}(b \text{ received} \mid a \text{ sent}) = \begin{cases} 1-p, & b = a, \\ \frac{p}{q-1}, & b \neq a, \end{cases}$$

where $\mathcal{P}(b \text{ received} \mid a \text{ sent})$ is the conditional probability that b is received, given that a is sent. For a q-ary code C, when it is used on such a channel, it is possible that the decoder fails to detect the existence of the errors. Thus, P_{ue}, the function in terms of the weight distribution of C is given in Equation (2). Clearly, this is a difficult computational problem for large parameters n, k, d, and q (see [2]). Hence, it is better to give bounds for P_{ue}. For example, here are some trivial bounds.

Theorem 1. *For every q-ary code C with* $|C| = q^k$, *if* $p < (q-1)(1-p)$, *then*

$$(q^k - 1){p_q}^n \leqslant P_{ue}(C,p) \leqslant (q^k - 1){p_q}^d (1-p)^{n-d},$$

where $p_q = \frac{p}{q-1}$. *Especially, when* $q = 2$ *and* $0 < p < \frac{1}{2}$, *we have*

$$(2^k - 1)p^n \leqslant P_{ue}(C,p) \leqslant (2^k - 1)p^d (1-p)^{n-d}.$$

Proof. It is easy to check that ${p_q}^j(1-p)^{n-j} > {p_q}^{j+1}(1-p)^{n-j-1}$ if and only if $p < (q-1)(1-p)$. Hence,

$$P_{ue} = \sum_{j=d}^{n} A_j {p_q}^j (1-p)^{n-j} \leqslant {p_q}^d (1-p)^{n-d} \sum_{j=d}^{n} A_j = (q^k - 1){p_q}^d (1-p)^{n-d},$$

since ${p_q}^j(1-p)^{n-j} \leqslant {p_q}^d(1-p)^{n-d}$ when $j \geqslant d$. The lower bound can be obtained similarly. □

The above bounds are trivial. However, they are both tight, because simplex codes over the finite field $\mathbb{F}_q$ attain these bounds.

2.3. Some Special Bounds

It is clear that the general bounds given by Theorem 1 will be much larger (or smaller) than the true value of P_{ue} for a fixed code. If the distance distribution is known, one computes $P_{ue}(C,p)$ (as a function of p), and if we know some particular information about the distance distribution, then we may get some bounds. The following is a special case and more thoughts can be seen in Section 4.

Theorem 2. *Let C be a binary code with* $A_n = 1$ *and* $A_i = A_{n-i}$ *for* $1 \leqslant i \leqslant n-1$, *then*

$$P_{ue} = \begin{cases} p^n + \sum_{j=d}^{t} A_j (p^j(1-p)^{n-j} + p^{n-j}(1-p)^j), & n = 2t+1, \\ p^n + A_t p^t (1-p)^t + \sum_{j=d}^{t-1} A_j (p^j(1-p)^{n-j} + p^{n-j}(1-p)^j), & n = 2t. \end{cases} \quad (7)$$

Moreover, when $d \leqslant t$, *we have*

$$P_{ue} \leqslant \begin{cases} p^n + \left(2^{k-1} - 1\right)\left(p^d(1-p)^{n-d} + p^{t+1}(1-p)^t\right), & n = 2t+1, \\ p^n + A_t p^t (1-p)^t + \left(2^{k-1} - \frac{A_t}{2} - 1\right)\left(p^d(1-p)^{n-d} + p^{t+1}(1-p)^{t-1}\right), & n = 2t, \end{cases}$$

and

$$P_{ue} \geqslant \begin{cases} p^n + \left(2^{k-1} - 1\right)\left(p^t(1-p)^{t+1} + p^{n-d}(1-p)^d\right), & n = 2t+1, \\ p^n + A_t p^t (1-p)^t + \left(2^{k-1} - \frac{A_t}{2} - 1\right)\left(p^{t-1}(1-p)^{t+1} + p^{n-d}(1-p)^d\right), & n = 2t, \end{cases}$$

where $0 < p < \frac{1}{2}$ *and* $d \leqslant t$.

Proof. By the definition of P_{ue}, Equation (7) holds if $A_i = A_{n-i}$ and $A_n = 1$. Due to $0 < p < \frac{1}{2}$, It is easy to check that $p^{n-j}(1-p)^j \leqslant p^j(1-p)^{n-j}$, where $0 \leqslant j \leqslant \lfloor n/2 \rfloor$. In addition, if $n = 2t+1$, then $\sum_{j=d}^{t} A_j = (2^k - 2)/2 = 2^{k-1} - 1$. Similarly for the case $n = 2t$. Hence, we get the bounds. □

Remark 1. *If the binary code C satisfies $A_i = A_{n-i}$ and $A_n = 0$, we can get the following bounds:*

$$P_{ue} \leqslant \begin{cases} 2^{k-1}\left(p^d(1-p)^{n-d}+p^{t+1}(1-p)^t\right), & n=2t+1, \\ A_t p^t(1-p)^t+\left(2^{k-1}-\frac{A_t+A_0}{2}\right)\left(p^d(1-p)^{n-d}+p^{t+1}(1-p)^{t-1}\right), & n=2t, \end{cases}$$

and

$$P_{ue} \geqslant \begin{cases} 2^{k-1}\left(p^t(1-p)^{t+1}+p^{n-d}(1-p)^d\right), & n=2t+1, \\ A_t p^t(1-p)^t+\left(2^{k-1}-\frac{A_t+A_0}{2}\right)\left(p^{t-1}(1-p)^{t+1}+p^{n-d}(1-p)^d\right), & n=2t. \end{cases}$$

Here, **0***, the all zero vector, may not be a codeword.*

Example 1. *For a binary linear code, if the all-one vector* **1** *is a codeword, then $A_i = A_{n-i}$. So, Theorem 2 can be applied to many codes, for example, Hamming codes. It is known that the binary Hamming code $\mathcal{H}_m$ is a linear $[n = 2^m - 1, k = 2^n - 1 - m, 3]$ code. The distance distribution of the* [15, 11, 3] *Hamming code $\mathcal{H}_4$ is listed in Table 1. According to Theorem 2, the values of the bounds and true probability can be seen in Figure 1.*

Table 1. Distance Distribution of the Hamming Code $\mathcal{H}_4$.

i	0	3	4	5	6	7	8	9	10	11	12	15
A_i	1	35	105	168	280	435	435	280	168	105	35	1

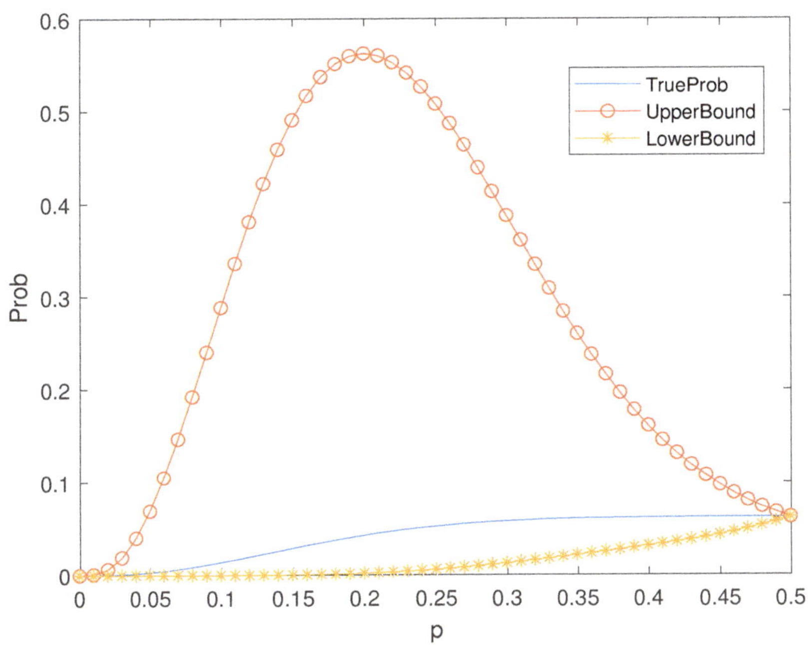

Figure 1. Bounds in Theorem 2 of P_{ue} for the Hamming Code $\mathcal{H}_4$.

3. Universal Bounds for q-Ary Codes

In this section, we will discuss the bounds for P_{ue} using different methods. These bounds are for general codes, thus they do not look so good. Meanwhile, compared with some known bounds, they do not perform better. However, it is the first as far as we know to give bounds for P_{ue} using the following two methods, though they have been shown in [21,22] due to different thoughts.

3.1. Linear Programming Bounds

Consider the linear programming problem $M(n,k,d,p)$ that maximizes the objective function

$$\sum_{j=1}^{n} A_j {p_q}^j (1-p)^{n-j}$$

under the constraints:

(1) $A_j \geqslant 0$,

(2) $\sum_{j=1}^{n} A_j = q^k - 1$,

(3) $\sum_{j=1}^{n} A_j P_i(j) \geqslant -P_i(0)$,

(4) $A_1 = A_2 = \cdots = A_{d-1} = 0$.

Likewise, let $m(n,k,d,p)$ be the minimization of the same objective function under the same constraints.

Theorem 3. *If C is a q-ary code of parameters (n, q^k, d), then $m(n,k,d,p) \leqslant P_{ue} \leqslant M(n,k,d,p)$.*

Proof. The objective function expression comes from (2). Constraint (1) is immediate by the definition of the distance distribution. Constraints (2) and (3) come from Equation (6) and Equation (5), respectively. Constraint (4) is a consequence of the definition of minimum distance. □

Remark 2. *Let $f(x)$ and $g(x)$ be two functions of x, then $f \lesssim g$ if $f < g$ or $f \sim g$, when $x \to 0$, where $0 < x < 1$. For example, let $f(x) = x^2 + x$ and $g(x) = x^3 + x$, then $f(x) > g(x)$ when $0 < x < 1$. But $f(x) \sim g(x)$, then $f(x) \lesssim g(x)$ when $0 < x < 1$ and $x \to 0$.*

Motivated by Equation (3) and [17], we have the following result.

Theorem 4. *Let C be a q-ary $[n,k,d]_q$ linear code, then when $p \to 0$,*

$$(q^k - 1 - \lfloor L \rfloor){p_q}^d (1-p)^{n-d} \leqslant P_{ue}(C,p) \lesssim (q^k - 1 - \lceil S \rceil){p_q}^d (1-p)^{n-d}, \quad (8)$$

where L (resp. S) denotes the maximum (resp. minimum) of $\sum_{j=d+1}^{n} A_j$ subject to the $2n-d$ constraints

$$-P_i(0) - (q^k - 1)P_i(d) \leqslant \sum_{j=d+1}^{n} A_j(P_i(j) - P_i(d)),$$

for $i = 1,2,\ldots,n$ and $j = d+1, d+2, \ldots, n$.

Proof. It is clear that $P_{ue}(C,p) \geqslant A^d {p_q}^d (1-p)^{n-d}$, then by [17], we get the left side of Equation (8). As for the right side, if $A_d < q^k - 1 - \lceil S \rceil$ and p is small enough, then by Equation (3), $P_{ue}(C,p) < (q^k - 1 - \lceil S \rceil){p_q}^d (1-p)^{n-d}$. Otherwise, $A_d = q^k - 1 - \lceil S \rceil$ and then, $P_{ue}(C,p) \sim (q^k - 1 - \lceil S \rceil){p_q}^d (1-p)^{n-d}$. □

Table 2 is a part of Table I in [17], which is helpful to give bounds for P_{ue}.

Table 2. Bounds of A_d for Some Binary Codes.

Parameters	[9, 4, 4]	[10, 4, 4]	[11, 4, 5]	[12, 4, 6]	[13, 4, 6]	[14, 4, 7]	[15, 4, 8]
Upper Bound	14	15	7	14	14	8	15
Lower Bound	6	12	5	11	4	8	15

Example 2. *Let C_1 be a binary [15, 4, 8] code, then*

$$P_{ue}(C_1, p) \sim 15p^8(1-p)^7.$$

As for the binary [12, 4, 6] code C_2, we have

$$11p^6(1-p)^6 < P_{ue}(C_2, p) < 14p^6(1-p)^6.$$

Obviously, for any [n, k, d] code, one can give bounds for its P_{ue}.

Remark 3. *From the above discussion, it is clear that our bounds depend solely on the three parameters [n, k, d] of the code, and [n, k, d] is the minimal requirement to use a code in practice.*

3.2. Polynomial Method

In this section, we will give some general bounds for P_{ue} for any binary $(n, 2^k, d)$ code. Recall the definition of the Krawtchouk polynomials and some properties. The following identity is a Polynomial Method of expressing the duality of LP.

Lemma 1. *Let $\beta(x) \in \mathbb{Q}[x]$ be the polynomial whose Krawtchouk expansion is*

$$\beta(x) = \sum_{j=0}^{n} \beta_j P_j(x).$$

Then we have the following identity

$$\sum_{i=0}^{n} \beta(i) A_i = q^k \sum_{j=0}^{n} \beta_j A'_j. \tag{9}$$

Proof. Immediate by Equation (4), upon swapping the order of summation. □

From now on, we denote the coefficient of Krawtchouk expansion of the polynomial $f(x)$ of degree n by $f_j, j = 0, 1, \cdots, n$, i.e., $f(x) = \sum_{j=0}^{n} f_j P_j(x)$.

The first main result of this section is inspired by Theorem 1 in [23], and given as follows.

Theorem 5. *Let $\beta(x)$ and $\gamma(x)$ be polynomials over $\mathbb{Q}$ such that $\beta_j \leqslant 0$, $\gamma_j \geqslant 0$ for $j \geqslant 1$ and $\gamma(i) \leqslant {p_q}^i (1-p)^{n-i} \leqslant \beta(i)$ for all i with $A_i \neq 0$. Then we have the upper bound*

$$P_{ue} \leqslant q^k \beta_0 - \beta(0), \tag{10}$$

and the lower bound

$$P_{ue} \geqslant q^k \gamma_0 - \gamma(0). \tag{11}$$

Proof. By Lemma 1, we have

$$\sum_{j=0}^{n} A_j \beta(j) \leqslant \beta_0 q^k.$$

Returning to the definition of P_{ue} and using the property of $\beta(j) \geqslant {p_q}^j (1-p)^{n-j}$, we get

$$P_{ue} = \sum_{j=1}^{n} A_j {p_q}^j (1-p)^{n-j} \leqslant \sum_{j=1}^{n} A_j \beta(j) \leqslant q^k \beta_0 - \beta(0).$$

The proof of the lower bound is analogous and ommitted. □

Remark 4. *The above result is a special case of Proposition 5 in [22]. More general setting of the linear programming bounds from Section 3 (Theorem 5) were already considered in [21,22].*

The following are some properties of the Krawtchouk expansion, and we omit the proof, since they are not difficult.

Lemma 2 ([24] Corollary 3.13). *Let $f(x) = \sum_{j=0}^{n} f_j P_j(x)$ and $g(x) = \sum_{j=0}^{n} g_j P_j(x)$ be polynomials over $\mathbb{Q}$, where $f_j \geqslant 0, g_j \geqslant 0, 0 \leqslant j \leqslant n$. Then the coefficients of the Krawtchouk expansion of $\lambda f(x) + \mu g(x)$ are nonnegative, where λ, μ are nonnegative rational numbers.*

3.2.1. Upper Bounds

For convenience, let $\delta_{i,j}$ be the Kronecker symbol, i.e.,

$$\delta_{i,j} = \begin{cases} 1, & \text{if } i = j, \\ 0, & \text{if } i \neq j. \end{cases}$$

Lemma 3. *For general q, the coefficients of the Krawtchouk expansion of the following polynomial*

$$g_i(x) = \frac{(-1)^{i-1}}{(i-1)!(n-i)!} \frac{\prod_{j=1}^{n}(j-x)}{i-x},$$

are all nonnegative if and only if i is odd, where $1 \leqslant i \leqslant n$ is an integer and $0! = 1$. Moreover, $g_i(j) = \delta_{i,j}$.

Proof. Let

$$h(x) = \frac{q^{n-d+1}}{s-x} \prod_{j=d}^{n} \left(1 - \frac{x}{j}\right) = \sum_{j=0}^{n} h_j P_j(x),$$

where $d \leqslant s \leqslant n$. Then, by Proposition 5.8.2 in [20],

$$\begin{aligned} h_i &= \frac{1}{q^n} \sum_{j=0}^{n} h(j) P_j(i) = \frac{1}{q^{d-1}} \sum_{j=0}^{d-1} \binom{n-j}{n-d+1} \frac{P_j(i)}{s-j} \Big/ \binom{n}{d-1} \\ &\geqslant \frac{1}{q^{d-1}s} \sum_{j=0}^{d-1} \binom{n-j}{n-d+1} P_j(i) \Big/ \binom{n}{d-1} \\ &= \frac{1}{s} \binom{n-i}{d-1} \Big/ \binom{n}{d-1} \geqslant 0. \end{aligned}$$

Note that if $d = 1$, we have

$$h(x) = \frac{q^n}{n!} (-1)^{i-1} (i-1)!(n-i)! g_s(x).$$

According to Lemma 2, the coefficients of the Krawtchouk expansion of $(-1)^{i-1} g_i(x)$ are all nonnegative.

Obviously, for any $j \neq i$, $g_i(j) = 0$, because j is a root of $g_i(x)$. Moreover,

$$\begin{aligned} g_i(i) &= \frac{(-1)^{i-1}}{(i-1)!(n-i)!} \prod_{\ell=1}^{i-1} (\ell - i) \prod_{\ell=i+1}^{n} (\ell - i) \\ &= \frac{(-1)^{i-1}}{(i-1)!(n-i)!} \left((-1)^{i-1} (i-1)!(n-i)! \right) = 1, \end{aligned}$$

which means $g_i(j) = \delta_{i,j}$. □

Theorem 6. *Let C be a binary code with the distance distribution A_j, where $A_j = 0$ for all possible odd j, then*

$$P_{ue} \leqslant \sum_{\text{even } i} p^i(1-p)^{n-i}\binom{n}{i}\left(\frac{1}{2^{n-k}}+1\right), \tag{12}$$

where even i means that i runs through the even intergers between d and n.

Proof. According to Lemma 3, the coefficients of the Krawtchouk expansion of the following polynomial:

$$g_i(x) = \frac{(-1)^{i-1}}{(i-1)!(n-i)!}\frac{\prod_{j=1}^{n}(j-x)}{i-x}$$

are nonnegative if and only if i is odd. Then, let

$$f(x) = \sum_{\text{even } i} p^i(1-p)^{n-i}g_i(x) = \sum_{j=0}^{n} f_j P_j(x).$$

Hence, $f_j \leqslant 0$, $f(i) = p^i(1-p)^{n-i}$ for even i and $f(i) = 0$ for odd i. By the proof of Theorem 5,

$$P_{ue} \leqslant 2^k f_0 - f(0),$$

where

$$f(0) = \sum_{\text{even } i} (-1)p^i(1-p)^{n-i}\binom{n}{i},$$

and

$$f_0 = \frac{1}{2^n}\sum_{\text{even } i} p^i(1-p)^{n-i}\binom{n}{i}.$$

Thus, the upper bound follows from Theorem 5. □

Remark 5. *If C is linear, then A_i is the number of codewords of weight i, which implies that $A_i \leqslant \binom{n}{i}$. Hence,*

$$P_{ue} \leqslant \sum_{i\in I} p^i(1-p)^{n-i}\binom{n}{i},$$

where $I = \{i | A_i \neq 0\}$. Moreover, if $A_i = 0$ for all odd i, then

$$P_{ue} \leqslant \sum_{\text{even } i} p^i(1-p)^{n-i}\binom{n}{i}. \tag{13}$$

Example 3. *Consider the Nordstrom–Robinson code, it is a binary nonlinear code with the distance distribution in Table 3. Moreover, the weight distribution is the same as the distance distribution. By Equation (2),*

$$P_{ue} = 112p^6(1-p)^{10} + 30p^8(1-p)^8 + 112p^{10}(1-p)^6 + p^{16}.$$

According to Theorem 6, the values of the upper bound and true probability can be seen in Figure 2.

Table 3. Distance Distribution of the Nordstrom–Robinson Code.

i	0	6	8	10	16
A_i	1	112	30	112	1

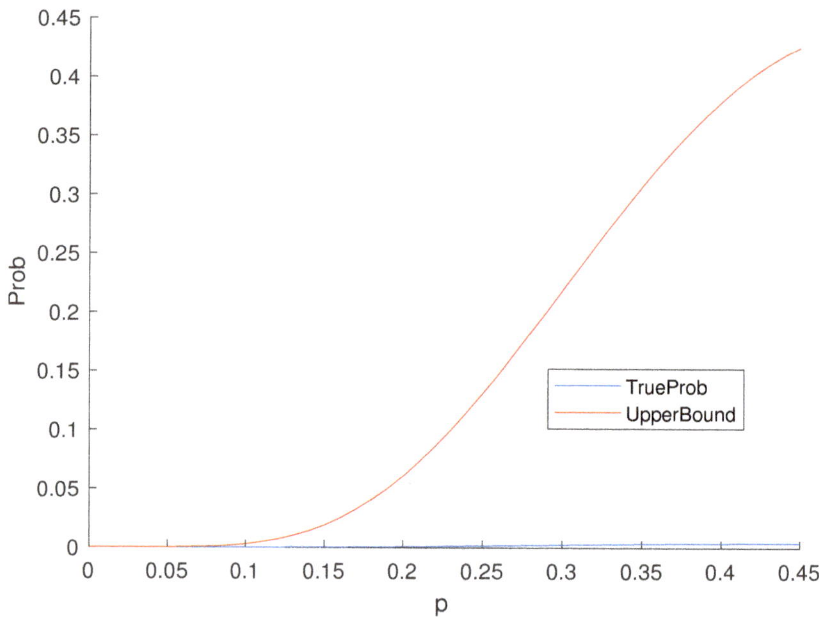

Figure 2. The Probability of Undetected Error of the Nordstrom–Robinson Code.

Example 4. *Let $\mathcal{E}$ be the set of binary vectors of length n and even weight, then it is actually the Reed–Muller code $RM(n-1,n)$ in Problem 5 in [2] and is generated by all the binary vectors of weight 2. Hence,*

$$P_{ue}(\mathcal{E},p) = \sum_{i=1}^{\lfloor n/2 \rfloor} \binom{n}{2i} p^{2i}(1-p)^{n-2i}.$$

Remark 6. *The bound is suitable for many codes, and thus it seems not good. In fact, there exists some code C, whose P_{ue} is very large.*

Motivated by [17], we have the following upper bounds for linear codes over $\mathbb{F}_2$.

Proposition 1. *When C is a q-ary linear $[n,\ k,\ d]$ code and p is small enough, we have the following statements:*

(1) *If $n+1+qd-nq>0$, then*

$$P_{ue} \lesssim \frac{q^k+nq-n-1}{n-nq+1+qd} {p_q}^d (1-p)^{n-d};$$

(2) *If $n+qd-nq-1<0$, then*

$$P_{ue} \lesssim \frac{q^{k-2}n(qn-n-qd+1)+n(d-1)}{n-d} {p_q}^d (1-p)^{n-d};$$

(3) *If $q=2$, $n-2d>0$, $(n-2d+2)^2>n$, and $A_i \neq 0$ only if $d \leqslant i \leqslant n-2d$, then*

$$P_{ue} \lesssim \frac{2^{k-2}((n-2d+2)^2-n)+(d-1)(n-d+1)}{n+1-2d} p^d (1-p)^{n-d}.$$

Proof. These three bounds can be deduced easily by Equation (3) and Corollaries 4–6 in [17]. □

Remark 7. *The results in Corollary 4–6 in [17] are actually the upper bounds of A_d under different conditions. Considering Equation (3), it is necessary to make p small enough. According to the proof of Theorem 4, if A_d does not meet such bounds, then "<" holds.*

3.2.2. Lower Bounds

Similar to Proposition 1, by Corollaries 1–3 in [17], we have

Proposition 2. *If C is a q-ary linear code, then we have the following statements:*

(1) *If $d = \lceil (n-1)(q-1)/q \rceil$, then*

$$P_{ue} \geqslant \frac{q^k - nq + n - 1}{(n-d)q - n + 1} {p_q}^d (1-p)^{n-d};$$

(2) *If $qd > nq - n - 2q + 1$, then*

$$P_{ue} \geqslant \frac{q^{k-2}n(n - qn + qd + 2q - 1) - nd - n}{n-d} {p_q}^d (1-p)^{n-d};$$

(3) *If $q = 2$ and all weights of C are in $[d, n-d]$, with $n - 2d > 0$ and $(n - 2d - 1)^2 < n + 1$, then*

$$P_{ue} \geqslant \left(\frac{2^{k-2}(n^2 - 4nd - 3n) + (2^k + 1)d(d+1)}{2d - n} - d - 1 \right) p^d (1-p)^{n-d}.$$

When using quadratic polynomials, we have the following bound.

Proposition 3. *Let f_0, f_1 and f_2 be nonnegative rational numbers such that*

$$f_0 - f_1 n + f_2 \binom{n}{2} \leqslant p^d (1-p)^{n-d} \quad \text{and} \quad f_1 + n f_2 \leqslant 2d f_2,$$

then, for a binary $(n, 2^k, d)$ code, we have

$$P_{ue} \geqslant 2^k f_0 - p^d (1-p)^{n-d} - 2 f_1 n,$$

where $0 \leqslant p \leqslant \frac{1}{2}$.

Proof. It is known that, when $q = 2$, $P_0(x) = 1$, $P_1(x) = n - 2x$ and $P_2(x) = 2x^2 - 2nx + \binom{n}{2}$. Let $f(x) = f_0 P_0(x) + f_1 P_1(x) + f_2 P_2(x)$ and then it is a quadratic function whose axis of symmetry is $\frac{f_1 + n f_2}{2 f_2}$. Considering that $p^{i+1}(1-p)^{n-i-1} \geqslant p^i (1-p)^{n-i}$, it is sufficient to show that

$$f(n) \leqslant p^d (1-p)^{n-d} \text{ and } \frac{f_1 + n f_2}{2 f_2} \leqslant d,$$

i.e., $f(i) \leqslant f(n) \leqslant p^d (1-p)^{n-d} \leqslant p^i (1-p)^{n-i}$ for $i \geqslant d$. Equivalently,

$$f_0 - f_1 n + f_2 \binom{n}{2} \leqslant p^d (1-p)^{n-d}, \quad f_1 + n f_2 \leqslant 2d f_2.$$

The result follows from Theorem 5. □

4. Good Bounds for Hamming Codes

Recall that the *weight enumerator* of the code C is the homogeneous polynomial

$$W_C(x, y) = \sum_{c \in C} x^{n - wt(u)} y^{wt(u)},$$

where $wt(\boldsymbol{u})$ means the Hamming weight the codeword $\boldsymbol{u}$. The binary Hamming code $\mathcal{H}_m$ is a $[n = 2^m - 1, k = n - m, d = 3]$ code, with the weight enumerator

$$\frac{(x+y)^n + n(x+y)^{(n-1)/2}(x-y)^{(n+1)/2}}{n+1},$$

whose distance distribution A_i satisfies

$$\sum_{i=1}^{n} iA_i y^{i-1} + \sum_{i=0}^{n} A_i y^i + \sum_{i=0}^{n-1} (n-i)A_i y^{i+1} = (1+y)^n,$$

and the recurrence $A_0 = 1$, $A_1 = 0$,

$$(i+1)A_{i+1} + A_i + (n-i+1)A_{i-1} = \binom{n}{i}.$$

Moreover,

$$\begin{aligned}(1+y)^n &= \frac{\sum_{i=1}^{n} iA_i y^i}{y} + \sum_{i=0}^{n} A_i y^i + ny\sum_{i=0}^{n-1} A_i y^i - y\sum_{i=0}^{n-1} iA_i y^i \\ &= \sum_{i=1}^{n-1} A_i y^i\left(\frac{i}{y} - iy\right) + (ny+1)\sum_{i=1}^{n-1} A_i y^i + y^n + ny^{n-1} + ny + 1.\end{aligned}$$

Let $\alpha \in \mathbb{F}_{2^m}$ be a primitive element and let $g(x) \in \mathbb{F}_2[x]$ be the minimal polynomial of α with respect to $\mathbb{F}_2$. According to Exercise 7.20 in [20], $g(x)$ can be regarded as the generator polynomial of a Hamming code. Since $\deg(g(x)) = m > 1$, then

$$g(x)\,\Big|\,\frac{x^n - 1}{x - 1} = 1 + x + x^2 + \cdots + x^{n-1},$$

which implies that the all-one vector is a codeword of the Hamming code and $A_n = 1$.

Note that

$$P_{ue} = \sum_{i=1}^{n} A_i p^i (1-p)^{n-i} = (1-p)^n \sum_{i=1}^{n} A_i \left(\frac{p}{1-p}\right)^i.$$

Hence,

$$\sum_{i=1}^{n-1} A_i \left(\frac{p}{1-p}\right)^i = \frac{P_{ue} - p^n}{(1-p)^n}.$$

Let $y = \varepsilon = \frac{p}{1-p}$, where $p \in (0, 1/2)$, then

$$\begin{aligned}&(n\varepsilon + 1)(P_{ue} - p^n) + (1-p)^n \sum_{i=1}^{n-1} A_i \varepsilon^i \left(\frac{i}{\varepsilon} - i\varepsilon\right) \\ &= 1 - p^n - np(1-p)^{n-1} - np^{n-1}(1-p) - (1-p)^n.\end{aligned}$$

According to Chapter 6, Exercise(E2), page 157 in [2], there are $n-4$ nonzero weights of $\mathcal{H}_m$. Considering that $A_n = 1$, we have $A_i = 0$ if and only if $i = 1, 2, n-1, n-2$. Since $0 < p < 1/2$, then $0 < \varepsilon < 1$ and we have

$$\frac{3}{\varepsilon} - 3\varepsilon \leqslant \frac{i}{\varepsilon} - i\varepsilon \leqslant \frac{n-3}{\varepsilon} - (n-3)\varepsilon.$$

Obviously,

$$\begin{aligned}(1-p)^n\sum_{i=1}^{n-1}A_i\varepsilon^i\left(\frac{i}{\varepsilon}-i\varepsilon\right) &\leqslant (1-p)^n\sum_{i=1}^{n-1}A_i\varepsilon^i\left(\frac{n-3}{\varepsilon}-(n-3)\varepsilon\right)\\ &=\left(\frac{n-3}{\varepsilon}-(n-3)\varepsilon\right)\sum_{i=1}^{n-1}A_ip^i(1-p)^{n-i}\\ &=\left(\frac{n-3}{\varepsilon}-(n-3)\varepsilon\right)(P_{ue}-p^n).\end{aligned}$$

Similarly,

$$(1-p)^n\sum_{i=1}^{n-1}A_i\varepsilon^i\left(\frac{i}{\varepsilon}-i\varepsilon\right)\geqslant\left(\frac{3}{\varepsilon}-3\varepsilon\right)(P_{ue}-p^n).$$

Thus,

$$\begin{aligned}P_{ue} &\leqslant \frac{1-p^n-np(1-p)^{n-1}-np^{n-1}(1-p)-(1-p)^n}{\frac{3}{\varepsilon}-3\varepsilon+n\varepsilon+1}+p^n \\ &= \frac{p(1-p)-p^{n+1}(1-p)-np^2(1-p)^n-np^n(1-p)^2-p(1-p)^{n+1}}{(n-1)p^2-5p+3}+p^n\end{aligned} \tag{14}$$

and

$$\begin{aligned}P_{ue} &\geqslant \frac{1-p^n-np(1-p)^{n-1}-np^{n-1}(1-p)-(1-p)^n}{\frac{n-3}{\varepsilon}-(n-3)\varepsilon+n\varepsilon+1}+p^n \\ &= \frac{p(1-p)-p^{n+1}(1-p)-np^2(1-p)^n-np^n(1-p)^2-p(1-p)^{n+1}}{(n-1)p^2-(2n-7)p+n-3}+p^n.\end{aligned} \tag{15}$$

Summarize the above discussions, we get

Theorem 7. *Let $\mathcal{H}_m$ be the binary $[n=2^m-1, k=n-m, 3]$ Hamming code, then when $0<p<1/2$ and $m\geqslant 3$, we have the upper bound Equation (14) and the lower bound Equation (15) for P_{ue}, respectively.*

Proof. Note that the upper bound should be larger or equal than the lower bound, then

$$(-(2n-7)p+n-3)-(-5p+3)=(n-6)(1-2p)\geqslant 0.$$

It is sufficient to solve the inequality $n=2^m-1>6$, due to $1-2p>0$. Hence, $m\geqslant 3$. □

Remark 8. *The difference of the upper bound and the lower bound is small.*

Let $U(n,p)=H_1/H$ and $L(n,p)=H_2/H$ be the bound given by Equation (14) and Equation (15), respectively, where $H_1=(n-1)p^2-5p+3$, $H_2=(n-1)p^2-(2n-7)p+n-3$ and

$$H=p(1-p)-p^{n+1}(1-p)-np^2(1-p)^n-np^n(1-p)^2-p(1-p)^{n+1}.$$

In fact, H is a polynomial of p whose degree $n+2$ and the leading coefficient is

$$h_{n+2}=1+(-1)^{n+2}n-n+(-1)^{n+2}=(1+(-1)^n)+n((-1)^n-1)\neq 0,$$

while the product H_1H_2 is just a polynomial whose degree is 4. Then,

$$U(n,p) - L(n,p) = \frac{(H_2 - H_1)H}{H_1H_2} = \frac{(n-6)(1-2p)H}{H_1H_2} \longrightarrow \frac{(n-6)(1-2p)h_{n+2}p^{n+2}}{(n-1)^2p^4} \longrightarrow 0 \quad (n \to +\infty).$$

That is to say, the lower bound and the upper bound are very close. On the other hand,

$$H_1 \geqslant \frac{12n-37}{4(n-1)} \quad \text{and} \quad H_2 \geqslant \frac{n+1}{4}.$$

Then,

$$\begin{aligned} U(n,p) - L(n,p) &= \frac{(H_2 - H_1)H}{H_1H_2} = \frac{(n-6)(1-2p)H}{H_1H_2} \\ &< \frac{(n-6)(1-2p)p(1-p)}{H_1H_2} < \frac{(n-6)(1-2p)p(1-p)}{\frac{12n-37}{4(n-1)}\frac{n+1}{4}} \\ &= \frac{16(n-1)(n-6)}{(n+1)(12n-37)}p(1-p)(1-2p) \\ &\leqslant \frac{\sqrt{3}}{18}\frac{16(n-1)(n-6)}{(n+1)(12n-37)} \longrightarrow \frac{2\sqrt{3}}{27} \approx 0.1283 \quad (n \to +\infty). \end{aligned}$$

Here, let $F(p) = p(1-p)(1-2p)$, then its derivative is $F'(p) = 6p^2 - 6p + 1$. Note that the roots of $F'(p)$ are $\frac{3\pm\sqrt{3}}{6}$. Since $0 < p < 1/2$, then we choose the root $p_0 = \frac{3-\sqrt{3}}{6}$. Hence,

$$F(p) \leqslant F(p_0) = \frac{\sqrt{3}}{18} \approx 0.0962.$$

Thus the difference of the upper bound and the lower bound is about 0.1283 at most, and tends to 0 when $n \to +\infty$.

Example 5. *Using the bounds in Theorem 7, the results in Figure 1 can be improved. See Figure 3.*

When $m = 5$, the bounds Equations (15) and (14) are also valid. See Figure 4.

Note that the difference of the bounds Equations (15) and (14) is about 0.05, which is much smaller than the given 0.1283.

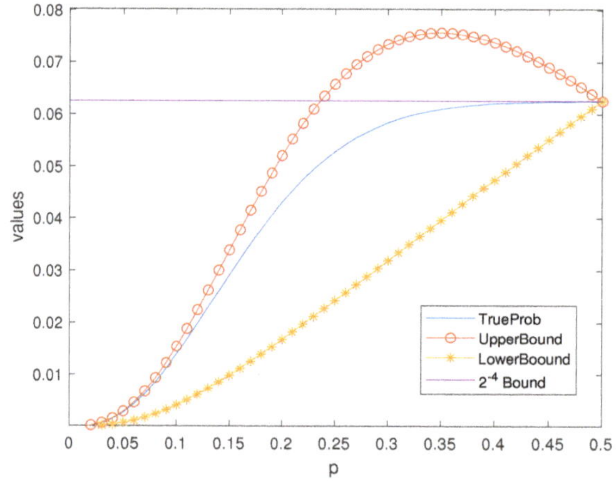

Figure 3. Bounds in Theorem 7 of P_{ue} for the Hamming Code $\mathcal{H}_4$.

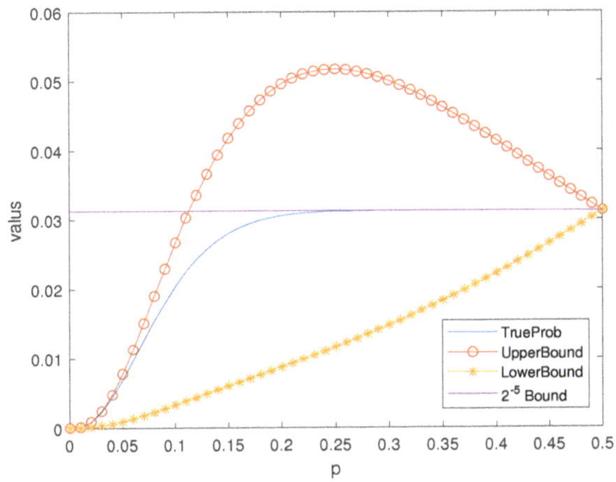

Figure 4. Bounds in Theorem 7 of P_{ue} for the Hamming Code $\mathcal{H}_5$.

It is known that the Hamming codes satisfy the 2^{-m} bound when $0 < p < 1/2$ i.e., $P_{ue} \leqslant 2^{-m}$. See [5] for more details. In fact, the obtained new bound is better than the ordinary 2^{-m} bound, when p is not large.

Theorem 8. *Let $\mathcal{H}_m$ be the binary $[n = 2^m - 1, k = n - m, 3]$ Hamming code, then when $0 < p < 1/2$ and $m \geq 3$, we have*

$$P_{ue} \leqslant \frac{p - p^2}{(n-1)p^2 - 5p + 3} + p^n. \tag{16}$$

Moreover, if $p < p_0$, this upper bound is better than the 2^{-m} bound, where p_0 is the smaller root of the equation $(2^{m+1} - 2)x^2 - (2^m + 5)x + 3 = 0$.

Proof. Assume that

$$\frac{p - p^2}{(n-1)p^2 - 5p + 3} < \frac{1}{2^m},$$

then it is sufficient to solve the inequality

$$(2^{m+1} - 2)p^2 - (2^m + 5)p + 3 > 0.$$

Obviously, the inequality holds when $p < p_0$, where

$$p_0 = \frac{(2^m + 5) - \sqrt{(2^m + 5)^2 - 12(2^{m+1} - 2)}}{2(2^{m+1} - 2)}$$

is the smaller root of the equation $(2^{m+1} - 2)x^2 - (2^m + 5)x + 3 = 0$. □

Example 6. *It is clear that when p is small enough, the new upper bound Equation (14) is smaller than the 2^{-m} bound in Figures 3 and 4.*

Remark 9. *Of course, the weight distribution of the binary Hamming codes can be computed and expressed by the sum of combinatorial numbers, which are usually very large when m is large. So, the method in this section is to estimate P_{ue} quickly. Compared with the 2^{-m} bound, our bounds are better when p is small enough.*

5. Conclusions

In this paper, we studied the probability of an undetected error P_{ue} and gave many bounds for P_{ue}. The main contributions of this paper are the following:

(1) The bounds obtained from the linear programming problem are given in Theorem 4. The bounds obtained from the Polynomial Method are given. According to the main Theorem 5, we get Theorem 6 (applied to the codes with even distances) and Proposition 3.
(2) Combining the results of [17], we give the bounds in Propositions 1 and 2.
(3) We find sharper bounds for binary Hamming codes (see Theorems 7 and 8).

To the best of our knowledge, that is the very first time that the LP method has been applied to bound P_{ue}. Even though computing P_{ue} exactly requires knowledge of the code weight spectrum, our bounds depend solely on the three parameters $[n,\ k,\ d]$, of the code. The weight frequencies are only used as variables in the LP program. Knowing the three parameters $[n,\ k,\ d]$ is the minimal requirement to use a code in applications.

To sum up, our bounds are most useful when the exact weight distribution is too hard to compute. Our bounds perform well when p is small enough and the kissing number A_d is known, and there are many such codes.

We mention the following open problems. The readers interested in Hamming codes are suggested to derive bounds for general q-ary Hamming codes with $q > 2$. Moreover, it is worth mentioning that the linear programming problem works better numerically than the Polynomial Method. The interest of the latter lies in producing bounds with closed formulas. It is a challenging open problem to derive better bounds with polynomials of degree higher than 2.

Author Contributions: Conceptualization, P.S.; methodology, P.S.; software, H.L.; validation, X.W. and P.S.; formal analysis, X.W. and P.S.; investigation, X.W. and P.S.; resources, H.L.; data curation, H.L.; writing—original draft preparation, X.W.; writing—review and editing, X.W. and P.S.; visualization, H.L.; supervision, P.S.; project administration, P.S. All authors have read and agreed to the published version of the manuscript.

Funding: This research received no external funding.

Institutional Review Board Statement: Not applicable.

Data Availability Statement: Data are available in a publicly accessible repository

Acknowledgments: The authors are grateful to Minjia Shi, Li Chen, and his colleagues for their helpful suggestions for improving the presentation of the material in this paper and pointing out the references [6,21,22,24].

Conflicts of Interest: The authors have no conflict of interest to declare that are relevant to the content of this article.

References

1. Dodunekova, R.; Dodunekov, S.M.; Nikolova, E. A survey on proper codes. *Discret. Appl. Math.* **2008**, *156*, 1499–1509. [CrossRef]
2. MacWilliams, F.J.; Sloane, N.J.A. *The Theory of Error Correcting Codes*; Elsevier: Amsterdam, The Netherlands, 1981.
3. Massey, J. Coding techniques for digital data networks. In Proceedings of the International Conference on Information Theory and Systems, NTG-Fachberichte, Berlin, Germany, 18–20 September 1978; Volume 65.
4. Wolf, J.K.; Michelson, A.M.; Levesque, A.H. On the probability of undetected error for linear block codes. *IEEE Trans. Commun.* **1982**, *30*, 317–324. [CrossRef]
5. Leung-Yan-Cheong, S.K.; Hellman, M.E. Concerning a bound on undetected error probability. *IEEE Trans. Inform. Theory* **1976**, *22*, 235–237. [CrossRef]
6. Baldi, M.; Bianchi, M.; Chiaraluce, F.; Kløve, T. A class of punctured Simplex codes which are proper for error detection. *IEEE Trans. Inform. Theory* **2012**, *58*, 3861–3880. [CrossRef]
7. Kasami, T.; Lin, S. On the probability of undetected error for the maximum distance separable codes. *IEEE Trans. Commun.* **1984**, *32*, 998–1006. [CrossRef]
8. Leung-Yan-Cheong, S.K.; Barnes, E.R.; Friedman, D.U. On some properties of the undetected error probability of linear codes. *IEEE Trans. Inform. Theory* **1979**, *25*, 110–112. [CrossRef]

9. Ong, C.; Leung, C. On the undetected error probability of triple-error-correcting BCH codes. *IEEE Trans. Inform. Theory* **1991**, *37*, 673–678. [CrossRef]
10. Kløve, T. Reed-Muller codes for error detection: The good the bad and the ugly. *IEEE Trans. Inform. Theory* **1996**, *42*, 1615–1622. [CrossRef]
11. Abdel-Ghaffar, K.A.S. A lower bound on the undetected error probability and strictly optimal codes. *IEEE Trans. Inform. Theory* **1997**, *43*, 1489–1502. [CrossRef]
12. Ashikhmin, A.; Barg, A. Binomial moments of the distance distribution: Bounds and applications. *IEEE Trans. Inform. Theory* **1999**, *45*, 438–452. [CrossRef]
13. Barg, A.; Ashikhmin, A. Binomial moments of the distance distribution and the probability of undetected error. *Des. Codes Cryptogr.* **1999**, *16*, 103–116. [CrossRef]
14. Xia, S.T.; Fu, F.W.; Jiang, Y.; Ling, S. The probability of undetected error for binary constant weight codes. *IEEE Trans. Inform. Theory* **2005**, *51*, 3364–3373. [CrossRef]
15. Xia, S.T.; Fu, F.W.; Ling, S. A lower bound on the probability of undetected error for binary constant weight codes. *IEEE Trans. Inform. Theory* **2006**, *52*, 4235–4243. [CrossRef]
16. Xia, S.T.; Fu, F.W. Undetected error probability of q-ary constant weight codes. *Des. Codes Cryptogr.* **2008**, *48*, 125–140. [CrossRef]
17. Solé, P.; Liu, Y.; Cheng, W.; Guilley, S.; Rioul, O. Linear programming bounds on the kissing number of q-ary Codes. In Proceedings of the 2021 IEEE Information Theory Workshop (ITW), Kanazawa, Japan, 17–21 October 2021; pp. 1–5.
18. Kløve, T. *Codes for Error Detection*; Kluwer: Singapore, 2007.
19. Van Lint, J.H. *Introduction to Coding Theory*, 3rd ed.; Springer: Berlin/Heidelberg, Germany; New York, NY, USA, 1999.
20. Xing, C.; Ling, S. *Coding Theory: A First Course*; Cambridge University Press: Cambridge, UK, 2003.
21. Boyvalenkov, P.; Dragnev, P.; Hardin, D.; Saff, E.; Stoyanova, M. Energy bounds for codes in polynomial metric spaces. *Anal. Math. Phys.* **2019**, *9*, 781–808. [CrossRef]
22. Cohn, H.; Zhao, Y. Energy-minimizing error-correcting codes. *IEEE Trans. Inform. Theory* **2014**, *60*, 7442–7450. [CrossRef]
23. Ashikmin, A.; Barg, A.; Litsyn, S. Estimates on the distance distribution of codes and designs. *IEEE Trans. Inform. Theory* **2001**, *47*, 1050–1061. [CrossRef]
24. Levenshtein, V. Universal bounds for codes and designs. In *Chapter 6 of Handbook of Coding Theory*; Pless, V.S., Huffman, W.C., Eds.; Elsevier: Amsterdam, The Netherlands, 1998; pp. 499–648.

entropy

MDPI

Article

The *c*-Differential-Linear Connectivity Table of Vectorial Boolean Functions

Said Eddahmani [1,2] and Sihem Mesnager [1,2,3,*]

[1] Department of Mathematics, University of Paris VIII, F-93526 Paris, France; said.eddahmani@etud.univ-paris8.fr
[2] Laboratory Geometry, Analysis and Applications (LAGA), University Sorbonne Paris Nord, CNRS, UMR 7539, F-93430 Villetaneuse, France
[3] Telecom Paris, Polytechnic Institute, F-91120 Palaiseau, France
* Correspondence: smesnager@univ-paris8.fr

Abstract: Vectorial Boolean functions and codes are closely related and interconnected. On the one hand, various requirements of binary linear codes are needed for their theoretical interests but, more importantly, for their practical applications (such as few-weight codes or minimal codes for secret sharing, locally recoverable codes for storage, etc.). On the other hand, various criteria and tables have been introduced to analyse the security of S-boxes that are related to vectorial Boolean functions, such as the Differential Distribution Table (DDT), the Boomerang Connectivity Table (BCT), and the Differential-Linear Connectivity Table (DLCT). In previous years, two new tables have been proposed for which the literature was pretty abundant: the *c*-DDT to extend the DDT and the *c*-BCT to extend the BCT. In the same vein, we propose extended concepts to study further the security of vectorial Boolean functions, especially the *c*-Walsh transform, the *c*-autocorrelation, and the *c*-differential-linear uniformity and its accompanying table, the *c*-Differential-Linear Connectivity Table (*c*-DLCT). We study the properties of these novel functions at their optimal level concerning these concepts and describe the *c*-DLCT of the crucial inverse vectorial (Boolean) function case. Finally, we draw new ideas for future research toward linear code designs.

Keywords: differential uniformity; vectorial function; S-box; linear codes; minimal codes

1. Introduction

Vectorial Boolean functions are intensively used to produce S-boxes in block ciphers such as DES [1], Rinjdael or AES [2], Blowfish [3], GOST [4], and Serpent [5]. Various criteria have been proposed to test the resistance of S-boxes and the corresponding vectorial Boolean functions to known cryptanalytical attacks, such as the differential attack [6], the linear attack [7], and some of their variants.

Let $F : \mathbb{F}_{2^n} \to \mathbb{F}_{2^m}$ be a (n, m)-vectorial Boolean function. The derivative of F in the direction of $a \in \mathbb{F}_{2^n}$ is the function $D_a(F)(x) = F(x) + F(x + a)$. The derivative is used to analyse the resistance of a vectorial Boolean function to the differential attack [6] and serves to build the Differential Distribution Table (DDT). The derivative is also used in the Boomerang Connectivity Table (BCT) [8] and in the Differential-Linear Connectivity Table (DLCT) [9,10]. The entry at $(a, b) \in \mathbb{F}_{2^n} \times \mathbb{F}_{2^m}$ of the DDT is defined by

$$\mathtt{DDT}_F(a, b) = \#\{x \in \mathbb{F}_{2^n} : F(x) + F(x + a) = b\}.$$

To measure the resistance of a vectorial Boolean function, Nyberg [11] introduced the differential uniformity as

$$\delta_F = \max\{\mathtt{DDT}_F(a, b) \mid (a, b) \in \mathbb{F}_{2^n} \times \mathbb{F}_{2^m}, \text{ and } a \neq 0\}.$$

The most resistant vectorial Boolean functions have small differential uniformities. The reader can consult the [12] for a complete background on vectorial Boolean functions with a deep analysis of their cryptographic aspects.

At FSE 2002, Borisov et al. [13] proposed a variant of the differential attack to study ciphers' resistance based on using modular multiplication as a primitive operation. This motivated Ellingsen et al. [14] to introduce the concept of c-differentials to study the resistance of a vectorial Boolean function to multiplicative variants of the differential attack. For a vectorial Boolean function $F : \mathbb{F}_{2^n} \to \mathbb{F}_{2^m}$ and $c \in \mathbb{F}_{2^m}$, the c-derivative F with respect to $a \in \mathbb{F}_{2^n}$ is the (n, m)-vectorial Boolean function ${}_cD_aF$ defined by ${}_cD_aF(x) = F(x + a) + cF(x)$ for all $x \in \mathbb{F}_{2^n}$. The c-derivative is used to study the resistance of ciphers based on popular vectorial Boolean functions such as the inverse function [15], the Gold function [16], and various other functions [17–21]. As for the DDT, a c-differential table was proposed in [14], where the entry at $(a, b) \in \mathbb{F}_{2^n} \times \mathbb{F}_{2^m}$ is defined by

$$ {}_c\mathrm{DDT}_F(a, b) = \#\{x \in \mathbb{F}_{2^n} \mid F(x + a) + cF(x) = b\}. $$

Also, a c-differential uniformity was proposed in [14] by

$$ {}_c\delta_F = \max\{{}_c\mathrm{DDT}_F(a, b) \mid (a, b) \in \mathbb{F}_{2^n} \times \mathbb{F}_{2^m}, \text{ and } a \neq 0 \text{ if } c = 1\}. $$

The construction of functions, particularly permutations, with low c-differential uniformity is an interesting problem, and recent work has focused heavily on this direction. Likewise, regarding the original notion of differential uniformity leading to optimal functions Perfect Nonlinear (PN) and Almost Perfect Nonlinear (APN) over finite fields in odd and even characteristics, respectively, optimal functions having the lowest possible values of a c-differential uniformity have also been introduced. One can refer to [19,22–27] and the references therein. Some of those functions with low c-differential uniformity have been investigated. There are relatively few known (non-trivial, nonlinear) optimal classes of PcN and APcN functions over finite fields with an even characteristic (see, e.g., [18,28–31] and the references therein).

Another popular cryptanalysis attack on S-boxes derived from Boolean functions is the boomerang attack, proposed by Wagner [32] in 1999. In connection with the boomerang attack, Cid et al. [8] proposed the Boomerang Connectivity Table (BCT) for a vectorial Boolean function where the entry at $(a, b) \in \mathbb{F}_{2^n} \times \mathbb{F}_{2^m}$ is defined by

$$ \mathrm{BCT}_F(a, b) = \#\{x \in \mathbb{F}_{2^n} : F^{-1}(F(x) + b) + F^{-1}(F(x + a) + b) = a\}. $$

Based on the BCT, Boura and Canteaut [33] introduced the boomerang uniformity of a vectorial Boolean function to measure its resistance against boomerang attack. The boomerang uniformity of F is defined by

$$ \beta_F = \max_{a \in \mathbb{F}_{2^n}^*, b \in \mathbb{F}_{2^m}^*} \mathrm{BCT}_F(a, b). $$

To extend the BCT and the boomerang uniformity of a vectorial Boolean function, Stănică [34] introduced the concept of the c-Boomerang Connectivity Table (c-BCT). For $c \in \mathbb{F}_{2^m}^*$, the c-BCT is defined at the entry $(a, b) \in \mathbb{F}_{2^n} \times \mathbb{F}_{2^m}$ by

$$ {}_c\mathrm{BCT}_F(a, b) = \#\{x \in \mathbb{F}_{2^n} : F^{-1}(cF(x) + b) + F^{-1}\left(c^{-1}F(x + a) + b\right) = a\}. $$

The corresponding c-boomerang uniformity is defined by

$$ {}_c\beta_F = \max_{a \in \mathbb{F}_{2^n}^*, b \in \mathbb{F}_{2^m}^*} {}_c\mathrm{BCT}_F(a, b). $$

More generalizations of the differential and boomerang uniformities can be found in [35].

In 2019, Bar-On et al. [10] (see also [9]) introduced the Differential-Linear Connectivity Table (DLCT) of a vectorial Boolean function where the entry at $(a,b) \in \mathbb{F}_{2^n} \times \mathbb{F}_{2^m}$ is defined by

$$DLCT_F(a,b) = \#\{x \in \mathbb{F}_{2^n} \mid b \cdot (F(x+a) + F(x)) = 0\} - 2^{n-1},$$

where $x \cdot y$ is the inner product of x and y on $\mathbb{F}_{2^m}$. To measure the resistance of an S-box connected to a vectorial Boolean function, the differential-linear uniformity of F can be used, as defined by Li et al. in [36],

$$\gamma_F = \max_{a \in \mathbb{F}_{2^n}^*, b \in \mathbb{F}_{2^m}^*} |DLCT_F(a,b)|.$$

Various links exist between the DLCT and the Autocorrelation Table (ACT) of a vectorial Boolean function F. The ACT is defined at $(a,b) \in \mathbb{F}_{2^n} \times \mathbb{F}_{2^m}$ by

$$\mathtt{ACT}_F(a,b) = \sum_{x \in \mathbb{F}_{2^n}} (-1)^{b \cdot (F(x) + F(x+a))}.$$

The corresponding absolute indicator is defined as

$$\Delta_F = \max_{\substack{u \in \mathbb{F}_{2^n}, u \neq 0, \\ b \in \mathbb{F}_{2^m}^*}} |\mathtt{ACT}_F(a,b)|.$$

In [37], Canteaut et al. showed that the DLCT and the ACT of a vectorial Boolean function satisfy $\gamma_F = \frac{1}{2}\Delta_F$ and $DLCT_F(a,b) = \frac{1}{2}\mathtt{ACT}_F(a,b)$ for all $(a,b) \in \mathbb{F}_{2^n} \times \mathbb{F}_{2^m}$.

One can observe that the derivative $D_a(F)(x) = F(x) + F(x+a)$ of a Boolean function F is used in various tables, such as the DDT, the BCT, and the DLCT. Motivated by the crucial role of the derivative in the former tables and the attacks related to them, we propose three new concepts towards the c-derivative ${}_cD_a(F)(x) = F(x+a) + cF(x)$:

- The c-Walsh transform of a vectorial Boolean function F: For $c \in \mathbb{F}_{2^m}^*$, it is defined for $a \in \mathbb{F}_{2^n}$ and $b \in \mathbb{F}_{2^m}$ by

$$_cW_F(a,b) = \sum_{x \in \mathbb{F}_{2^n}} (-1)^{a \cdot x + b \cdot cF(x)}.$$

- The c-autocorrelation of a vectorial Boolean function: Let $c \in \mathbb{F}_{2^m}$, $c \neq 0$. The c-autocorrelation of F at $(a,b) \in \mathbb{F}_{2^n} \times \mathbb{F}_{2^m}$ is the integer

$$_c\mathrm{AC}_F(a,b) = \sum_{x \in \mathbb{F}_{2^n}} (-1)^{b \cdot (F(x+a) + cF(x))}.$$

  The absolute indicator is

$$_c\Delta_F = \max_{\substack{u \in \mathbb{F}_{2^n}, u \neq 0 \text{ if } c=1, \\ b \in \mathbb{F}_{2^m}^*}} |{}_c\mathrm{AC}_F(a,b)|,$$

  and the autocorrelation spectrum is

$$_c\Lambda_F = \{{}_c\mathrm{AC}_F(a,b), a \in \mathbb{F}_{2^n}^*, b \in \mathbb{F}_{2^m}^*\}.$$

- The c-Differential-Linear Connectivity Table (c-DLCT) where we use the c-derivative: Let $c \in \mathbb{F}_{2^m}^*$. The c-DLCT of F is a $2^n \times 2^m$ table where the entry at $(a,b) \in \mathbb{F}_{2^n} \times \mathbb{F}_{2^m}$ is defined by

$$_cDLCT_F(a,b) = \#\{x \in \mathbb{F}_{2^n} \mid b \cdot (F(x+a) + cF(x)) = 0\} - 2^{n-1}.$$

We also define the c-differential-linear uniformity of F as

$$_c\gamma_F = \max_{\substack{u\in\mathbb{F}_{2^n}, u\neq 0 \text{ if } c=1, \\ b\in\mathbb{F}_{2^m}^*}} |_cDLCT_F(a,b)|,$$

and, also, we define the c-DLCT spectrum of F by

$$_c\Gamma_F = \{_cDLCT_F(a,b), a \in \mathbb{F}_{2^n}, b \in \mathbb{F}_{2^m}\}.$$

We show that there are numerous relationships between the three new concepts. Typically, we show that $_cDLCT_F(a,b) = \frac{1}{2}{}_c\mathtt{AC}_F(a,b)$ for all $(a,b) \in \mathbb{F}_{2^n} \times \mathbb{F}_{2^m}$ and $_c\gamma_F = \frac{1}{2}{}_c\Delta_F$.

Moreover, we focus on the inverse function defined on $\mathbb{F}_{2^n}$ by $F(x) = \frac{1}{x}$ if $x \neq 0$, and $F(0) = 0$. We study its c-DLCT and give an explicit value for the entries, including when $c = 1$.

We mention that there is an interesting connection between c differential uniformity and combinatorial designs, which has been highlighted in [38] by showing that the graph of a perfect c-nonlinear function (an optimal function concerning the c differential uniformity) is a set of differences in a quasigroup. Difference sets give rise to symmetric designs, which are known to build optimal self-complementary codes. Some types of designs also have concrete applications such as secret sharing and visual cryptography.

Finally, we emphasise that one of our practical applications in brother research lines is to use the derived (optimal) functions (see, e.g., [12]) to derive minimal binary linear codes (see, e.g., [39]) that are needed for their theatrical interests but, more importantly, for their practical applicants such as few-weight codes or minimal codes for secret sharing and securing two-party computation.

The rest of this paper is organized as follows. Section 2 presents some known results that will be used in this paper. In Section 3, we define the c-Walsh and the c-autocorrelation of a vectorial Boolean function and study some of their properties. In Section 4, we present the concept of the c-DLCT and study its properties. We investigate the c-DLCT of the inverse function in Section 5. Finally, Section 6 concludes the paper and presents new ideas for future research toward linear code designs along the same lines as designing (minimal) codes from Almost Perfect Nonlinear (APN) and recent achievements [40] on minimal codes from low differential uniformity.

2. Preliminaries

In this section, we present some results and definitions that will be used in the next sections, including the c-derivative and the c-differential uniformity of a vectorial Boolean function.

For $b \in \mathbb{F}_{2^n}$, we define the orthogonal space $b^\perp$ of b as follows.

Definition 1. *For $b \in \mathbb{F}_{2^n}$, the orthogonal space $b^\perp$ of b is defined by*

$$b^\perp = \{x \in \mathbb{F}_{2^n} \mid b \cdot x = 0\},$$

where $b \cdot x$ is the inner product of b and x on $\mathbb{F}_{2^n}$.

The following result gives an explicit value for $\#b^\perp$.

Proposition 1. *For $b \in \mathbb{F}_{2^n}$, the orthogonal space $b^\perp$ of b satisfies*

$$\#b^\perp = \begin{cases} 2^n & \text{if } b = 0, \\ 2^{n-1} & \text{if } b \neq 0. \end{cases}$$

Proof. It is obvious that $\#0^{\perp} = 2^n$. Suppose that $b \neq 0$. Then, the binary expansion of b is in the following form.

$$b = (b_{n-1}, b_{n-2}, \ldots, b_j, \ldots, b_0).$$

Suppose that $b_j = 1$ for some j with $0 \leq j \leq n-1$. Let $x \in \mathbb{F}_{2^n}$ such that $x \notin b^{\perp}$, that is $b \cdot x = 1$, with the binary expansion

$$x = (x_{n-1}, x_{n-2}, \ldots, x_j, \ldots, x_0).$$

Let $y \in \mathbb{F}_{2^n}$ with the binary expansion

$$y = (y_{n-1}, y_{n-2}, \ldots, x_j + 1 \pmod 2, \ldots, x_0).$$

Then,

$$b \cdot y = b \cdot x + b_j \equiv 1 + 1 \equiv 0 \pmod 2.$$

Hence, $y \in b^{\perp}$. It follows that for $b \neq 0$, each element x of $\mathbb{F}_{2^n}$ satisfying $b \cdot x = 1$ is in correspondence with one element y of $\mathbb{F}_{2^n}$ satisfying $b \cdot y = 0$. As a consequence, we have $\#b^{\perp} = 2^{n-1}$. □

For $n \geq 1$, let $\mathbb{F}_{2^n}$ be the finite field with 2^n elements. The trace of an element $x \in \mathbb{F}_{2^n}$ is given by

$$\mathrm{Tr}(x) = x + x^2 + \cdots + x^{2^{n-1}},$$

and satisfies $\mathrm{Tr}(x) \in \{0, 1\}$. The trace function satisfies $\mathrm{Tr}(x^2) = \mathrm{Tr}(x)$ for all $x \in \mathbb{F}_{2^n}$.

The following lemma is well known and is useful for our work.

Lemma 1. *Let n and k be positive integers and $e = \gcd(k, n)$. Then,*

$$\gcd\left(2^k + 1, 2^n - 1\right) = \begin{cases} 1 & \text{if } \frac{n}{e} \text{ is odd,} \\ 2^e + 1 & \text{if } \frac{n}{e} \text{ is even.} \end{cases}$$

Some specific equations on $\mathbb{F}_{2^n}$ may be involved. The following result deals with the quadratic equation.

Lemma 2. *(Proposition 1 of [41]) Let $a, b, c \in \mathbb{F}_{2^n}$. The equation $ax^2 + bx + c = 0$ has*

(i) One root if and only if $b = 0$.

(ii) Two roots if and only if $b \neq 0$ and $Tr\left(\frac{ac}{b^2}\right) = 0$.

(iii) No root if and only if $b \neq 0$ and $Tr\left(\frac{ac}{b^2}\right) = 1$.

The following lemma concerns another equation on $\mathbb{F}_{2^n}$.

Lemma 3. *Let k and n be positive integers such that $k < n$. Let $d = \gcd(k, n)$, $m = \frac{n}{d} > 1$, and $\beta_{m-1} = \mathrm{Tr}_d^n(B)$. Then, the trinomial $f(X) = X^{2^k} + X + B$ has no root if $\beta_{m-1} \neq 0$ and has 2^d roots $x + \delta\tau$ in $\mathbb{F}_{2^n}$ if $\beta_{m-1} = 0$, where $\delta \in \mathbb{F}_{2^d}$, $\tau \in \mathbb{F}_{2^n}$ is any element satisfying $\tau^{2^k - 1} = 1$, and*

$$x = \frac{1}{\mathrm{Tr}_d^n(c)} \sum_{i=0}^{m-1} \left(\sum_{j=0}^{i} c^{2^{kj}} \right) B^{2^{ki}},$$

with any $c \in \mathbb{F}_{2^n}^*$ satisfying $\mathrm{Tr}_d^n(c) \in \mathbb{F}_{2^d}^*$.

In [14], Ellingsen et al. proposed the concept of c-differentials. The following definitions are valid for binary finite fields.

Definition 2. *Let $F : \mathbb{F}_{2^n} \to \mathbb{F}_{2^m}$ be an (n,m)-vectorial Boolean function and $c \in \mathbb{F}_{2^m}$. The c-derivative F with respect to $a \in \mathbb{F}_{2^n}$ is the (n,m)-vectorial function ${}_cD_aF$ satisfying* ${}_tp_x$

$$ {}_cD_aF(x) = F(x+a) + cF(x) $$

for all $x \in \mathbb{F}_{2^n}$.

Definition 3. *Let $F : \mathbb{F}_{2^n} \to \mathbb{F}_{2^m}$ be a (n,m)-vectorial Boolean function, and $c \in \mathbb{F}_{2^m}$. The c-differential table of F is an $2^n \times 2^m$ table whose components are defined for $a \in \mathbb{F}_{2^n}$ and $b \in \mathbb{F}_{2^m}$ by*

$$ {}_c\Delta_F(a,b) = \#\{x \in \mathbb{F}_{2^n} \mid F(x+a) + cF(x) = b\}. $$

Definition 4. *Let $F : \mathbb{F}_{2^n} \to \mathbb{F}_{2^m}$ be a (n,m)-vectorial Boolean function, and $c \in \mathbb{F}_{2^m}$. The c-differential uniformity of F is*

$$ {}_c\Delta_F = \begin{cases} \max\limits_{a \in \mathbb{F}_{2^n}, b \in \mathbb{F}_{2^m}} {}_c\Delta_F(a,b) & \text{if } c \neq 1, \\ \max\limits_{a \in \mathbb{F}_{2^n} \setminus \{0\}, b \in \mathbb{F}_{2^m}} {}_c\Delta_F(a,b) & \text{if } c = 1. \end{cases} $$

3. The c-Walsh and c-Autocorrelation of a Vectorial Boolean Function

The Walsh transform of a Boolean function $f : \mathbb{F}_{2^n} \to \mathbb{F}_2$ is defined at $u \in \mathbb{F}_{2^n}$ by

$$ W_f(u) = \sum_{x \in \mathbb{F}_{2^n}} (-1)^{u \cdot x + f(x)}, $$

where $u \cdot x$ is the inner product of u and x. The Walsh transform serves to compute the linearity of f as

$$ \mathtt{L}(f) = \max_{u \in \mathbb{F}_{2^n}} |W_f(u)|. $$

For a vectorial Boolean function $F : \mathbb{F}_{2^n} \to \mathbb{F}_{2^m}$, the Walsh transform of F is defined for $u \in \mathbb{F}_{2^n}$ and $v \in \mathbb{F}_{2^m}$ by

$$ W_F(u,v) = \sum_{x \in \mathbb{F}_{2^n}} (-1)^{u \cdot x + v \cdot F(x)}, $$

and is used to compute the linearity of F by

$$ \mathtt{L}(F) = \max_{u \in \mathbb{F}_{2^n}, v \in \mathbb{F}_{2^n} \setminus \{0\}} |W_F(u,v)|. $$

We extend the Walsh transform of a vectorial Boolean function to the c-Walsh transform as follows.

Definition 5. *Let F be an (n,m)-vectorial Boolean function, and $c \in \mathbb{F}_{2^m}^*$. The c-Walsh transform of F is defined for $u \in \mathbb{F}_{2^n}$ and $v \in \mathbb{F}_{2^m}$ by*

$$ {}_cW_F(u,v) = \sum_{x \in \mathbb{F}_{2^n}} (-1)^{u \cdot x + v \cdot cF(x)}. $$

The autocorrelation function is used to study various properties of the Boolean functions (see [42]).

Definition 6. *Let f be Boolean function defined on $\mathbb{F}_{2^n}$. The autocorrelation of f at $u \in \mathbb{F}_{2^n}$ is the integer*

$$AC_f(u) = \sum_{x\in\mathbb{F}_{2^n}} (-1)^{f(x)+f(x+u)},$$

and its absolute indicator is $\Delta_f = \max_{u\in\mathbb{F}_{2^n},u\neq 0}\left|AC_f(u)\right|$.

We notice that $u = 0$ is excluded in the definition of the absolute indicator since $\mathrm{AC}_f(0) = \sum_{x\in\mathbb{F}_{2^n}}(-1)^{f(x)+f(x)} = 2^n$. The generalization of the autocorrelation to vectorial Boolean functions can be then defined as follows.

Definition 7. *Let F be an (n,m)-vectorial Boolean function defined on $\mathbb{F}_{2^n}$. The autocorrelation of F at $(u,v) \in \mathbb{F}_{2^n}\times\mathbb{F}_{2^m}$ is the integer*

$$AC_F(u,v) = \sum_{x\in\mathbb{F}_{2^n}} (-1)^{v\cdot(F(x)+F(x+u))}.$$

The absolute indicator is

$$\Delta_F = \max_{\substack{u\in\mathbb{F}_{2^n},u\neq 0,\\ v\in\mathbb{F}_{2^m},v\neq 0}} |AC_F(u,v)|,$$

and the autocorrelation spectrum is

$$\Lambda_F = \{AC_F(u,v), u\in\mathbb{F}_{2^n}, u\neq 0, v\in\mathbb{F}_{2^m}, v\neq 0\}.$$

The trivial values are not considered in the definition of the absolute indicator since $\mathrm{AC}_F(0,v) = \mathrm{AC}_F(u,0) = 2^n$.

Inspired by Definition 6, we introduce the notion of c-autocorrelation of a Boolean function.

Definition 8. *Let f be the Boolean function defined on $\mathbb{F}_{2^n}$, and $c\in\mathbb{F}_{2^m}$, $c\neq 0$. The c-autocorrelation of f at $u\in\mathbb{F}_{2^n}$ is the integer*

$${}_cAC_f(u) = \sum_{x\in\mathbb{F}_{2^n}} (-1)^{f(x+u)+cf(x)},$$

and the c-absolute indicator is ${}_c\Delta_f = \max_{u\in\mathbb{F}_{2^n}}\left|AC_f(u)\right|$.

Similarly, to generalize Definition 7, we define the c-autocorrelation of a vectorial Boolean function.

Definition 9. *Let F be an (n,m)-vectorial Boolean function defined on $\mathbb{F}_{2^n}$, and $c\in\mathbb{F}_{2^m}$, $c\neq 0$. The c-autocorrelation of F at $(u,v)\in\mathbb{F}_{2^n}\times\mathbb{F}_{2^m}$ is the integer*

$${}_cAC_F(u,v) = \sum_{x\in\mathbb{F}_{2^n}} (-1)^{v\cdot(F(x+u)+cF(x))}.$$

The absolute indicator is

$${}_c\Delta_F = \max_{\substack{u\in\mathbb{F}_{2^n},u\neq 0 \text{ if } c=1,\\ v\in\mathbb{F}_{2^m},v\neq 0}} |{}_cAC_F(u,v)|,$$

and the autocorrelation spectrum is

$${}_c\Lambda_F = \{{}_cAC_F(u,v), u\in\mathbb{F}_{2^n}, v\in\mathbb{F}_{2^m},\}.$$

To ease the study of the c-autocorrelation of a vectorial Boolean function F, we present its c-autocorrelation table defined at $(u,v)\in\mathbb{F}_{2^n}\times\mathbb{F}_{2^m}$ by

$${}_c\mathrm{ACT}_F(u,v) = \sum_{x\in\mathbb{F}_{2^n}} (-1)^{v\cdot(F(x+u)+cF(x))}.$$

The following result links the c-autocorrelation of a vectorial Boolean function and its c-Walsh transform.

Proposition 2. *Let F be an (n,m) Boolean function. Then, for any $u \in F_{2^n}$ and any $v \in F_{2^n}$,*

$$W_F(u,v)_c W_F(u,v) = \sum_{z \in \mathbb{F}_{2^n}} (-1)^{u \cdot z} {}_c AC_F(z,v).$$

Proof. We have

$$\begin{aligned} W_F(u,v)_c W_F(u,v) &= \sum_{x \in \mathbb{F}_{2^n}} (-1)^{u \cdot x + v \cdot F(x)} \sum_{y \in \mathbb{F}_{2^n}} (-1)^{u \cdot y + v \cdot cF(y)} \\ &= \sum_{x,y \in \mathbb{F}_{2^n}} (-1)^{u \cdot (x+y) + v \cdot (F(x) + cF(y)} \\ &= \sum_{y,z \in \mathbb{F}_{2^n}} (-1)^{u \cdot z + v \cdot (F(y+z) + cF(y))} \\ &= \sum_{z \in \mathbb{F}_{2^n}} (-1)^{u \cdot z} \sum_{y \in \mathbb{F}_{2^n}} (-1)^{v \cdot (F(y+z) + cF(y))} \\ &= \sum_{z \in \mathbb{F}_{2^n}} (-1)^{u \cdot z} {}_c AC_F(z,v). \end{aligned}$$

This finishes the proof. □

4. The c-Differential-Linear Connectivity Table of a Vectorial Boolean Function

In this section, we present a new concept, called the c-Differential-Linear Connectivity Table (c-DLCT), which generalizes the standard DLCT, independently defined in 2018 by Kim et al. [9] and Bar-On et al. [10]

We start by defining the standard Differential-Linear Connectivity Table (DLCT).

Definition 10. *Let F be an (n,m)-vectorial Boolean function. The DLCT of F is an $2^n \times 2^m$ table where the entry at $(u,v) \in \mathbb{F}_{2^n} \times \mathbb{F}_{2^m}$ is*

$$DLCT_F(u,v) = \#\{x \in \mathbb{F}_{2^n} \mid v \cdot (F(x+u) + F(x)) = 0\} - 2^{n-1}.$$

The DLCT is a tool that could analyse the relationships between differential and linear parts of a block cipher. One can observe that if $x \in \mathbb{F}_{2^n}$ is such that $v \cdot (F(x+u) + F(x)) = 0$, then $v \cdot (F((x+u)+u) + F(x+u)) = 0$. Consequently, $DLCT_F(u,v)$ is always even. Moreover, if $u = 0$, or if $v = 0$, then $DLCT_F(u,v) = 2^{n-1}$. This induces the following definition for differential-linear connectivity uniformity.

Definition 11. *Let F be an (n,m)-vectorial Boolean function. The differential-linear connectivity uniformity of F is*

$$\gamma_F = \max_{u \in \mathbb{F}_{2^n}^*, v \in \mathbb{F}_{2^m}^*} |DLCT_F(u,v)|.$$

The DLCT of a vectorial Boolean function is related to the autocorrelation function by the following relation.

$$\begin{aligned} AC_F(u,v) &= \#\{x \in \mathbb{F}_{2^n} \mid v \cdot (F(x) + F(x+u)) = 0)\} \\ &\quad - \#\{x \in \mathbb{F}_{2^n} \mid v \cdot (F(x) + F(x+u)) = 1\} \\ &= 2\#\{x \in \mathbb{F}_{2^n} \mid v \cdot (F(x) + F(x+u)) = 0\} - 2^n \\ &= 2DLCT_F(u,v). \end{aligned}$$

The DLCT is a tool to study the relationships between the linear and the differential properties of a block cipher. For $(u,v) \in \mathbb{F}_{2^n} \times \mathbb{F}_{2^m}$, it counts the number of elements

$x \in \mathbb{F}_{2^n}$ such that $v \cdot (F(x+u) + F(x)) = 0$. Let $a \in \mathbb{F}_{2^m}, a \neq 0$, and $b \in \mathbb{F}_{2^m}, b \neq 0$, be two fixed non-zero elements. It is possible to study the relationships between the linear and the differential properties of a block cipher by studying the number of solutions of the equation $v \cdot (aF(x+u) + bF(x)) = 0$ or equivalently $v \cdot (F(x+u) + cF(x)) = 0$, where $c = \frac{a}{b}$. This leads us to define a function's c-Differential-Linear Connectivity Table (c-DLCT).

Definition 12. *Let F be an (n, m)-vectorial Boolean function, and $c \in \mathbb{F}_{2^m}$, $c \neq 0$. The c-DLCT of F is an $2^n \times 2^m$ table where the entry at $(u, v) \in \mathbb{F}_{2^n} \times \mathbb{F}_{2^m}$ is*

$$ {}_cDLCT_F(u,v) = \#\{x \in \mathbb{F}_{2^n} \mid v \cdot (F(x+u) + cF(x)) = 0\} - 2^{n-1}. $$

Moreover, the c-differential-linear connectivity uniformity of F is

$$ {}_c\gamma_F = \max_{\substack{u \in \mathbb{F}_{2^n}, u \neq 0 \text{ if } c=1, \\ v \in \mathbb{F}_{2^m}, v \neq 0}} |{}_cDLCT_F(u,v)|, $$

and the c-DLCT spectrum of F is defined for $(u, v) \in \mathbb{F}_{2^n} \times \mathbb{F}_{2^m}$ by

$$ {}_c\Gamma_F = \{{}_cDLCT_F(u,v), u \in \mathbb{F}_{2^n}, v \in \mathbb{F}_{2^m}\}. $$

From Definitions 9 and 12, we obtain the following connection between the ${}_c$ACT and the ${}_cDLCT$ of a vectorial Boolean function.

Proposition 3. *Let F be (n, m)-vectorial Boolean function. Then, for all $u \in \mathbb{F}_{2^n}$ and $v \in \mathbb{F}_{2^m}$,*

$$ {}_cDLCT_F(u,v) = \frac{1}{2} {}_c\mathrm{AC}_F(u,v), \text{ and } {}_c\gamma_F = \frac{1}{2} {}_c\Delta_F. $$

Proof. We have

$$ \begin{aligned} {}_c\mathrm{AC}_F(u,v) &= \#\{x \in \mathbb{F}_{2^n} \mid v \cdot (F(x+u) + cF(x)) = 0)\} \\ &\quad - \#\{x \in \mathbb{F}_{2^n} \mid v \cdot (F(x+u) + cF(x)) = 1\} \\ &= 2\#\{x \in \mathbb{F}_{2^n} \mid v \cdot (F(x+u) + cF(x)) = 0\} - 2^n \\ &= 2{}_cDLCT_F(u,v). \end{aligned} $$

which gives ${}_cDLCT_F(u,v) = \frac{1}{2} {}_c\mathrm{AC}_F(u,v)$. On the other hand, we have

$$ {}_c\Delta_F = \max_{\substack{u \in \mathbb{F}_{2^n}, u \neq 0 \text{ if } c=1, \\ v \in \mathbb{F}_{2^m}, v \neq 0}} |{}_c\mathrm{AC}_F(u,v)| = 2 \max_{\substack{u \in \mathbb{F}_{2^n}, u \neq 0 \text{ if } c=1, \\ v \in \mathbb{F}_{2^m}, v \neq 0}} {}_cDLCT_F(u,v) = 2{}_c\gamma_F, $$

and ${}_c\gamma_F = \frac{1}{2} {}_c\Delta_F$. This finishes the proof. □

As a consequence of the former proposition, the following result connects the c-DLCT and the c-derivative of a vectorial Boolean function via the Walsh transform.

Proposition 4. *Let F be an (n, m)-vectorial Boolean function, and $c \in \mathbb{F}_{2^m}$, $c \neq 0$. Then, for any $(u, v) \in \mathbb{F}_{2^n} \times \mathbb{F}_{2^m}$,*

$$ {}_cDLCT_F(u,v) = \frac{1}{2} W_{({}_cD_uF)}(0,v). $$

Proof. Combining Definition 2 and the definition of the Walsh transform, we obtain

$$ W_{({}_cD_uF)}(0,v) = \sum_{x \in \mathbb{F}_{2^n}} (-1)^{v \cdot (F(x+u) + cF(x))} = {}_c\mathrm{AC}_F(u,v). $$

Then, using Proposition 3, we have

$$W_{{}_cD_uF}(0,v) = {}_c\mathtt{AC}_F(u,v) = 2{}_cDLCT_F(u,v),$$

and ${}_cDLCT_F(u,v) = \frac{1}{2}W_{({}_cD_uF)}(0,v)$. □

The following result shows a connection between the c-DLCT and the c-derivative of a vectorial Boolean function via the Walsh transform.

Proposition 5. *Let F be an (n,m)-vectorial Boolean function, and $c \in \mathbb{F}_{2^m}$, $c \neq 0$. Then, for any $(u,v) \in \mathbb{F}_{2^n} \times \mathbb{F}_{2^m}$,*

$$W_F(u,v)_cW_F(u,v) = 2\sum_{\omega\in\mathbb{F}_{2^n}} (-1)^{u\cdot\omega}{}_cDLCT_F(\omega,v).$$

Proof. Combining Proposition 2 and Proposition 5, we obtain

$$\begin{aligned} W_F(u,v)_cW_F(u,v) &= \sum_{z\in\mathbb{F}_{2^n}} (-1)^{u\cdot z}{}_c\mathtt{AC}_F(z,v) \\ &= 2\sum_{\omega\in\mathbb{F}_{2^n}} (-1)^{u\cdot\omega}{}_cDLCT_F(\omega,v), \end{aligned}$$

as claimed. □

The following result gives a link between ${}_cDLCT_F$ and ${}_c\Delta_F(a,b)$.

Proposition 6. *Let F be an (n,m)-vectorial Boolean function, and $c \in \mathbb{F}_{2^m}$, $c \neq 0$. Then, for any $(u,v) \in \mathbb{F}_{2^n} \times \mathbb{F}_{2^m}$,*

$${}_cDLCT_F(u,v) = \frac{1}{2}\sum_{\omega\in\mathbb{F}_{2^n}} (-1)^{\omega\cdot v}{}_c\Delta_F(u,\omega).$$

Proof. By Proposition 3, we have

$$\begin{aligned} 2{}_cDLCT_F(u,v) &= {}_c\mathtt{AC}_F(u,v) \\ &= \#\{x \in \mathbb{F}_{2^n} \mid v\cdot(F(x+u)+cF(x)) = 0)\} \\ &\quad - \#\{x \in \mathbb{F}_{2^n} \mid v\cdot(F(x+u)+cF(x)) = 1\} \\ &= \sum_{\omega\in\mathbb{F}_{2^n},\omega\cdot v=0} \#\{x \in \mathbb{F}_{2^n} \mid F(x+u)+cF(x) = \omega\} \\ &\quad - \sum_{\omega\in\mathbb{F}_{2^n},\omega\cdot v=1} \#\{x \in \mathbb{F}_{2^n} \mid F(x+u)+cF(x) = \omega\} \\ &= \sum_{\omega\in\mathbb{F}_{2^n}} (-1)^{\omega\cdot v}\#\{x \in \mathbb{F}_{2^n} \mid F(x+u)+cF(x) = \omega\} \\ &= \sum_{\omega\in\mathbb{F}_{2^n}} (-1)^{\omega\cdot v}{}_c\Delta_F(u,\omega). \end{aligned}$$

This leads to

$${}_cDLCT_F(u,v) = \frac{1}{2}\sum_{\omega\in\mathbb{F}_{2^n}} (-1)^{\omega\cdot v}{}_c\Delta_F(u,\omega),$$

which finishes the proof. □

5. The c-DLCT of the Inverse Function

In this section, we give the explicit values of the entries of the c-DLCT, including the case $c = 1$, and give some numerical results on $\mathbb{F}_{2^n}$ with $3 \leq n \leq 8$.

5.1. The 1-DLCT of the Inverse Function

For $c = 1$, the 1-DLCT satisfies the following result.

Theorem 1. *Let $F : \mathbb{F}_{2^n} \to \mathbb{F}_{2^n}$ be the inverse function defined by $F(0) = 0$, and $F(x) = x^{2^n-2}$ for $x \neq 0$. For $a, b \in \mathbb{F}_{2^n}$, define the set*

$$E_0(a,b) = \left\{ z \in b^{\perp} \mid z \neq 0, Tr\left(\frac{1}{az}\right) = 0 \right\},$$

where $b^{\perp}$ is the orthogonal space of b. Then,

$$_1DLCT_F(a,b) = \begin{cases} 2^{n-1} & \text{if } a = 0, \text{ or } b = 0, \\ 2\#E_0(a,b) + 2 - 2^{n-1} & \text{if } \frac{1}{a} \in b^{\perp}, \\ 2\#E_0(a,b) - 2^{n-1} & \text{if } \frac{1}{a} \notin b^{\perp}. \end{cases}$$

Proof. We use the definition

$$_1DLCT_F(a,b) = \#\{x \in \mathbb{F}_{2^n} \mid b \cdot (F(x+a) + F(x)) = 0\} - 2^{n-1}.$$

We consider the following cases.
Case 1. Suppose that $b = 0$. Then, for all $x \in \mathbb{F}_{2^n}$, $b \cdot (F(x+a) + F(x)) = 0$. Hence,

$$_1DLCT_F(a,0) = 2^n - 2^{n-1} = 2^{n-1}.$$

Case 2. Suppose that $b \neq 0$ and $a = 0$. Then, for all $x \in \mathbb{F}_{2^n}$, $b \cdot (F(x+a) + F(x)) = b \cdot 0 = 0$. This leads to

$$_1DLCT_F(0,b) = 2^n - 2^{n-1} = 2^{n-1}.$$

Case 3. Suppose that $b \neq 0$ and $a \neq 0$. Consider the equation

$$b \cdot (F(x+a) + F(x)) = 0. \tag{1}$$

Case 3.1. If $x = 0$, then

$$b \cdot (F(x+a) + F(x)) = b \cdot F(a) = b \cdot \frac{1}{a}.$$

Hence, $x = 0$ is a solution of the Equation (1) if and only if $\frac{1}{a} \in b^{\perp}$.
Case 3.2. If $x = a$, then

$$b \cdot (F(x+a) + F(x)) = b \cdot F(a) = b \cdot \frac{1}{a}.$$

Hence, $x = a$ is a solution of the Equation (1) if and only if $\frac{1}{a} \in b^{\perp}$.
Case 3.3. Suppose that $x \neq 0$ and $x \neq a$. We have

$$F(a+x) + F(x) = \frac{1}{a+x} + \frac{1}{x} = \frac{a}{x^2 + ax}.$$

If $b \cdot (F(a+x) + F(x)) = 0$, then $F(a+x) + F(x) = z$ for some $z \in b^{\perp}$, that is $\frac{a}{x^2+ax} = z$, or equivalently

$$zx^2 + azx + a = 0. \tag{2}$$

Case 3.3.1. If $z = 0$, then the Equation (2) reduces to $a = 0$, which is not possible.
Case 3.3.2. Suppose that $z \neq 0$. If $\text{Tr}\left(\frac{1}{az}\right) = 1$, then, by Lemma 2, the Equation (2) has no

solution, and if $\mathrm{Tr}\left(\frac{1}{az}\right) = 0$, it has two solutions.
Define the set

$$E_0(a,b) = \left\{ z \in b^{\perp} \mid z \neq 0, \mathrm{Tr}\left(\frac{1}{az}\right) = 0 \right\}.$$

The ${}_1DLCT$ in Case 3 is then

$${}_1DLCT_F(a,b) = \begin{cases} 2\#E_0(a,b) + 2 - 2^{n-1} & \text{if } \frac{1}{a} \in b^{\perp}, \\ 2\#E_0(a,b) - 2^{n-1} & \text{if } \frac{1}{a} \notin b^{\perp}, \end{cases}$$

which finishes the proof. □

5.2. The c-DLCT of the Inverse Function for $c \neq 1$

Theorem 2. *Let $F : \mathbb{F}_{2^n} \to \mathbb{F}_{2^n}$ be the inverse function defined by $F(0) = 0$, and $F(x) = \frac{1}{x}$ for $x \neq 0$. Let $c \in \mathbb{F}_{2^n}$ with $c \neq 0$ and $c \neq 1$. For $a, b \in \mathbb{F}_{2^n}$, define the set*

$$E_0(a,b,c) = \left\{ z \in b^{\perp} \mid z \neq 0, z \neq \frac{1+c}{a}, Tr\left(\frac{acz}{(1+c+az)^2}\right) = 0 \right\},$$

where $b^{\perp}$ is the orthogonal space of b. Then,

$${}_cDLCT_F(a,b) = \begin{cases} 2^{n-1} & \text{if } b = 0, \\ 0 & \text{if } a = 0, b \neq 0, \\ 2\#E_0(a,b,c) + 2 - 2^{n-1} & \text{if } \frac{1}{a} \in b^{\perp}, \frac{c}{a} \notin b^{\perp}, \\ 2\#E_0(a,b,c) + 2 - 2^{n-1} & \text{if } \frac{1}{a} \notin b^{\perp}, \frac{c}{a} \in b^{\perp}, \\ 2\#E_0(a,b,c) + 4 - 2^{n-1} & \text{if } \frac{1}{a} \in b^{\perp}, \frac{c}{a} \in b^{\perp}, \\ 2\#E_0(a,b,c) + 2 - 2^{n-1} & \text{if } \frac{1}{a} \notin b^{\perp}, \frac{c}{a} \notin b^{\perp}. \end{cases}$$

Proof. Suppose that $c \neq 0$ and $c \neq 1$. We use the definition

$${}_cDLCT_F(a,b) = \#\{x \in \mathbb{F}_{2^n} \mid b \cdot (F(x+a) + cF(x)) = 0\} - 2^{n-1}.$$

We consider the following cases.
Case 1. Suppose that $b = 0$. Then, for all $x \in \mathbb{F}_{2^n}$, $b \cdot (F(x+a) + cF(x)) = 0$. Hence,

$${}_cDLCT_F(a,0) = 2^n - 2^{n-1} = 2^{n-1}.$$

Case 2. Suppose that $b \neq 0$ and $a = 0$. If $b \cdot (F(x+a) + cF(x)) = 0$, then $b \cdot (1+c)F(x) = 0$, and $(1+c)F(x) \in b^{\perp}$. Observe that $x = 0$ is a possible solution. If $x \neq 0$, then there exists $z \in b^{\perp} \backslash \{0\}$ such that $(1+c)F(x) = z$, that is $\frac{1+c}{x} = z$, and $x = \frac{1+c}{z}$. This leads to

$${}_cDLCT_F(0,b) = \#b^{\perp} - 2^{n-1} = 0.$$

Case 3. Suppose that $a \neq 0$ and $b \neq 0$. Consider the equation

$$b \cdot (F(x+a) + cF(x)) = 0. \quad (3)$$

Case 3.1. If $x = 0$, then

$$b \cdot (F(x+a) + cF(x)) = b \cdot F(a) = b \cdot \frac{1}{a}.$$

Hence, $x = 0$ is a solution of the Equation (3) if and only if $\frac{1}{a} \in b^{\perp}$.
Case 3.2. If $x = a$, then

$$b \cdot (F(x+a) + cF(x)) = b \cdot cF(a) = b \cdot \frac{c}{a}.$$

Hence, $x = a$ is a solution of the Equation (3) if and only if $\frac{c}{a} \in b^{\perp}$.
Case 3.3. Suppose that $x \neq 0$ and $x \neq a$. We have

$$F(a+x) + cF(x) = \frac{1}{a+x} + \frac{c}{x} = \frac{(1+c)x + ac}{x^2 + ax}.$$

If $b \cdot (F(a+x) + cF(x)) = 0$, then $F(a+x) + cF(x) = z$ for some $z \in b^{\perp}$, that is $\frac{(1+c)x+ac}{x^2+ax} = z$, or equivalently

$$zx^2 + (1 + c + az)x + ac = 0. \tag{4}$$

Case 3.3.1. If $z = 0$, then the Equation (4) reduces to $(1+c)x + ac = 0$, which has one solution $x = \frac{ac}{1+c}$.
Case 3.3.2. If $z_0 = \frac{1+c}{a} \in b^{\perp}$, then for z_0, the Equation (4) reduces to $z_0x^2 + ac = 0$, which, by Lemma 2, has one solution.
Case 3.3.3. Suppose that $z \neq 0$ and $z \neq \frac{1+c}{a}$. If $\mathrm{Tr}\left(\frac{acz}{(1+c+az)^2}\right) = 1$, then, by Lemma 2, the Equation (4) has no solution, and if $\mathrm{Tr}\left(\frac{acz}{(1+c+az)^2}\right) = 0$, it has two solutions.
To summarize all the cases, we define the set

$$E_0(a,b,c) = \left\{ z \in b^{\perp} \mid z \neq 0, z \neq \frac{1+c}{a}, \mathrm{Tr}\left(\frac{acz}{(1+c+az)^2}\right) = 0 \right\}.$$

The ${}_cDLCT$ in Case 3 is then

$${}_cDLCT_F(a,b) = \begin{cases} 2\#E_0(a,b,c) + 2 - 2^{n-1} & \text{if } \frac{1}{a} \in b^{\perp}, \frac{c}{a} \notin b^{\perp}, \\ 2\#E_0(a,b,c) + 2 - 2^{n-1} & \text{if } \frac{1}{a} \notin b^{\perp}, \frac{c}{a} \in b^{\perp}, \\ 2\#E_0(a,b,c) + 4 - 2^{n-1} & \text{if } \frac{1}{a} \in b^{\perp}, \frac{c}{a} \in b^{\perp}, \\ 2\#E_0(a,b,c) + 2 - 2^{n-1} & \text{if } \frac{1}{a} \notin b^{\perp}, \frac{c}{a} \notin b^{\perp}, \end{cases}$$

which finishes the proof. □

5.3. Numerical Results for the c-DLCT of the Inverse Function

We have computed the c-DLCT of the inverse function over $\mathbb{F}_{2^n}$ for $3 \leq n \leq 7$, and all $c \in \mathbb{F}_{2^n}^*$, while for $n = 8$, we only compute it for $c = 1, 2, \ldots, 10$. The inversion and multiplication in $\mathbb{F}_{2^n}$ are processed modulo the polynomials presented in Table 1.

In Table 2, we present the values of ${}_cDLCT_F(u,v)$ of the inverse function over $\mathbb{F}_{2^4}$ with $c = 0 \times 9$.

For the inverse function over $\mathbb{F}_{2^n}$, we present in Table 3 the c-DLCT spectrum ${}_c\Gamma_F$ and c-differential-linear uniformity ${}_c\gamma_F$ for $3 \leq n \leq 8$ and for small values of c. All the other c-DLCT spectrums reduce to one of the listed ones in the table.

Table 1. The polynomials of $\mathbb{F}_{2^n}$ for $3 \leq n \leq 8$.

$\mathbb{F}_{2^n}$	Polynomial
$\mathbb{F}_{2^3}$	x^3+x+1
$\mathbb{F}_{2^4}$	x^4+x+1
$\mathbb{F}_{2^5}$	x^5+x^3+1
$\mathbb{F}_{2^6}$	x^6+x^3+1
$\mathbb{F}_{2^7}$	x^7+x^3+1
$\mathbb{F}_{2^8}$	$x^8+x^4+x^3+x^2+1$

Table 2. The values of ${}_cDLCT_F(u,v)$ of the c-DLCT of the inverse function over $\mathbb{F}_{2^4}$ for $c = 0 \times 9$.

$u \backslash v$	0	1	2	3	4	5	6	7	8	9	a	b	c	d	e	f
0	8	0	0	0	0	0	0	0	0	0	0	0	0	0	0	0
1	8	0	2	2	0	−4	2	−2	2	−4	0	2	2	0	0	−2
2	8	2	0	−2	2	2	2	−2	0	2	−4	2	−4	0	0	0
3	8	0	2	0	−2	−4	0	0	−2	0	2	2	2	2	2	−4
4	8	−2	2	−2	0	2	−4	0	2	0	2	2	2	−4	0	0
5	8	2	0	2	0	0	−2	2	−4	0	2	2	−2	0	2	−4
6	8	0	−2	0	−2	2	2	−4	0	2	−4	0	0	2	2	2
7	8	2	−4	−4	2	−2	0	2	2	0	2	−2	0	0	2	0
8	8	−2	0	0	2	2	2	0	−2	2	2	−4	0	2	−4	0
9	8	2	−4	0	2	0	2	2	0	2	0	−4	2	0	−2	−2
a	8	2	0	2	−4	2	−2	−4	2	0	0	−2	0	2	0	2
b	8	−4	0	2	0	2	2	2	0	−2	0	0	−2	2	−4	2
c	8	0	−2	−4	0	0	0	2	0	−2	2	2	2	−4	2	2
d	8	0	2	2	−4	0	−4	0	2	2	0	0	2	−2	−2	2
e	8	−4	2	2	2	−2	0	0	2	−4	−2	0	0	2	0	2
f	8	2	2	0	2	0	0	2	−4	2	−2	0	−4	−2	2	0

Table 3. The c-DLCT spectrum and the c-differential-linear connectivity uniformity of the inverse function over $\mathbb{F}_{2^n}$ for $3 \leq n \leq 8$ and small c.

$\mathbb{F}_{2^n}$	c	${}_c\Gamma_F$	${}_c\gamma_F$
$\mathbb{F}_{2^3}$	1	$\{-4,0,4\}$	4
$\mathbb{F}_{2^3}$	2	$\{-2,0,2,4\}$	2
$\mathbb{F}_{2^4}$	1	$\{-4,0,4,8\}$	4
$\mathbb{F}_{2^4}$	2	$\{-4,-2,0,2,8\}$	4
$\mathbb{F}_{2^4}$	6	$\{-2,0,2,4,8\}$	4
$\mathbb{F}_{2^5}$	1	$\{-4,0,4,16\}$	4
$\mathbb{F}_{2^5}$	2	$\{-6,-4,-2,0,2,4,6,16\}$	6
$\mathbb{F}_{2^5}$	3	$\{-6,-4,-2,0,2,4,16\}$	6
$\mathbb{F}_{2^5}$	7	$\{-4,-2,0,2,4,16\}$	4
$\mathbb{F}_{2^6}$	1	$\{-8,-4,0,4,8,32\}$	8
$\mathbb{F}_{2^6}$	2	$\{-8,-6,-4,-2,0,2,4,6,8,32\}$	8
$\mathbb{F}_{2^6}$	6	$\{-8,-6,-4,-2,0,2,4,6,32\}$	8
$\mathbb{F}_{2^6}$	8	$\{-6,-4,-2,0,2,6,8,32\}$	8
$\mathbb{F}_{2^7}$	1	$\{-12,-8,-4,0,4,8,64\}$	12
$\mathbb{F}_{2^7}$	2	$\{-12,-10,-8,-6,-4,-2,0,2,4,6,8,10,64\}$	12
$\mathbb{F}_{2^8}$	1	$\{-16,-12,-8,-4,0,4,8,12,16,128\}$	16
$\mathbb{F}_{2^8}$	2	$\{-16,-14,-12,-10,-8,-6,-4,-2,0,2,4,6,8,10,12,14,16,128\}$	16
$\mathbb{F}_{2^8}$	6	$\{-16,-14,-12,-10,-8,-6,-4,-2,0,2,4,6,8,10,12,14,128\}$	16
$\mathbb{F}_{2^8}$	10	$\{-14,-12,-10,-8,-6,-4,-2,0,2,4,6,8,10,12,14,16,128\}$	16

6. Conclusions

In this paper, we introduced and studied new cryptographic tools and parameters to help us quantify the security of S-boxes (mathematically, vectorial Boolean functions) involving block ciphers as main components: the c-Walsh transform, the c-autocorrelation, and the c-differential-linear uniformity. We also introduced a new table called the c-Differential-Linear Connectivity Table (c-DLCT) to analyse attacks related to the differential and the linear attacks. We considered various S-box family properties associated with the above-mentioned notion and presented the values of the c-DLCT of the particular crucial case of the inverse function. Finally, recall that codes over finite fields have been studied extensively because of their linear structures and practical implementations. It is the basis of the research on various kinds of codes. One well-known construction method of linear codes is derived from special functions (essentially from cryptographic functions which play a crucial role in symmetric cryptography) over finite fields (see the book [12]). Cryptographic multi-output Boolean functions and codes have essential data communication and storage applications. These two areas are closely related and have had a fascinating interplay (see, e.g., the book chapter in [43] and the references therein). Cryptographic functions and linear codes are closely related and have had a fascinating interplay. Cryptographic functions (e.g., highly nonlinear functions, Perfect Nonlinear (PN), Almost Perfect Nonlinear (APN), Bent, Almost Bent (AB), and Plateaued) have essential applications in coding theory. For instance, Perfect Nonlinear (APN or PN) functions have been employed to construct optimal linear codes (see, e.g., [44–48] and the references therein). Very recently, Mesnager, Shi, and Zhu [40] proposed several constructions of minimal (cyclic) codes from low differential uniform functions. Given these works, the derived functions from this paper would help design new families of binary minimal codes. We will keep an in-depth study of them in future work and cordially invite interested readers to investigate them.

Author Contributions: Conceptualization, S.E. and S.M.; Methodology, S.E. and S.M.; Validation, S.E. and S.M.; Formal analysis, S.E. and S.M.; Investigation, S.E. and S.M.; Writing—original draft, S.E.; Writing—review and editing, S.M. All authors have read and agreed to the published version of the manuscript.

Funding: This research received no external funding.

Institutional Review Board Statement: Not applicable.

Data Availability Statement: No new data were created or analyzed in this study. Data sharing is not applicable to this article.

Acknowledgments: The authors thank the anonymous reviewers for their comments and P. Solé for his kind invitation to contribute to this Special Issue.

Conflicts of Interest: The authors declare no conflict of interest.

References

1. *NBS FIPS PUB 46*; Data Encryption Standard. National Bureau of Standards: Gaithersburg, MD, USA; U.S. Department of Commerce: Washington, DC, USA, 15 January 1977.
2. Daemen, J.; Rijmen, V. *The Design of Rijndael: AES–The Advanced Encryption Standard*; Information Security and Cryptography; Springer: Berlin/Heidelberg, Germany, 2002.
3. Schneier, B. Description of a New Variable-Length Key, 64-bit Block Cipher (Blowfish). In *Fast Software Encryption*; Anderson, R., Ed.; Lecture Notes in Computer Science; Springer: Berlin/Heidelberg, Germany, 1994; Volume 809, pp. 191–204.
4. *GOST 28147-89*; Cryptographic Protection for Data Processing Systems, Cryptographic Transformation Algorithm. Inv. No. 3583, UDC 681.325.6:006.354. Government Standard of the USSR: Moscow, Soviet, 1998. (In Russian)
5. Biham, E.; Anderson, R.J.; Knudsen, L.R. Serpent: A new block cipher proposal. In *Fast Software Encryption, Proceedings of the 5th International Workshop, FSE'98, Paris, France, 23–25 March 1998*; Vaudenay, S., Ed.; Lecture Notes in Computer Science; Springer: Berlin/Heidelberg, Germany, 1998; Volume 1372, pp. 222–238.
6. Biham, E.; Shamir, A. Differential cryptanalysis of DES-like cryptosystems. *J. Cryptol.* **1991**, *4*, 3–72. [CrossRef]
7. Matsui, M. Linear Cryptanalysis Method for DES Cipher. In *Advances in Cryptology-EUROCRYPT'93* ; Helleseth, T., Ed.; Lecture Notes in Computer Science; Springer: Berlin/Heidelberg, Germany, 1994; Volume 765, pp. 386–397.

8. Cid, C.; Huang, T.; Peyrin, T.; Sasaki, Y.; Song, L. Boomerang Connectivity Table: A New Cryptanalysis Tool. In Proceedings of the Advances in Cryptology–EUROCRYPT 2018, Tel Aviv, Israel, 29 April– 3 May 2018; Nielsen, J.B., Rijmen, V., Eds.; Proceedings, Part II; Lecture Notes in Computer Science; Springer: Cham, Switzerland, 2018; Volume 10821, pp. 683–714.
9. Kim, H.; Kim, S.; Hong, D.; Sung, J.; Hong, S. Improved Differential-Linear Cryptanalysis Using DLCT. *J. Korea Inst. Inf. Secur. Cryptol.* **2018**, *28*, 11379–1392.
10. Bar-On, A.; Dunkelman, O.; Keller, N.; Weizman, A. DLCT: A new tool for differential-linear cryptanalysis. In Proceedings of the EUROCRYPT 2019, Darmstadt, Germany, 19–23 May 2019; Ishai, Y., Rijmen, V., Eds.; Springer: Berlin/Heidelberg, Germany, 2019; Volume 11476, pp. 313–342.
11. Nyberg, K. Differentially uniform mappings for cryptography. In *Advances in Cryptology–EUROCRYPT'93*; Helleseth, T., Ed.; Lecture Notes in Computer Science; Springer: Berlin/Heidelberg, Germany, 1994; Volume 765, pp. 55–64.
12. Carlet, C. *Boolean Functions for Cryptography and Coding Theory*; Cambridge University Press: Cambridge, UK, 2021.
13. Borisov, N.; Chew, M.; Johnson, R.; Wagner, D. Multiplicative differentials. In *Fast Software Encryption, Proceedings of the 9th International Workshop, FSE 2002, Leuven, Belgium, 4–6 February 2002*; Daemen, J., Rijmen, V., Eds.; Springer: Berlin/Heidelberg, Germany, 2002; Volume 2365, pp. 17–33.
14. Ellingsen, P.; Felke, P.; Riera, C.; Stănică, P.; Tkachenko, A. C-differentials, multiplicative uniformity and (almost) perfect c-nonlinearity. *IEEE Trans. Inf. Theory* **2020**, *66*, 5781–5789. [CrossRef]
15. Stănică, P.; Geary, A. The *c*-differential behavior of the inverse function under the EA-equivalence. *Cryptogr. Commun.* **2021**, *13*, 295–306. [CrossRef]
16. Stănică, P. Low c-differential uniformity for the Gold function modified on a subfield. In Proceedings of the International Conference on Security and Privacy (ICSP 2020), Valletta, Malta, 25–27 February 2020; Springer: Singapore, 2021; Volume 744, pp. 131–137.
17. Bartoli, D.; Calderini, M.; Riera, C.; Stănică, P. Low c-differential uniformity for functions modified on subfields. *Cryptogr. Commun.* **2022**, *14*, 1211–1227. [CrossRef]
18. Tu, Z.; Li, N.; Wu, Y.; Zeng, X.; Tang, X.; Jiang, Y. On the Differential Spectrum and the AP*c*N Property of a Class of Power Functions Over Finite Fields. *IEEE Trans. Inf. Theory* **2023**, *69*, 582–597. [CrossRef]
19. Wang, X.; Zheng, D.; Hu, L. Several classes of PcN power functions over finite fields. *Discret. Appl. Math.* **2022**, *322*, 171–182. [CrossRef]
20. Wang, Z.; Mesnager, S.; Li, N.; Zeng, X. On the *c*-differential uniformity of a class of Niho-type power functions. *arXiv* **2023**, arXiv:2305.05231.
21. Yan, H.; Zhang, K. On the c-differential spectrum of power functions over finite fields. *Des. Codes Cryptogr.* **2022**, *90*, 2385–2405. [CrossRef]
22. Garg, K.; Hasan, S.U.; Stănică, P. Several classes of permutation polynomials and their differential uniformity properties. *arXiv* **2022**, arXiv:2212.01931.
23. Hasan, S.U.; Pal, M.; Riera, C.; Stănică, P. On the *c*-differential uniformity of certain maps over finite fields. *Des. Codes Cryptogr.* **2021**, *89*, 221–239. [CrossRef]
24. Jeong, J.; Koo, N.; Kwon, S. Investigations of *c*-differential uniformity of permutations with Carlitz rank 3. *Finite Fields Appl.* **2023**, *86*, 102145. [CrossRef]
25. Li, C.; Riera, C.; Stănică, P. Low *c*-differentially uniform functions via an extension of Dillon's switching method. *arXiv* **2022**, arXiv:2204.08760.
26. Wu, Y.; Li, N.; Zeng, X. New PcN and APcN functions over finite fields. *Des. Codes Cryptogr.* **2021**, *89*, 2637–2651. [CrossRef]
27. Zha, Z.; Hu, L. Some classes of power functions with low *c*-differential uniformity over finite fields. *Des. Codes Cryptogr.* **2021**, *89*, 1193–1210. [CrossRef]
28. Hasan, S.U.; Pal, M.; Stănică, P. On the *c*-differential uniformity and boomerang uniformity of two classes of permutation polynomials. *IEEE Trans. Inf. Theory* **2022**, *68*, 679–691. [CrossRef]
29. Jeong, J.; Koo, N.; Kwon, S. On non-monomial AP*c*N permutations over finite fields of even characteristic. *arXiv* **2022**, arXiv:2205.11418.
30. Pal, M. Some new classes of (almost) perfect *c*-nonlinear permutations. *arXiv* **2022**, arXiv:2208.01004.
31. Tu, Z.; Zeng, X.; Jiang, Y.; Tang, X. A class of AP*c*N power functions over finite fields of even characteristic. *arXiv* **2021**, arXiv:2107.06464v1.
32. Wagner, D. The Boomerang Attack. In Proceedings of the Fast Software Encryption, Rome, Italy, 24–26 March 1999; Knudsen, L.R., Ed.; Lecture Notes in Computer Science; Springer: Berlin/Heidelberg, Germany, 1999; Volume 1636, pp. 156–170.
33. Boura, C.; Canteaut, A. On the Boomerang Uniformity of Cryptographic Sboxes. *IACR Trans. Symmetr. Cryptol. Ruhr Univ. Boch.* **2018**, *2018*, 290–310. [CrossRef]
34. Stănică, P. Investigations on c-boomerang uniformity and perfect nonlinearity. *arXiv* **2021**, arXiv:2004.11859.
35. Mesnager, S.; Mandal, B.; Msahli, M. Survey on recent trends towards generalized differential and boomerang uniformities. *Cryptogr. Commun.* **2021**, *14*, 691–735. [CrossRef]
36. Li, K.; Li, C.; Li, C.; Qu, L. On the differential linear connectivity table of vectorial boolean functions. *arXiv* **2019**, arXiv:1907.05986.
37. Canteaut, A.; Kölsch, L.; Li, C.; Li, C.; Li, K.; Qu, L.; Wiemer, F. On the differential-linear connectivity table of vectorial boolean functions. *arXiv* **2019**, arXiv:1908.07445.

38. Anbar, N.; Kalayci, T.; Meidl, W.; Riera, C.; Stănică, P. PcN functions, complete mappings and quasi-group difference sets. *arXiv* **2022**, arXiv:2212.12943.
39. Huffman, W.C.; Pless, V. *Fundamentals of Error-Correcting Codes;* Cambridge University Press: Cambridge, UK, 2003.
40. Mesnager, S.; Shi, M.; Zhu, H. Cyclic codes from low differentially uniform functions. *arXiv* **2022**, arXiv:2210.12092.
41. Pommerening, K. Quadratic Equations in Finite Fields of Characteristic 2. February 2012. Available online: http://www.staff.uni-mainz.de/pommeren/MathMisc/QuGlChar2.pdf (accessed on 1 January 2024).
42. Canteaut, A.; Kölsch, L.; Li, C.; Li, C.; Li, K.; Qu, L.; Wiemer, F. Autocorrelations of Vectorial Boolean Functions. Cryptology ePrint Archive, Paper 2021/947. 2021. Available online: https://eprint.iacr.org/2021/947 (accessed on 1 January 2024).
43. Mesnager, S. Chapter 20–Linear codes from functions. In *Concise Encyclopedia of Coding Theory;* Huffman, W.-C., Kim, J.-L., Solé, P., Eds.; CRC Press/Taylor and Francis Group: London, UK, 2021; 94p.
44. Mesnager, S. Linear codes with few weights from weakly regular bent functions based on a generic construction. *Cryptogr. Commun.* **2017**, *9*, 71–84. [CrossRef]
45. Mesnager, S.; Özbudak, F.; Sınak, A. Linear codes from weakly regular plateaued functions and their secret sharing schemes. *Des. Codes Cryptogr.* **2019**, *87*, 463–480. [CrossRef]
46. Mesnager, S.; Qi, Y.; Ru, H.; Tang, C. Minimal linear codes from characteristic functions. *IEEE Trans. Inf. Theory* **2020**, *66*, 5404–5413. [CrossRef]
47. Mesnager, S.; Sınak, A. Several classes of minimal linear codes with few weights from weakly regular plateaued functions. *IEEE Trans. Inf. Theory* **2020**, *66*, 2296–2310. [CrossRef]
48. Mesnager, S.; Sınak, A.; Yayla, O. Minimal linear codes with few weights and their Secret Sharing. *Int. J. Inf. Secur. Sci.* **2019**, *8*, 44–52.

entropy

MDPI

Article

Non-Projective Two-Weight Codes

Sascha Kurz [1,2]

[1] Mathematisches Institut, Universität Bayreuth , D-95440 Bayreuth, Germany; sascha.kurz@uni-bayreuth.de
[2] Department of Data Science, Friedrich-Alexander-Universitäät Erlangen-Nürnberg, D-91058 Erlangen, Germany; sascha.kurz@fau.de

Abstract: It has been known since the 1970's that the difference of the non-zero weights of a projective $\mathbb{F}_q$-linear two-weight code has to be a power of the characteristic of the underlying field. Here, we study non-projective two-weight codes and, e.g., show the same result under mild extra conditions. For small dimensions we give exhaustive enumerations of the feasible parameters in the binary case.

Keywords: linear codes; two-weight codes; two-character sets

MSC: 94B05; 05B25; 68R01

1. Introduction

It has been known since the 1970s that the two non-zero weights of a projective $\mathbb{F}_q$-linear two-weight code C can be written as $w_1 = up^t$ and $w_2 = (u+1)p^t$, where $u \in \mathbb{N}_{\geq 1}$ and p is the characteristic of the underlying finite field $\mathbb{F}_q$; see Corollary 2 [1]. So, especially the weight difference $w_2 - w_1$ is a power of the characteristic p. Here, we want to consider $\mathbb{F}_q$-linear two-weight codes C with non-zero weights $w_1 < w_2$ which are not necessarily projective. In [2], it was observed that if $w_2 - w_1$ is not a power of the characteristic p, then the code C has to be non-projective, which settles a question in [3]. Here, we prove the stronger statement that C is repetitive, i.e., C is the l-fold repetition of a smaller two-weight code C', where l is the largest factor of $w_2 - w_1$ that is coprime to the field size q, if C does not have full support, cf. [4]. Moreover, if a two-weight code C is non-repetitive and does not have full support, then its two non-zero weights can be written as $w_1 = up^t$ and $w_2 = (u+1)p^t$, where again p is the characteristic of the underlying finite field $\mathbb{F}_q$; see Theorem 3.

Constructions for projective two-weight codes can be found in the classical survey paper [5]. Many research papers considered these objects since they, e.g., yield strongly regular graphs (srgs), and we refer the reader to [6] for a corresponding monograph on srgs. For a few more recent papers on constructions for projective two-weight codes, we refer, e.g., to [7–10]. In, e.g., [9], the author uses geometric language and speaks of constructions for two-character sets, i.e., sets of points in a projective space $\mathrm{PG}(k-1,q)$ with just two different hyperplane multiplicities; call them s and t. In general, each (full-length) linear code is in one-to-one correspondence to a (spanning) multiset of points in some projective space $\mathrm{PG}(k-1,q)$. Here, we will also mainly use the geometric language and consider a few general constructions for two-character multisets of points corresponding to two-weight codes (possibly non-projective). For each subset $\overline{\mathcal{H}}$ of hyperplanes in $\mathrm{PG}(k-1,q)$ we construct a multiset of points $\mathcal{M}(\overline{\mathcal{H}})$ such that all hyperplanes $H \in \overline{\mathcal{H}}$ have the same multiplicity, say s, and also all other hyperplanes $H \notin \overline{\mathcal{H}}$ have the same multiplicity, say t. Actually, we characterize the full set of such multisets with at most two different hyperplane multiplicities given $\overline{\mathcal{H}}$; see Theorems 1 and 2. Using this correspondence we have classified all two-weight codes up to symmetry for small parameters. For projective two-weight codes such enumerations can be found in [11].

Brouwer and van Eupen give a correspondence between arbitrary projective codes and arbitrary two-weight codes via the so-called BvE dual transform. The correspondence can be said to be 1–1, even though there are choices for the involved parameters to be made in both directions. In [12], the dual transform was, e.g., applied to the unique projective $[16,5,9]_3$-code. For parameters $\alpha = \frac{1}{3}$ and $\beta = -3$ the result is a $[69,5,45]_3$ two-weight code, and for $\alpha = -\frac{1}{3}$ and $\beta = 5$ the result is a $[173,5,108]_3$ two-weight code. This resembles the fact that we have some freedom when constructing a two-weight code from a given projective code, e.g., we can take complements or add simplex codes of the same dimension. Our obtained results may be rephrased in the language of the BvE dual transform by restricting to a canonical choice of the involved parameters. For further literature on the dual transform, see, e.g., [12–15]. For a variant that is rather close to our presentation we refer the reader to [16].

With respect to further related studies in the literature we remark that a special subclass of (non-projective) two-weight codes was completely characterized in [17]. A conjecture by Vega [18] states that all two-weight cyclic codes are the "known" ones, cf. [19]. Another stream of the literature considers the problem of whether all projective two-weight codes that have the parameters of partial k-spreads indeed have to be partial k-spreads. Those results can be found in papers considering extendability results for partial k-spreads or classifying minihypers; see, e.g., [20]. Two-weight codes have also been considered over rings instead of finite fields; see, e.g., [21].

The remaining part of this paper is structured as follows. In Section 2, we introduce the necessary preliminaries for linear two-weight codes and their geometric counterpart called two-character multisets in projective spaces. In general, multisets of points, corresponding to general linear codes, can be described via so-called characteristic functions and we collect some of their properties in Section 3. Examples and constructions for two-character multisets are given in Section 4. In Section 5, we present our main results. We close with enumeration of the results for two-character multisets in $\mathrm{PG}(k-1,q)$ for small parameters in Section 6. We will mainly use geometric language and arguments. For the ease of the reader we only use elementary arguments and give (almost) all details.

2. Preliminaries

An $[n,k]_q$-code C is a k-dimensional subspace of $\mathbb{F}_q^n$, i.e., C is assumed to be $\mathbb{F}_q$-linear. Here, n is called the length and k is called the dimension of C. Elements $c \in C$ are called codewords and the weight $\mathrm{wt}(c)$ of a codeword is given by the number of non-zero coordinates. Clearly, the all-zero vector $\mathbf{0}$ has weight zero and all other codewords have a positive integer weight. A two-weight code is a linear code with exactly two non-zero weights. A generator matrix for C is a $k \times n$ matrix G such that its rows span C. We say that C is of full length if for each index $1 \le i \le n$ there exists a codeword $c \in C$ whose ith coordinate c_i is non-zero, i.e., all columns of a generator matrix of C are non-zero. The dual code $C^\perp$ of C is the $(n-k)$-dimensional code consisting of the vectors orthogonal to all codewords of C with respect to the inner product $\langle u, v\rangle = \sum_{i=1}^n u_i v_i$.

Now, let C be a full-length $[n,k]_q$-code with generator matrix G. Each column g of G is an element of $\mathbb{F}_q^k$ and since $g \neq \mathbf{0}$ we can consider $\langle g \rangle$ as a point in the projective space $\mathrm{PG}(k-1,q)$. Using the geometric language we call 1-, 2-, 3-, and $(k-1)$-dimensional subspaces of $\mathbb{F}_q^k$ points, lines, planes, and hyperplanes in $\mathrm{PG}(k-1,q)$. Instead of an l-dimensional space we also speak of an l-space. By $\mathcal{P}$ we denote the set of points and by $\mathcal{H}$ we denote the set of hyperplanes of $\mathrm{PG}(k-1,q)$ whenever k and q are clear from the context. A multiset of points in $\mathrm{PG}(k-1,q)$ is a mapping $\mathcal{M}\colon \mathcal{P} \to \mathbb{N}$, i.e., to each point $P \in \mathcal{P}$ we assign its multiplicity $\mathcal{M}(P) \in \mathbb{N}$. By $\#\mathcal{M} = \sum_{P\in\mathcal{P}} \mathcal{M}(P)$ we denote the cardinality of $\mathcal{M}$. The support $\mathrm{supp}(\mathcal{M})$ is the set of all points with non-zero multiplicity. We say that $\mathcal{M}$ is spanning if the set of points in the support of $\mathcal{M}$ span $\mathrm{PG}(k-1,q)$. Clearly permuting columns of a generator matrix G or multiplying some columns with non-zero elements in $\mathbb{F}_q^\star := \mathbb{F}_q \backslash \{0\}$ yields an equivalent code. In addition to that we obtain a one-to-one correspondence between full-length $[n,k]_q$-codes and spanning multisets of points $\mathcal{M}$ in $\text{PG}(k-1,q)$ with cardinality $\#\mathcal{M} = n$. Moreover, two linear $[n,k]_q$-codes C and C' are equivalent if their corresponding multisets of points $\mathcal{M}$ and $\mathcal{M}'$ are. For details we refer, e.g., to [22]. A linear code C is projective if its corresponding multiset of points satisfies $\mathcal{M}(P) \in \{0,1\}$ for all $P \in \mathcal{P}$. We also speak of a set of points in this case. The multisets of points with $\mathcal{M}(P) = 0$ for all $P \in \mathcal{P}$ are called trivial.

Geometrically, for a non-zero codeword $c \in C$ the set $c \cdot \mathbb{F}_q^\star$ corresponds to a hyperplane $H \in \mathcal{H}$ and $\text{wt}(c) = \#\mathcal{M} - \mathcal{M}(H)$, where we extend the function $\mathcal{M}$ additively, i.e., $\mathcal{M}(S) := \sum_{P \in S} \mathcal{M}(P)$ for every subset $S \subseteq \mathcal{P}$ of points. We call $\mathcal{M}(H)$ the multiplicity of hyperplane $H \in \mathcal{H}$ and have $\mathcal{M}(V) = \#\mathcal{M}$ for the entire ambient space $V := \mathcal{P}$. The number of hyperplanes $\#\mathcal{H}$, as well as the number of points $\#\mathcal{P}$, in $\text{PG}(k-1,q)$ is given by $[k]_q := \frac{q^k-1}{q-1}$. A two-character multiset is a multiset of points $\mathcal{M}$ such that exactly two different hyperplane multiplicities $\mathcal{M}(H)$ occur. i.e., a multiset of points $\mathcal{M}$ is a two-character multiset if its corresponding code C is a two-weight code. If $\mathcal{M}$ actually is a set of points, i.e., if we have $\mathcal{M}(P) \in \{0,1\}$ for all points $P \in \mathcal{P}$, then we speak of a two-character set. We say that an $[n,k]_q$-code C is Δ-divisible if the weights of all codewords are divisible by Δ. A multiset of points $\mathcal{M}$ is called Δ-divisible if the corresponding linear code is. More directly, a multiset of points $\mathcal{M}$ is Δ-divisible if we have $\mathcal{M}(H) \equiv \#\mathcal{M} \pmod{\Delta}$ for all $H \in \mathcal{H}$.

A one-weight code is an $[n,k]_q$-code C such that all non-zero codewords have the same weight w. One-weight codes have been completely classified in [23] and are given by repetitions of so-called simplex codes. Geometrically, the multiset of points $\mathcal{M}$ in $\text{PG}(k-1,q)$ corresponding to a one-weight code C satisfies $\mathcal{M}(P) = l$ for all $P \in \mathcal{P}$, i.e., we have $\#\mathcal{M} = n = [k]_q \cdot l$, $\mathcal{M}(H) = [k-1]_q \cdot l$ for all $H \in \mathcal{H}$, and $w = \#\mathcal{M} - \mathcal{M}(H) = q^{k-1} \cdot l$. We say that a linear $[n,k]_q$-code C is repetitive if it is the l-fold repetition of an $[n/l,k]_q$-code C', where $l > 1$, and non-repetitive otherwise. A given multiset of points $\mathcal{M}$ is called repeated if its corresponding code is. More directly, a non-trivial multiset of points $\mathcal{M}$ is repeated if the greatest common divisor of all point multiplicities is larger than one. We say that a multiset of points $\mathcal{M}$ or its corresponding linear code C has full support if $\text{supp}(\mathcal{M}) = \mathcal{P}$, i.e., if $\mathcal{M}(P) > 0$ for all $P \in \mathcal{P}$. So, for each non-repetitive one-weight code C with length n, dimension k, and non-zero weight w we have $n = [k]_q$ and $w = q^{k-1}$. Each non-trivial one-weight code, i.e., one with dimension at least 1, has full support. The aim of this paper is to characterize the possible parameters of non-repetitive two-weight codes (with or without full support). For the correspondence between $[n,k]_q$-codes and multisets of points $\mathcal{M}$ in $\text{PG}(k-1,q)$ we have assumed that $\mathcal{M}$ is spanning. If $\mathcal{M}$ is not spanning, then there exists a hyperplane containing the entire support, so that $\mathcal{M}$ is two-character multiset if $\mathcal{M}$ induces a one-character multiset in the span of $\text{supp}(\mathcal{M})$, cf. Proposition 1. The structure of the set of all two-character multisets where the larger hyperplane multiplicity is attained for a prescribed subset of the hyperplanes is considered in Section 5.

3. Characteristic Functions

Fixing the field size q and the dimension k of the ambient space, a multiset of points in $\text{PG}(k-1,q)$ is a mapping $\mathcal{M}\colon \mathcal{P} \to \mathbb{N}$. By $\mathcal{F}$ we denote the $\mathbb{Q}$-vector space consisting of all functions $F\colon \mathcal{P} \to \mathbb{Q}$, where addition and scalar multiplication is defined pointwise. i.e., $(F_1 + F_2)(P) := F_1(P) + F_2(P)$ and $(x \cdot F_1)(P) := x \cdot F_1(P)$ for all $P \in \mathcal{P}$, where $F_1, F_2 \in \mathcal{F}$, and $x \in \mathbb{Q}$ are arbitrary. For each non-empty subset $S \subseteq \mathcal{P}$ the characteristic function χ_S is defined by $\chi_S(P) = 1$ if $P \in S$ and $\chi_S(P)$ otherwise. Clearly the set of functions χ_P for all $P \in \mathcal{P}$ forms a basis of $\mathcal{F}$ for ambient space $\text{PG}(k-1,q)$ for all $k \geq 1$. Note that there are no hyperplanes if $k = 1$ and hyperplanes coincide with points for $k = 2$. We also extend the functions $F \in \mathcal{F}$ additively, i.e., we set $F(S) = \sum_{P \in S} F(P)$ for all $S \subseteq \mathcal{P}$. Our next aim is to show the well-known fact that also the set of functions χ_H for all hyperplanes $H \in \mathcal{H}$ forms a basis of $\mathcal{F}$ for ambient space $\text{PG}(k-1,q)$ for all $k \geq 2$. In other words, also $\mathcal{M}(P)$ can be reconstructed from the $\mathcal{M}(H)$:

Lemma 1. *Let $\mathcal{M} \in \mathcal{F}$ for ambient space $\mathrm{PG}(k-1,q)$, where $k \geq 2$. Then, we have*

$$\mathcal{M}(P) = \sum_{H \in \mathcal{H}\,:\,P \in H} \frac{1}{[k-1]_q} \cdot \mathcal{M}(H) + \sum_{H \in \mathcal{H}\,:\,P \notin H} \frac{1}{q^{k-1}} \cdot \left(\frac{1}{[k-1]_q} - 1 \right) \cdot \mathcal{M}(H) \quad (1)$$

for all points $P \in \mathcal{P}$.

Proof. Without loss of generality we assume $k \geq 3$. Since each point $P' \in \mathcal{P}$ is contained in $[k-1]_q$ of the $\#\mathcal{H} = [k]_q$ hyperplanes and each point $P' \neq P$ is contained in $[k-2]_q$ of the $[k-1]_q$ hyperplanes that contain P, we have

$$\sum_{H \in \mathcal{H}\,:\,P \in H} \mathcal{M}(H) = [k-2]_q \cdot |\mathcal{M}| + ([k-1]_q - [k-2]_q)\mathcal{M}(P) = [k-2]_q \cdot |\mathcal{M}| + q^{k-2}\mathcal{M}(P)$$

so that

$$\sum_{H \in \mathcal{H}\,:\,P \in H} \mathcal{M}(H) - \frac{[k-2]_q}{[k-1]_q} \cdot \sum_{H \in \mathcal{H}} \mathcal{M}(H) = q^{k-2}\mathcal{M}(P)$$

using $[k-1]_q \cdot \#\mathcal{M} = \sum_{H \in \mathcal{H}} \mathcal{M}(H)$. Thus, we can conclude the stated formula using

$$\frac{1}{q^{k-2}} \cdot \left(1 - \frac{[k-2]_q}{[k-1]_q} \right) = \frac{1}{q^{k-2}} \cdot \frac{[k-1]_q - [k-2]_q}{[k-1]_q} = \frac{1}{[k-1]_q}$$

and

$$-\frac{[k-2]_q}{[k-1]_q \cdot q^{k-2}} = \frac{1 - [k-1]_q}{[k-1]_q \cdot q^{k-1}} = \frac{1}{q^{k-1}} \cdot \left(\frac{1}{[k-1]_q} - 1 \right).$$

□

As an example we state that in $\mathrm{PG}(3-1,2)$ we have

$$\mathcal{M}(P) = \frac{1}{3} \cdot \sum_{H \in \mathcal{H}\,:\,P \in H} \mathcal{M}(H) - \frac{1}{6} \cdot \sum_{H \in \mathcal{H}\,:\,P \notin H} \mathcal{M}(H).$$

Lemma 2. *Let $\mathcal{M} \in \mathcal{F}$ for ambient space $\mathrm{PG}(k-1,q)$, where $k \geq 2$. Then, there exist $\alpha_H \in \mathbb{Q}$ for all hyperplanes $H \in \mathcal{H}$ such that*

$$\mathcal{M} = \sum_{H \in \mathcal{H}} \alpha_H \cdot \chi_H. \quad (2)$$

Moreover, the coefficients α_H are uniquely determined by $\mathcal{M}$.

Proof. Each point $P \in \mathcal{P}$ is contained in $[k-1]_q$ hyperplanes and for each point $Q \neq P$ there are exactly $[k-2]_q$ hyperplanes that contain both P and Q, so that

$$\sum_{H \in \mathcal{H}\,:\,P \in H} \chi_H - \frac{[k-2]_q}{[k-1]_q} \cdot \sum_{H \in \mathcal{H}} \chi_H = q^{k-2} \cdot \chi_P.$$

Using

$$\mathcal{M} = \sum_{P \in \mathcal{P}} \mathcal{M}(P) \cdot \chi_P$$

we conclude the existence of the $\alpha_H \in \mathbb{Q}$. Since the functions $(\chi_P)_{P \in \mathcal{P}}$ form a basis of the $\mathbb{Q}$-vector space $\mathcal{F}$, which is also generated by the functions $(\chi_H)_{H \in \mathcal{H}}$, counting $\#\mathcal{P} = [k]_q = \#\mathcal{H}$ yields that also $(\chi_H)_{H \in \mathcal{H}}$ forms a basis and the coefficients α_H are uniquely determined by $\mathcal{M}$. □

If $\mathcal{M} \in \mathcal{F}$ is given by the representation

$$\mathcal{M} = \sum_{P \in \mathcal{P}} \alpha_P \cdot \chi_P$$

with $\alpha_P \in \mathbb{Q}$ we can easily decide whether $\mathcal{M}$ is a multiset of points. The necessary and sufficient conditions are given by $\alpha_P \in \mathbb{N}$ for all $P \in \mathcal{P}$ (including the case of a trivial multiset of points). If a multiset of points is characterized by coefficients α_H for all hyperplanes $H \in \mathcal{H}$, as in Lemma 2, then some α_H may be fractional or negative. For two-character multisets we will construct a different unique representation, involving the characteristic functions χ_H of hyperplanes; see Theorem 1.

Let us state a few observations about operations for multisets of points that yield multisets of points again.

Lemma 3. *For two multisets of points $\mathcal{M}_1$ and $\mathcal{M}_2$ of $\mathrm{PG}(k-1,q)$ and each non-negative integer $n \in \mathbb{N}$ the functions $\mathcal{M}_1 + \mathcal{M}_2$ and $n \cdot \mathcal{M}_1$ are multisets of points of $\mathrm{PG}(k-1,q)$.*

In order to say something about the subtraction of multisets of points we denote the minimum point multiplicity of a multiset of points $\mathcal{M}$ by $\mu(\mathcal{M})$ and the maximum point multiplicity by $\gamma(\mathcal{M})$. Whenever $\mathcal{M}$ is clear from the context we also just write μ and γ instead of $\mu(\mathcal{M})$ and $\mu(\gamma)$.

Lemma 4. *Let $\mathcal{M}_1$ and $\mathcal{M}_2$ be two multisets of points of $\mathrm{PG}(k-1,q)$. If $\mu(\mathcal{M}_1) \ge \gamma(\mathcal{M}_2)$, then $\mathcal{M}_1 - \mathcal{M}_2$ is a multiset of points of $\mathrm{PG}(k-1,q)$.*

Definition 1. *Let $\mathcal{M}$ be a multiset of points in $\mathrm{PG}(k-1,q)$. If l is an integer with $l \ge \gamma(\mathcal{M})$, then the l-complement $\mathcal{M}^{l-C}$ of $\mathcal{M}$ is defined by $\mathcal{M}^{l-C}(P) := l - \mathcal{M}(P)$ for all points $P \in \mathcal{P}$.*

One can easily check that $\mathcal{M}^{l-C}$ is a multiset of points with cardinality $l \cdot [k]_q - \#\mathcal{M}$, maximum point multiplicity $\gamma\left(\mathcal{M}^{l-C}\right) = l - \mu(\mathcal{M})$, and minimum point multiplicity $\mu\left(\mathcal{M}^{l-C}\right) = l - \gamma(\mathcal{M})$. Using characteristic functions we can write $\mathcal{M}^{l-C} = l \cdot \chi_V - \mathcal{M}$, where $V = \mathcal{P}$ denotes the set of all points of the ambient space.

Given an arbitrary function $\mathcal{M} \in \mathcal{F}$ there always exist $\alpha \in \mathbb{Q}\backslash\{0\}$ and $\beta \in \mathbb{Z}$ such that $\alpha \cdot \mathcal{M} + \beta \cdot \chi_V$ is a multiset of points.

4. Examples and Constructions for Two-Character Multisets

The aim of this section is to list a few easy constructions for two-character multisets of points $\mathcal{M}$ in $\mathrm{PG}(k-1,q)$. We will always abbreviate $n = \#\mathcal{M}$ and denote the two occurring hyperplane multiplicities by s and t, where we assume $s > t$ by convention.

Proposition 1. *For integers $1 \le l < k$, let L be an arbitrary l-space in $\mathrm{PG}(k-1,q)$. Then, χ_L is a two-character set with $n = [l]_q$, $\gamma = 1$, $\mu = 0$, $s = [l]_q$, and $t = [l-1]_q$.*

Note that for the case $l = k$ we have the one-character set χ_V, which can be combined with any two-character multiset.

Lemma 5. *Let $\mathcal{M}$ be a two-character multiset of points in $\mathrm{PG}(k-1,q)$. Then, for each integer $0 \le a \le \mu(\mathcal{M})$, each $b \in N$, and each integer $c \ge \gamma(\mathcal{M})$ the functions $\mathcal{M} - a \cdot \chi_V$, $\mathcal{M} + b \cdot \chi_V$, $b \cdot \mathcal{M}$, and $c \cdot \chi_V - \mathcal{M}$ are two-character multisets of points.*

For the first and the fourth construction we also spell out the implications for the parameters of a given two-character multiset:

Lemma 6. *Let $\mathcal{M}$ be a multiset of points in $\mathrm{PG}(k-1,q)$ such that $\mathcal{M}(H) \in \{s,t\}$ for every hyperplane $H \in \mathcal{H}$. If $\mathcal{M}(P) \ge l$ for every point $P \in \mathcal{P}$, i.e., $l \le \mu(\mathcal{M})$, then $\mathcal{M}' := \mathcal{M} - l \cdot \chi_V$*

is a multiset of points in PG$(k-1,q)$ *such that* $\mathcal{M}'(H) \in \{s-[k-1]_q \cdot l, t-[k-1]_q \cdot l\}$ *for every hyperplane* $H \in \mathcal{H}$.

Lemma 7. *Let* $\mathcal{M}$ *be a multiset of points in* PG$(k-1,q)$ *such that* $\mathcal{M}(H) \in \{s,t\}$ *for every hyperplane* $H \in \mathcal{H}$. *If* $\mathcal{M}(P) \le u$, *i.e.,* $\le \gamma(\mathcal{M})$ *for every point* $P \in \mathcal{P}$, *then the u-complement* $\mathcal{M}' := u \cdot \chi_V - \mathcal{M}$ *of* $\mathcal{M}$ *is a multiset of points in* PG$(k-1,q)$ *such that* $\mathcal{M}'(H) \in \{u[k-1]-s, u[k-1]-t\}$ *for every hyperplane* $H \in \mathcal{H}$.

We can also use two (almost) arbitrary subspaces to construct two-character multisets:

Proposition 2. *Let* $a \ge b \ge 1$ *and* $0 \le i \le b-1$ *be arbitrary integers, A be an a-space, and B be a b-space with* $\dim(A \cap B) = i$ *in* PG$(k-1,q)$, *where* $k = a+b-i$. *Then,* $\mathcal{M} = \chi_A + q^{a-b} \cdot \chi_B$ *satisfies* $\mathcal{M}(H) \in \{s,t\}$ *for all* $H \in \mathcal{H}$, *where* $s = [a-1]_q + q^{a-b} \cdot [b-1]_q$ *and* $t = s + q^{a-1}$. *If* $i = 0$, *then* $\gamma = q^{a-b}$, *and* $\gamma = q^{a-b}+1$ *otherwise. In general, we have* $n = [a]_q + q^{a-b} \cdot [b]_q$ *and* $\mu = 0$.

Proof. For each $H \in \mathcal{H}$ we have $\mathcal{M}(H \cap A) \in \{[a-1]_q, [a]_q\}$ and $\mathcal{M}(H \cap B) \in \{[b-1]_q, [b]_q\}$. Noting that we cannot have both $\mathcal{M}(H \cap A) = [a]_q$ and $\mathcal{M}(H \cap B) = [b]_q$, we conclude $\mathcal{M}(H) \in \left\{[a-1]_q + q^{a-b} \cdot [b-1]_q, [a]_q + q^{a-b} \cdot [b-1]_q, [a-1]_q + q^{a-b} \cdot [b]_q\right\} = \{s,t\}$. □

A partial k-spread is a set of k-spaces in PG$(v-1,q)$ with pairwise trivial intersection.

Proposition 3. *Let* $\mathcal{S}_1, \ldots, \mathcal{S}_r$ *be a partial parallelism of* PG$(2k-1,q)$, *i.e., the* $\mathcal{S}_i$ *are partial k-spreads that are pairwise disjoint. Then,*

$$\mathcal{M} = \sum_{i=1}^{r} \sum_{S \in \mathcal{S}_i} \chi_S$$

is a two-character multiset of PG$(2k-1,q)$ *with* $n = r \cdot [k]_q$ *and hyperplane multiplicities* $s = r \cdot [k-1]_q$, $t = r \cdot [k-1]_q + q^{k-1}$, *where* $r = \sum_{i=1}^{r} |\mathcal{S}_i|$.

Cf. example SU2 in [5]. Field changes work similarly to those explained in Section 6 [5] for two-character sets.

Based on hyperplanes we can construct large families of two-character multisets:

Lemma 8. *Let* $\emptyset \ne \mathcal{H}' \subsetneq \mathcal{H}$ *be a subset of the hyperplanes of* PG$(k-1,q)$, *where* $k \ge 3$, *then*

$$\mathcal{M} = \sum_{H \in \mathcal{H}'} \chi_H \tag{3}$$

is a two-character multiset with $n = r[k-1]_q$, $s = r[k-2]_q + q^{k-2}$, *and* $t = r[k-2]_q$, *where* $r = \#\mathcal{H}'$.

By allowing $\mathcal{H}'$ to be a multiset of hyperplanes we end up with $(\tau+1)$-character sets, where τ is the maximum number of occurrences of a hyperplane in $\mathcal{H}'$.

Applying Lemma 6 yields:

Lemma 9. *Let* $\emptyset \ne \mathcal{H}' \subsetneq \mathcal{H}$ *be a subset of the hyperplanes of* PG$(k-1,q)$, *where* $k \ge 3$. *If each point* $P \in \mathcal{P}$ *is contained in at least* $\mu \in N$ *elements of* $\mathcal{H}'$, *then*

$$\mathcal{M} = \sum_{H \in \mathcal{H}'} \chi_H - \mu \cdot \chi_V \tag{4}$$

is a two-character multiset with $n = r[k-1]_q - \mu[k]_q$, $s = r[k-2]_q + q^{k-2} - \mu[k-1]_q$ *and* $t = r[k-2]_q - \mu[k-1]_q$, *where* $r = |\mathcal{H}'|$.

In some cases we obtain two-character multisets where all point multiplicities have a common factor $g > 1$. Here, we can apply the following general construction:

Lemma 10. *Let $\mathcal{M}$ be a multiset of points in $\mathrm{PG}(k-1,q)$ such that $\mathcal{M}(H) \in \{s,t\}$ for every hyperplane $H \in \mathcal{H}$. If $\mathcal{M}(P) \equiv 0 \pmod{g}$ for every point $P \in \mathcal{P}$, then $\mathcal{M}' := \frac{1}{g} \cdot \mathcal{M}$ is a multiset of points in $\mathrm{PG}(k-1,q)$ such that $\mathcal{M}'(H) \in \left\{\frac{1}{g} \cdot s, \frac{1}{g} \cdot t\right\}$ for every hyperplane $H \in \mathcal{H}$. Moreover, we have $\#\mathcal{M}' = \frac{1}{g} \cdot \#\mathcal{M}$, $\mu(\mathcal{M}') = \frac{1}{g} \cdot \mu(\mathcal{M})$, and $\gamma(\mathcal{M}') = \frac{1}{g} \cdot \gamma(\mathcal{M})$.*

Interestingly enough, it will turn out that we can construct all two-character multisets by combining Lemma 8 with Lemmas 5 and 10; see Theorems 1 and 2.

5. Geometric Duals and Sets of Feasible Parameters for Two-Character Multisets

To each two-character multiset $\mathcal{M}$ in $\mathrm{PG}(k-1,q)$, i.e., $\{\mathcal{M}(H) : H \in \mathcal{H}\} = \{s,t\}$ for some $s,t \in \mathbb{N}$, we can assign a set of points $\overline{\mathcal{M}}$ by using the geometric dual, i.e., interchanging hyperplanes and points. More precisely, fix a non-degenerated billinear form $\perp$ and consider pairs of points and hyperplanes (P,H) that are perpendicular with respect to $\perp$ (different choices of $\perp$ lead to isomorphic configurations). We write $H = P^{\perp}$ for the geometric dual of a point. We define $\overline{\mathcal{M}}$ via $\overline{\mathcal{M}}(P) = 1$ if $\mathcal{M}(H) = s$, where $H = P^{\perp}$, and $\overline{\mathcal{M}}(P) = 0$ otherwise, i.e., if $\mathcal{M}(H) = t$ (a generalization of the notion of the geometric dual has been introduced by Brouwer and van Eupen [12] for linear codes and formulated for multisets of points by Dodunekov and Simonis [22]). Of course we have some freedom in how we order s and t. So, we may also write $\overline{\mathcal{M}}(P) = (\mathcal{M}(H) - t)/(s-t) \in \{0,1\}$ for all $P \in \mathcal{P}$, where $H = P^{\perp}$. Noting the asymmetry in s and t we may also interchange the role of s and t or replace $\overline{\mathcal{M}}$ by its complement. Note that in principle several multisets of points with two hyperplane multiplicities can have the same corresponding point set $\overline{\mathcal{M}}$.

For the other direction we can start with an arbitrary set of points $\overline{\mathcal{M}}$, i.e., $\overline{\mathcal{M}}(P) \in \{0,1\}$ for all $P \in \mathcal{P}$. The multiset of points with two hyperplane multiplicities $\mathcal{M}$ is then defined via $\mathcal{M}(H) = s$ if $\overline{\mathcal{M}}(P) = 1$, where $H = P^{\perp}$, and $\mathcal{M}(H) = t$ if $\overline{\mathcal{M}}(P) = 0$. i.e., we may set

$$\mathcal{M}(H) = t + (s-t) \cdot \overline{\mathcal{M}}(H^{\perp}). \tag{5}$$

While we have $\mathcal{M}(H) \in \mathbb{N}$ for all $s,t \in \mathbb{N}$, the point multiplicities $\mathcal{M}(P)$ induced by the hyperplane multiplicities $\mathcal{M}(H)$ (see Lemma 1) are not integral or non-negative in general. For suitable choices of s and t they are, while for others they are not.

Definition 2. *Let $\overline{\mathcal{M}}$ be a set of points in $\mathrm{PG}(k-1,q)$. By $\mathbb{L}(\overline{\mathcal{M}}) \subseteq \mathbb{N}^2$ we denote the set of all pairs $(s,t) \in \mathbb{N}^2$ with $s \geq t$ such that a multiset of points $\mathcal{M}$ in $\mathrm{PG}(k-1,q)$ exists with $\mathcal{M}(H) = s$ if $\overline{\mathcal{M}}(H^{\perp}) = 1$ and $\mathcal{M}(H) = t$ if $\overline{\mathcal{M}}(H^{\perp}) = 0$ for all hyperplanes $H \in \mathcal{H}$.*

Directly from Lemma 5 we can conclude:

Lemma 11. *Let $\overline{\mathcal{M}}$ be a set of points in $\mathrm{PG}(k-1,q)$. If $(s,t) \in \mathbb{L}(\overline{\mathcal{M}})$, then we have*

$$\langle (s,t) \rangle_{\mathbb{N}} + \left\langle \left([k-1]_q, [k-1]_q\right) \right\rangle_{\mathbb{N}} = \left\{ \left(us + v[k-1]_q, ut + v[k-1]_q\right) \,:\, u,v \in \mathbb{N} \right\} \subseteq \mathbb{L}(\overline{\mathcal{M}}). \tag{6}$$

Before we study the general structure of $\mathbb{L}(\overline{\mathcal{M}})$ and show that it can be generated by a single element (s_0,t_0) in the above sense, we consider all non-isomorphic examples in $\mathrm{PG}(3-1,2)$ (ignoring the constraint $s \geq t$).

Example 1. *Let $\mathcal{M}$ be a multiset of points in $\mathrm{PG}(2,2)$ uniquely characterized by $\mathcal{M}(L) = s \in \mathbb{N}$ for some line L and $\mathcal{M}(L') = t \in \mathbb{N}$ for all other lines $L' \neq L$. For each point $P \in L$, we have*

$$\mathcal{M}(P) = \frac{s+2t}{3} - \frac{4t}{6} = \frac{s}{3} \tag{7}$$

and for each point $Q \notin L$, we have

$$\mathcal{M}(Q) = \frac{3t}{3} - \frac{s+3t}{6} = \frac{3t-s}{6}. \tag{8}$$

Since $\mathcal{M}(P), \mathcal{M}(Q) \in \mathbb{N}$ we set $x := \mathcal{M}(P) = \frac{s}{3}$ and $y := \mathcal{M}(Q) = \frac{3t-s}{6}$, so that $s = 3x$ and $t = 2y + x$. With this we have $n = 3x + 4y$, $\gamma = \max\{x, y\}$, and $s - t = 2(x - y)$. If $x \geq y$, then we can write $\mathcal{M} = y \cdot \chi_E + (x - y) \cdot \chi_L$. If $x \leq y$, then we can write $\mathcal{M} = y \cdot \chi_E - (y - x) \cdot \chi_L$.

For Example 1 the set of all feasible (s,t)-pairs, assuming $s \geq t$, is given by $\langle(3,1)\rangle_{\mathbb{N}} + \langle(3,3)\rangle_{\mathbb{N}}$. If we assume $t \geq s$, then the set of feasible (s,t)-pairs is given by $\langle(0,2)\rangle_{\mathbb{N}} + \langle(3,3)\rangle_{\mathbb{N}}$. The vector $(0,2)$ can be computed from $(3,1)$ by computing a suitable complement.

Due to Lemma 6 we can always assume the existence of a point of multiplicity 0 as a normalization. So, in Example 1 we may assume $x = 0$ or $y = 0$, so that $\mathcal{M} = y \cdot \chi_E - y \cdot \chi_L$ or $\mathcal{M} = x \cdot \chi_L$.

Due to Lemma 10 we can always assume that the greatest common divisor of all point multiplicities is 1 as a normalization (excluding the degenerated case of an empty multiset of points). Applying both normalizations to the multisets of points in Example 1 leaves the two possibilities χ_L and $\chi_E - \chi_L$, i.e., point sets.

Due to Lemma 7 we always can assume $\#\mathcal{M} \leq \gamma(\mathcal{M}) \cdot [k]_q/2$. Applying also the third normalization to the multisets of points in Example 1 leaves only the possibility χ_L, i.e., a subspace construction; see Proposition 1, where $s = 3$, $t = 1$, $n = 3$, and $s - t = 2$.

Example 2. *Let $\mathcal{M}$ be a multiset of points in $\mathrm{PG}(2,2)$ uniquely characterized by $\mathcal{M}(L_1) = \mathcal{M}(L_2) = s \in \mathbb{N}$ for two different lines L_1, L_2 and $\mathcal{M}(L') = t \in \mathbb{N}$ for all other lines $L' \notin \{L_1, L_2\}$. For $P := L_1 \cap L_2$, we have*

$$\mathcal{M}(P) = \frac{2s+t}{3} - \frac{4t}{6} = \frac{2s-t}{3}, \tag{9}$$

for each point $Q \in (L_1 \cup L_2) \backslash \{P\}$, we have

$$\mathcal{M}(Q) = \frac{s+2t}{3} - \frac{s+3t}{6} = \frac{s+t}{6}, \tag{10}$$

and for each point $R \notin L_1 \cup L_2$, we have

$$\mathcal{M}(R) = \frac{3t}{3} - \frac{2s+2t}{6} = \frac{2t-s}{3}. \tag{11}$$

Since $\mathcal{M}(Q), \mathcal{M}(R) \in \mathbb{N}$ we set $x := \mathcal{M}(Q) = \frac{s+t}{6}$ and $y := \mathcal{M}(R) = \frac{2t-s}{3}$, so that $s = 4x - y$ and $t = 2x + y$. With this we have $n = 6x + 7y$ and $s - t = 2(x - y)$. Of course we need to have $y \leq 2x$ so that $\mathcal{M}(P) \geq 0$, which implies $s \geq 0$.

- *$\mathcal{M}(P) = 0$: $y = 2x$, so that $\mathcal{M}(P) = 0$, $\mathcal{M}(Q) = x$, $\mathcal{M}(R) = 2x$, and the greatest common divisor of $\mathcal{M}(P)$, $\mathcal{M}(Q)$, and $\mathcal{M}(R)$ is equal to x. Thus, we can assume $x = 1$, $y = 2$, so that $s = 2$, $t = 4$, $n = 8$, $\gamma = 2$, $t - s = 2$, and $\mathcal{M} = 2\chi_E - \chi_{L_1} - \chi_{L_2}$ for two different lines L_1, L_2.*
- *$\mathcal{M}(Q) = 0$: $x = 0$, so that also $y = 0$ and $\mathcal{M}$ is the empty multiset of points.*
- *$\mathcal{M}(R) = 0$: $y = 0$, $\mathcal{M}(P) = 2x$, $\mathcal{M}(Q) = x$, so that $\gcd(\mathcal{M}(P), \mathcal{M}(Q), \mathcal{M}(R)) = x$ and we can assume $x = 1$. With this we have $s = 4$, $t = 2$, $n = 6$, $\gamma = 2$, $s - t = 2$, and $\mathcal{M} = \chi_{L_1} + \chi_{L_2}$ for two different lines L_1, L_2.*

So, Example 2 can be explained by the construction in Proposition 2.

Example 3. *Let $\mathcal{M}$ be a multiset of points in* PG(2,2) *uniquely characterized by $\mathcal{M}(L_1) = \mathcal{M}(L_2) = \mathcal{M}(L_3) = s \in \mathbb{N}$ for three different lines L_1, L_2, L_3 with a common intersection point $P = L_1 \cap L_2 \cap L_3$ and $\mathcal{M}(L') = t \in \mathbb{N}$ for all other lines. We have*

$$\mathcal{M}(P) = \frac{3s}{3} - \frac{4t}{6} = s - \frac{2t}{3} \tag{12}$$

and

$$\mathcal{M}(Q) = \frac{s+2t}{3} - \frac{2s+2t}{6} = \frac{t}{3} \tag{13}$$

for all points $Q \neq P$. Since $\mathcal{M}(P), \mathcal{M}(Q) \in \mathbb{N}$ we set $x := \mathcal{M}(P) = s - \frac{2t}{3}$ and $y := \mathcal{M}(Q) = \frac{t}{3}$, so that $s = x + 2y$ and $t = 3y$. With this we have $n = x + 6y$ and $s - t = x - y$.

- *$\mathcal{M}(P) = 0$: $x = 0$, so that we can assume $y = 1$, which implies $s = 2$, $t = 3$, $\gamma = 1$, $n = 6$, $t - s = 1$, and $\mathcal{M} = \chi_E - \chi_P$ for some point P.*
- *$\mathcal{M}(Q) = 0$: $y = 0$, so that we can assume $x = 1$, which implies $s = 1$, $t = 0$, $\gamma = 1$, $n = 1$, $s - t = 1$, and $\mathcal{M} = \chi_P$ for some point P.*

So, also Example 3 can be explained by the subspace construction in Proposition 1.

Example 4. *Let $\mathcal{M}$ be a multiset of points in* PG(2,2) *uniquely characterized by $\mathcal{M}(L_1) = \mathcal{M}(L_2) = \mathcal{M}(L_3) = s \in \mathbb{N}$ for three different lines L_1, L_2, L_3 without a common intersection point, i.e., $L_1 \cap L_2 \cap L_3 = \emptyset$, and $\mathcal{M}(L') = t \in \mathbb{N}$ for all other lines. For each point P that is contained on exactly two lines L_i, we have*

$$\mathcal{M}(P) = \frac{2s+t}{3} - \frac{s+3t}{6} = \frac{3s-t}{6}, \tag{14}$$

for each point Q that is contained on exactly one line L_i, we have

$$\mathcal{M}(Q) = \frac{s+2t}{3} - \frac{2s+2t}{6} = \frac{t}{3}, \tag{15}$$

and for the unique point R that is contained on none of the lines L_i, we have

$$\mathcal{M}(R) = \frac{3t}{3} - \frac{3s+t}{6} = \frac{5t-3s}{6}. \tag{16}$$

Since $\mathcal{M}(P), \mathcal{M}(Q) \in \mathbb{N}$, we set $x := \mathcal{M}(P) = \frac{3s-t}{6}$ and $y := \mathcal{M}(Q) = \frac{t}{3}$, so that $s = 2x + y$ and $t = 3y$. With this we have $n = 2x + 5y$ and $s - t = 2(x - y)$.

- *$\mathcal{M}(P) = 0$: $x = 0$, so that we can assume $y = 1$, which implies $s = 1$, $t = 3$, $t - s = 2$, $\gamma = 2$, $n = 5$, and $\mathcal{M} = \chi_L + 2\chi_P$ for some line L and some point $P \notin L$.*
- *$\mathcal{M}(Q) = 0$: $y = 0$, so that $x = 0$ and $\mathcal{M}$ is the empty multiset of points.*
- *$\mathcal{M}(R) = 0$: $x = 2y$, so that we can assume $y = 1$, which implies $x = 2$, $s = 4$, $t = 6$, $t - s = 2$, $\gamma = 2$, $n = 9$, and the 2-complement of $\mathcal{M}$ equals $\mathcal{M} = \chi_L + 2\chi_P$ for some line L and some point $P \notin L$; see the case $\mathcal{M}(P) = 0$.*

So, also Example 4 can be explained by the construction in Proposition 2.

In Examples 1–4 we have considered all cases of $1 \le \#\overline{\mathcal{M}} \le 3$ up to symmetry. The cases $\#\overline{\mathcal{M}} \in \{0, 7\}$ give one-character multisets. By considering the complement $\mathcal{M}' = \chi_V - \overline{\mathcal{M}}$ we see that examples for $4 \le \#\overline{\mathcal{M}} \le 6$ do not give anything new. Since the dimension of the ambient space is odd, we cannot apply the construction in Proposition 3.

Now, let us consider the general case. Given the set $\overline{\mathcal{M}}$ of hyperplanes with multiplicity s we obtain an explicit expression for the multiplicity $\mathcal{M}(P)$ of every point $P \in \mathcal{P}$ depending on the two unknown hyperplane multiplicities s and t.

Lemma 12. *Let $\overline{\mathcal{M}}$ be a set of points in* $\mathrm{PG}(k-1,q)$, *where* $k \geq 3$, *and* $\mathcal{M}$ *be a multiset of points in* $\mathrm{PG}(k-1,q)$ *such that* $\mathcal{M}(H) = s$ *if* $\overline{\mathcal{M}}(H^\perp) = 1$ *and* $\mathcal{M}(H) = t$ *if* $\overline{\mathcal{M}}(H^\perp) = 0$ *for all hyperplanes* $H \in \mathcal{H}$. *Denoting the number of hyperplanes* $H \ni P$ *with* $\mathcal{M}(H) = s$ *by* $\varphi(P)$ *and setting* $r := \#\overline{\mathcal{M}}$, $\Delta := s - t \in \mathbb{Z}$, *we have*

$$\mathcal{M}(P) = \frac{t + \Delta \cdot \varphi(P)}{[k-1]_q} - \frac{\Delta}{q^{k-2}} \cdot \frac{[k-2]_q}{[k-1]_q} \cdot (r - \varphi(P)). \tag{17}$$

Proof. Counting gives that $[k-1]_q - \varphi(P)$ hyperplanes through P have multiplicity t, from the q^{k-1} hyperplanes not containing P exactly $r - \varphi(P)$ have multiplicity $\mathcal{M}(H) = s$ and $q^{k-1} - r + \varphi(P)$ have multiplicity $\mathcal{M}(H) = t$. With this we can use Lemma 1 to compute

$$\begin{aligned}
\mathcal{M}(P) &= \sum_{H\in\mathcal{H}\,:\,P\in H} \frac{1}{[k-1]_q} \cdot \mathcal{M}(H) + \sum_{H\in\mathcal{H}\,:\,P\notin H} \frac{1}{q^{k-1}} \cdot \left(\frac{1}{[k-1]_q} - 1\right) \cdot \mathcal{M}(H) \\
&= \sum_{H\in\mathcal{H}\,:\,P\in H} \frac{1}{[k-1]_q} \cdot \mathcal{M}(H) - \sum_{H\in\mathcal{H}\,:\,P\notin H} \frac{1}{q^{k-1}} \cdot \frac{q[k-2]_q}{[k-1]_q} \cdot \mathcal{M}(H) \\
&= t + \frac{\Delta}{[k-1]_q} \cdot \varphi(P) - \frac{q[k-2]_q}{[k-1]_q} \cdot t - \frac{\Delta}{q^{k-1}} \cdot \frac{q[k-2]_q}{[k-1]_q} \cdot (r - \varphi(P)) \\
&= \frac{t + \Delta \cdot \varphi(P)}{[k-1]_q} - \frac{\Delta}{q^{k-2}} \cdot \frac{[k-2]_q}{[k-1]_q} \cdot (r - \varphi(P)).
\end{aligned}$$

□

Note that $\varphi(P) = \overline{\mathcal{M}}(P^\perp)$ for all $P \in \mathcal{P}$.

Lemma 13. *Let $\overline{\mathcal{M}}$ be a set of points in* $\mathrm{PG}(k-1,q)$, *where* $k \geq 3$, *and* $\mathcal{M}$ *be a multiset of points in* $\mathrm{PG}(k-1,q)$ *such that* $\mathcal{M}(H) = s$ *if* $\overline{\mathcal{M}}(H^\perp) = 1$ *and* $\mathcal{M}(H) = t$ *if* $\overline{\mathcal{M}}(H^\perp) = 0$ *for all hyperplanes* $H \in \mathcal{H}$. *Denote the number of hyperplanes* $H \ni P$ *with* $\mathcal{M}(H) = s$ *by* $\varphi(P)$ *and uniquely choose* $m \in \mathbb{N}$, $\mathcal{I} \subseteq \mathbb{N}$ *with* $0 \in \mathcal{I}$ *such that* $\{\varphi(P) : P \in \mathcal{P}\} = \{m + i : i \in \mathcal{I}\}$. *If* $s > t$ *and there exists a point* $Q \in \mathcal{P}$ *with* $\mathcal{M}(Q) = 0$, *then we have*

$$t = \frac{\Delta}{q^{k-2}} \cdot [k-2]_q \cdot (r - m) - \Delta \cdot m \tag{18}$$

and

$$\mathcal{M}(P) = \frac{\Delta \cdot i}{q^{k-2}} \tag{19}$$

for all points $P \in \mathcal{P}$ *where* $i := \varphi(P) - m$, $r := \#\overline{\mathcal{M}}$, *and* $\Delta := s - t \in \mathbb{N}_{\geq 1}$. *If* $\mathcal{M}$ *is non-repetitive, then* Δ *divides* q^{k-2}.

Proof. Using $\Delta > 0$ we observe that the expression for $\mathcal{M}(P)$ in Equation (17) is increasing in $\varphi(P)$. So, we need to choose a point $Q \in \mathcal{P}$ which minimizes $\varphi(Q)$ to normalize using $\mathcal{M}(Q) = 0$, since otherwise we will obtain points with negative multiplicity. So, choosing a point $Q \in \mathcal{P}$ with $\varphi(Q) = m$ we require

$$0 = \mathcal{M}(Q) = \frac{t + \Delta \cdot m}{[k-1]_q} - \frac{\Delta}{q^{k-1}} \cdot \frac{q[k-2]_q}{[k-1]_q} \cdot (r - m),$$

which yields Equation (18). Using $i := \varphi(P) - m$ and the expression for t we compute

$$\begin{aligned}\mathcal{M}(P) &= \frac{t+\Delta\cdot(m+i)}{[k-1]_q} - \frac{\Delta}{q^{k-2}}\cdot\frac{[k-2]_q}{[k-1]_q}\cdot(r-m-i) \\ &= \frac{\Delta}{q^{k-2}}\cdot\frac{[k-2]_q}{[k-1]_q}\cdot(r-m) - \frac{\Delta\cdot m}{[k-1]_q} + \frac{\Delta\cdot(m+i)}{[k-1]_q} - \frac{\Delta}{q^{k-2}}\cdot\frac{[k-2]_q}{[k-1]_q}\cdot(r-m-i) \\ &= \frac{\Delta\cdot i}{[k-1]_q} + \frac{\Delta\cdot i}{q^{k-2}}\cdot\frac{[k-2]_q}{[k-1]_q} = \frac{\Delta\cdot i}{q^{k-2}}\end{aligned}$$

for all $P \in \mathcal{P}$. Note that if $f > 1$ is a divisor of Δ that is coprime to q, then all point multiplicities of $\mathcal{M}$ are divisible by f. If $\Delta = q^{k-2}\cdot f$ for an integer $f > 1$, then all point multiplicities of $\mathcal{M}$ are divisible by f. Thus, we have that Δ divides q^{k-2}. □

Note that $\mathcal{I} = \{\overline{\mathcal{M}}(H) - \overline{\mathcal{M}}(H') \,:\, H \in \mathcal{H}\}$, where $H' \in \mathcal{H}$ is a minimizer of $\overline{\mathcal{M}}(H)$.

Lemma 14. *Let $\overline{\mathcal{M}}$ be a set of points in $\mathrm{PG}(k-1,q)$, where $k \ge 3$ and $\mathcal{M}$ be a multiset of points in $\mathrm{PG}(k-1,q)$ such that $\mathcal{M}(H) = s$ if $\overline{\mathcal{M}}(H^\perp) = 1$ and $\mathcal{M}(H) = t$ if $\overline{\mathcal{M}}(H^\perp) = 0$ for all hyperplanes $H \in \mathcal{H}$. Using the notation from Lemma 13 we set*

$$g = gcd\Big(\{i \in \mathcal{I}\} \cup \{q^{k-2}\}\Big), \tag{20}$$

$$\Delta_0 = q^{k-2}/g, \tag{21}$$

$$t_0 = \frac{1}{g}\cdot[k-2]_q\cdot(r-m) - \Delta_0\cdot m, \text{ and} \tag{22}$$

$$s_0 = t+\Delta_0. \tag{23}$$

If $s > t$, then we have

$$\mathbb{L}(\overline{\mathcal{M}}) = \langle (s_0,t_0)\rangle_{\mathbb{N}} + \langle([k-1]_q,[k-1]_q)\rangle_{\mathbb{N}}.$$

Proof. Setting $\mu = \mu(\mathcal{M}) \in \mathbb{N}$ we have that $\mathcal{M}' := \mathcal{M} - \mu\cdot\chi_V$ is a two-character multiset corresponding to $(s',t') := (s-\mu[k-1]_q, t-\mu[k-1]_q) \in \mathbb{L}(\overline{\mathcal{M}})$ and there exists a point $Q \in \mathcal{P}$ with $\mathcal{M}'(Q) = 0$. Clearly, we have $(s',t') \in \mathbb{N}^2$ and $s' > t'$. From Lemma 13 we conclude the existence of an integer $\Delta' \in \mathbb{N}_{\ge 1}$ such that $t' = \frac{\Delta'}{q^{k-2}}\cdot[k-2]_q\cdot(r-m) - \Delta'\cdot m$, $s' = t'+\Delta'$, and $\mathcal{M}'(P) = \frac{\Delta'\cdot i}{q^{k-2}}$ for all $P \in \mathcal{P}$. Since $\mathcal{M}'(P) \in \mathbb{N}$ for all $P \in \mathcal{P}$ we have that q^{k-2} divides $\Delta'\cdot g$, so that $\Delta_0 \in \mathbb{N}$ divides Δ'. For $f := \Delta'/\Delta_0 \in \mathbb{N}_{\ge 1}$ we observe that $\mathcal{M}'(P)$ is divisible by f and we set $\mathcal{M}'' := \frac{1}{f}\cdot\mathcal{M}'$. With this, we can check that $\mathcal{M}''$ is a two-character multiset corresponding to $(s_0,t_0) \in \mathbb{L}(\overline{\mathcal{M}})$. □

Note that it is not necessary to explicitly check $t_0 \in \mathbb{N}$ since $\mathcal{M}''(P) \in \mathbb{N}$ is sufficient to this end.

Before we consider the problem whether $\mathbb{L}(\overline{\mathcal{M}}) \subseteq \mathbb{N}^2$ contains an element (s,t) with $s > t$, we treat the so-far-excluded case $k = 2$ separately.

Lemma 15. *Let $\overline{\mathcal{M}}$ be a set of points in $\mathrm{PG}(1,q)$. Then, we have*

$$\mathbb{L}(\overline{\mathcal{M}}) = \langle (s_0,0)\rangle_{\mathbb{N}} + \langle(q+1,q+1)\rangle_{\mathbb{N}},$$

where $s_0 = 0$ if $\#\overline{\mathcal{M}} \in \{0,q+1\}$ and $s_0 = 1$ otherwise.

Proof. If $\#\overline{\mathcal{M}} \in \{0,q+1\}$, then a two-character multiset $\mathcal{M}$ corresponding to $(s,t) \in \overline{\mathcal{M}}$ actually is a one-character multiset and there exists some integer $x \in \mathbb{N}$ such that $\mathcal{M} = x\cdot\chi_v$.

Otherwise, we observe that in $\mathrm{PG}(1,q)$ points and hyperplanes coincide and the image of $\overline{\mathcal{M}}$ is $\{0,1\}$. Note that we have $\mathcal{M} = t\cdot\chi_V + \sum_{P\in\mathcal{P}}(s-t)\cdot\overline{\mathcal{M}}(P)\cdot\chi_P$ for each two-character multiset $\mathcal{M}$ corresponding to $(s,t) \in \mathbb{L}(\overline{\mathcal{M}})$ by definition. We can easily check $(s,t) \in \langle(1,0)\rangle_{\mathbb{N}} + \langle(q+1,q+1)\rangle_{\mathbb{N}}$. The proof is completed by choosing $s = 1$ and $t = 0$ in our representation of $\mathcal{M}$. □

Theorem 1. *Let $\overline{\mathcal{M}}$ be a set of points in* $\mathrm{PG}(k-1,q)$ *with* $\#\overline{\mathcal{M}} \notin \{0,[k]_q\}$, *where* $k \geq 2$. *Then,*

$$\mathcal{M} := \sum_{H \in \mathcal{H}} \overline{\mathcal{M}}(H^\perp) \cdot \chi_H \tag{24}$$

is a two-character multiset corresponding to $(s,t) \in \mathbb{L}(\overline{\mathcal{M}})$ *with* $n = \#\mathcal{M} = r[k-1]_q$, *where* $r := \#\overline{\mathcal{M}}$, $t = r[k-2]_q$, *and* $s = r[k-2]_q + q^{k-2}$. *Setting* $\mu := \mu(\mathcal{M})$ *and* $g := \gcd(\{\mathcal{M}(P) - \mu : P \in \mathcal{P}\})$ *the function*

$$\mathcal{M}' := \frac{1}{g} \cdot \left(-\mu \cdot \chi_V + \sum_{H \in \mathcal{H}} \overline{\mathcal{M}}(H^\perp) \cdot \chi_H \right) = \frac{1}{g} \cdot (\mathcal{M} - \mu \cdot \chi_V) \tag{25}$$

is a two-character multiset corresponding to $(s_0,t_0) \in \mathbb{L}(\overline{\mathcal{M}})$ *with* $n' = \#\mathcal{M}' = \frac{1}{q} \cdot (r[k-1]_q - \mu[k]_q)$, *where* $r := \#\overline{\mathcal{M}}$, $t_0 = \frac{1}{g} \cdot (r[k-2]_q - \mu[k-1]_q)$, *and* $s_0 = \frac{1}{g} \cdot \left(r[k-2]_q - \mu[k-1]_q + q^{k-2}\right)$, *and* g *divides* q^{k-2}. *Moreover, we have*

$$\mathbb{L}(\overline{\mathcal{M}}) = \langle (s_0,t_0) \rangle_{\mathbb{N}} + \langle ([k-1]_q,[k-1]_q) \rangle_{\mathbb{N}}. \tag{26}$$

Proof. We can easily check $\mathcal{M}(H) = r[k-2]_q = t$ if $\mathcal{M}(H^\perp) = 0$ and $\mathcal{M}(H) = r[k-2]_q + q^{k-2} = s$ if $\mathcal{M}(H^\perp) = 1$ for all $H \in \mathcal{H}$ as well as $\#\mathcal{M} = r[k-1]_q$ directly from the definition of $\mathcal{M}$. Using Lemmas 6 and 10 we conclude that $\mathcal{M}'$ is a two-character multiset with the stated parameters.

For $k = 2$, Lemma 15 is our last statement. For $k \geq 3$ we can apply Lemma 13 to conclude $g = \gcd(\{i \in \mathcal{I}\})$ and use the proof of Lemma 14 to conclude our last statement. Since $s,t \in \mathbb{N}$ and $s > t$ we have that g divides $g(s-t) = q^{k-2}$. □

Using the notation from Lemma 13 applied to the multiset of points $\mathcal{M} - \mu \cdot \chi_V$ from Theorem 1 we observe $\#\mathcal{I} \geq 2$ for $\#\overline{\mathcal{M}} \notin \{0,[k]_q\}$. Using the facts that $g := \gcd(\{\mathcal{M}(P) - \mu : P \in \mathcal{P}\})$, that g divides q^{k-2}, and Equation (19) we conclude

$$g = gcd(\{i \in \mathcal{I}\}) = gcd(\{\overline{\mathcal{M}}(H) - \overline{\mathcal{M}}(H') : H \in \mathcal{H}\}), \tag{27}$$

where $H' \in \mathcal{H}$ is a minimizer of $\overline{\mathcal{M}}(H)$.

Using the classification of one-character multisets we conclude from Theorem 1:

Corollary 1. *Let $\overline{\mathcal{M}}$ be a set of points in* $\mathrm{PG}(k-1,q)$, *where* $k \geq 2$. *Then, there exist* $(s_0,t_0) \in \mathbb{N}^2$ *such that* $\mathbb{L}(\overline{\mathcal{M}}) = \langle (s_0,t_0) \rangle_{\mathbb{N}} + \langle ([k-1]_q,[k-1]_q) \rangle_{\mathbb{N}}$.

Theorem 2. *Let $\widetilde{\mathcal{M}}$ be a two-character multiset in* $\mathrm{PG}(k-1,q)$, *where* $k \geq 2$. *Then, there exist unique* $u,v \in \mathbb{N}$ *such that* $\widetilde{\mathcal{M}} = u \cdot \mathcal{M}' + v \cdot \chi_V$, *where $\mathcal{M}'$ is given by Equation (25).*

Proof. Let $s > t$ be the two hyperplane multiplicities of $\widetilde{\mathcal{M}}$. With this, define $\overline{\mathcal{M}}$ such that $\overline{\mathcal{M}}(H^\perp) = 1$ if $\widetilde{\mathcal{M}}(H) = s$ and $\overline{\mathcal{M}}(H^\perp) = 0$ if $\widetilde{\mathcal{M}}(H) = t$ for all $H \in \mathcal{H}$. So, $(s,t) \in \mathbb{L}(\overline{\mathcal{M}})$ and Theorem 1 yields the existence of $u,v \in \mathbb{N}$ with $(s,t) = u \cdot (s_0,t_0) + v \cdot ([k-1]_q,[k-1]_q)$, where s_0, t_0 are as in Theorem 1. From Lemma 1 we then conclude $\widetilde{\mathcal{M}} = u \cdot \mathcal{M}' + v \cdot \chi_V$. Note that $\mu(\mathcal{M}')$ and $\mu(\chi_V) = 1$ imply $\mu(\widetilde{\mathcal{M}}) = v$, so that u can be computed from $\gamma(\widetilde{\mathcal{M}}) = u \cdot \gamma(\mathcal{M}') + v$, i.e., u and v are uniquely determined. □

Note that for a one-character multiset $\widetilde{\mathcal{M}}$ there exists a unique $v \in \mathbb{N}$ such that $\widetilde{\mathcal{M}} = v \cdot \chi_V$. Given a set of points $\overline{\mathcal{M}}$ we call $\mathcal{M}'$ the canonical representant of the set of two-character multisets $\mathcal{M}$ corresponding to $(s,t) \in \mathbb{L}(\overline{\mathcal{M}})$. If $\mathcal{M} = \mathcal{M}'$ we just say that $\mathcal{M}$ is the canonical two-character multiset.

Theorem 3. *Let $w_1 < w_2$ be the non-zero weights of a non-repetitive $[n,k]_q$ two-weight code C without full support. Then, there exist integers f and u such that $w_1 = up^f$ and $w_2 = (u+1)p^f$, where p is the characteristic of the underlying field $\mathbb{F}_q$.*

Proof. Let $\mathcal{M}$ be the two-character multiset in $\mathrm{PG}(k-1,q)$ corresponding to C. Choose unique $u, v \in \mathbb{N}$ such that $\mathcal{M} = u \cdot \mathcal{M}' + v \cdot \chi_V$, as in Theorem 2. Since C does not have full support, we have $v = 0$ and since C is non-repetitive we have $u = 1$. With this we can use Theorem 1 to compute

$$w_1 = n - s = \frac{1}{g} \cdot \left(r \cdot q^{k-2} - \mu \cdot q^{k-1} - q^{k-2}\right) = (r - q\mu - 1) \cdot p^f \tag{28}$$

and

$$w_2 = n - t = \frac{1}{g} \cdot \left(r \cdot q^{k-2} - \mu \cdot q^{k-1}\right) = (r - q\mu) \cdot p^f, \tag{29}$$

where f is chosen such that $\frac{q^{k-2}}{g} = p^f$, i.e., we can choose $u = r - q\mu - 1$. □

We have seen in Equation (27) that we can compute the parameter g directly from the set of points $\overline{\mathcal{M}}$. If we additionally assume that $\overline{\mathcal{M}}$ is spanning, then we can consider the corresponding projective $[n,k]_q$-code $\overline{C}$, where $n = \#\overline{\mathcal{M}}$ (if $\overline{\mathcal{M}}$ is not spanning, then we can consider the lower-dimensional subspace spanned by $\mathrm{supp}(\overline{\mathcal{M}})$). Note that we have $\overline{\mathcal{M}}(H) \equiv m \pmod{g}$ for all $H \in \mathcal{H}$ and that g is maximal with this property. If $m \equiv n \pmod{g}$, then g would simply be the maximal divisibility constant of the weights of $\overline{C}$. From theorem 7 in [24] or theorem 3 in [25] we can conclude $m \equiv n \pmod{g}$. Thus, we have

$$g = \gcd(\{\mathrm{wt}(c) \,:\, c \in \overline{C}\}). \tag{30}$$

The argument may also be based on the following lemma (using the fact that $\overline{C}$ is projective):

Lemma 16. *Let C be an $[n,k]_q$-code of full length such that we have $\mathrm{wt}(c) \equiv m \pmod{\Delta}$ for all non-zero codewords $c \in C$. If Δ is a power of the characteristic of the underlying field $\mathbb{F}_q$, then we have $m \equiv 0 \pmod{\min\{\Delta, q\}}$. Moreover, if additionally q divides Δ and $k \geq 2$, then the non-zero weights in each residual code are congruent to m/q modulo Δ/q.*

Proof. Let $\mathcal{M}$ be the multiset of points in $\mathrm{PG}(k-1,q)$ corresponding to C. For each hyperplane H we have $n - \mathcal{M}(H) \equiv m \pmod{\Delta}$, which is equivalent to $\mathcal{M}(H) \equiv n - m \pmod{\Delta}$. The weight of a non-zero codeword in a residual code is given by a subspace K of codimension 2 and a hyperplane H with $K \leq H$. With this, the weight is given by $\mathcal{M}(H) - \mathcal{M}(K) \equiv n - m - \mathcal{M}(K) \pmod{\Delta}$. Counting the hyperplane multiplicities of the $q+1$ hyperplanes that contain K yields

$$\sum_{H \in \mathcal{H} : K \leq H} \mathcal{M}(H) = \#\mathcal{M} + q \cdot \mathcal{M}(K) = \#\mathcal{M} + q \cdot \mathcal{M}(K) \tag{31}$$

and

$$\sum_{H \in \mathcal{H} : K \leq H} \mathcal{M}(H) \equiv (q+1)(n-m) \pmod{\Delta}, \tag{32}$$

so that

$$m \equiv q \cdot (n - m - \mathcal{M}(K)) \pmod{\Delta}. \tag{33}$$

□

Given Equation (30) we might be interested in projective divisible codes (with a large divisibility constant). For enumerations for the binary case we refer the reader to [26] and for a more general survey we refer the reader to, e.g., [27]. Note that the only point sets $\mathcal{M}$ in $\mathrm{PG}(k-1,q)$ that are q^{k-1}-divisible are given by $\#\mathcal{M} \in \{0, [k]_q\}$, i.e., the empty and the full set. All other point sets are at most q^{k-2}-divisible, as implied by Theorem 1.

6. Enumeration of Two-Character Multisets in PG$(k-1, q)$ for Small Parameters

Since all two-character multisets in PG$(1, q)$ can be parameterized as $\mathcal{M} = b \cdot \chi_V + \sum_{P \in \mathcal{P}} (a-b) \cdot \overline{\mathcal{M}}(P) \cdot \chi_P$ for integers $a > b \geq 0$ and a set of points $\overline{\mathcal{M}}$ in PG$(k-1, q)$ (see Lemma 15 and its proof), we assume $k \geq 3$ in the following. Due to Theorem 2, every two-character multiset in PG$(k-1, q)$ can be written as $u \cdot \mathcal{M}' + v \cdot \chi_V$, where $u, v \in \mathbb{N}$ and $\mathcal{M}'$ is characterized in Theorem 1. So, we further restrict out considerations on canonical two-character multisets where we have $u = 1$ and $v = 0$. For $k = 2$, all canonical two-character multisets in PG$(k-1, q)$ are indeed sets of points and given by the construction in Proposition 3 (with $r = 1$).

It can be easily checked that two isomorphic sets of points in PG$(k-1, q)$ yield isomorphic canonical two-character multisets $\mathcal{M}'$. So, for the full enumeration of canonical two-character multisets in PG$(k-1, q)$ we just need to loop over all non-isomorphic sets of points $\overline{\mathcal{M}}$ in PG$(k-1, q)$ and use Theorem 1 to determine $\mathcal{M}$, $\mathcal{M}'$, and their parameters. We remark that the numbers of non-isomorphic projective codes per length, dimension, and field size are, e.g., listed in tables 6.10–6.12 in [28] (for small parameters). For the binary case and at most six dimensions some additional data can be found in [29]. Here, we utilize the software package LinCode [30] to enumerate these codes.

In Tables 1 and 2 we list the feasible parameters for canonical two-character multisets in PG$(2, 2)$ and in PG$(3, 2)$, respectively, where $n' := \#\mathcal{M}'$ and $\gamma' := \gamma(\mathcal{M}')$. The two hyperplane multiplicities for $\mathcal{M}'$ are denoted by s_0, t_0 and those of $\mathcal{M}$ by s, t. The parameters g, μ, r are as in (25) and $n = \#\mathcal{M}$. For PG$(2, 2)$ we can also state more direct constructions:

- $(n', s_0, t_0, \gamma') = (1, 1, 0, 1)$: characteristic function of a point (not spanning);
- $(n', s_0, t_0, \gamma') = (3, 3, 1, 1)$: characteristic function of a line (not spanning);
- $(n', s_0, t_0, \gamma') = (4, 2, 0, 1)$: complement of the characteristic function of a line;
- $(n', s_0, t_0, \gamma') = (6, 3, 2, 1)$: complement of the characteristic function of a point;
- $(n', s_0, t_0, \gamma') = (5, 3, 1, 2)$: $\chi_L + 2\chi_P$ for a line L and a point P with $P \notin L$;
- $(n', s_0, t_0, \gamma') = (6, 4, 2, 2)$: $\chi_L + \chi'_L$ for two different lines L and L';
- $(n', s_0, t_0, \gamma') = (8, 4, 2, 2)$: $\chi_V - \chi_L - \chi'_L$ for two different lines L and L';
- $(n', s_0, t_0, \gamma') = (9, 5, 3, 2)$: $2\chi_V - \chi_L + -\chi_P$ for a line L and a point P with $P \notin L$.

Table 1. Feasible parameters for canonical two-character multisets in PG$(2, 2)$.

g	μ	r	n	γ	s	t	s_0	t_0	n'	γ'
2	1	3	9	3	5	3	1	0	1	1
1	0	1	3	1	3	1	3	1	3	1
1	2	6	18	3	8	6	2	0	4	1
2	0	4	12	2	6	4	3	2	6	1
1	1	4	12	3	6	4	3	1	5	2
1	0	2	6	2	4	2	4	2	6	2
1	1	5	15	3	7	5	4	2	8	2
1	0	3	9	2	5	3	5	3	9	2

Table 2. Feasible parameters for canonical two-character multisets in PG$(3, 2)$.

g	μ	r	n	γ	s	t	s_0	t_0	n'	γ'
4	3	7	49	7	25	21	1	0	1	1
2	1	3	21	3	13	9	3	1	3	1
2	4	10	70	6	34	30	3	1	5	1
2	2	6	42	4	22	18	4	2	6	1
1	0	1	7	1	7	3	7	3	7	1
1	6	14	98	7	46	42	4	0	8	1
2	3	9	63	5	31	27	5	3	9	1
2	1	5	35	3	19	15	6	4	10	1
2	4	12	84	6	40	36	6	4	12	1
4	0	8	56	4	28	24	7	6	14	1

Table 2. *Cont.*

g	μ	r	n	γ	s	t	s_0	t_0	n'	γ'
2	2	8	56	6	28	24	7	5	13	2
1	0	2	14	2	10	6	10	6	14	2
2	0	4	28	4	16	12	8	6	14	2
1	5	13	91	7	43	39	8	4	16	2
2	3	11	77	7	37	33	8	6	16	2
2	1	7	49	5	25	21	9	7	17	2
1	1	4	28	4	16	12	9	5	13	3
1	4	11	77	7	37	33	9	5	17	3
1	3	9	63	6	31	27	10	6	18	3
1	2	7	49	5	25	21	11	7	19	3
1	1	5	35	4	19	15	12	8	20	3
1	0	3	21	3	13	9	13	9	21	3
1	4	12	84	7	40	36	12	8	24	3
1	3	10	70	6	34	30	13	9	25	3
1	2	8	56	5	28	24	14	10	26	3
1	1	6	42	4	22	18	15	11	27	3
1	0	4	28	3	16	12	16	12	28	3
1	3	11	77	6	37	33	16	12	32	3
1	3	8	56	7	28	24	7	3	11	4
1	2	6	42	6	22	18	8	4	12	4
1	3	9	63	7	31	27	10	6	18	4
1	2	7	49	6	25	21	11	7	19	4
1	1	5	35	5	19	15	12	8	20	4
1	3	10	70	7	34	30	13	9	25	4
1	2	8	56	6	28	24	14	10	26	4
1	1	6	42	5	22	18	15	11	27	4
1	2	9	63	6	31	27	17	13	33	4
1	1	7	49	5	25	21	18	14	34	4
1	0	5	35	4	19	15	19	15	35	4
1	2	10	70	6	34	30	20	16	40	4
1	1	8	56	5	28	24	21	17	41	4
1	0	6	42	4	22	18	22	18	42	4
1	1	9	63	5	31	27	24	20	48	4
1	0	7	49	4	25	21	25	21	49	4

Of course, also for $\mathrm{PG}(3,2)$ some of the examples have nicer descriptions:

- $(n', s_0, t_0, \gamma') = (1,1,0,1)$: characteristic function of a point (not spanning);
- $(n', s_0, t_0, \gamma') = (3,3,1,1)$: characteristic function of a line (not spanning);
- $(n', s_0, t_0, \gamma') = (7,7,3,1)$: characteristic function of a plane (not spanning);
- $(n', s_0, t_0, \gamma') = (5,3,1,1)$: projective base; spanning projective 2-weight code;
- $(n', s_0, t_0, \gamma') = (6,4,2,1)$: characteristic function of two disjoint lines; spanning projective 2-weight code;
- $(n', s_0, t_0, \gamma') = (14,10,6,2)$: characteristic function of two different planes;
- $(n', s_0, t_0, \gamma') = (21,13,9,3)$: characteristic function of three planes intersecting in a common point but not a common line.

Note that we may restrict our considerations to $r < [k]_q/2$, since if $\mathcal{M}'$ is the a canonical two-character multiset for a set of points $\overline{\mathcal{M}}$ with $\#\overline{\mathcal{M}} = r$, then the complement of $\mathcal{M}'$ is the a canonical two-character multiset for a set of points which is the complement of $\overline{\mathcal{M}}$ and has cardinality $[k]_q - r$.

From the data in Tables 1 and 2 we can guess the maximum possible point multiplicity $\gamma(\mathcal{M}')$ of $\mathcal{M}'$:

Proposition 4. *Let $\mathcal{M}$ be a canonical two-character multiset in $\mathrm{PG}(k-1,q)$, where $k \geq 2$. Then, we have $\gamma(\mathcal{M}) \leq q^{k-2}$.*

Proof. Choose a suitable set $\mathcal{H}' \subseteq \mathcal{H}$ and $g, \nu \in \mathbb{N}$ such that

$$\mathcal{M} = \frac{1}{g} \cdot \left(\sum_{H \in \mathcal{H}'} \chi_H - \mu \cdot \chi_V \right).$$

Let $P \in \mathcal{P}$ be a point with $\mathcal{M}(P) = \gamma$ and $Q \in \mathcal{P}$ be a point with $\mathcal{M}(Q) = 0$. With this we have $\lambda \ge |\{H \in \mathcal{H}' : Q \le H\}|$. Since P is contained in $[k-1]_q$ hyperplanes in $\mathcal{H}$ and $\langle P, Q \rangle$ is contained in $[k-2]_q$ hyperplanes in $\mathcal{H}$, we have $\mathcal{M}(P) \le q^{k-2}$. □

We can easily construct an example showing that the stated upper bound is tight. To this end, let P, Q be two different points in $\mathrm{PG}(k-1, q)$, where $k \ge 3$, and H' be an arbitrary hyperplane neither containing P nor Q. With this, we choose $\mathcal{H}'$ as the set of all q^{k-2} hyperplanes that contain P but do not contain Q and additionally the hyperplane H'. For the corresponding multiset of points $\mathcal{M}$ we then have $\mathcal{M}(P) = q^{k-2}$ and $\mathcal{M}(Q) = 0$, so that $\mu(\mathcal{M}) = 0$. For an arbitrary point $R \in H'$ we have $\mathcal{M}(R) = q^{k-2} - q^{k-3} + 1 = (q-1)q^{k-3} + 1$, so that $\gcd(\mathcal{M}(R), \mathcal{M}(P)) = 1$ if $k \ge 4$ or $k = 3$ and $q \ne 2$. For $(k, q) = (3, 2)$ we have already seen examples of canonical two-character multisets with maximum point multiplicity 2.

In Tables 3 and 4, we list the feasible parameters for canonical two-character multisets in $\mathrm{PG}(4, 2)$ with point multiplicity at most 4.

Table 3. Feasible parameters for canonical two-character multisets in $\mathrm{PG}(4, 2)$ with $\gamma' \le 4$—part 1.

g	μ	r	n	γ	s	t	s_0	t_0	n'	γ'
8	7	15	225	15	113	105	1	0	1	1
4	3	7	105	7	57	49	3	1	3	1
2	1	3	45	3	29	21	7	3	7	1
1	0	1	15	1	15	7	15	7	15	1
1	14	30	450	15	218	210	8	0	16	1
2	12	28	420	14	204	196	12	8	24	1
4	8	24	360	12	176	168	14	12	28	1
8	0	16	240	8	120	112	15	14	30	1
2	2	6	90	6	50	42	10	6	14	2
2	5	13	195	9	99	91	12	8	20	2
2	3	9	135	7	71	63	13	9	21	2
2	1	5	75	5	43	35	14	10	22	2
2	8	20	300	12	148	140	14	10	26	2
2	6	16	240	10	120	112	15	11	27	2
2	4	12	180	8	92	84	16	12	28	2
2	2	8	120	6	64	56	17	13	29	2
4	0	8	120	8	64	56	16	14	30	2
2	0	4	60	4	36	28	18	14	30	2
1	0	2	30	2	22	14	22	14	30	2
4	7	23	345	15	169	161	16	14	32	2
2	11	27	405	15	197	189	16	12	32	2
1	13	29	435	15	211	203	16	8	32	2
2	9	23	345	13	169	161	17	13	33	2
2	7	19	285	11	141	133	18	14	34	2
2	5	15	225	9	113	105	19	15	35	2
2	3	11	165	7	85	77	20	16	36	2
2	10	26	390	14	190	182	20	16	40	2
2	8	22	330	12	162	154	21	17	41	2
2	6	18	270	10	134	126	22	18	42	2
2	9	25	375	13	183	175	24	20	48	2
2	4	10	150	10	78	70	9	5	13	3
2	9	21	315	15	155	147	10	6	18	3
2	3	9	135	9	71	63	13	9	21	3
2	6	16	240	12	120	112	15	11	27	3

Table 3. *Cont.*

g	μ	r	n	γ	s	t	s_0	t_0	n'	γ'
2	4	12	180	10	92	84	16	12	28	3
2	2	8	120	8	64	56	17	13	29	3
1	1	4	60	4	36	28	21	13	29	3
2	7	19	285	13	141	133	18	14	34	3
2	5	15	225	11	113	105	19	15	35	3
2	3	11	165	9	85	77	20	16	36	3
2	1	7	105	7	57	49	21	17	37	3
2	6	18	270	12	134	126	22	18	42	3
2	4	14	210	10	106	98	23	19	43	3
2	2	10	150	8	78	70	24	20	44	3
1	0	3	45	3	29	21	29	21	45	3
1	12	28	420	15	204	196	24	16	48	3
2	7	21	315	13	155	147	25	21	49	3

Table 4. Feasible parameters for canonical two-character multisets in PG(4, 2) with $\gamma' \leq 4$—part 2.

g	μ	r	n	γ	s	t	s_0	t_0	n'	γ'
2	5	17	255	11	127	119	26	22	50	3
2	3	13	195	9	99	91	27	23	51	3
2	8	24	360	14	176	168	28	24	56	3
2	6	20	300	12	148	140	29	25	57	3
2	4	16	240	10	120	112	30	26	58	3
2	2	12	180	8	92	84	31	27	59	3
1	11	27	405	14	197	189	32	24	64	3
2	7	23	345	13	169	161	32	28	64	3
2	5	19	285	11	141	133	33	29	65	3
2	3	15	225	9	113	105	34	30	66	3
2	6	22	330	12	162	154	36	32	72	3
2	0	10	150	6	78	70	39	35	75	3
2	5	21	315	11	155	147	40	36	80	3
2	4	12	180	12	92	84	16	12	28	4
1	2	6	90	6	50	42	20	12	28	4
2	3	11	165	11	85	77	20	16	36	4
2	4	14	210	12	106	98	23	19	43	4
1	2	7	105	6	57	49	27	19	43	4
1	1	5	75	5	43	35	28	20	44	4
1	11	26	390	15	190	182	25	17	49	4
1	10	24	360	14	176	168	26	18	50	4
1	9	22	330	13	162	154	27	19	51	4
1	8	20	300	12	148	140	28	20	52	4
1	7	18	270	11	134	126	29	21	53	4
1	5	14	210	9	106	98	31	23	55	4
2	6	20	300	14	148	140	29	25	57	4
1	3	10	150	7	78	70	33	25	57	4
2	4	16	240	12	120	112	30	26	58	4
1	2	8	120	6	64	56	34	26	58	4
1	1	6	90	5	50	42	35	27	59	4
1	0	4	60	4	36	28	36	28	60	4
1	11	27	405	15	197	189	32	24	64	4
1	10	25	375	14	183	175	33	25	65	4
2	3	15	225	11	113	105	34	30	66	4
1	9	23	345	13	169	161	34	26	66	4
2	1	11	165	9	85	77	35	31	67	4
1	8	21	315	12	155	147	35	27	67	4
1	6	17	255	10	127	119	37	29	69	4
1	4	13	195	8	99	91	39	31	71	4
1	3	11	165	7	85	77	40	32	72	4

Table 4. *Cont.*

g	μ	r	n	γ	s	t	s_0	t_0	n'	γ'
1	2	9	135	6	71	63	41	33	73	4
1	1	7	105	5	57	49	42	34	74	4
1	0	5	75	4	43	35	43	35	75	4
1	10	26	390	14	190	182	40	32	80	4
2	3	17	255	11	127	119	41	37	81	4
1	9	24	360	13	176	168	41	33	81	4
2	4	20	300	12	148	140	44	40	88	4
2	3	19	285	11	141	133	48	44	96	4
1	9	25	375	13	183	175	48	40	96	4

Funding: This research received no external funding.

Institutional Review Board Statement: Not applicable.

Data Availability Statement: No new data were created or analyzed in this study. Data sharing is not applicable to this article.

Conflicts of Interest: The author declares no conflicts of interest.

References

1. Delsarte, P. Weights of linear codes and strongly regular normed spaces. *Discret. Math.* **1972**, *3*, 47–64. [CrossRef]
2. Brouwer, A.E. Two-weight codes. In *Concise Encyclopedia of Coding Theory*; Chapman and Hall/CRC: Boca Raton, FL, USA, 2021; pp. 449–462.
3. Luo, G.; Cao, X. A construction of linear codes and strongly regular graphs from q-polynomials. *Discret. Math.* **2017**, *340*, 2262–2274. [CrossRef]
4. Boyvalenkov, P.; Delchev, K.; Zinoviev, D.V.; Zinoviev, V.A. On two-weight codes. *Discret. Math.* **2021**, *344*, 112318. [CrossRef]
5. Calderbank, R.; Kantor, W.M. The geometry of two-weight codes. *Bull. Lond. Math. Soc.* **1986**, *18*, 97–122. [CrossRef]
6. Brouwer, A.E.; Maldeghem, H.V. *Strongly Regular Graphs*; Cambridge University Press: Cambridge, UK, 2022; Volume 182.
7. Heng, Z.; Li, D.; Du, J.; Chen, F. A family of projective two-weight linear codes. *Des. Codes Cryptogr.* **2021**, *89*, 1993–2007. [CrossRef]
8. Kohnert, A. Constructing two-weight codes with prescribed groups of automorphisms. *Discret. Appl. Math.* **2007**, *155*, 1451–1457. [CrossRef]
9. Pavese, F. Geometric constructions of two-character sets. *Discret. Math.* **2015**, *338*, 202–208. [CrossRef]
10. Zhu, C.; Liao, Q. Two new classes of projective two-weight linear codes. *Finite Fields Their Appl.* **2023**, *88*, 102186. [CrossRef]
11. Bouyukliev, I.; Fack, V.; Willems, W.; Winne, J. Projective two-weight codes with small parameters and their corresponding graphs. *Des. Codes Cryptogr.* **2006**, *41*, 59–78. [CrossRef]
12. Brouwer, A.E.; Eupen, M.V. The correspondence between projective codes and 2-weight codes. *Des. Codes Cryptogr.* **1997**, *11*, 261–266. [CrossRef]
13. Bouyukliev, I.; Bouyuklieva, S. Dual transform and projective self-dual codes. *Adv. Math. Commun.* **2024**, *18*, 328–341. [CrossRef]
14. Bouyukliev, I.G. Classification of Griesmer codes and dual transform. *Discret. Math.* **2009**, *309*, 4049–4068. [CrossRef]
15. Takenaka, M.; Okamoto, K.; Maruta, T. On optimal non-projective ternary linear codes. *Discret. Math.* **2008**, *308*, 842–854. [CrossRef]
16. Bouyuklieva, S.; Bouyukliev, I. Dual transform through characteristic vectors. In Proceedings of the International Workshop OCRT, Sofia, Bulgaria, 7–8 December 2017; pp. 43–48.
17. Jungnickel, D.; Tonchev, V.D. The classification of antipodal two-weight linear codes. *Finite Fields Their Appl.* **2018**, *50*, 372–381. [CrossRef]
18. Vega, G.; Vázquez, C.A. The weight distribution of a family of reducible cyclic codes. In *Arithmetic of Finite Fields, Proceedings of the 4th International Workshop, WAIFI 2012, Bochum, Germany, 16–19 July 2012*; Springer: Berlin/Heidelberg, Germany, 2012; Proceedings 4, pp. 16–28.
19. Duc, T.D. Non-projective cyclic codes whose check polynomial contains two zeros. *arXiv* **2019**, arXiv:1903.07321.
20. Govaerts, P.; Storme, L. On a particular class of minihypers and its applications. I. The result for general q. *Des. Codes Cryptogr.* **2003**, *28*, 51–63. [CrossRef]
21. Byrne, E.; Greferath, M.; Honold, T. Ring geometries, two-weight codes, and strongly regular graphs. *Des. Codes Cryptogr.* **2008**, *48*, 1–16. [CrossRef]
22. Dodunekov, S.; Simonis, J. Codes and projective multisets. *Electron. J. Comb.* **1998**, *5*, R37. [CrossRef]
23. Bonisoli, A. Every equidistant linear code is a sequence of dual Hamming codes. In *ARS Combinatoria*; Charles Babbage Research Centre: Manitoba, ON, Canada, 1984; Volume 18, pp. 181–186.

24. Honold, T.; Kiermaier, M.; Kurz, S. Partial spreads and vector space partitions. In *Network Coding and Subspace Designs*; Greferath, M., Pavčević, M.O., Silberstein, N., Vázquez-Castro, M.Á., Eds.; Springer: Berlin/Heidelberg, Germany, 2018; pp. 131–170.
25. Ward, H.N. An introduction to divisible codes. *Des. Codes Cryptogr.* **1999**, *17*, 73–79. [CrossRef]
26. Heinlein, D.; Honold, T.; Kiermaier, M.; Kurz, S.; Wassermann, A. Projective divisible binary codes. In Proceedings of the 10th International Workshop on Coding and Cryptography, Saint Petersburg, Russia, 18–22 September 20017; pp. 1–10.
27. Kurz, S. Divisible codes. *arXiv* **2021**, arXiv:2112.11763.
28. Betten, A.; Braun, M.; Fripertinger, H.; Kerber, A.; Kohnert, A.; Wassermann, A. *Error-Correcting Linear Codes: Classification by Isometry and Applications*; Springer Science & Business Media: Berlin/Heidelberg, Germany, 2006; Volume 18.
29. Bouyukliev, I. On the binary projective codes with dimension 6. *Discret. Appl. Math.* **2006**, *154*, 1693–1708. [CrossRef]
30. Bouyukliev, I.; Bouyuklieva, S.; Kurz, S. Computer classification of linear codes. *IEEE Trans. Inf. Theory* **2021**, *67*, 7807–7814. [CrossRef]

entropy

MDPI

Article

Some Constructions and Mathematical Properties of Zero-Correlation-Zone Sonar Sequences

Xiaoxiang Jin, Gangsan Kim, Sangwon Chae and Hong-Yeop Song *,†

School of Electrical and Electronic Engineering, Yonsei University, Seoul 03722, Republic of Korea; xxjin@yonsei.ac.kr (X.J.); gs.kim@yonsei.ac.kr (G.K.); sw.chae@yonsei.ac.kr (S.C.)
* Correspondence: hysong@yonsei.ac.kr
† In memory of Herbert Taylor.

Abstract: In this paper, we propose the zero-correlation-zone (ZCZ) of radius r on two-dimensional $m \times n$ sonar sequences and define the (m, n, r) ZCZ sonar sequences. We also define some new optimality of an (m, n, r) ZCZ sonar sequence which has the largest r for given m and n. Because of the ZCZ for perfect autocorrelation, we are able to relax the distinct difference property of the conventional sonar sequences, and hence, the autocorrelation of ZCZ sonar sequences outside ZCZ may not be upper bounded by 1. We may sometimes require such an ideal autocorrelation outside ZCZ, and we define ZCZ-DD sonar sequences, indicating that it has an additional distinct difference (DD) property. We first derive an upper bound on the ZCZ radius r in terms of m and $n \geq m$. We next propose some constructions for (m, n, r) ZCZ sonar sequences, which leads to some very good constructive lower bound on r. Furthermore, this construction suggests that for m and r, the parameter n can be as large as possible indefinitely. We present some exhaustive search results on the existence of (m, n, r) ZCZ sonar sequences for some small values of r. For ZCZ-DD sonar sequences, we prove that some variations of Costas arrays construct some ZCZ-DD sonar sequences with ZCZ radius $r = 2$. We also provide some exhaustive search results on the existence of (m, n, r) ZCZ-DD sonar sequences. Lots of open problems are listed at the end.

Keywords: sonar sequences; zero-correlation-zone; costas arrays; distinct difference property

1. Introduction

Sonar sequences are two-dimensional synchronizing patterns of dots and blanks with minimal ambiguity [1]. Rectangular array representation of sonar sequences is defined by having only one dot per column and the distinct difference properties of the dots. They are used in active sonar systems to improve target detection performance. They are also useful in radar [2] and many other applications where optimal 2-dimensional autocorrelation is required. Costas arrays as sonar sequences were introduced by J. P. Costas in 1984 [3]. Subsequently, research interest was aroused in the existence [4], enumeration, construction [5–8], and mathematical properties [9–12] of Costas arrays and also sonar sequences. It is further generalized into various shapes, for example, honeycomb array, maintaining the distinct difference properties [13].

Numerous studies have delved into the structural properties of sonar sequences. The properties of symmetry were discussed for Welch and Golomb constructions in [14]. S. W. Golomb and H. Taylor had previously proposed a weakened version of the conjecture, asserting that single periodicity was characteristic of Welch construction of the Costas array. Subsequently, in [15], the concept of cyclic Costas sequences was introduced, along with the conjecture that a Costas sequence is cyclic if and only if it is Welch.

With the introduction of Costas arrays, the search for the number of Costas arrays began using computers, even though computers were not well developed at the time. R. Games and M. Chao were the first to report exact values for order $n \leq 10$, the values for $n \leq 12$ were found by J. P. Costas, and J. Robbins furthered the search up to $n = 13$ in 1984 [8]. In 1988, Silverman et al. reported a further extension to $n = 17$, and developed a probabilistic estimation formula for the number of Costas arrays [16]. In 2011, K. Drakakis and S. Rickard et al. published results enumerating Costas arrays up to $n = 29$ [17].

In one dimension, a binary sequence is called to have an ideal autocorrelation when the out-of-phase autocorrelation magnitude is at most 1 or 2 according to the period of the sequence [18,19]. In [20], P. Fan proposed the concept of zero-correlation-zone (ZCZ) in which the autocorrelation is zero (perfect). As one-dimensional CDMA sequences, binary or non-binary ZCZ sequences can be used to perfectly eliminate co-channel and multipath interference for quasi-synchronous CDMA systems [21]. Therefore, they do not care for the autocorrelation values of ZCZ sequences outside ZCZ. It would have been mathematically or theoretically desirable if the autocorrelation magnitudes of ZCZ sequences were also very low or even close to zero, which is not at all required for QS-CDMA systems using ZCZ sequences since the system performance depends only on the autocorrelation magnitudes inside ZCZ [21,22]. In addition, several studies on the construction and bounds of these one-dimensional ZCZ sequences have been published [22–24].

Sonar sequences are two-dimensional synchronizing patterns since their autocorrelation properties are well-described in two dimensions. We now propose for the first time the concept of ZCZ into sonar sequences, and we emphasize that we do care for the autocorrelation value zero inside ZCZ (except for the in-phase, of course) and we do not care for the value outside ZCZ. As we have mentioned in the previous paragraph, it would have been great if we could define a ZCZ sonar sequence that has not only the zero autocorrelation value inside ZCZ but also the value of at most 1 outside ZCZ. We will call such a ZCZ sonar sequence a ZCZ-DD sonar sequence, which is itself a sonar sequence. We note, therefore, that a ZCZ sonar sequence may not be a (conventional) sonar sequence since it may lack the so called distinct difference property that defines sonar sequences.

In this paper, we propose the zero-correlation-zone (ZCZ) of radius r on two-dimensional $m \times n$ sonar sequences and define the (m, n, r) ZCZ sonar sequences. We also define some new optimality of an (m, n, r) ZCZ sonar sequence which has the largest r for given m and n. Because of the ZCZ for perfect autocorrelation, we are able to relax the distinct difference property of the conventional sonar sequences, and hence, the autocorrelation of ZCZ sonar sequences outside ZCZ may not be upper bounded by 1. We may sometimes require such an ideal autocorrelation outside ZCZ, and we call this a ZCZ-DD sonar sequence, indicating that it has an additional distinct difference (DD) property.

It is to be noted that, for conventional sonar sequences (without considering ZCZ), one has to increase the value n for a given m in order to increase the overall autocorrelation performance [25,26]. This gives the definition of (conventional) optimal (m, n) sonar sequences with largest n for a given m [26]. Now, we emphasize that it is quite appropriate to think of the new optimality of (m, n, r) ZCZ sonar sequences with largest value of r given m and n, since now it has perfect autocorrelation inside ZCZ and hence it is desirable to have as large ZCZ as possible for given size $m \times n$. It is because we may be able to limit the operating range (of active sonar systems) inside ZCZ, as is the case for the one-dimensional sequences with ZCZ [20].

In Section 2, we review sonar sequences, encompassing essential definitions, properties, autocorrelation properties, and some well-known constructions. We introduce the Manhattan metric, which will be used in subsequent discussions to represent the ZCZ radius. Section 3 contains some main results on ZCZ sonar sequences. Section 4 discusses some theory only on ZCZ-DD sonar sequences. Section 6 discusses some open problems of both ZCZ sonar sequences and ZCZ-DD sonar sequences.

2. Preliminary

Definition 1. *(Sonar Sequences, Sonar Arrays and Costas Arrays [1,26]) Let $m \leq n$ be positive integers. A function $f : \{1,2,\ldots,n\} \rightarrow \{1,2,\ldots,m\}$ has the distinct difference (DD) property if*

$$f(u+h) - f(u) = f(v+h) - f(v) \quad \textit{implies} \quad u = v$$

for $1 \leq h \leq n-1$ and $1 \leq u,v \leq n-h$.

An (m,n) sonar sequence is a function $f : \{1,2,\ldots,n\} \rightarrow \{1,2,\ldots,m\}$ with the DD property. It can be written as

$$f = [f(1), f(2), \ldots, f(n)],$$

where $1 \leq f(j) \leq i$, for $j = 1,2,\ldots,n$. This can also be represented as an $m \times n$ sonar array $A = [A(i,j)]$, where

$$A(i,j) = \begin{cases} 1, & f(j) = i \\ 0, & \textit{otherwise} \end{cases}, 1 \leq i \leq m, 1 \leq j \leq n.$$

It is a usual convention to represent "1" with a dot and "0" with a blank in A.

An (m,n) sonar sequence is called optimal if n is the largest with m rows.

The Costas array is a sonar array of square size with an additional condition that there is only one "dot" in each row.

There are some well-known constructions of Costas arrays as sonar sequences.

- **Lempel construction** [1,5,8]: Let $q > 2$ be a prime or a prime power and let α be a primitive element of $\mathbb{F}_q$ which is the finite field of size q. Then $f : \{1,2,\ldots,q-2\} \rightarrow \{1,2,\ldots,q-2\}$ defined by the relation $\alpha^j + \alpha^{f(j)} = 1$, for $j = 1,2,\ldots,q-1$, is a $(q-2) \times (q-2)$ Costas array.
- **(Exponential) Welch construction** [1,5,8]: Let α be a primitive element of $\mathbb{F}_p$ where p is a prime. Then $f : \{1,2,\ldots,p-1\} \rightarrow \{1,2,\ldots,p-1\}$ defined by $f(i) = \alpha^i$, for $i = 1,2,\ldots,p-1$, is a $(p-1) \times (p-1)$ Costas array. Furthermore, if $[f(1), f(2), \ldots, f(p-1)]$ is the exponential Welch Costas array, then so is

$$[f(j), f(j+1), \ldots, f(p-1), f(1), f(2), \ldots, f(j-1)]$$

for each $j = 2,3,\ldots,p-1$. This property is called the single periodicity of the Costas array.

There are also Quadratic constructions [25], Shift construction [27], Golomb construction [5,8], the constructions using Sidon set [28] and their extensions.

We note that attaching i empty rows, for any integer $i = 1,2,\ldots$, to the above $n \times n$ Costas array gives an $(n+i) \times n$ sonar array. We note also that rotating the rows of the result any number of times is still an $(n+i) \times n$ sonar array. If we start from the exponential Welch Costas array, then rotating the columns of the result any number of times is still an $(n+i) \times n$ sonar array because of its single periodicity. This will be used later for the some new construction of ZCZ-DD sonar sequences with radius 2.

Another variation on any $n \times n$ Costas array is to delete any corner dot and obtain the $(n-1) \times (n-1)$ Costas array. Deleting the corner dots twice gives the size $(n-2) \times (n-2)$. Two corner dots in the diagonal position can be deleted once to produce the size $(n-2) \times (n-2)$. This will also be used later for ZCZ-DD sonar sequence construction.

The discrete non-periodic autocorrelation function [8] $C(\tau, \varphi)$ of an $m \times n$ sonar array $[A(i,j)]$ where $i = 1,2,\ldots,m$, $j = 1,2,\ldots,n$ is defined to be the number of coincidences between dots in $A(i,j)$ and its shift $A(i+\varphi, j+\tau)$ where τ is the amount of horizontal shift and φ is the amount of vertical shift. The set of all the values of $C(\tau, \varphi)$ can be represented as an array of size $(2m-1) \times (2n-1)$, and it has a center-symmetric structure:

$$C(\tau, \varphi) = C(-\tau, -\varphi), \quad \text{for all} \quad (\tau, \varphi) \in \mathbb{Z}^2.$$

When $(\tau, \varphi) = (0,0)$, the correlation has the peak value $C(0,0) = n$, since all the dots coincide. The DD property implies that

$$C(\tau, \varphi) \leq 1, \quad \text{for all} \quad (\tau, \varphi) \neq (0,0).$$

In this paper, we will define ZCZ in the Manhattan metric. The Manhattan metric is also known as the taxicab metric [29]. In a 2-dimensional plain, the Manhattan distance D between two dots in positions $a = (x_1, y_1)$ and $b = (x_2, y_2)$ is defined by

$$D(a,b) = |x_1 - x_2| + |y_1 - y_2|. \tag{1}$$

We will use the terms "sonar array" and "sonar sequence" interchangeably, and hence, the autocorrelation of a sonar sequence has to be understood as that of the sonar array.

This induces an integer-valued lattice in the 2-dimensional plain, which will be denoted by $\mathbb{Z}^2$. For a positive integer r, we consider the Manhattan-circle of radius r centered at the origin in $\mathbb{Z}^2$ and the set $M(r)$ of all the integer points inside, i.e.,

$$M(r) = \left\{(x,y) \in \mathbb{Z}^2 : |x| + |y| \leq r\right\}.$$

Lemma 1. *The area of a Manhattan-circle $M(r)$ of radius r is given as*

$$|M(r)| = 1 + 2r + 2r^2. \tag{2}$$

Proof. The first term in (2) counts the center. The remaining size is given by 4 times $(1 + 2 + \cdots + r)$ as shown in Figure 1. □

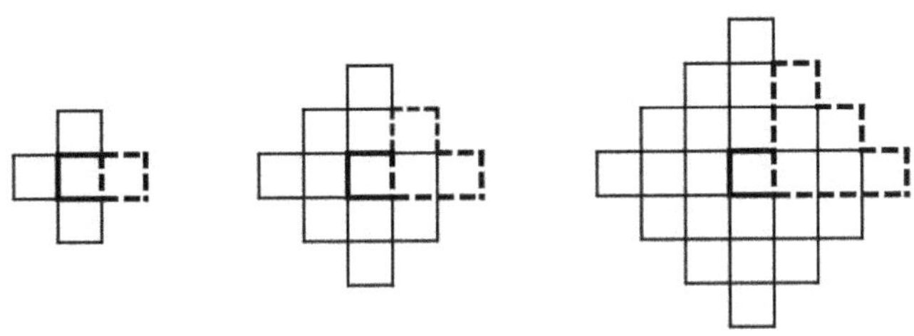

$1 + 4(1)$ $\quad$ $1 + 4(1 + 2)$ $\quad$ $1 + 4(1 + 2 + 3)$

Figure 1. Manhattan-circles of radius $r = 1, 2, 3$ and its area.

3. Main Results on ZCZ Sonar Sequences

Definition 2. *For positive integers r and $m \leq n$, an (m, n, r) ZCZ sonar sequence is a function $f : \{1, 2, \ldots, n\} \to \{1, 2, \ldots, m\}$ such that its autocorrelation $C(\tau, \varphi) = 0$ for all $(\tau, \varphi) \neq (0,0)$ with $|\varphi| + |\tau| \leq r$ where r is the radius of ZCZ in the Manhattan metric.*

For clarity, it is important to note that a ZCZ sonar sequence, although termed a "sonar sequence", does not necessarily satisfy the DD property of sonar sequences. A special case of ZCZ sonar sequences is a ZCZ-DD sonar sequence, which is a sonar sequence with ZCZ of some radius.

Definition 3. *An (m, n, r) ZCZ-DD sonar sequence is an (m, n, r) ZCZ sonar sequence that has the DD property, in addition.*

Remark 1. *A ZCZ-DD sonar sequence is a sonar sequence. A ZCZ-DD sonar sequence is always a ZCZ sonar sequence, but not conversely. A ZCZ sonar sequence may not have the DD property.*

Example 1. *The first example in Figure 2 is a* $(5,5)$ *Costas array (sonar sequence) and its autocorrelation. The second example is a* $(5,5,2)$ *ZCZ-DD sonar sequence and its autocorrelation showing the ZCZ of radius 2. We note that it is a sonar sequence. The third example is a* $(5,5,2)$ *ZCZ sonar sequence. Observe that it is not a sonar sequence because it does not have the DD property. This can be seen by the value 2 at some out-of-phase shifts* $(\tau,\varphi) \neq (0,0)$.

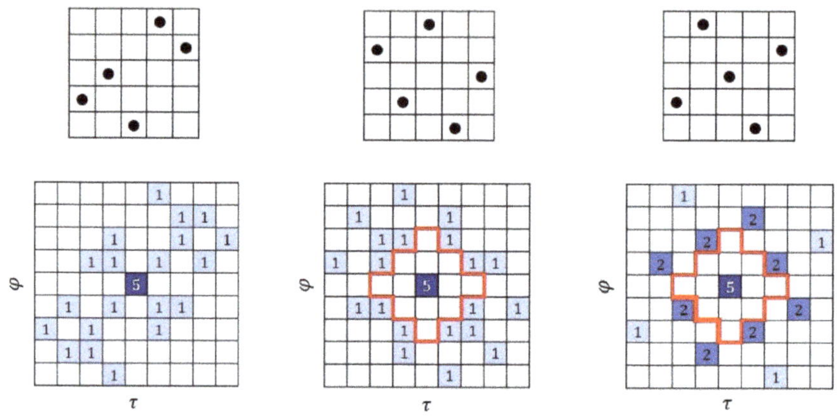

Figure 2. Three 5×5 arrays in Example 1.

Given an (m,n,r) ZCZ sonar array, we define D_{min} to be the minimum Manhattan distance among all the distances between the pairs of dots. The following is obvious:

Lemma 2. *For a ZCZ sonar sequence with its ZCZ radius r, the distance D of any pair of dots satisfies*

$$D \geq D_{min} = r + 1.$$

This lemma gives some trivial upper bound on r of any (m,n,r) ZCZ sonar sequences. That is,

$$r = D_{min} - 1 \leq D - 1.$$

The following upper bound on r is the best in terms of m and $n \geq m$ that we could prove. The main idea is analogous to the proof of Hamming bound on binary linear block codes:

Theorem 1. *For an* (m,n,r) *ZCZ sonar sequence with* $n \geq m \geq 2$, *we have*

$$r \leq \left\lfloor \sqrt{2m-4} \right\rfloor. \tag{3}$$

Proof. Consider the $m \times n$ array corresponding to an (m,n,r) ZCZ sonar sequence. Then, any two Manhattan-circles of radius ρ with dots at the center will not intersect with each other when $\rho \geq \lfloor \frac{r}{2} \rfloor$. Therefore, the sum of the area of all the Manhattan-circles of radius ρ cannot be more than the total area of the array. Here, we may have to consider the dots in the edges so that the Manhattan-circle may cover the area beyond the $m \times n$ sonar array. For this, we increase the total area of the array from $m \times n$ to $(m+2\rho) \times (n+2\rho)$, since the dot in the edges could reach the distance ρ for both horizontally and vertically. By carefully counting the number of cells in these additional areas, we see that we only have to increase in one direction. Therefore, we have the bound (similar to Hamming bound in algebraic coding theory)

$$n|M(\rho)| \leq (m+2\rho)n,$$

or

$$|M(\rho)| \leq (m+2\rho).$$

We substitute $\rho = r/2$ on LHS and $\rho = (r-1)/2$ on RHS by carefully counting again the additional areas outside the $m \times n$ array. This gives the bound in the theorem. □

In [30], the maximum number of disjoint non-attacking Queens (NAQ) patterns that can sit on an $n \times n$ chessboard is proposed, where each pattern consists of n NAQs placed symmetrically around the center. NAQ means that for each dot in the pattern, there are no other dots in the horizontal, vertical and diagonal directions. We cite one of NAQ patterns and calculate the autocorrelation as shown in Figure 3. From its autocorrelation, it can be seen that it is an $(11, 11, 2)$ ZCZ sonar sequence. The following construction of (m, n, r) ZCZ sonar sequence essentially comes from this idea from [30].

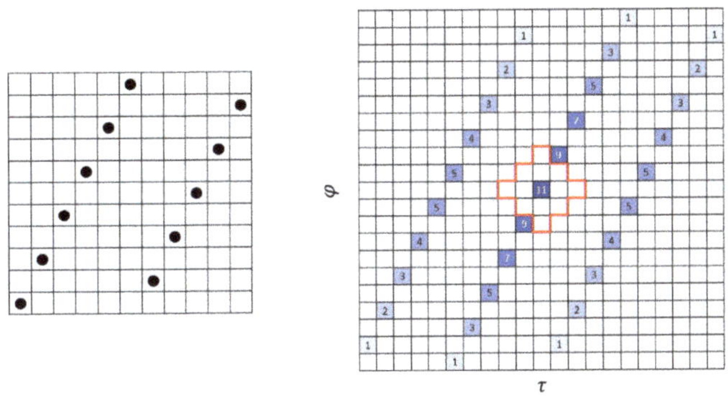

Figure 3. An 11×11 NAQ pattern from [30] is an $(11, 11, 2)$ ZCZ sonar sequence.

Theorem 2. *The function* $f : \{0, 1, \ldots, n-1\} \to \{0, 1, \ldots, m-1\}$ *defined by* $f(j) = rj \pmod{m}$ *is an* (m, n, r) *ZCZ sonar sequence for any positive integers* $m, n \geq m$ *and* $r \geq 3$ *with* $m = r^2 - 1$.

Proof. We will focus on a section containing consecutive r columns inside. For $j = 0, 1, 2, \ldots, r-1$ and also $j = r$, the function f is shown in Figure 4. We claim that the Manhattan distance between any two dots is at least $r+1$ as shown below, and since this one period of r columns can repeat indefinitely, the proof is completed:

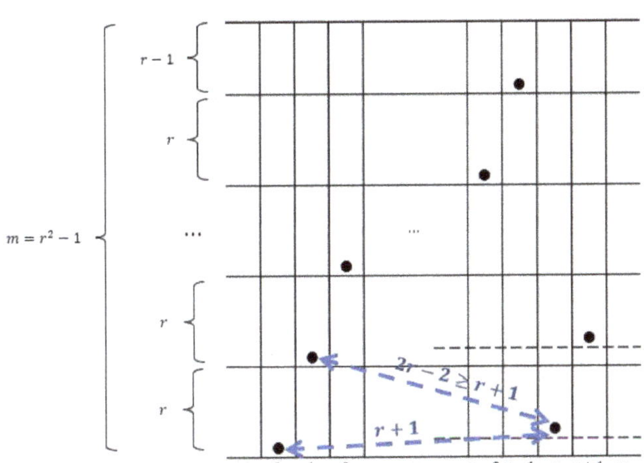

Figure 4. Proof of Theorem 2.

Consider the columns from 0 to $r-1$ in Figure 4. Any two adjacent dots have Manhattan distance $r+1$. Consider the dot in column r in Figure 4. Since $m = r^2 - 1$, it is located one row up relative to the dot in column 0. Therefore, the Manhattan distance (of lower arrow in the figure) is $r+1$. The Manhattan distance of the dot from the dot in column 1 is $r-1+r-1 = 2r-2 \geq r+1$ since $r \geq 3$ (upper arrow in the figure). □

The above construction gives a constructive lower bound on the parameter r for (m,n,r) ZCZ sonar sequences:

Corollary 1. *There exists an (m,n,r) ZCZ sonar sequence such that*

$$r \geq \sqrt{m+1}.$$

In an attempt to improve the lower bound in the above corollary, we propose another construction for (m,n,r) ZCZ sonar sequences in which the first repeat of the dot in the lowest block of size r is not in column r (which is the case in Figure 4 for the proof of Theorem 2) but in some column t where $t << r$ where we assume that $r \geq 3$. Since the total number of rows is m, its row index must be $rt \pmod{m}$ which is equal to $rt - m$. Therefore, we are trying to find the minimum $t \in \{0,1,\ldots,n-1\}$ such that $rt - m > 0$, where the function $f : \{0,1,\ldots,n-1\} \to \{0,1,\ldots,m-1\}$ defined as $f(j) = rj \pmod{m}$ is shown in Figure 5.

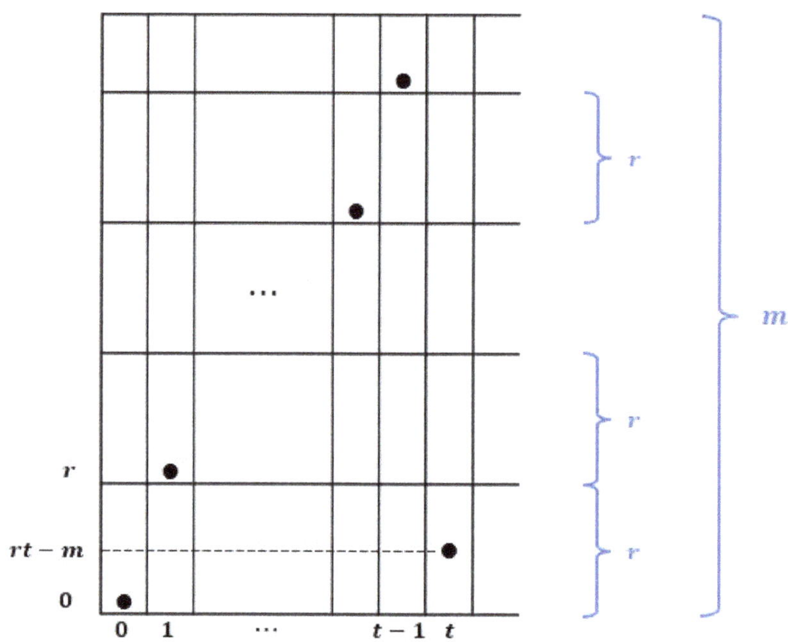

Figure 5. Proof of Theorem 3 where $\frac{(r+3)}{2} \leq t$ and $(r-1)t+2 \leq m \leq (r+1)(t-1)$.

Since any two adjacent dots in the first t columns have the Manhattan distance of $r+1$, we need to check only the distances between the dot in column t and the dots in the first and second columns. This gives the following inequalities:

$$r+1 \leq t+rt-m \tag{4}$$

and

$$r + 1 \le t - 1 + r - (rt - m). \tag{5}$$

By combining (4) and (5), we obtain the following range of m:

$$(r-1)t + 2 \le m \le (r+1)(t-1) \tag{6}$$

or the inequality

$$(r-1)t + 2 \le (r+1)(t-1)$$

which implies that

$$\frac{r+3}{2} \le t. \tag{7}$$

Now, a ZCZ sonar sequence can be constructed for (m, n, r) as follows: Choose a positive integer $r \ge 3$, and select the parameter t satisfying $t \ge \lceil \frac{r+3}{2} \rceil$. The pair of integers r and t determines the range of m by (6). Select an appropriate value of m in this range. Then, for any positive integer n, we have an (m, n, r) ZCZ sonar sequence $f(j) = rj \pmod{m}$ for $j = 1, 2, \ldots, n$.

As an example, the case where $t = r$ yields

$$r^2 - r + 2 \le m \le r^2 - 1$$

for $r \ge 3$. Taking the value $m = r^2 - 1$ in this range for $t = r$ is exactly the case of Theorem 2. Taking the value $m = r^2 - r + 2$ on the other hand for the same $t = r$ gives another (m, n, r) ZCZ sonar sequence for any positive integer n.

For some specific example, we consider $r = 6$. Then $t \ge 5$ and $5t + 2 \le m \le 7(t-1)$. Therefore, we may construct the $(m, n, 6)$ ZCZ sonar sequences for any positive integer n and the value m in the following range:

$$\begin{array}{ccc} t = 5 & \rightarrow & 27 \le m \le 28 \\ t = 6 & \rightarrow & 32 \le m \le 35 \\ t = 7 & \rightarrow & 37 \le m \le 42 \\ etc. & & \end{array}$$

We summarize the discussions above as our main construction for a family of (m, n, r) ZCZ sonar sequences:

Theorem 3 (Main construction for ZCZ sonar sequences). *The function $f : \{0, 1, \ldots, n-1\} \rightarrow \{0, 1, \ldots, m-1\}$ defined by $f(j) \equiv rj \pmod{m}$, as shown in Figure 5, is an (m, n, r) ZCZ sonar sequence for any positive integers $n \ge m$ and $r \ge 3$ where the value m must be in the range (6) in which t satisfies the inequality (7).*

Example 2. *When $r = 3$, the value of m can be 8 according to Theorem 3. Figure 6 depicts the $(8, 8, 3)$ ZCZ sonar sequence with their autocorrelation on the left side.*

When $r = 4$, the construction derived from Theorem 3 produces the square array depicted on the right side of the figure with its autocorrelation. It becomes apparent that the top $\frac{r}{2} - 1 = 1$ row of the array does not contain any dots. Thus, by removing this top row, we arrive at the construction for the size 13×14 with $r = 4$.

Both examples can be repeated any number of times so that the result becomes either $(8, n, 3)$ ZCZ sonar sequence or $(13, n, 4)$ ZCZ sonar sequence for any positive integer n.

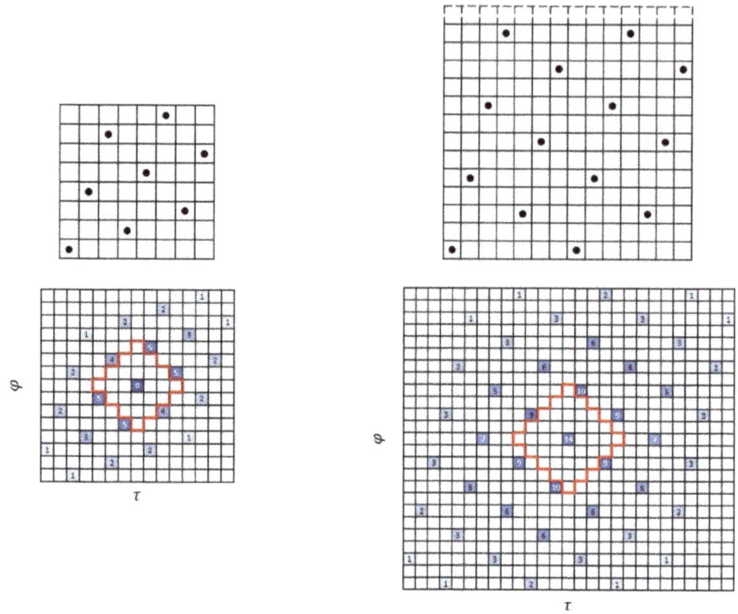

Figure 6. The $(8,8,3)$ and $(13,14,4)$ ZCZ sonar sequences from the construction in Theorem 3.

By selecting the minimum value of $t = \lceil \frac{r+3}{2} \rceil$ for $r \geq 3$ from the above construction, we derive the minimum value of m and hence the best constructive lower bound on r:

Corollary 2. *The minimum value of m in Theorem 3 becomes the following*

$$m = \begin{cases} \frac{r^2+2r+1}{2}, & r \text{ is odd} \\ \frac{r^2+2r+2}{2}, & r \text{ is even} \end{cases},$$

for the value $t = \lceil \frac{r+3}{2} \rceil$*. This gives a constructive lower bound as follows: for any positive integer* $m \geq 3$*, there exists an* (m,n,r) *ZCZ sonar sequence (for any* $n \geq m$*) with the value r satisfying*

$$r \geq \sqrt{2m-1} - 1. \tag{8}$$

Proof. The case of an odd r is obvious. When r is even, the theorem says the minimum value of $m = \frac{r^2+3r}{2}$, and the construction gives an $m \times n$ ZCZ sonar array for any $n \geq m$ where the top $r/2-1$ rows are empty. These rows can be further removed to make m smaller. The resulting value of m becomes $\frac{r^2+2r+2}{2}$. □

We show an example of a $(61,52,10)$ ZCZ sonar sequence in Figure 7 found by computer. This is an interesting example since the construction in Theorem 3 for $r = 10$ gives a ZCZ sonar sequence with the smallest value $m = 61$. It is also very special in that it has a periodic structure of a period of 13 columns repeating 4 times. We note that this period can be repeated any number of times to make a $(61, 13a+b, 10)$ ZCZ sonar sequence for any integers a and b. Essentially, it gives a family of examples of $(61,n,10)$ ZCZ sonar sequences for any positive integer $n \geq 1$.

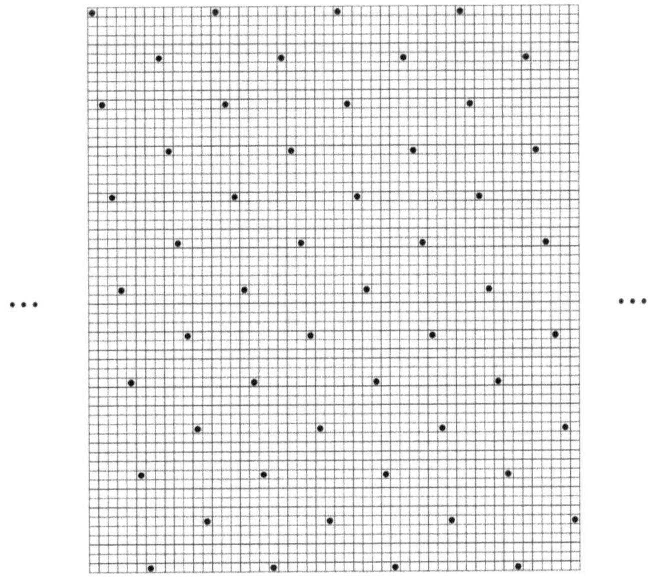

Figure 7. A $(61, 52, 10)$ ZCZ sonar sequence by computer search.

Remark 2. *It is obvious that one can find a family of* (m, n, r) *ZCZ sonar sequences for some given values of m and r with infinitely many values of n. Some evidence we discussed so far can be summarized as follows:*

1. *The example of* $(11, 11, 2)$ *ZCZ sonar sequence in Figure 3 from [30] can be repeated any number of times and the result can be an* $(11, n, 2)$ *ZCZ sonar sequence for any positive integer n.*
2. *The example of* $(61, 52, 10)$ *ZCZ sonar sequence in Figure 7 can be repeated any number of times and the result can be an* $(61, n, 10)$ *ZCZ sonar sequence for any positive integer n.*
3. *Theorem 2 gives a family of* (m, n, r) *ZCZ sonar sequences for any* $r \geq 3$ *and* $m = r^2 - 1$ *but with infinitely many values of the positive integer n.*
4. *Theorem 3 generalizes Theorem 2. Corollary 2 gives one specific case for m and r with any positive integer n, which is different from those by Theorem 2. Two examples from this construction are shown in Example 2.*

Therefore, it becomes meaningless to talk about the 'optimal' (m, n, r) *ZCZ sonar sequence with the maximum value of n for given m and r. Instead, we may define the optimality of an* (m, n, r) *ZCZ sonar sequence if it has the maximum r for given m and n.*

Definition 4. *The ZCZ sonar sequence with the maximum r is called optimal for given m and n. In other words, an* (m, n, r) *ZCZ sonar sequence is optimal when there does not exist an* $(m, n, r + 1)$ *ZCZ sonar sequence.*

We have searched by computer for the true maximum r in (m, n, r) ZCZ sonar sequences for m up to 78 and n in the range from m to $m + 2$. We show this result in Table 1. The value r in this table is the maximum in the sense of Definition 4. This has been checked exhaustively. Therefore, they all are optimal ZCZ sonar sequences for given m and n. It is to be noted further that the upper bound in Theorem 1 is not tight since there are cases where this value is not attained. However, we argue that it is quite good since some other many times, this bound or one less value is attained.

Table 1. The maximum r in (m, n, r) ZCZ sonar sequence found by computer.

m \ n	m	$m+1$	$m+2$	u.bnd (Theorem 1)	l.bnd (Corollary 2)	m \ n	m	$m+1$	$m+2$	u.bnd (Theorem 1)	l.bnd (Corollary 2)
3	1	1	1	1	1	41	8	8	8	8	8
4	2	1	1	2	1	42	8	8	8	8	8
5	2	2	2	2	2	43	8	8	8	9	8
6	2	2	2	3	2	44	8	8	8	9	8
7	3	2	2	3	2	45	8	8	8	9	8
8	3	3	3	3	2	46	8	8	8	9	8
9	3	3	3	3	3	47	8	8	8	9	8
10	3	3	3	4	3	48	8	8	8	9	8
11	3	3	3	4	3	49	9	9	9	9	8
12	4	3	3	4	3	50	9	9	9	9	8
13	4	4	4	4	4	51	9	9	9	9	9
14	4	4	4	4	4	52	9	9	9	10	9
15	4	4	4	5	4	53	9	9	9	10	9
16	4	4	4	5	4	54	9	9	9	10	9
17	5	4	4	5	4	55	9	9	9	10	9
18	5	5	5	5	4	56	9	9	9	10	9
19	5	5	5	5	5	57	9	9	9	10	9
20	5	5	5	6	5	58	9	9	9	10	9
21	5	5	5	6	5	59	9	9	9	10	9
22	5	5	5	6	5	60	10	10	9	10	9
23	5	5	5	6	5	61	10	10	10	10	10
24	6	5	5	6	5	62	10	10	10	10	10
25	6	6	6	6	6	63	10	10	10	11	10
26	6	6	6	6	6	64	10	10	10	11	10
27	6	6	6	7	6	65	10	10	10	11	10
28	6	6	6	7	6	66	10	10	10	11	10
29	6	6	6	7	6	67	10	10	10	11	10
30	6	6	6	7	6	68	10	10	10	11	10
31	7	6	6	7	6	69	10	10	10	11	10
32	7	7	7	7	6	70	10	10	10	11	10
33	7	7	7	7	7	71	11	11	11	11	10
34	7	7	7	8	7	72	11	11	11	11	10
35	7	7	7	8	7	73	11	11	11	11	11
36	7	7	7	8	7	74	11	11	11	12	11
37	7	7	7	8	7	75	11	11	11	12	11
38	7	7	7	8	7	76	11	11	11	12	11
39	7	7	7	8	7	77	11	11	11	12	11
40	8	8	7	8	7	78	11	11	11	12	11

We also show the upper bound on r from Theorem 1 for comparison. Therefore, any max value in the table must be equal to or smaller than this upper bound. We also show the constructive lower bound from Corollary 2 as well in the last column. As n increases from m, the max r will be non-increasing. When it reaches the lower bound, it will stay forever as n increases indefinitely. Therefore, it is enough to show the values of n in the range $m \leq n \leq m+2$ for $3 \leq m \leq 78$.

In this range of values of m, we see that the difference between the upper bound and the constructive lower bound is either 0 or 1. When they are the same, the max r is this value for any $n \geq m$. When they differ by 1, then the max r starts either from the upper bound and decreases by 1 somewhere and stays forever or from the lower bound and stays forever. The example of the former case is when $m = 17$ and those of the latter is when $m = 20$.

For example, for $m = 17$, the max r for $n = 17$ is 5 which is the upper bound. Since the constructive lower bound is 4 for $m = 17$ and this value is reached at $n = 18 = m + 1$, we know that the max $r = 4$ stays the same as n increases from 18 indefinitely. For the case

$m = 20$, the max r at $n = 20$ is 5 which is already equal to the lower bound. Therefore, the max $r = 5$ for n stays the same as n increases indefinitely. We show the three ZCZ sonar sequences with parameters $(17,17,5)$, $(17,18,4)$ and $(20,20,5)$ as follows:

$$\begin{aligned}(17,17,5):&\quad [5,10,15,1,7,12,17,4,9,14,1,6,11,16,3,8,13]\\(17,18,4):&\quad [1,5,9,13,2,6,10,14,1,5,9,13,2,6,10,14,1,17]\\(20,20,5):&\quad [7,12,1,16,5,10,19,2,7,12,17,4,9,14,1,6,11,16,3,20]\end{aligned}$$

These are shown in Figure 8. These are examples of optimal ZCZ sonar sequences.

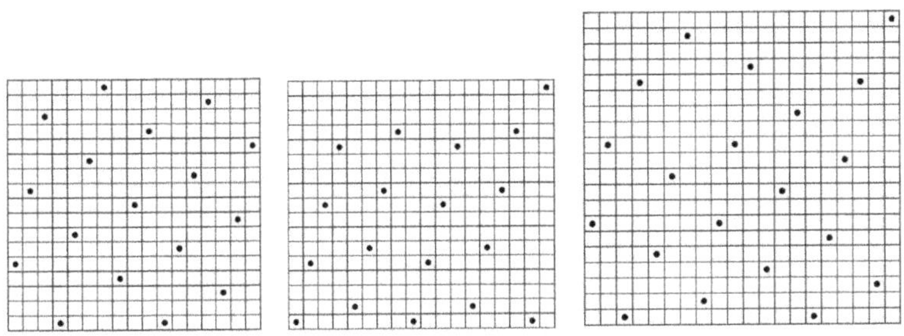

Figure 8. The optimal $(17,17,5)$, $(17,18,4)$ and $(20,20,5)$ ZCZ sonar sequences by computer search.

4. Two Constructions for Zcz-Dd Sonar Sequences with $R = 2$

Theorem 4. *Let q be a prime or a prime power and α be a primitive element of $\mathbb{F}_q$ which is the finite field of size q. Consider the Lempel Costas array $(j, f(j))$ for $j = 1,2,\ldots,q-2$ given by $\alpha^j + \alpha^{f(j)} = 1$. If α satisfies $\alpha^2 + \alpha = 1$, then deleting the two corner dots at $(1,2)$ and $(2,1)$ gives a $(q-4, q-4, 2)$ ZCZ-DD sonar sequence.*

Proof. The Lempel Costas array has only one dot in each row and column and is symmetric along the main diagonal [8]. Therefore, there are two types of dot pairs with a Manhattan distance of 2, as shown in Figure 9. One type consists of two consecutive dots along the diagonal (white dot pair), while the other type consists of two adjacent dots on either side of the diagonal (black dot pair).

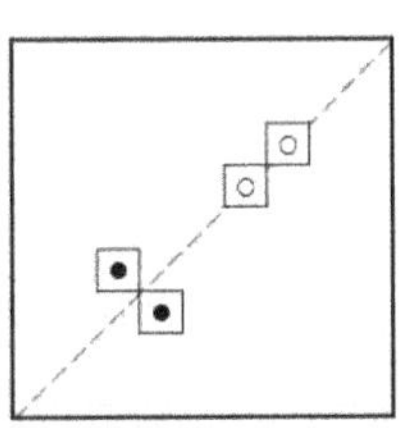

Figure 9. Dot pair types with Manhattan distance 2 in the Lempel construction.

We now claim that the pair of white dots do not exist in Lempel construction for any q. When q is even, $\alpha^j + \alpha^j = 0 \neq 1$ for all j. Therefore, no dot may come on the diagonal. In odd q, $\alpha^j + \alpha^j$ are all distinct for $j = 1,2,\ldots,q-2$, with a unique j satisfying $\alpha^j + \alpha^j = 1$. Therefore, there exists only one dot on the diagonal. Consequently, only black dot pair type exists in the array and no white dot pairs.

When $\alpha^2 + \alpha = 1$, the dots at positions $(2,1)$ and $(1,2)$ constitute the type of black dot pair. Due to the DD property, this is the only dot pair of this type. Thus, removing the dots at positions $(2,1)$ and $(1,2)$ ensures that the Manhattan distance between the remaining pair of dots is at least 3 and hence $r = 2$. The remaining array is a Costas array and maintains the DD property. □

Example 3. *Figure 10 shows a* $(7,7)$ *Lempel Costas array from* $q = 9$. *Deleting the dots* $(1,2)$ *and* $(2,1)$ *gives a* $(5,5,2)$ *ZCZ-DD sonar sequence.*

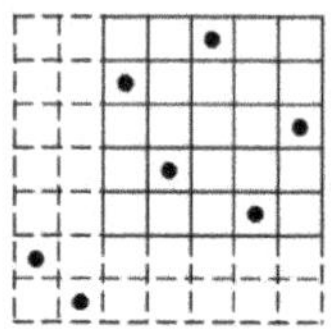

Figure 10. The $(5,5,2)$ ZCZ-DD sonar sequence from the construction in Theorem 4.

For the second type construction of ZCZ-DD sonar sequence with $r = 2$ from the exponential Welch construction for Costas arrays, we observe the following:

Lemma 3. *Let* p *be a prime and* α *be a primitive root mod* p. *There must exist unique* j $\pmod{p-1}$ *satisfying*

$$\alpha^j - \alpha^{j-1} = 1 \text{ or } -1 \pmod{p}.$$

Proof. Consider the case $\alpha^j - \alpha^{j-1} = 1 \pmod{p}$ or $\alpha^{j-1}(\alpha - 1) = 1 \pmod{p}$. Since any non-zero element is some power of α, we let $\alpha - 1 = \alpha^u$ for some u with $2 \le u \le p-2$. This gives

$$\alpha^{j-1+u} = 1 \pmod{p}.$$

Then $j - 1 + u = 0 \pmod{p-1}$ or $j = p - u$ is the unique integer mod $p-1$. The other case is similar. □

Theorem 5. *Consider the exponential Welch Costas array* $f(j) = \alpha^j$ *for any consecutive* $p-1$ *values of* j. *Let* $j_0 \pmod{p-1}$ *satisfy* $\alpha^{j_0} - \alpha^{j_0-1} = 1 \pmod{p}$ *and* $i_0 \pmod{p-1}$ *satisfy* $\alpha^{i_0} - \alpha^{i_0-1} = -1 \pmod{p}$. *Then*

$$f(j) = \alpha^j - 1 - \alpha^{i_0} \pmod{p}$$

for $j = j_0, j_0+1, \ldots, j_0+p-2$ *is a* $(p, p-1, 2)$ *ZCZ-DD sonar sequence.*

Proof. The Welch construction satisfies the DD property. According to Lemma 3, since there is a unique j_0 that satisfies $\alpha^{j_0} - \alpha^{j_0-1} = 1 \pmod{p}$, take j when starting from j_0, the rest of the dots are all at a Manhattan distance greater than 2 from the point (j_0, α^{j_0}). And of the rest of the dots, only the Manhattan distance between the dot pair (i_0, α^{i_0}) and $(i_0 - 1, \alpha^{i_0-1})$ is 2 since $\alpha^{i_0} - \alpha^{i_0-1} = -1 \pmod{p}$. By adding an empty row at the bottom of the array, called the 0-th row, and cyclically rotating the rows of the array, once the dot (i_0, α^{i_0}) moves to the top row of the array, then the pairs of dots with a Manhattan distance of 2 are avoided. Consequently, the Manhattan distance between the dots becomes at least 3. After adding a row, the array consists of a total of p rows, it retains the DD property because of its single periodicity. □

Example 4. *There exists a unique integer* $i_0 \pmod{p-1}$ *satisfying* $\alpha^{i_0} - \alpha^{i_0-1} = -1 \pmod{p}$ *from Lemma 3. Similarly, there exists a unique integer* $j_0 \pmod{p-1}$ *satisfying* $\alpha^{j_0} - \alpha^{j_0-1} = 1 \pmod{p}$. *As shown in Figure 11, when* $p = 7$, *we have* $\alpha = 3$, *and hence,* $i_0 = 2$ *and* $j_0 = 5$ *both mod 6. Therefore, we take the exponential Welch Costas array given as* $f(j) = 3^j \pmod{7}$ *for* $j = j_0 = 5, 6, \ldots, 10$. *This* 6×6 *array has two adjacent dots in some two consecutive columns whose row indices are* $\alpha^{i_0-1} = 3$ *and* $\alpha^{i_0} = 2$ *both mod 7. We will make this a* 7×6 *sonar array by adjoining an empty row at the bottom. Now, rotating all* $p = 7$ *rows downward* $1 + \alpha^{i_0} = 3$ *times will place the dot in column* i_0 *at the top. The resulting* 7×6 *array becomes a* $(7, 6, 2)$ *ZCZ-DD sonar sequence.*

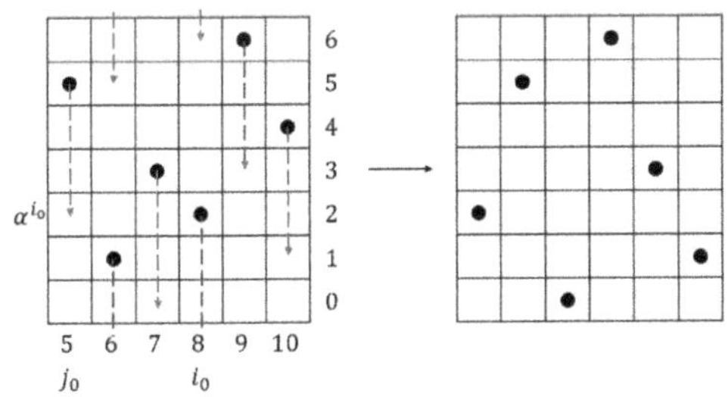

Figure 11. The $(7,6,2)$ ZCZ-DD sonar sequence from the construction in Theorem 5.

Remark 3. *The upper bound on r for (m,n,r) ZCZ sonar sequences can be an upper bound on r for (m,n,r) ZCZ-DD sonar sequences, only because any (m,n,r) ZCZ-DD sonar sequence is an (m,n,r) ZCZ sonar sequence. We expect that this upper bound must be quite loose.*

Some search results for the max r in (m,n,r) ZCZ-DD sequences are documented initially in [31] for $m \leq 17$ and we extend the search for $m \leq 20$ and show the results in Table 2. Where the parameters $m = 10$, $n = m+4$, and $r = 2$ represent the existence of an optimal $(10,14,2)$ ZCZ-DD sonar sequence. It also implies that there does not exist a $(10,14,3)$ ZCZ-DD sonar sequence.

Table 2. The maximum r in (m,n,r) ZCZ-DD sonar sequence.

m \ n	m	$m+1$	$m+2$	$m+3$	$m+4$
2	1	1	0	–	–
3	1	1	1	0	–
4	1	1	1	1	0
5	2	1	1	1	1
6	2	2	1	1	1
7	2	2	2	1	1
8	2	2	2	1	1
9	2	2	2	1	1
10	2	2	2	2	2
11	2	2	2	2	2
12	3	3	2	2	2
13	3	3	2	2	2
14	3	3	3	2	2
15	3	3	3	3	2
16	3	3	3	3	2
17	3	3	3	3	2
18	3	3	3	3	2
19	3	3	3	3	2
20	3	3	3	3	?

5. Some Relations with Results in [26,30]

This subsection is newly added as a result of some analysis from the comments of the initial reviewers of this manuscript. All of the authors would like to express sincere appreciation for these comments. We have investigated most of the results in both [26] and [30], with emphasis on some possibility of having ZCZ sonar sequences from theirs. Following is some conclusion from this analysis.

Most of the best known $m \times n$ sonar sequences in [26] for m up to 100 turned out to have no ZCZ at all. We show only two cases here for $m = 10$ and $m = 30$ from [26]. These are 10×16 and 30×37 sonar sequences as shown in Figure 12. These have the largest value of n for the given value of $m = 10$ and $m = 30$. The fact that they do not have ZCZ can be seen easily by observing that there exist two adjacent dots of (Manhattan) distance 1.

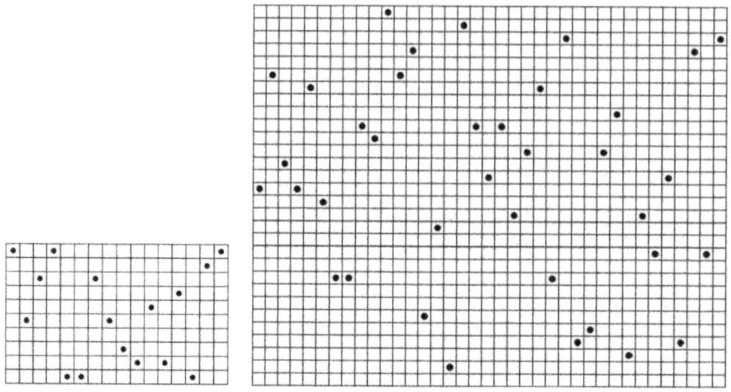

Figure 12. Best known sonar sequences from [26] without ZCZ ($m = 10$ and $m = 30$).

The main topic of [30] is to find the maximum number of disjoint nonattacking-n-queen patterns that simultaneously pack the $n \times n$ board. We find one of interesting relation there when $n > 7$ is an odd prime. One of the solution in this case gives not only an $(n, n, 3)$ ZCZ sonar sequence, but a family of disjoint n ZCZ sonar sequences (which are also n disjoint nonattacking-n-queen patterns) of the same parameters that simultaneously pack $n \times n \times n$ cube without attacking each other in three dimensional space as n-queen patterns. We may formulate a theorem from this construction as follows. We skip the proof which is quite straightforward. The first conclusion is from [30]. The second conclusion is the relation with ZCZ sonar sequences.

Theorem 6. *Let $n > 7$ be a prime. Construct the $n \times n$ matrix $Q = (q_{i,j})$ with integers mod n for $i, j = 0, 1, \ldots, n-1$ as follows:*

- *Put $q_{0,j} = 1$ for $j = (n-1)/2$.*
- *Put $q_{0,j+2} = q_{0,j} + 1 \pmod{n}$ where the subscript $j+2$ is computed mod n, for $j = (n-1)/2, (n-1)/2 + 2, \ldots$.*
- *For each $j = 0, 1, \ldots, n-1$, put $q_{i+1,j} = q_{i,j} + 2 \pmod{n}$ where the subscript $i+1$ is computed mod n for $i = 0, 1, \ldots$.*

Then, the first conclusion from [30] is that Q is a packing of an $n \times n$ board by n disjoint nonattacking-n-queen patterns, which is three-dimensionally nonattacking queens also. Second (new) conclusion: for each symbol $k = 0, 1, \ldots, n-1$, the pattern of the constant symbol k in Q is an $(n, n, 3)$ ZCZ sonar sequence.

6. Concluding Remarks

Some immediate open problems on (m, n, r) ZCZ sonar sequences are the following:

1. Describe the values of m for which the upper bound on r is the same as its constructive lower bound. Some of the smaller such values of m from Table 1 are $m = 5$, $m = 9$, $m = 13$, $m = 14$, etc.
2. Describe the values of m for which the upper bound on r is one more than its constructive lower bound. Some examples of such values of m from Table 1 are $m = 6$, $m = 10$, $m = 15$, $m = 16$, etc.
3. Prove that the difference between the upper bound and the constructive lower bound is at most 1 for all positive integers $n \geq m$ or else find the values of m for which the difference is more than 1.
4. Find the formula for the max r for the optimal $m \times m$ ZCZ sonar sequence.
5. Prove that the max r as $n = m, m+1, m+2, \ldots$ is non-increasing. We know that it eventually reaches and stays at the constructive lower bound in Cor.2.
6. Find any new construction for ZCZ sonar sequences $(j, f(j))$ for $j = 1, 2, \ldots, n$ which is not of the type $f(j) = rj \pmod{m}$. Note that the construction in Theorem 6 is

of the form $f(j) = rj \pmod{n}$ where $r = -4$ for all n disjoint patterns with some appropriate initial condition. See Figure 13.

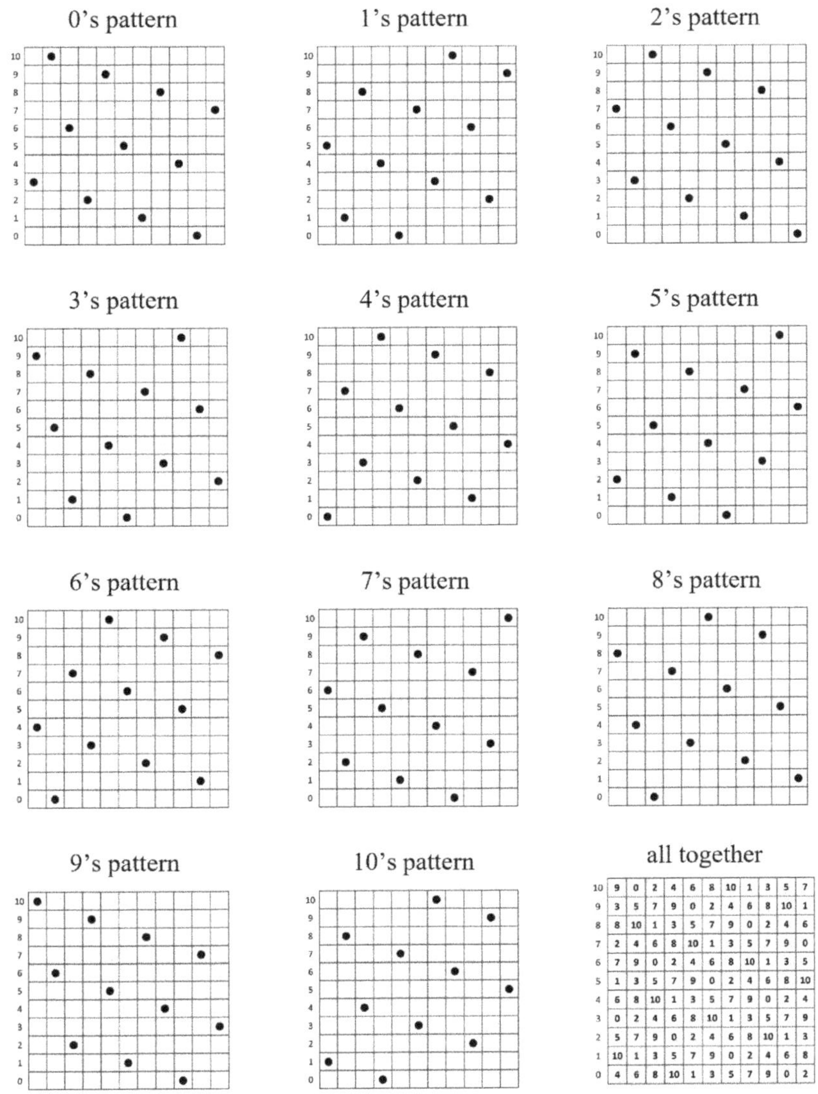

Figure 13. Disjoint nonattacking-n-queen patterns ($n = 11$) where each pattern of the constant symbol is an $(n, n, 3)$ ZCZ sonar sequence.

For (m, n, r) ZCZ-DD sonar sequences, we have a lot of open problems. Only some of them are listed here:

1. Find the max r for given m and n.
2. Prove that the max r as $n = m, m + 1, m + 2, \ldots$ is non-increasing.
3. Find the max n for given m and r.
4. Find the max $n \geq m$ such that $r = 2$ for a given m. Some small cases are $n = m = 5$, $n = m + 1 = 7$, $n = m + 2 = 9$, and $n = m + 2 = 10$, etc.
5. Find the relation of n and r for a given m.

6. Find a systematic construction for (m, n, r) ZCZ-DD sonar sequences for $r > 2$.
7. Improve the upper bound on r in Remark 3 for given m and n.

Author Contributions: Conceptualization, X.J., G.K. and H.-Y.S.; methodology, X.J., G.K. and H.-Y.S.; software, X.J. and S.C.; writing—original draft preparation, X.J.; writing—review and editing, X.J., G.K. and H.-Y.S.; supervision, H.-Y.S. All authors have read and agreed to the published version of the manuscript.

Funding: This work was supported by the National Research Foundation of Korea (NRF) Grant by the Korean Government through Ministry of Sciences and ICT (MSIT) under Grant RS-2023-00209000.

Institutional Review Board Statement: Not applicable.

Informed Consent Statement: Not applicable.

Data Availability Statement: Data is contained within the article.

Conflicts of Interest: The authors declare no conflicts of interest.

References

1. Golomb, S.W.; Taylor, H. Two-Dimensional Synchronization Patterns for Minimum Ambiguity. *IEEE Trans. Inf. Theory* **1982**, *28*, 600–604. [CrossRef]
2. Levanon, N.; Mozeson, E. *Radar Signals*; Wiley: Hoboken, NY, USA, 2004; pp. 74–86.
3. Costas, J.P. A study of a class of detection waveforms having nearly ideal range—Doppler ambiguity properties. *Proc. IEEE* **1984**, *72*, 996–1009. [CrossRef]
4. Drakakis, K. A review of Costas arrays. *J. Appl. Math.* **2006**, *2006*, 1–32. [CrossRef]
5. Golomb, S.W. Algebraic constructions for Costas arrays. *J. Comb. Theory, Ser.* **1984**, *37*, 13–21. [CrossRef]
6. Golomb, S.W. The T_4 and G_4 constructions for Costas arrays. *IEEE Trans. Inf. Theory* **1992**, *38*, 1404–1406. [CrossRef]
7. Golomb, S.W.; Gong, G. The status of Costas arrays. *IEEE Trans. Inf. Theory* **2007**, *53*, 4260–4265. [CrossRef]
8. Golomb, S.W.; Taylor, H. Constructions and properties of Costas arrays. *Proc. IEEE* **1984**, *72*, 1143–1163. [CrossRef]
9. Correll, B. A new structural property of Costas arrays. In Proceedings of the 2018 IEEE Radar Conference, Oklahoma City, OK, USA, 23–27 April 2018; pp. 748–753.
10. Correll, B. More new structural properties of Costas arrays. In Proceedings of the 2019 IEEE Radar Conference, Boston, MA, USA, 22–26 April 2019; pp. 1–6.
11. Correll, B.; Swanson, C.N. Difference-based structural properties of Costas arrays. *Des. Codes Cryptogr.* **2023**, *91*, 779–794. [CrossRef]
12. Jedwab, J.; Wodlinger, J. Structural properties of Costas arrays. *Adv. Math. Commun.* **2014**, *8*, 241–256. [CrossRef]
13. Blackburn, S.R.; Etzion, T.; Martin, K.M.; Paterson, M.B. Two-dimensional patterns with distinct differences-constructions, bounds, and maximal anticodes. *IEEE Trans. Inf. Theory* **2010**, *56*, 1216–1229. [CrossRef]
14. Drakakis, K.; Gow, R.; O'Carroll, L. On the symmetry of Welchand Golomb-constructed Costas arrays. *Discret. Math.* **2009**, *309*, 2559–2563. [CrossRef]
15. Golomb, S.W.; Moreno, O. On periodicity properties of Costas arrays and a conjecture on permutation polynomials. *IEEE Trans. Inf. Theory* **1996**, *42*, 2252–2253. [CrossRef]
16. Silverman, J.; Vickers, V.E. On the number of Costas arrays as a function of array size. *Proc. IEEE* **1988**, *76*, 851–853. [CrossRef]
17. Drakakis, K.; Iorio, F.; Rickard, S.; Walsh, J. Results of the enumeration of Costas arrays of order 29. *Adv. Math. Commun.* **2011**, *5*, 547–553. [CrossRef]
18. Fan, P.; Darnell, M. *Sequence Design for Communications Applications*; Wiley: Hoboken, NJ, USA, 1996.
19. Golomb, S.W.; Gong, G. *Signal Design for Good Correlation: For Wireless Communications, Cryptography, and Radar*; Cambridge University Press: Cambridge, UK, 2005.
20. Fan, P.Z.; Suehiro, N.; Kuroyanagi, N.; Deng, X.M. Class of binary sequences with zero correlation zone. *Electron. Lett.* **1999**, *35*, 777–779. [CrossRef]
21. Suehiro, N. A signal design without co-channel interference for approximately synchronized CDMA systems. *IEEE J. Sel. Areas Commun.* **1994**, *12*, 837–841. [CrossRef]
22. Tang, X.; Fan, P.Z.; Matsufuji, S. Lower Bounds on Correlation of Spreading Sequence set with Low or Zero Correlation Zone. *Electron. Lett.* **2000**, *36*, 551–552. [CrossRef]
23. Matsufuji, S.; Suehiro, N.; Kuroyanagi, N.; Fan, P.Z.; Takatsukasa, K. A binary sequence pair with zero correlation zone derived from complementary pairs. In Proceedings of the ISCTA'99, Ambleside, UK, 11–16 July 1999; pp. 223–224.
24. Tang, X.; Fan, P.Z. Bounds on aperiodic and odd correlations of spreading sequences with low or zero correlation zone. *Electron. Lett.* **2001**, *37*, 1201–1202. [CrossRef]
25. Gagliardi, R.; Robbins, J.; Taylor, H. Acquisition sequences in PPM communications. *IEEE Trans. Inf. Theory* **1987**, *33*, 738–744. [CrossRef]

26. Moreno, O.; Games, R.A.; Taylor, H. Sonar Sequences from Costas Arrays and the Best Known Sonar Sequences with up to 100 Symbols. *IEEE Trans. Inf. Theory* **1993**, *39*, 1985–1987. [CrossRef]
27. Games, R.A. An algebraic construction of sonar sequences using M-sequences. *Siam J. Algebr. Discret. Methods* **1987**, *8*, 753–761. [CrossRef]
28. Ruiz, D.; Trujillo, C.; Caicedo, Y. New Constructions of Sonar Sequences. *Int. J. Basic Appl. Sci.* **2014**, *14*, 12–16.
29. Kraus, E.F. *Taxicab Geometry: An Adventure in Non-Euclidean Geometry*; Dover Publications: New York, NY, USA, 1986; pp. 1–5.
30. Taylor, H. Packing Centrosymmetric Patterns of n Nonattacking Queens on an $n \times n$ Board. In Proceedings of the Sequences, Subsequences, and Consequences, Los Angeles, CA, USA, 31 May–2 June 2007.
31. Chae, S.-W.; Kim, H.-J.; Jin, X.; Song, H.-Y. Properties and optimization of sonar codes. In Proceedings of the 2023 KICS Winter Conference, Pyeongchang, Republic of Korea, 8–10 February 2023.

entropy

MDPI

Article

Evaluating the Gilbert–Varshamov Bound for Constrained Systems †

Keshav Goyal and Han Mao Kiah *

School of Physical and Mathematical Sciences, Nanyang Technological University, Singapore 637121, Singapore; keshav002@ntu.edu.sg

* Correspondence: hmkiah@ntu.edu.sg

† The paper was presented in part at the 2022 IEEE International Symposium on Information Theory (ISIT), Espoo, Finland, 26 Jun–1 July 2022.

Abstract: We revisit the well-known Gilbert–Varshamov (GV) bound for constrained systems. In 1991, Kolesnik and Krachkovsky showed that the GV bound can be determined via the solution of an optimization problem. Later, in 1992, Marcus and Roth modified the optimization problem and improved the GV bound in many instances. In this work, we provide explicit numerical procedures to solve these two optimization problems and, hence, compute the bounds. We then show that the procedures can be further simplified when we plot the respective curves. In the case where the graph presentation comprises a single state, we provide explicit formulas for both bounds.

Keywords: Gilbert–Varshamov bound; constrained codes; asymptotic rates; sliding window constrained codes

1. Introduction

From early applications in magnetic recording systems to recent applications in DNA-based data storage [1–4] and energy-harvesting [5–10], constrained codes have played a central role in enhancing reliability in many data storage and communications systems (see also [11] for an overview). Specifically, for most data storage systems, certain substrings are more prone to errors than others. Thus, by forbidding the appearance of such strings, that is, by imposing constraints on the codewords, the user is able to reduce the likelihood of error. We refer to the collection of words that satisfy the constraints as the *constrained space* $\mathcal{S}$.

To further reduce the error probability, one can impose certain distance constraints on the codebook. In this work, we focus on the *Hamming metric* and consider the maximum size of a codebook whose words belong to the constrained space $\mathcal{S}$ and whose pairwise distance is at least of a certain value d. Specifically, we study one of the most well-known and fundamental lower bounds of this quantity—the *Gilbert–Varshamov (GV) bound*.

To determine the GV bound, one requires two quantities: the size of the constrained space, $|\mathcal{S}|$, and, also, the *ball volume*, that is, the number of words with a distance of at most $d-1$ from a "center" word. In the case where the space is unconstrained, i.e., $\mathcal{S} = \{0,1\}^n$, the ball volume does not depend on the center. Then, the GV bound is simply $|\mathcal{S}|/V$, where V is the ball volume of a center. However, for most constrained systems, the ball volume varies with the center. Nevertheless, Kolesnik and Krachkovsky showed that the GV lower bound can be generalized to $|\mathcal{S}|/4\overline{V}$, where $\overline{V}$ is the *average ball volume* [12]. This was further improved by Gu and Fuja to $|\mathcal{S}|/\overline{V}$ in [13] (see pp. 242–243 in [11] for additional details). In the same paper [12], they showed the asymptotic rate of average ball volume can be computed via an optimization problem. Later, Marcus and Roth modified the optimization problem by including an additional constraint and variable [14], and the resulting bound, which we refer to as *GV-MR bound*, improves the usual GV bound. Furthermore, in most cases, the improvement is strictly positive.

However, about three decades later, very few works have evaluated these bounds for specific constrained systems. To the best of our knowledge, in all works that numerically computed the GV bound and/or GV-MR bound, the constrained systems of interest have, at most, eight states [15]. In [15], the authors wrote that "evaluation of the bound required considerable computation", referring to the GV-MR bound.

In this paper, we revisit the optimization problems defined by Kolesnik and Krachkovsky [12] and Marcus and Roth [14] and develop a suite of explicit numerical procedures that solve these problems. In particular, to demonstrate the feasibility of our methods, we evaluated and plotted the GV and GV-MR bounds for a constrained system involving 120 states in Figure 1b.

(a) Lower bounds for $R(\delta;\mathcal{S})$ where $\mathcal{S}$ is the class of $(3,2)$-SWCC

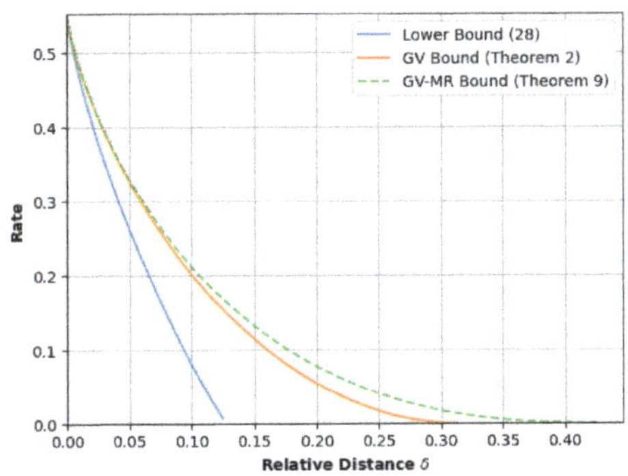

(b) Lower bounds for $R(\delta;\mathcal{S})$ where $\mathcal{S}$ is the class of $(10,7)$-SWCC

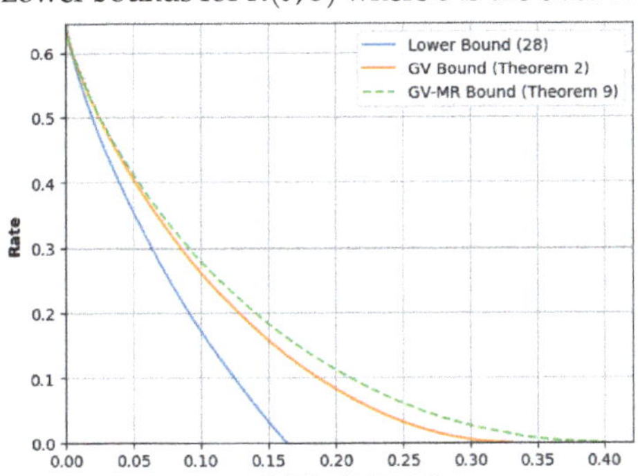

Figure 1. Lower bounds for optimal asymptotic code rates $R(\delta;\mathcal{S})$ for the class of sliding-window constrained codes

We provide a high-level description of our approach. For both optimization problems, we first characterized the optimal solutions as roots of certain equations. Then, using the celebrated *Newton–Raphson* iterative procedure, we proceeded to find the roots of these equations. However, as the latter equations involved the largest eigenvalues of certain matrices, each Newton–Raphson iteration required the (partial) derivatives of these eigenvalues (in some variables). To resolve this, we made modifications to another celebrated iterative procedure—the *power iteration* method—and the resulting procedures computed the GV and GV-MR bounds efficiently for a specific relative distance δ. Interestingly, if we plot the bounds for $0 \leq \delta \leq 1$, the numerical procedure can be further simplified. Specifically, by exploiting certain properties of the optimal solutions, we provided procedures that use less Newton–Raphson iterations.

Parts of this paper were presented in the IEEE International Symposium on Information Theory (ISIT 2022) [16]. In the next section, we provide the formal definitions and state the optimization problems that compute the GV bound.

2. Preliminaries

Let $\Sigma = \{0,1\}$ be the binary alphabet and let Σ^n denote the set of all words of length n over Σ. A *labeled graph* $\mathcal{G} = (\mathcal{V}, \mathcal{E}, \mathcal{L})$ is a finite directed graph with *states* $\mathcal{V}$, *edges* $\mathcal{E} \subseteq \mathcal{V} \times \mathcal{V}$, and an *edge labeling* $\mathcal{L} : \mathcal{E} \to \Sigma^s$ for some $s \geq 1$. Here, we use $v_i \xrightarrow{\sigma} v_j$ to mean that there is an edge from v_i to v_j with label σ. The labeled graph $\mathcal{G}$ is *deterministic* if, for each state, the outgoing edges have distinct labels.

A *constrained system* $\mathcal{S}$ is, then, the set of all words obtained by reading the labels of paths in a labeled graph $\mathcal{G}$. We say that $\mathcal{G}$ is a *graph presentation* of $\mathcal{S}$. We further denote the set of all n-length words $\mathcal{S}$ by $\mathcal{S}_n$. Alternatively, $\mathcal{S}_n$ is the set of all words obtained by reading the labels of (n/s)-length paths in $\mathcal{G}$. Then, the *capacity of* $\mathcal{S}$, denoted by $\mathrm{Cap}(\mathcal{S})$, is given by $\mathrm{Cap}(\mathcal{S}) \triangleq \limsup_{n\to\infty} \log|\mathcal{S}_n|/n$. It is well-known that $\mathrm{Cap}(\mathcal{S})$ corresponds to the largest eigenvalue of the *adjacency matrix* $\boldsymbol{A}_{\mathcal{G}}$ (see, for example, [11]). Here, $\boldsymbol{A}_{\mathcal{G}}$ is a $(|\mathcal{V}| \times |\mathcal{V}|)$-matrix whose rows and columns are indexed by $\mathcal{V}$. For each entry $(u,v) \in \mathcal{V} \times \mathcal{V}$, we set the corresponding entry to be one if (u,v) is an edge, and zero otherwise.

Every constrained system can be presented by a deterministic graph $\mathcal{G}$. Furthermore, any deterministic graph can be transformed into a primitive deterministic graph $\mathcal{H}$ such that the capacity of $\mathcal{G}$ is same as the capacity of the constrained system presented by some irreducible component (maximal irreducible subgraph) of $\mathcal{H}$ (see, for example, Marcus et al. [11]). It should be noted that a graph $\mathcal{G}$ is primitive if there exists a positive integer ℓ such that $(\boldsymbol{A}_{\mathcal{G}})^\ell$ is strictly positive. Therefore, we henceforth assume that our graphs are deterministic and primitive. When $|\mathcal{V}| = 1$, we call this a *single-state graph presentation* and study these graphs in Section 5.

For $\boldsymbol{x}, \boldsymbol{y} \in \mathcal{S}$, $d_H(\boldsymbol{x}, \boldsymbol{y})$ is the Hamming distance between $\boldsymbol{x}$ and $\boldsymbol{y}$. We fix $1 \leq d \leq n$, and a fundamental problem in coding theory is finding the largest subset $\mathcal{C}$ of $\mathcal{S}_n$ such that $d_H(\boldsymbol{x}, \boldsymbol{y}) \geq d$ for all distinct $\boldsymbol{x}, \boldsymbol{y} \in \mathcal{C}$. Let $A(n, d; \mathcal{S})$ denote the size of largest subset $\mathcal{C}$.

In terms of asymptotic rates, we fix $0 \leq \delta \leq 1$, and our task is to find the highest attainable rate, denoted by $R(\delta)$, which is given by $R(\delta; \mathcal{S}) \triangleq \limsup_{n\to\infty} \log A(n, \lfloor \delta n \rfloor; \mathcal{S})/n$.

2.1. Review of Gilbert–Varshamov Bound

To define the GV bound, we need to determine the total ball size. Specifically, for $\boldsymbol{x} \in \mathcal{S}_n$ and $0 \leq r \leq n$, we define $V(\boldsymbol{x}, r; \mathcal{S}) \triangleq |\{\boldsymbol{y} \in \mathcal{S}_n : d_H(\boldsymbol{x}, \boldsymbol{y}) \leq r\}|$. We further define $T(n, d; \mathcal{S}) = \sum_{\boldsymbol{x}\in\mathcal{S}_n} V(\boldsymbol{x}, d-1; \mathcal{S})$. Then, the GV bound, as given by Gu and Fuja [13,17], states that there exists an $(n, d; \mathcal{S})$ code of size at least $|\mathcal{S}_n|^2/T(n, d; \mathcal{S})$.

In terms of asymptotic rates, there exists a family of $(n, \lfloor \delta n \rfloor; \mathcal{S})$ codes such that their rates approach

$$R_{\mathrm{GV}}(\delta) = 2\mathrm{Cap}(\mathcal{S}) - \widetilde{T}(\delta), \quad (1)$$

where $\widetilde{T}(\delta) \triangleq \limsup_{n\to\infty} \log T(n, \lfloor \delta n \rfloor; \mathcal{S})/n$.

In this paper, our main task is to determine $R_{\mathrm{GV}}(\delta)$ *efficiently*. We observe that since $\mathrm{Cap}(\mathcal{S}) = \widetilde{T}(0)$, it suffices to find efficient ways of determining $\widetilde{T}(\delta)$. It turns out that $\widetilde{T}(\delta)$ can be found via the solution of a convex optimization problem. Specifically, given a labeled graph $\mathcal{G} = (\mathcal{V}, \mathcal{E}, \mathcal{L})$, we define its *product graph* $\mathcal{G}' = (\mathcal{V}', \mathcal{E}', \mathcal{L}')$ as follows:

- $\mathcal{V}' \triangleq \mathcal{V} \times \mathcal{V}$.
- For $(v_i, v_j), (v_k, v_\ell) \in \mathcal{V}'$, and $(\sigma_1, \sigma_2) \in \Sigma^s \times \Sigma^s$, we draw an edge $(v_i, v_j) \xrightarrow{(\sigma_1,\sigma_2)} (v_k, v_\ell)$ if and only if both $v_i \xrightarrow{\sigma_1} v_k$ and $v_j \xrightarrow{\sigma_2} v_\ell$ belong to $\mathcal{E}$.
- Then, we label the edges in $\mathcal{E}'$ with the function $\mathcal{L}' : \mathcal{E}' \to \mathbb{Z}_{\geq 0}$, where $\mathcal{L}'\Big((v_i, v_j) \xrightarrow{(\sigma_1,\sigma_2)} (v_k, v_\ell)\Big) = d_H(\sigma_1, \sigma_2)/s$.

A stationary Markov chain P on a graph $\mathcal{G} = (\mathcal{V}, \mathcal{E}, \mathcal{L})$ is a probability distribution function $P : \mathcal{E} \to [0,1]$ such that $\sum_{e \in E} P(e) = 1$ and, for any state $u \in \mathcal{G}$, the sum of the probabilities of the outgoing edges equals the sum of the probabilities of the incoming edges. We denote by $\mathcal{M}(\mathcal{G})$ the set of all stationary Markov chains on $\mathcal{G}$. For a state $u \in \mathcal{V}$, let $\mathcal{E}_u$ denote the set of outgoing edges from u in $\mathcal{G}$. The state vector $\pi^T = (\pi_u)_{u \in V}$ of a stationary Markov chain P on $\mathcal{G}$ is defined by $\pi_u = \sum_{e \in E_u} P(e)$. The entropy rate of a stationary Markov chain is defined by

$$H(P) = -\sum_{u \in \mathcal{V}} \sum_{e \in \mathcal{E}_u} \pi_u P(e) \log(P(e))$$

Furthermore, $\widetilde{T}(\delta)$ can be obtained by solving the following optimization problem [12,14]:

$$\widetilde{T}(\delta) = \sup\left\{ H(P) : P \in \mathcal{M}(\mathcal{G} \times \mathcal{G}),\ \sum_{e \in \mathcal{E}'} P(e)D(e) \leq \delta \right\}. \tag{2}$$

To this end, we consider the dual problem of (2). Specifically, we define a $(|\mathcal{V}|^2 \times |\mathcal{V}|^2)$-*distance matrix* $\boldsymbol{T}_{\mathcal{G}\times\mathcal{G}}(y)$ whose rows and columns are indexed by $\mathcal{V}'$. For each entry indexed by $e \in \mathcal{V}' \times \mathcal{V}'$, we set the entry to be zero if $e \notin \mathcal{E}'$ and we set it to be $y^{D(e)}$ if $e \in \mathcal{E}'$. Then, the dual problem can be stated in terms of the dominant eigenvalue of the matrix $\boldsymbol{T}_{\mathcal{G}\times\mathcal{G}}(y)$.

By applying the reduction techniques from [14], we can reduce the problem size by a factor of two. Formally, in the case of $s = 1$, we define a $\binom{|\mathcal{V}|+1}{2} \times \binom{|\mathcal{V}|+1}{2}$-*reduced distance matrix* $\boldsymbol{B}_{\mathcal{G}\times\mathcal{G}}(y)$ whose rows and columns are indexed by $\mathcal{V}^{(2)} \triangleq \{(v_i, v_j) : 1 \leq i \leq j \leq |\mathcal{V}|\}$ using the following procedure.

Two states $s_1 = (v_i, v_j)$ and $s_2 = (v_k, v_\ell)$ in $\mathcal{G} \times \mathcal{G}$ are said to be *equivalent* if $v_i = v_\ell$ and $v_j = v_k$. The matrix $\boldsymbol{B}_{\mathcal{G}\times\mathcal{G}}(y)$ is then obtained by merging all pairs of equivalent states s_1 and s_2. That is, we add the column indexed by v_2 to the column indexed by v_1 and then remove the row and column which are indexed by v_2. It should be noted that it may be possible to reduce the size of this matrix $\boldsymbol{B}_{\mathcal{G}\times\mathcal{G}}(y)$ further. However, for the ease of exposition, we did not consider this case in this work.

Following this procedure, we observe that the entries in the matrix $\boldsymbol{B}_{\mathcal{G}\times\mathcal{G}}(y)$ can be described by the rules in Table 1. Moreover, the dominant eigenvalue of $\boldsymbol{B}_{\mathcal{G}\times\mathcal{G}}(y)$ is the same as that of $\boldsymbol{T}_{\mathcal{G}\times\mathcal{G}}(y)$. Then, by strong duality, computing (2) is equivalent to solving the following dual problem [18,19] (see also, [20]):

$$\widetilde{T}(\delta) = \inf\{-\delta \log y + \log \Lambda(\boldsymbol{B}_{\mathcal{G}\times\mathcal{G}}(y)) : 0 \leq y \leq 1\}. \tag{3}$$

Here, we use $\Lambda(\boldsymbol{M})$ to denote the dominant eigenvalue of matrix $\boldsymbol{M}$. To simplify further, we write $\Lambda(y; \boldsymbol{B}) \triangleq \Lambda(\boldsymbol{B}_{\mathcal{G}\times\mathcal{G}}(y))$.

Since the objective function in (3) is convex, it follows from standard calculus that any local minimum solution y^* in the interval $[0,1]$ is also a global minimum solution. Furthermore, y^* is a zero of the first derivative of the objective function. If we consider the numerator of this derivative, then y^* is a root of the function

$$F(y) \triangleq y\Lambda'(y; \boldsymbol{B}) - \delta\Lambda(y; \boldsymbol{B}). \tag{4}$$

In Corollary 1, we showed that there is only one y^* such that $F(y^*) = 0$ and $F'(y)$ is strictly positive for all values of y. Therefore, to evaluate the GV bound for a fixed δ, it suffices to determine y^*.

Later, Marcus and Roth [14] improved the GV bound (1) by considering certain subsets of the constrained space $\mathcal{S}$. This entails the inclusion of an additional constraint defined in the optimization problem (2), and, correspondingly, an additional variable in the dual problem (3). Specifically, they considered certain subsets $\mathcal{S}(p) \subseteq \mathcal{S}$ where each symbol in the words of $\mathcal{S}(p)$ appears with a certain frequency dependent on the parameter p. We describe this in more detail in Section 4.

Table 1. We set the $\big((v_i, v_j), (v_k, v_\ell)\big)$ entry of the matrix $\boldsymbol{B}_{\mathcal{G}\times\mathcal{G}}(y)$ according to subgraph induced by the states v_i,v_j,v_k Gilbert–Varshamov v_ℓ. Here, $\bar{\sigma}$ denotes the complement of σ.

$\boldsymbol{B}_{\mathcal{G}\times\mathcal{G}}(y)$ at Entry $((v_i,v_j),(v_k,v_\ell))$	Subgraph Induced by the States $\{v_i, v_j, v_k, v_\ell\}$
0	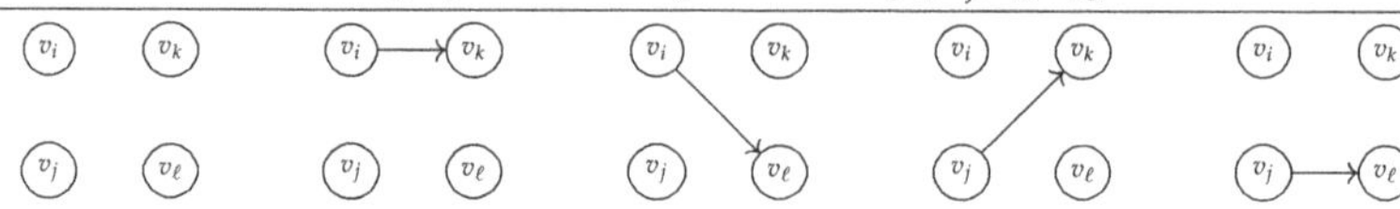
1	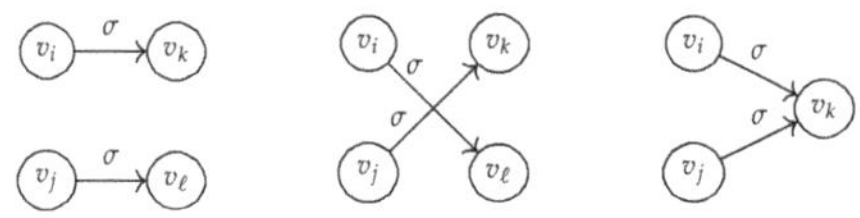
y	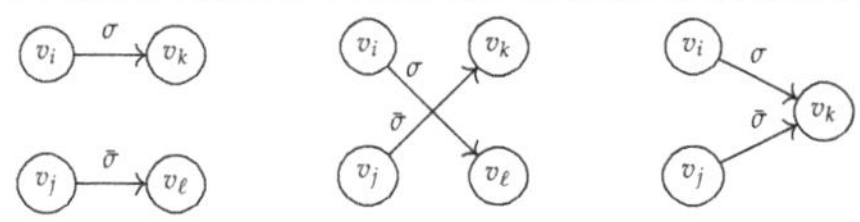
$2y$	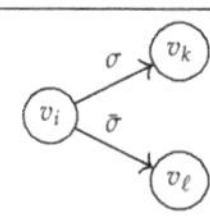

2.2. Our Contributions

(A) In Section 3, we develop the numerical procedures to compute $\widetilde{T}(\delta)$ for a fixed δ and, hence, determine the GV bound (1). Our procedure modifies the well-known *power iteration method* to compute the derivatives of $\Lambda(y; \boldsymbol{B})$. After that, using these derivatives, we apply the classical Newton–Raphson method to determine the root of (4). In the same section, we also study procedures to plot the GV curve, that is, the set $\{(\delta, R_{\mathrm{GV}}(\delta)) : 0 \le \delta \le 1\}$. Here, we demonstrate that the GV curve can be plotted without any Newton–Raphson iterations.

(B) In Section 4, we then develop similar power iteration methods and numerical procedures to compute the GV-MR bound. Similar to the GV curve, we also provide a plotting procedure that uses significantly less Newton–Raphson iterations.

(C) In Section 5, we provide explicit formulas for the computation of the GV bound and GV-MR bound for graph presentations that have exactly one state but multiple parallel edges.

(D) In Section 6, we validate our methods by computing the GV and the GV-MR bounds for some specific constrained systems. For comparison purposes, we also plot a simple lower bound that is obtained by using an upper estimate of the ball size. From the plots in Figures 1–3, it is also clear that the GV and GV-MR bounds are significantly better. We also observe that the GV bound and GV-MR bound for *subblock energy-constrained codes (SECCs)* obtained through our procedures improve the GV-type bound given by Tandon et al. (Proposition 12 in [21]).

(a) Lower bounds for $R(\delta; \mathcal{S})$ where $\mathcal{S}$ is the class of $(1,3)$-RLL

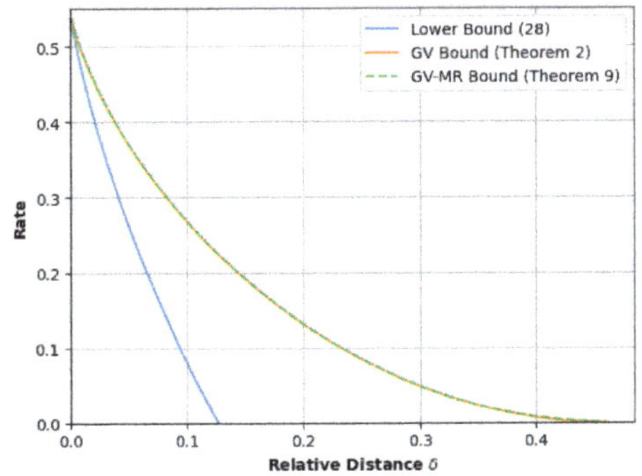

(b) Lower bounds for $R(\delta; \mathcal{S})$ where $\mathcal{S}$ is the class of $(3,7)$-RLL

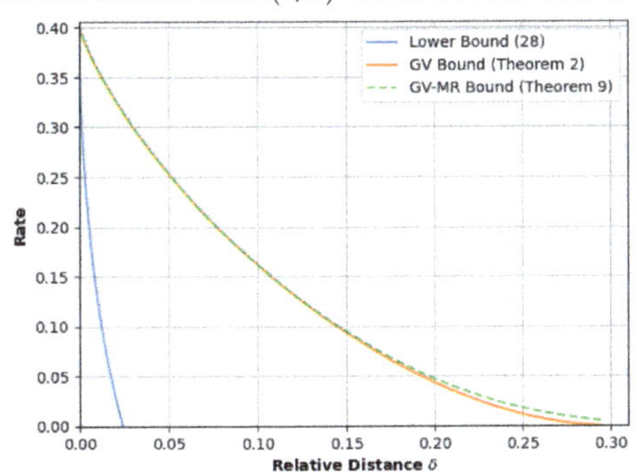

Figure 2. Lower bounds for optimal asymptotic code rates $R(\delta; \mathcal{S})$ for the class of runlength limited codes.

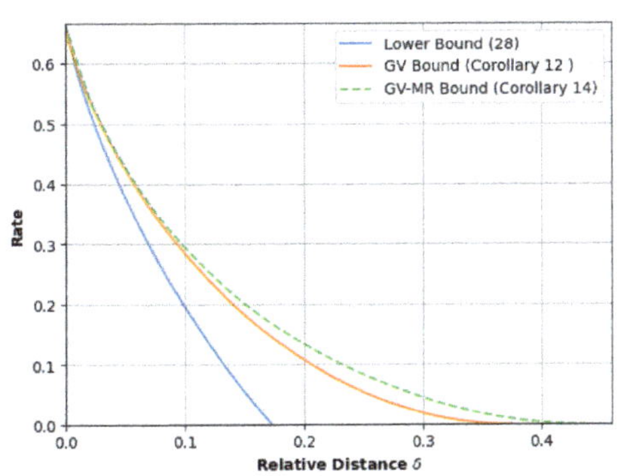

Figure 3. Lower bounds for optimal asymptotic code rates $R(\delta; \mathcal{S})$ where $\mathcal{S}$ is the class of $(3,2)$-SECCs (subblock energy-constrained codes).

3. Evaluating the Gilbert–Varshamov Bound

In this section, we first describe a numerical procedure that solves (3) and, hence, determine $R_{\rm GV}(\delta)$ for fixed values of δ. Then, we show that the procedure can be simplified when we compute the GV curve, that is, the set of points $\{(\delta, R_{\rm GV}(\delta)) : \delta \in [0,1]\}$. Here, we eschew notation and use $[a,b]$ to denote the interval $\{x : a \le x \le b\}$, if $a < b$, and the interval $\{x : b \le x \le a\}$ otherwise.

Below, we provide formal description of our procedure to obtain the GV bound for a fixed relative distance δ.

Procedure 1 (GV bound for fixed relative distance) .

INPUT: Adjacency matrix $A_{\mathcal{G}}$, reduced distance matrix $B_{\mathcal{G}\times\mathcal{G}}(y)$, and relative minimum distance δ

OUTPUT: GV bound, that is, $R_{\rm GV}(\delta)$ as defined in (1)

(1) Apply the Newton–Raphson method to obtain y^* such that $F(y^*)$ is approximately zero.
- Fix the tolerance value ϵ.
- Set $t = 0$ and pick an initial guess $0 \le y_t \le 1$.
- While $|y_t - y_{t-1}| > \epsilon$,
  - Compute the next guess y_{t+1} as follows:

$$y_{t+1} = y_t - \frac{F(y_t)}{F'(y_t)} = y_t - \frac{y_t\Lambda'(y_t;\boldsymbol{B}) - \delta\Lambda(y_t;\boldsymbol{B}))}{(1-\delta)\Lambda'(y_t;\boldsymbol{B}) + y_t\Lambda''(y_t;\boldsymbol{B})}.$$

  - In this step, apply the power iteration method to compute $\Lambda(y_t;\boldsymbol{B})$, $\Lambda'(y_t;\boldsymbol{B})$, and $\Lambda''(y_t;\boldsymbol{B})$.
  - Increment t by one.
- Set $y^* \leftarrow y_t$.

(2) Determine $R_{\rm GV}(\delta)$ using y^*. Specifically, compute $\widetilde{T}(\delta) \triangleq -\delta\log y^* + \log\Lambda(y^*;\boldsymbol{B})$, $\mathrm{Cap}(\mathcal{S}) \triangleq \log\Lambda(A_{\mathcal{G}})$, and $R_{\rm GV}(\delta) \triangleq 2\mathrm{Cap}(\mathcal{S}) - \widetilde{T}(\delta)$.

Throughout Sections 3 and 4, we illustrate our numerical procedures via a running example using the class of *sliding window-constrained codes (SWCCs)*. Formally, we fix a *window length L* and *window weight w*, and say that a binary word satisfies the (L,w)-*sliding window weight constraint* if the number of ones in every consecutive L bits is at least w. We refer to the collection of words that meet this constraint as an (L,w)-*SWCC constrained system*. The class of SWCCs was introduced by Tandon et al. for the application of simultaneous energy and information transfer [7,10]. Later, Immink and Cai [8,9] studied encoders for this constrained system and provided a simple graph presentation that uses only $\binom{L}{w}$ states.

In the next example, we illustrate how the numerical procedure can be used to compute the GV bound for the value when $\delta = 0.1$.

Example 1. *Let $L = 3$ and $w = 2$, and we consider a $(3,2)$-SWCC constrained system. From [8], we have the following graph presentation with states* x11, 101, *and* 110*:*

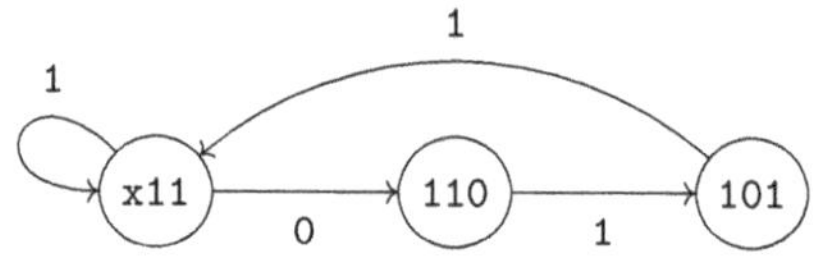

Then, the corresponding adjacency and reduced distance matrices are as follows:

$$A_{\mathcal{G}} = \begin{bmatrix} 1 & 1 & 0 \\ 0 & 0 & 1 \\ 1 & 0 & 0 \end{bmatrix},\ B_{\mathcal{G}\times\mathcal{G}}(y) = \begin{bmatrix} 1 & 2y & 0 & 1 & 0 & 0 \\ 0 & 0 & 1 & 0 & y & 0 \\ 1 & y & 0 & 0 & 0 & 0 \\ 0 & 0 & 0 & 0 & 0 & 1 \\ 0 & 0 & 1 & 0 & 0 & 0 \\ 1 & 0 & 0 & 0 & 0 & 0 \end{bmatrix}.$$

To determine the GV bound at $\delta = 0.1$, we first approximate the optimal point y^* for which $-\delta\log y + \log\Lambda(y;\boldsymbol{B})$ is minimized.

We apply the Newton–Raphson method to find a zero of the function $F(y)$. Now, with the initial guess $y_0 = 0.3$, we apply the power iteration method to determine

$$\Lambda(0.3;\boldsymbol{B}) = 1.659,\ \Lambda'(0.3;\boldsymbol{B}) = 0.694,\ \Lambda''(0.3;\boldsymbol{B}) = 0.183.$$

Then, we compute that $y_1 \approx 0.238$. Repeating the computations, we have that $y_2 \approx 0238$. Since $|y_2 - y_1|$ is less than the tolerance value 10^{-5}, we set $y^* = 0.238$. Hence, we have that $\widetilde{T}(0.1) = 0.9$. Applying the power iteration method to either $\boldsymbol{A}_{\mathcal{G}}$ or $\boldsymbol{B}_{\mathcal{G}\times\mathcal{G}}(0)$, we compute the capacity of the $(3,2)$-SWCC constrained system to be $\mathrm{Cap}(\mathcal{S}) = 0.551$. Then, the GV bound is given by $R_{\mathrm{GV}}(0.1) = 2(0.551) - 0.9 = 0.202$.

We discuss the convergence issues arising from Procedure 1. We observe that there are two different iterative processes in Step 1, namely, (a) the power iteration method to compute the values $\Lambda(y_t;\boldsymbol{B})$, $\Lambda'(y_t;\boldsymbol{B})$, and $\Lambda''(y_t;\boldsymbol{B})$, and (b) the Newton–Raphson method that determines the zero of $F(y)$.

(a) We recall that $\Lambda(y;\boldsymbol{B})$ is the largest eigenvalue of the reduced distance matrix $\boldsymbol{B}_{\mathcal{G}\times\mathcal{G}}(y)$. If we apply naive methods to compute this dominant eigenvalue, the computational complexity increases very rapidly with the matrix size. Specifically, if $\mathcal{G}$ has M states, then the reduced distance matrix has dimensions $\Theta(M^2) \times \Theta(M^2)$ and finding its characteristic equation takes $O(M^6)$ time. Even then, determining the exact roots of characteristic equations with at least five degrees is generally impossible. Therefore, we turn to the numerical procedures like the ubiquitous power iteration method [22]. However, the standard power iteration method is only able to compute the dominant eigenvalue $\Lambda(y;\boldsymbol{B})$. Nevertheless, we can modify the power iteration method to compute $\Lambda(y;\boldsymbol{B})$ and its higher order derivatives. In Appendix A, we demonstrate that under certain mild assumptions, the modified power iteration method always converges. Moreover, using the sparsity of the reduced distance matrix, we have that each iteration can be completed in $O(M^2)$ time.

(b) Next, we discuss whether we can guarantee that y_t converges to y^* as t approaches infinity. Even though the Newton–Raphson method converges in all our numerical experiments, we are unable to demonstrate that it always converges for $F(y)$. Nevertheless, we can circumvent this issue if we are interested in *plotting the GV curve*. Specifically, if our objective is to determine the curve $\{(\delta, R_{\mathrm{GV}}(\delta)) : \delta \in [0,1]\}$, it turns out that we do not need to implement the Newton–Raphson iterations and we discuss this next.

We fix some constrained system $\mathcal{S}$. Let us define its corresponding *GV curve* to be the set of points $\mathcal{GV}(\mathcal{S}) \triangleq \{(\delta, R_{\mathrm{GV}}(\delta)) : \delta \in [0,1]\}$. Here, we demonstrate that the GV curve can be plotted without any Newton–Raphson iterations.

To this end, we observe that when $F(y^*) = 0$, we have that $\delta = y^*\Lambda'(y^*;\boldsymbol{B})/\Lambda(y^*;\boldsymbol{B})$. Hence, we eschew notation and define the function

$$\delta(y) \triangleq y\Lambda'(y;\boldsymbol{B})/\Lambda(y;\boldsymbol{B})\,. \tag{5}$$

We further define $\delta_{\max} = \delta(1) = \Lambda'(1;\boldsymbol{B})/\Lambda(1;\boldsymbol{B})$. In this section, we prove the following theorem.

Theorem 1. *Let $\mathcal{G}$ be the graph presentation for the constrained system $\mathcal{S}$. If we define the function*

$$\rho_{\mathrm{GV}}(y) \triangleq 2\mathrm{Cap}(\mathcal{S}) + \delta(y)\log y - \log\Lambda(y;\boldsymbol{B})\,, \tag{6}$$

then the corresponding GV curve is given by

$$\mathcal{GV}(\mathcal{S}) = \big\{(\delta(y), \rho_{\mathrm{GV}}(y)) : y \in [0,1]\big\} \cup \big\{(\delta, 0) : \delta \geq \delta_{\max}\big\}\,. \tag{7}$$

Before we prove Theorem 1, we discuss its implications. It should be noted that to compute $\delta(y)$ and $\rho(y)$, it suffices to determine $\Lambda(y;\boldsymbol{B})$ and $\Lambda'(y;\boldsymbol{B})$ using the modified power iteration methods described in Appendix A. In other words, no Newton–Raphson iterations are required. We also have additional computational savings, as we do not need to apply the power iteration method to compute the second derivative $\Lambda''(y;\boldsymbol{B})$.

Example 2. *We continue our example and plot the GV curve for the* $(3,2)$*-SWCC constrained system in Figure 1a. Before plotting, we observe that when* $y=0$*, we have* $(\delta(0),\rho(0)) = (0, 0.551) = (0, \mathrm{Cap}(\mathcal{S}))$*, as expected. When* $y=1$*, we have* $\delta(1)=\delta_{\max}=0.313$*. Indeed, both* $\rho(1)$ *and* $R_{\mathrm{GV}}(\delta_{\max})$ *are equal to zero and we have that* $R_{\mathrm{GV}}(\delta)=0$ *for* $\delta \geq \delta_{\max}$*.*

Next, we compute a set of 100 points on the GV curve. If we apply Procedure 1 to compute $R_{\mathrm{GV}}(\delta)$ *for 100 values of* δ *in the interval* $[0,\delta_{\max}]$*, we require 275 Newton–Raphson iterations and 6900 power iterations to find these points. In contrast, applying Theorem 1, we compute* $(\delta(y),\rho(y))$ *for 100 values of* y *in the interval* $[0,1]$*. This does not require any Newton–Raphson iterations and involves only 2530 power iterations.*

To prove Theorem 1, we demonstrate the following lemmas. Our first lemma is immediate from the definitions of R_{GV}, δ, and ρ in (1), (5), and (6), respectively.

Lemma 1. $R_{\mathrm{GV}}(\delta(y)) = \rho(y)$ *for all* $y \in [0,1]$*.*

The next lemma studies the behaviour of both δ and ρ as functions in y.

Lemma 2. *In terms of* y*, the functions* $\delta(y)$ *and* $\rho(y)$ *are monotone increasing and decreasing, respectively. Furthermore, we have that* $(\delta(0),\rho(0)) = (0,\mathrm{Cap}(\mathcal{S}))$*,* $(\delta(1),\rho(1)) = (\delta_{\max}, 0)$ *and* $R_{\mathrm{GV}}(\delta)=0$ *for* $\delta \geq \delta_{\max}$*.*

Proof. To simplify notation, we write $\Lambda(y;\boldsymbol{B})$, $\Lambda'(y;\boldsymbol{B})$, and $\Lambda''(y;\boldsymbol{B})$ as Λ, Λ', and Λ'', respectively.

First, we show that $\delta'(y)$ is positive for $0 \leq y < 1$. Differentiating the expression in (5), we have that $\delta'(y) > 0$ is equivalent to

$$\Lambda(\Lambda' + y\Lambda'') - y(\Lambda')^2 > 0. \tag{8}$$

We recall that (3) is a convex minimization problem. Hence, the second order derivative of the objective function is always positive. In other words,

$$\frac{\delta}{y^2} + \frac{\Lambda''\Lambda - (\Lambda')^2}{\Lambda^2} > 0.$$

Substituting δ with $y\Lambda'/\Lambda$ and multiplying by $y\Lambda^2$, we obtain (8), as desired.

Next, we show that ρ is monotone decreasing. We recall that $\rho(y) = R_{\mathrm{GV}}(\delta(y)) = \mathrm{Cap}(\mathcal{S}) - \widetilde{T}(\delta)$. Since $\widetilde{T}(\delta)$ yields the asymptotic rate of the total ball size, we have that as y increases, $\delta(y)$ increases and so, $\widetilde{T}(\delta)$ increases. Therefore, $\rho(y)$ decreases, as desired.

Next, we show that $\rho(1)=0$. When $y=1$, we have from (6) that $\rho(1) = 2\mathrm{Cap}(\mathcal{S}) - \log\Lambda(1;\boldsymbol{B})$. Now, we recall that $\boldsymbol{B}_{\mathcal{G}\times\mathcal{G}}(y)$ shares the same dominant eigenvalue as the matrix $\boldsymbol{T}_{\mathcal{G}\times\mathcal{G}}(y)$ [12]. Furthermore, it can be verified that when $y=1$, $\boldsymbol{T}_{\mathcal{G}\times\mathcal{G}}(1)$ is tensor product of $\boldsymbol{A}_{\mathcal{G}}$ and $\boldsymbol{A}_{\mathcal{G}}$. That is, $\boldsymbol{T}_{\mathcal{G}\times\mathcal{G}}(1) = \boldsymbol{A}_{\mathcal{G}} \otimes \boldsymbol{A}_{\mathcal{G}}$. It then follows from standard linear algebra that $\Lambda(1;\boldsymbol{B}) = \Lambda(1;\boldsymbol{T}) = \Lambda(\boldsymbol{A}_{\mathcal{G}})^2$. Thus, $\log\Lambda(1;\boldsymbol{B}) = 2\mathrm{Cap}(\mathcal{S})$ and $\rho(1)=0$. In this instance, we also have that $\widetilde{T}(\delta_{\max}) = 2\mathrm{Cap}(\mathcal{S})$.

Finally, for $\delta \geq \delta_{\max}$, we have that $\widetilde{T}(\delta_{\max}) = 2\mathrm{Cap}(\mathcal{S})$ and thus, $R_{\mathrm{GV}}(\delta) = 0$, as required. □

Theorem 1 is then immediate from Lemmas 1 and 2.

We have the following corollary that immediately follows from Lemma 2. This corollary then implies that y^* yields the global minimum for the optimization problem.

Corollary 1. *When* $0 \le \delta \le \delta_{max} = \frac{\Lambda'(1,\boldsymbol{B})}{\Lambda(1,\boldsymbol{B})}$, $F(y) \triangleq y\Lambda'(y;\boldsymbol{B}) - \delta\Lambda(y;\boldsymbol{B})$ *has a unique zero in* $[0,1]$. *Furthermore,* $F'(y)$ *is strictly positive for all* $y \in [0,1]$.

4. Evaluating Marcus and Roth's Improvement of the Gilbert–Varshamov Bound

In [14], Marcus and Roth improved the GV lower bound for most constrained systems by considering subsets $\mathcal{S}(p)$ of $\mathcal{S}$ where p is some parameter. Here, we focus on the case $s = 1$ and set p to be the normalized frequency of edges whose labels correspond to one. Specifically, we set $\mathcal{S}(p) \triangleq \{\boldsymbol{x} \in \mathcal{S} : \mathrm{wt}(\boldsymbol{x}) = \lfloor p|\boldsymbol{x}| \rfloor\}$.

Next, let $\mathcal{S}_n(p)$ be the set of all words/paths of length n in $\mathcal{S}(p)$ and we define $S(p) \triangleq \limsup_{n\to\infty} \frac{1}{n}\log|\mathcal{S}_n(p)|$.

Similar to before, we define $\widetilde{T}(p,\delta) = \limsup_{n\to\infty} \frac{1}{n}\log T(\lfloor \delta n \rfloor, n; \mathcal{S}_n(p))$. Since $\mathcal{S}_n(p)$ is a subset of $\mathcal{S}_n$, it follows from the usual GV argument that there exists a family of $(n, \lfloor \delta n \rfloor; \mathcal{S})$ codes whose rates approach $2S(p) - \widetilde{T}(p,\delta)$ for all $0 \le p \le 1$. Therefore, we have the following lower bound on asymptotic achievable code rates:

$$R_{\mathrm{MR}}(\delta) = \sup\{2S(p) - \widetilde{T}(p,\delta) : 0 \le p \le 1\}. \tag{9}$$

Now, a key result from [14] is that both $S(p)$ and $\widetilde{T}(p,\delta)$ can be obtained via two different convex optimization problems. For succinctness, we state the *dual* formulations of these optimization problems.

First, $S(p)$ can be obtained from the following problem:

$$S(p) = \inf\{-p\log z + \log\Lambda(\boldsymbol{C}_{\mathcal{G}}(z)) : z \ge 0\}. \tag{10}$$

Here, $\boldsymbol{C}_{\mathcal{G}}(z)$ is the following $(|\mathcal{V}| \times |\mathcal{V}|)$ matrix $\boldsymbol{C}_{\mathcal{G}}(z)$ whose rows and columns are indexed by $\mathcal{V}$. For each entry indexed by e, we set $(\boldsymbol{C}_{\mathcal{G}}(z))_e$ to be zero if $e \notin \mathcal{E}$, and $z^{\mathcal{L}(e)}$ if $e \in \mathcal{E}$.

As before, we simplify notation by writing $\Lambda(z;\boldsymbol{C}) \triangleq \Lambda(\boldsymbol{C}_{\mathcal{G}}(z))$. Again, following the convexity of (10), we are interested in finding the zero of the following function:

$$G_1(z) \triangleq z\Lambda'(z;\boldsymbol{C}) - p\Lambda(z;\boldsymbol{C}). \tag{11}$$

Next, $\widetilde{T}(p,\delta)$ can be obtained via the following optimization:

$$\widetilde{T}(p,\delta) = \inf\{-2p\log x - \delta\log y + \log\Lambda(\boldsymbol{D}_{\mathcal{G}\times\mathcal{G}}(x,y)) : x \ge 0,\ 0 \le y \le 1\}. \tag{12}$$

Here, $\boldsymbol{D}_{\mathcal{G}\times\mathcal{G}}(x,y)$ is a $\binom{|\mathcal{V}|+1}{2} \times \binom{|\mathcal{V}|+1}{2}$-reduced distance matrix indexed by $\mathcal{V}^{(2)}$. To define the entry of matrix $\boldsymbol{D}_{\mathcal{G}\times\mathcal{G}}(x,y)$ indexed by $((v_i,v_j),(v_k,v_\ell))$, we look at the vertices v_i, v_j, v_k, and v_ℓ and follow the rules given in Table 2.

Again, we write $\Lambda(x,y;\boldsymbol{D}) \triangleq \Lambda(\boldsymbol{D}_{\mathcal{G}\times\mathcal{G}}(x,y))$. Furthermore, following the convexity of (12), we have that if the optimal solution is obtained at x and y, then

$$G_2(x,y) \triangleq x\Lambda_x(x,y;\boldsymbol{D}) - 2p\Lambda(x,y;\boldsymbol{D}) = 0. \tag{13}$$

$$G_3(x,y) \triangleq y\Lambda_y(x,y;\boldsymbol{D}) - \delta\Lambda(x,y;\boldsymbol{D}) = 0. \tag{14}$$

To this end, we consider the function $\Delta(x) = \Lambda_y(x,1;\boldsymbol{D})/\Lambda(x,1;\boldsymbol{D})$ for $x > 0$ and set $\delta_{\max} = \sup\{\Delta(x) : x > 0\}$. As with the previous section, we develop a numerical procedure to solve the optimization problem (9). To this end, we have the following critical observation.

Table 2. We set the $\big((v_i, v_j), (v_k, v_\ell)\big)$ entry of the matrix $D_{\mathcal{G}\times\mathcal{G}}(x, y)$ according to the subgraph induced by the states v_i,v_j,v_k, and v_ℓ.

$D_{\mathcal{G}\times\mathcal{G}}(x,y)$ at Entry $((v_i,v_j),(v_k,v_\ell))$	Subgraph Induced by the States $\{v_i,v_j,v_k,v_\ell\}$
0	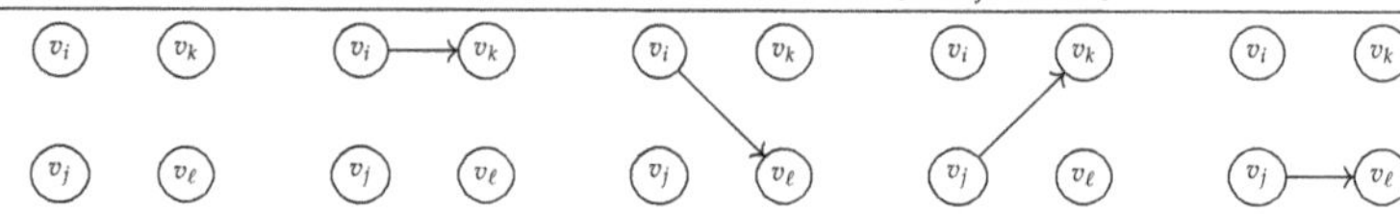
1	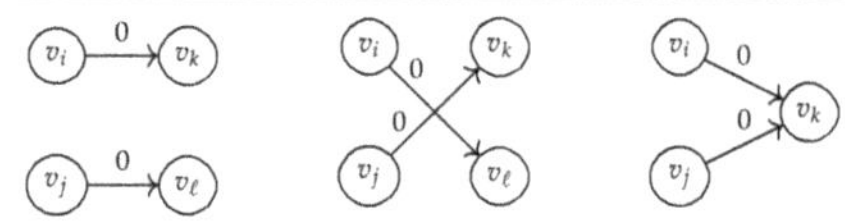
x^2	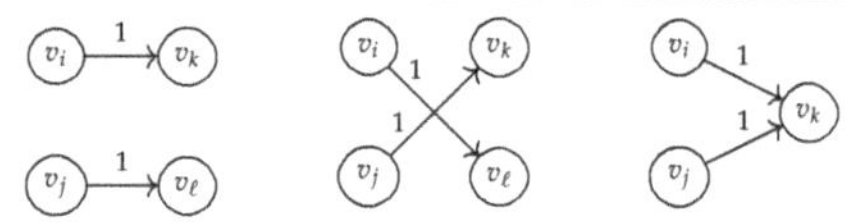
xy	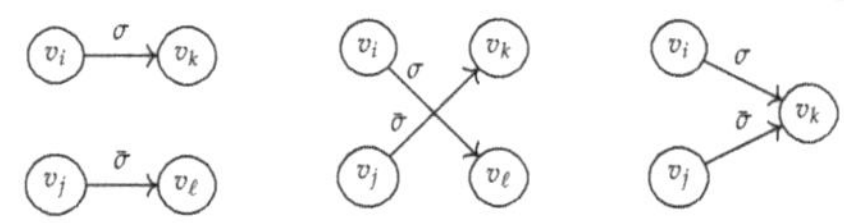
$2xy$	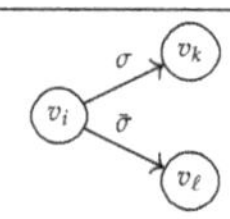

Theorem 2. *For a given $\delta < \delta_{\max}$, consider the optimization problem*

$$\begin{aligned}&\sup\Big\{ -2p\log z + 2\log\Lambda(z;\boldsymbol{C}) + 2p\log x + \delta\log y - \log\Lambda(x,y;\boldsymbol{D}) :\\ &G_1(z) = G_2(x,y) = G_3(x,y) = 0\Big\}.\end{aligned}$$

If (p^*, x^*, y^*, z^*) is an optimal solution, then $x^* = z^*$. Furthermore, if $0 \le p^* \le 1$, then $x^*, z^* \ge 0$ and $0 \le y^* \le 1$.

Proof. Let λ_1, λ_2, and λ_3 be real-valued variables and we define $L(p,x,y,z,\lambda_1,\lambda_2,\lambda_3) \triangleq G(p,x,y,z) + \lambda_1 G_1(z) + \lambda_2 G_2(x,y) + \lambda_3 G_3(x,y)$. Using the Lagrangian multiplier theorem, we have that $\partial L/\partial p = \partial L/\partial x = \partial L/\partial y = \partial L/\partial z = 0$ for any optimal solution. Solving these equations with the constraints $G_1(z) = G_2(x,y) = G_3(x,y) = 0$, we have that $\lambda_1 = \lambda_2 = \lambda_3 = 0$ and $x = z$ for any optimal solution.

Now, when $p^* \in [0,1]$, using $G_1(z) = 0$, let us define $z(p) \triangleq z\Lambda'(z;\ \boldsymbol{C})/\Lambda(z;\ \boldsymbol{C})$. Then, proceeding as with the proof of Lemma 2, we see that $z(p)$ is monotone increasing with $z(0) = 0$. Therefore, $z^* = z(p^*)$ is zero.

Similarly, given p^* and x^*, we use $G_3(x^*,\ y) = 0$ to define $\delta(y) = y\Lambda_y(x^*,\ y;\ \boldsymbol{D})/\Lambda(x^*,\ y;\ \boldsymbol{D})$. Again, we can proceed as with the proof of Lemma 2 to show that $\delta(y)$ is monotone increasing. Furthermore, since $\delta(y^*) < \delta_{\max} = \delta(1)$, we have that $y^* \in [0,1]$. □

Therefore, to determine $R_{\text{MR}}(\delta)$ for any fixed δ, it suffices to find x, y, z, and p such that $G_1(z) = G_2(x,\ y) = G_3(x,\ y) = 0$ and $x = z$.

Now, the optimization in Theorem 2 does not constrain the values of p. Furthermore, for certain constrained systems, there are instances where p falls outside the interval $[0,1]$. In this case, instead of solving the optimization problem (9), we set p to be either zero or one, and we solve the corresponding optimization problems (10) and (12). Specifically, if we have $p^* < 0$, then we set $p^* = 0$ and $x^* = 0$, or if $p^* > 1$, then we set $p^* = 1$ and $x^* = \infty$. Hence, the resulting rates that we obtain are a *lower bound* for the GV-MR bound.

Procedure 2 $\left(R_{\mathrm{MR}}(\delta)\ \textbf{for fixed}\ \delta \le \delta_{\max}\right)$.

INPUT: Matrices $C_{\mathcal{G}}(x), D_{\mathcal{G}}(x,y)$

OUTPUT: $R_{\mathrm{MR}}(\delta)$ or $R_{\mathrm{LB}}(\delta)$, where $R_{\mathrm{MR}}(\delta) \ge R_{\mathrm{LB}}(\delta)$.

(1) Apply the Newton–Raphson method to obtain p^*, x^*, and y^* such that $G_1(x^*), G_2(x^*,y^*)$, and $G_3(x^*,y^*)$ are approximately zero. Specifically, do the following:
- Fix a tolerance value ϵ
- Set $t = 0$ and pick an initial guess $p_t \ge 0$, $x_t \ge 0$, $0 \le y_t \le 1$.
- While $|p_t - p_{t-1}| + |x_t - x_{t-1}| + |y_t - y_{t-1}| > \epsilon$,
  - Compute the next guess $p_{t+1}, x_{t+1}, y_{t+1}$:

$$\begin{bmatrix} p_{t+1} \\ x_{t+1} \\ y_{t+1} \end{bmatrix} = \begin{bmatrix} p_t \\ x_t \\ y_t \end{bmatrix} - \begin{bmatrix} \frac{\partial G_1}{\partial p} & \frac{\partial G_1}{\partial x} & \frac{\partial G_1}{\partial y} \\ \frac{\partial G_2}{\partial p} & \frac{\partial G_2}{\partial x} & \frac{\partial G_2}{\partial y} \\ \frac{\partial G_3}{\partial p} & \frac{\partial G_3}{\partial x} & \frac{\partial G_3}{\partial y} \end{bmatrix}^{-1} \begin{bmatrix} G_1(x_t) \\ G_2(x_t, y_t) \\ G_3(x_t, y_t) \end{bmatrix}.$$

  - Here, apply the power iteration method to compute $\Lambda(x_t;\ C)$, $\Lambda'(x_t;\ C)$, $\Lambda''(x_t;\ C)$, $\Lambda(x_t, y_t;\ D)$, $\Lambda_x(x_t, y_t;\ D)$, $\Lambda_y(x_t, y_t;\ D)$, $\Lambda_{xx}(x_t, y_t;\ D)$, $\Lambda_{yy}(x_t, y_t;\ D)$, and $\Lambda_{xy}(x_t, y_t;\ D)$.
  - Increment t by one.
- Set $p^* \leftarrow p_t$, $x^* \leftarrow x_t$, $y^* \leftarrow y_t$.

(2A) If $0 \le p^* \le 1$, set $R_{\mathrm{MR}}(\delta) \leftarrow 2\log\Lambda(x^*;\ C) + \delta\log y^* - \log\Lambda(x^*, y^*; D)$.

(2B) Otherwise,
- If $p^* < 0$, set $p^* \leftarrow 0$, $x^* \leftarrow 0$, and $y^* \leftarrow$ solution of $G_3(0, y) = 0$.
- If $p^* > 1$, set $p^* \leftarrow 1$, $x^* \leftarrow \infty$, and $y^* \leftarrow$ solution of $G_3(\infty, y) = 0$.

Finally, set $R_{\mathrm{LB}}(\delta) \leftarrow 2\log\Lambda(x^*; C) + \delta\log y^* - \log\Lambda(x^*, y^*;\ D)$.

Remark 1. *Let p^* be the value computed at Step 1. When p^* falls outside the interval $[0,1]$, we set $p^* \in \{0,1\}$, and we argued earlier that the value returned $R_{\mathrm{LB}}(\delta)$ (at Step 2B) is, at most, $R_{\mathrm{MR}}(\delta)$. Nevertheless, we* conjecture *that $R_{\mathrm{LB}}(\delta) = R_{\mathrm{MR}}(\delta)$.*

As before, we develop a plotting procedure that minimizes the use of Newton–Raphson iterations.

We note that we have three scenarios for $\Delta(x)$. If $\Delta(x)$ is monotone decreasing, then $\delta_{\max} = \lim_{x\to 0}\Delta(x)$ and we set $x^\# = 0$. If $\Delta(x)$ is monotone increasing, then $\delta_{\max} = \lim_{x\to\infty}\Delta(x)$ and we set $x^\# = \infty$. Otherwise, $\Delta(x)$ is maximized for some positive value and we set $x^\#$ to be this value. Next, to obtain the GV-MR curve (see Remark 2); we iterate over $x \in [1, x^\#]$. It should be noted that if $y(x^\#) < 1$ or, equivalently, $\delta(x^\#) < \delta_{\max}$, we obtain a lower bound on the GV-MR curve by iterating over $y \in [y(x^\#), 1]$. Similar to Theorem 1, we define

$$\rho_{\mathrm{MR}}(x) \triangleq 2\log\Lambda(x; C) + \delta(x)\log y(x) - \log\Lambda(x, y(x); D), \tag{15}$$

and

$$\rho_{\mathrm{LB}}(y) \triangleq 2\log\Lambda(x^\#; C) + \delta(y)\log y - \log\Lambda(x^\#, y; D). \tag{16}$$

Finally, we state the following analogue of Theorem 1.

Theorem 3. *We define $\delta_{\max}$, $x^\#$ as before. For $x \in [1, x^\#]$, we set*

$$p(x) \leftarrow x\Lambda'(x;\mathbf{C})/\Lambda(x;\mathbf{C}),$$
$$y(x) \leftarrow \textit{solution of } G_2(x,y)=0,$$
$$\delta(x) \leftarrow y(x)\Lambda_y(x,y(x);\mathbf{D})/\Lambda(x,y(x);\mathbf{D}),$$

If $y(x^{\#}) < 1$, *then for* $y \in \left[y(x^{\#}),1\right]$, *we set*

$$\delta(y) \leftarrow y\Lambda_y(x^{\#},y;\mathbf{D})/\Lambda(x^{\#},y;\mathbf{D}),$$

then, the corresponding GV-MR curve is given by

$$\left\{(\delta(x),\rho_{\rm MR}(x)) : x \in \left[1,x^{\#}\right]\right\} \cup \left\{(\delta(y),\rho_{\rm LB}(y)) : y \in \left[y(x^{\#}),1\right]\right\} \cup \left\{(\delta,0) : \delta \geq \delta_{\max}\right\}. \tag{17}$$

where $\rho_{\rm MR}$ *and* $\rho_{\rm LB}$ *are defined in* (15) *and* (16), *respectively.*

Example 3. *We continue our example and evaluate the GV-MR bound for the* (3,2)*-SWCC constrained system. In this case, the matrices of interest are*

$$\mathbf{C}_{\mathcal{G}}(z) = \begin{bmatrix} z & 1 & 0 \\ 0 & 0 & z \\ z & 0 & 0 \end{bmatrix} \text{ and } \mathbf{D}_{\mathcal{G}\times\mathcal{G}}(x,y) = \begin{bmatrix} x^2 & 2xy & 0 & 1 & 0 & 0 \\ 0 & 0 & x^2 & 0 & xy & 0 \\ x^2 & xy & 0 & 0 & 0 & 0 \\ 0 & 0 & 0 & 0 & 0 & x^2 \\ 0 & 0 & x^2 & 0 & 0 & 0 \\ x^2 & 0 & 0 & 0 & 0 & 0 \end{bmatrix}.$$

Here, we observe that $\Delta(x)$ *is a monotone decreasing function and so, we set* $x^{\#} = 0.01$ *and* $\delta_{\max} = \lim_{x\to 0}\Delta(x) \approx 0.426$. *If we apply Procedure 2 to compute* $R_{\rm MR}(\delta)$ *for 100 points in* $[0,\delta_{\max}]$, *we require 437 Newton–Raphson iterations and 85,500 power iterations. In contrast, we use Theorem 3 to compute* $(\delta(x),\rho_{\rm MR}(x))$ *for 100 values of* x *in the interval* $\left[1,x^{\#}\right]$. *This requires 323 Newton–Raphson iterations and involves 22,296 power iterations. The resulting GV-MR curve is given in Figure 1a.*

Remark 2. *Strictly speaking, the GV-MR curve described by* (17) *may not be equal to the curve defined by the optimization problem* (15). *Nevertheless, the curve provides a lower bound for the optimal asymptotic code rates and we conjecture that the GV-MR curve described by* (17) *is a lower bound for the curve defined by the optimization problem* (15).

5. Single-State Graph Presentation

In this section, we focus on graph presentations that have exactly one state. Here, we allow these single-state graph presentations to contain the parallel edges and their labels to be binary strings of length possibly greater than one. Now, for these constrained systems, the procedures to evaluate the GV bound and its MR improvements can be greatly simplified. This is because the matrices $\mathbf{B}_{\mathcal{G}\times\mathcal{G}}(y)$, $\mathbf{C}_{\mathcal{G}}(z)$, and $\mathbf{D}_{\mathcal{G}\times\mathcal{G}}(x,y)$ are all of dimensions one by one. Therefore, determining their respective dominant eigenvalues is straightforward and does not require the power iteration method. The results in this section follow directly from previous sections and our objective is to provide explicit formulas whenever possible.

Formally, let $\mathcal{S}$ be the constrained system with graph presentation $\mathcal{G} = (\mathcal{V},\mathcal{E},\mathcal{L})$ such that $|V| = 1$ and $\mathcal{L} : \mathcal{E} \to \Sigma^s$ with $s \geq 1$ (existing methods that determine the GV bound for constrained systems with $|V| \geq 1$ assume that the edge-labels have single letters, i.e., $s = 1$. In other words, previous methods developed in [12,14] do not apply).

We further define $\alpha_t \triangleq \#\{(\boldsymbol{x},\boldsymbol{y}) \in \mathcal{L}(\mathcal{E})^2 : d_H(\boldsymbol{x},\boldsymbol{y}) = t\}$ for $0 \leq t \leq s$. Then. the corresponding adjacency and reduced distance matrices are as follows:

$$\mathbf{A}_{\mathcal{G}} = \left[|\mathcal{E}|\right] \text{ and } \mathbf{B}_{\mathcal{G}\times\mathcal{G}}(y) = \left[\textstyle\sum_{t\geq 0}\alpha_t y^t\right].$$

Then, we compute the capacity using its definition as $\mathrm{Cap}(\mathcal{S}) = (\log|\mathcal{E}|)/s$.

To compute $\widetilde{T}(\delta)$, we consider the following extension of the optimization problem (3) for the case $s \geq 1$:

$$\begin{aligned} \widetilde{T}(\delta) &= \frac{1}{s}\inf\{-\delta s \log y + \log \lambda(y; \boldsymbol{B}) : 0 \leq y \leq 1\} \\ &= \frac{1}{s}\inf\left\{-\delta s \log y + \log\left(\sum_{t\geq 0} \alpha_t y^t\right) : 0 \leq y \leq 1\right\}. \end{aligned} \tag{18}$$

As before, following the convexity of the objective function in (18), we have that the optimal y is the zero (in the interval $[0,1]$) of the function

$$F(y) \triangleq \sum_{t\geq 0}(t - \delta s)\alpha_t y^t. \tag{19}$$

So, for fixed values of δ, we can use the Newton–Raphson procedure to compute the root y of (19), and, hence, evaluate $R_{\mathrm{GV}}(\delta)$. It should be noted that the power iteration method is not required in this case.

On the other hand, to plot the GV curve, we have the following corollary of Theorem 1.

Corollary 2. *Let $\mathcal{G}$ be the single-state graph presentation for a constrained system $\mathcal{S}$. Then, the corresponding GV curve is given by*

$$\mathcal{GV}(\mathcal{S}) \triangleq \{(\delta, R_{\mathrm{GV}}(\delta)) : \delta \in [0,1]\} = \{(\delta(y), \rho(y)) : y \in [0,1]\} \cup \{(\delta, 0) : \delta \geq \delta_{\max}\}, \tag{20}$$

where

$$\begin{aligned} \delta_{\max} &= \frac{\sum_{t\geq 0} t\alpha_t}{s|\mathcal{E}|^2}, \\ \delta(y) &= \frac{\sum_{t\geq 0} t\alpha_t y^t}{s\left(\sum_{t\geq 0}\alpha_t y^t\right)}, \\ \rho(y) &= \frac{1}{s}\left(\log\frac{|\mathcal{E}|^2}{\sum_{t\geq 0}\alpha_t y^t} - \frac{\sum_{t\geq 0} t\alpha_t y^t}{\sum_{t\geq 0}\alpha_t y^t}\log y\right). \end{aligned}$$

We illustrate this evaluation procedure via an example of the class of *subblock energy-constrained codes (SECCs)*. Formally, we fix a *subblock length* L and *energy constraint* w. A binary word $\boldsymbol{x}$ of length mL is said to satisfy the (L, w)*-subblock energy constraint* if we partition $\boldsymbol{x}$ into m subblocks of length L, then the number of ones in every subblock is at least w. We refer to the collection of words that meet this constraint as an (L, w)*-SECC constrained system*. The class of SECCs was introduced by Tandon et al. for the application of simultaneous energy and information transfer [7]. Later, in [21], a GV-type bound was introduced (see Proposition 12 in [21] and also, (28)) and we make comparisons with the GV bound (20) in the following example.

Example 4. *Let $L = 3$ and $w = 2$ and we consider a $(3,2)$-SECC constrained system. It is straightforward to observe that the graph presentation is as follows with the single state* x. *Here,* $s = L = 3$.

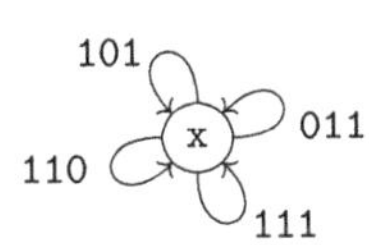

Then, the corresponding adjacency and reduced distance matrices are as follows:

$$\boldsymbol{A}_{\mathcal{G}} = [4],\ \boldsymbol{B}_{\mathcal{G}\times\mathcal{G}}(y) = \left[4 + 6y + 6y^2\right].$$

First, we determine the GV bound at $\delta = 1/3$. We observe that $F(y) = -4 + 6y^2$ and, so, the optimal point y for (18) *is $\sqrt{2/3}$ (the unique solution to $F(y)$ in the interval $[0,1]$). Hence, we have that $\widetilde{T}(1/3) \approx 1.327$. On the other hand, the capacity of a $(3,2)$-SECC constrained system is* $\mathrm{Cap}(\mathcal{S}) = 2/3$. *Therefore, the GV bound is given by $R_{\mathrm{GV}}(1/3) = 0.006$.*

In contrast, the GV-type lower bound given by Proposition 12 in [21] is zero for $\delta > 0.174$. Hence, the evaluation of the GV bound yields a significantly better lower bound. In fact, we can show that $R_{\mathrm{GV}}(\delta) > 0$ for all $\delta \leq \delta_{\max} = 3/8$.

To plot the GV curve, using the fact that $\delta_{\max} = 3/8$, we have that

$$\mathcal{GV}(\mathcal{S}) = \left\{ \left(\frac{y+2y^2}{2+3y+3y^2}, \frac{1}{3}\log\frac{8}{2+3y+3y^2} + \frac{3y+6y^2}{2+3y+3y^2}\log y \right) : y \in [0,1] \right\} \cup \left\{ (\delta, 0) : \delta \geq \frac{3}{8} \right\}.$$

We plot the curve in Section 6.

From this example, we see that our methods yield better lower bounds in terms of asymptotic coding rates *for a specific pair of (L,w). It is open to determine how much improvement can be achieved for general pairs of L and w.*

Next, we evaluate the GV-MR bound. To this end, we consider some proper subset $\mathcal{P} \subset \mathcal{E}$ and define

$$\begin{aligned}
\alpha_t &\triangleq \#\{(\boldsymbol{x},\boldsymbol{y}) \in \mathcal{L}(\mathcal{E})^2 : d_H(\boldsymbol{x},\boldsymbol{y}) = t,\ \boldsymbol{x},\boldsymbol{y} \in \mathcal{P}\}, \\
\beta_t &\triangleq \#\{(\boldsymbol{x},\boldsymbol{y}) \in \mathcal{L}(\mathcal{E}) : d_H(\boldsymbol{x},\boldsymbol{y}) = t,\ (\boldsymbol{x} \in \mathcal{P}, \boldsymbol{y} \notin \mathcal{P}) \text{ or } (\boldsymbol{x} \notin \mathcal{P}, \boldsymbol{y} \in \mathcal{P})\}, \\
\gamma_t &\triangleq \#\{(\boldsymbol{x},\boldsymbol{y}) \in \mathcal{L}(\mathcal{E}) : d_H(\boldsymbol{x},\boldsymbol{y}) = t,\ \boldsymbol{x},\boldsymbol{y} \notin \mathcal{P}\}.
\end{aligned}$$

Then, we consider the following matrices:

$$\boldsymbol{C}_{\mathcal{G}}(z) = \left[|\mathcal{E}| - |\mathcal{P}| + |\mathcal{P}|z \right] \text{ and } \boldsymbol{D}_{\mathcal{G}\times\mathcal{G}}(x,y) = \left[\textstyle\sum_{t\geq 0} (\alpha_t x^2 + \beta_t x + \gamma_t) y^t \right].$$

Setting p to be the normalized frequency of edges in $\mathcal{P}$, we obtain $S(p)$ by solving the optimization problem (10).

Specifically, we have that

$$S(p) = \frac{1}{s}\left(H(p) + p + \log|\mathcal{P}| + (1-p)\log(|\mathcal{E}| - |\mathcal{P}|) \right), \tag{21}$$

and this value is achieved when

$$z = \frac{p(|\mathcal{E}| - |\mathcal{P}|)}{(1-p)|\mathcal{P}|}. \tag{22}$$

To compute $\widetilde{T}(p,\delta)$, we consider the following extension of the optimization problem (12) for the case $s \geq 1$.

$$\begin{aligned}
\widetilde{T}(p,\delta) &= \frac{1}{s}\inf\{-2p\log x - \delta s \log y + \log \lambda(y;\boldsymbol{D}) : 0 \leq y \leq 1\} \\
&= \frac{1}{s}\inf\left\{ -2p\log x - \delta s\log y + \log\left(\sum_{t\geq 0} (\alpha_t x^2 + \beta_t x + \gamma_t) y^t \right) : 0 \leq y \leq 1 \right\}.
\end{aligned} \tag{23}$$

As before, following the convexity of the objective function in (23), we have that the optimal x and y are the zeroes (in the interval $[0,1]$) of the functions

$$\begin{aligned}
G_2(x,y) &\triangleq 2(1-p)(\sum_{t\geq 0}\alpha_t y^t)x^2 + (1-2p)(\sum_{t\geq 0}\beta_t y^t)x - 2p(\sum_{t\geq 0}\gamma_t y^t) \\
G_3(x,y) &\triangleq \sum_{t\geq 0}(t - \delta s)(\alpha_t x^2 + \beta_t x + \gamma_t)y^t
\end{aligned} \tag{24}$$

So, for fixed values of p and δ, we can use the Newton–Raphson procedure to compute the roots x and y of (24), and, hence, evaluate $R_{\rm GV}(p,\delta)$. It should be noted that the power iteration method is not required in this case. We find $x^{\#}$ as defined in Section 4 and set

$$\rho_{\rm MR}(x) \triangleq 2\log(|\mathcal{E}| - |\mathcal{P}| + |\mathcal{P}|x) + \delta(x)\log y(x) - \log\sum_{t\geq 0}(\alpha_t x^2 + \beta_t x + \gamma_t)y(x)^t\,. \quad (25)$$

Furthermore, if $y(x^{\#}) < 1$, we set

$$\rho_{\rm LB}(y) \triangleq 2\log(|\mathcal{E}| - |\mathcal{P}| + |\mathcal{P}|x^{\#}) + \delta(y)\log y - \log\sum_{t\geq 0}(\alpha_t (x^{\#})^2 + \beta_t x^{\#} + \gamma_t)y^t\,. \quad (26)$$

Next, to plot the GV-MR curve, we have the following corollary of Theorem 3.

Corollary 3. *Let $\mathcal{G}$ be the single-state graph presentation for a constrained system $\mathcal{S}$. For $x \in [1, x^{\#}]$, we set*

$$p(x) = \frac{|\mathcal{P}|x}{(|\mathcal{E}| - |\mathcal{P}|) + |\mathcal{P}|x},$$
$$\delta(x) = \frac{\sum_{t\geq 1} t(\alpha_t x^2 + \beta_t x + \gamma_t)y(x)^t}{s\sum_{t\geq 0}(\alpha_t x^2 + \beta_t x + \gamma_t)y(x)^t},$$

where $y(x)$ is the smallest root of the equation

$$2(|\mathcal{E}| - |\mathcal{P}|)(\sum_{t\geq 0}\alpha_t y^t)x + (|\mathcal{E}| - |\mathcal{P}| - |\mathcal{P}|x)(\sum_{t\geq 0}\beta_t y^t) - 2|\mathcal{P}|(\sum_{t\geq 0}\gamma_t y^t) = 0.$$

If $y(x^{\#}) < 1$, then for $y \in [y(x^{\#}), 1]$, we set

$$\delta(y) = \frac{\sum_{t\geq 1} t(\alpha_t (x^{\#})^2 + \beta_t x^{\#} + \gamma_t)y^t}{s\sum_{t\geq 0}(\alpha_t (x^{\#})^2 + \beta_t x^{\#} + \gamma_t)y^t},$$

Then, the corresponding GV-MR curve is given by

$$\{(\delta(x), \rho_{\rm MR}(x)) : x \in [1, x^{\#}]\} \cup \{(\delta(y), \rho_{\rm LB}(y)) : y \in [y(x^{\#}), 1]\} \cup \{(\delta, 0) : \delta \geq \delta_{\max}\}\,. \quad (27)$$

where $\rho_{\rm MR}$ and $\rho_{\rm LB}$ are defined in (25) *and* (26)*, respectively.*

Example 5. *We continue our example and evaluate the GV-MR bound for the* (3,2)*-SECC constrained system. We have the following single-state graph presentation:*

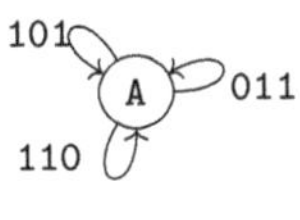

Then, the matrices of interest are:

$$\boldsymbol{C}_{\mathcal{G}} = [1 + 3z],\ \boldsymbol{D}_{\mathcal{G}\times\mathcal{G}}(x,y) = [(3 + 6y^2)x^2 + 6xy + 1]\,.$$

Since $\boldsymbol{C}_{\mathcal{G}}$ and $\boldsymbol{D}_{\mathcal{G}\times\mathcal{G}}(x,y)$ are both singleton matrices, we have $\Lambda(z;\boldsymbol{C}) = 1 + 3z$ and $\Lambda(x,y;\boldsymbol{D}) = (3 + 6y^2)x^2 + 6xy + 1$. Then, $G_1(z) = -p(1+3z) + 3z$, $G_2(x,y) = 3(1+2y^2)x^2(1-p) + 3xy(1-2p) - p$ and $G_3(x,y) = 4x^2y^2 - 3\delta(1+2y^2)x^2 + 2xy(1-3\delta) - \delta$. Now, we apply Theorem 2 and express p, y, and δ in terms of x where $x \in [1, x^{\#}]$ where $x^{\#} \to \infty$.

$$p = \frac{3x}{(1+3x)}$$
$$y = \frac{x-1}{2x}$$
$$\delta = \frac{2x(x-1)}{(9x^2-1)}$$

Now, we observe that we have $y(x^{\#}) = 1/2$. Since we can still increase y to 1, we apply the GV bound with $p = 1$ and $x = z = x^{\#}$ once we reach the boundary that is $p = 1$. Hence, at the boundary, we solve the following problem:

$$\begin{aligned} S(1) &= 2\log 3 \\ \widetilde{T}(1,\delta) &= \inf\{-2\log x - 3\delta\log y + \log(3(1+2y^2)x^2 + 6xy + 1) : 1/2 \le y \le 1; x = x^{\#} \to \infty\} \\ &= \inf\{-3\delta\log y + \log 3 + \log(1+2y^2) : 1/2 \le y \le 1\} \\ R_{\mathrm{MR}}(\delta) &= S(1) - \widetilde{T}(1,\delta). \end{aligned}$$

By setting $F(y) = -3\delta(1+2y^2) + 4y^2 = 0$, we get $\delta = 4y^2/3(1+2y^2)$ where $y \in [1/2, 1]$ and we plot the respective curve.

6. Numerical Plots

In this section, we apply our numerical procedures to compute the GV and the GV-MR bounds for some specific constrained systems. In particular, we consider the (L,w)-SWCC constrained systems defined in Section 3, the ubiquitous (d,k)-runlength limited systems (see, for example, p. 3 in [11]) and the (L,w)-subblock energy constrained codes recently introduced in [7]. In addition to the GV and GV-MR curves, we also plot a simple lower bound. For each $\delta \in [0, 1/2]$, any ball size is at most $2^{\mathbb{H}(\delta n)}$. So, for any constrained system $\mathcal{S}$, we have that $\widetilde{T}(\delta) \le \mathrm{Cap}(\mathcal{S}) + \mathbb{H}(\delta)$. Therefore, we have that

$$R(\delta;\mathcal{S}) \le \mathrm{Cap}(\mathcal{S}) - \mathbb{H}(\delta)\,. \tag{28}$$

From the plots in Figures 1–3, it is also clear that the computations of (7) and (17) yield a significantly better lower bound.

6.1. (L,w)-Sliding Window Constrained Codes

We fix L and w. We recall from Section 3 that a binary word satisfies the (L,w)-sliding window weight constraint if the number of ones in every consecutive L bits is at least w and the (L,w)-SWCC constrained system refers to the collection of words that meet this constraint. From [8,9], we have a simple graph presentation that uses only $\binom{L}{w}$ states. To validate our methods, we choose $(L,w) \in \{(3,2),(10,7)\}$ and the corresponding graph presentations have 3 and 120 states, respectively. Applying the plotting procedures described in Theorems 1 and 3, we obtain Figure 1.

6.2. (d,k)-Runlength Limited Codes

Next, we revisit the ubiquitous runlength constraint. We fix d and k. We say that a binary word satisfies the *(d,k)-RLL constraint* if each run of zeroes in the word has a length of at least d and at most k. Here, we allow the first and last runs of zeroes to have a length of less than d . We refer to the collection of words that meet this constraint as a *(d,k)-RLL constrained system*. It is well known that a *(d,k)-RLL constrained system* has the graph presentation with $k+1$ states (see, for example, [11]). Here, we choose $(d,k) \in \{(1,3),(3,7)\}$ to validate our methods and apply Theorems 1 and 3 to obtain Figure 2. For $(d,k) = (3,7)$, we corroborate our results with those derived in [15]. Specifically, Winick and Yang determined the GV bound (1) for the $(3,7)$-RLL constraint and remarked that the "evaluation of the (GV-MR) bound required considerable computation" for "a small improvement". In Table 3, we verify this statement.

Table 3. Comparison of the GV-MR bound with lower bound [15] for (3,7)-RLL constrained systems.

δ	**GV-MR Bound** (15)	**GV Bound [15] (see Equation** (1)**)**
0	0.406	0.406
0.05	0.255	0.225
0.1	0.163	0.163
0.15	0.095	0.094
0.2	0.048	0.044
0.25	0.018	0.012

6.3. (L, w)-Subblock Energy-Constrained Codes

We fix L and w. We recall from Section 5 that a binary word satisfies the (L, w)-subblock energy constraint if each subblock of length L has a weight of at least w and the (L, w)-SECC constrained system refers to the collection of words that meet this constraint. Then, the corresponding graph presentation has a single state x with $\sum_{i=0}^{w} \binom{L}{i}$ edges, where each edge is labeled by a word of length L and weight at least w. We apply the methods in Section 5 to determine the GV and GV-MR bounds.

For the GV bound, we provide the explicit formula for α_t and proceed as in Example 4.

$$\alpha_t = \binom{L}{t}(|\mathcal{E}| - \sum_{j=1}^{t} \sum_{k=0}^{\lceil \frac{j}{2} \rceil - 1} \binom{L-t}{w-j+k}\binom{t}{k}) \tag{29}$$

Similarly, for GV-MR bound, we provide the explicit formula for α_t, β_t, and γ_t and proceed as in Example 5.

$$\alpha_t = \binom{L}{w}\binom{L-w}{i/2}\binom{w}{i/2} \text{ if } t \text{ is even, otherwise, } \alpha_t = 0. \tag{30}$$

$$\beta_t = 2\binom{L}{w}\sum_{j=1}^{\lfloor \frac{t}{2} \rfloor}\binom{L-w}{t-j}\binom{w}{j} - 2\alpha_t \tag{31}$$

$$\gamma_t = \binom{L}{t}(|\mathcal{E}| - \sum_{j=1}^{t} \sum_{k=0}^{\lceil \frac{j}{2} \rceil - 1} \binom{L-t}{w-j+k}\binom{t}{k}) - \alpha_t - \beta_t \tag{32}$$

In Figure 3, we plot the GV bound and GV-MR bounds. We remark that the simple lower bound (28) corresponds to Proposition 12 in [21].

Author Contributions: Conceptualization, K.G. and H.M.K.; software, K.G.; writing—original draft preparation, K.G.; writing—review and editing, K.G. and H.M.K. All authors have read and agreed to the published version of the manuscript.

Funding: The work of Han Mao Kiah was supported by the Ministry of Education, Singapore, under its MOE AcRF Tier 2 Award under Grant MOE-T2EP20121-0007 and MOE AcRF Tier 1 Award under Grant RG19/23.

Institutional Review Board Statement: Not applicable.

Data Availability Statement: No new data were created or analyzed in this study. Data sharing is not applicable to this article.

Acknowledgments: The authors would also like to thank the assistant editor for her skillful handling and the anonymous reviewers for their valuable suggestions.

Conflicts of Interest: The authors declare no conflict of interest. The funders had no role in the design of the study; in the collection, analyses, or interpretation of data; in the writing of the manuscript, or in the decision to publish the results.

Appendix A. Power Iteration Method for Derivatives of Dominant Eigenvalues

Throughout this appendix, we assume that A is a diagonalizable matrix with dominant eigenvalue λ_1 and whose corresponding eigenspace has dimension one. Let e_1 be the unit eigenvector whose entries are positive in this space. Then, the power iteration method is a well-known numerical procedure that finds the dominant eigenvalue λ_1 and the corresponding eigenvector e_1 efficiently.

Now, in the preceding sections, the entries in the matrix A are given functions in either one or two variables and, thus, the dominant eigenvalue λ_1 is a function in the same variables. Moreover, the numerical procedures in these sections require us to compute the higher order (partial) derivatives of this dominant eigenvalue function λ_1. To the best of our knowledge, we are unaware of any algorithms or numerical procedures that estimate the values of these derivatives. Hence, in this appendix, we modify the power iteration method to compute these estimates.

Formally, let A be an irreducible nonnegative diagonalizable square matrix with dominant eigenvalue λ_1 and corresponding unit eigenvector e_1. Since A is diagonalizable, A has n eigenvectors $e_1, e_2, \ldots, e_n$ that form an orthonormal basis for $\mathbb{R}^n$. Let $\lambda_1, \lambda_2, \ldots, \lambda_n$ be the corresponding eigenvalues and, so, we have that

$$Ae_i = \lambda_i e_i \text{ for all } i = 1, 2, \ldots, n. \tag{A1}$$

Since A is irreducible, the dominant eigenspace has dimension one and, also, the dominant eigenvalue is real and positive. Therefore, we can assume that $\lambda_1 > |\lambda_2| \geq \cdots \geq |\lambda_n|$.

We first assume that the entries of A are functions in the variable z. Hence, λ_i and the entries of e_i are functions in z too. Then Power Iteration I then evaluates both λ_1 and λ_1' for some fixed value of z, while Power Iteration II additionally evaluates the second order derivative λ_1''.

The case where the entries of A are functions in two variables x and y is discussed at the end of the appendix. Here, Power Iteration III evaluates higher order partial derivatives of λ_1 for certain fixed values of x and y. For ease of exposition, we provide detailed proofs for the correctness of Power Iteration I and the proofs can be extended for Power Iteration II and Power Iteration III.

We continue our discussion where the entries of A are univariate functions in z. We differentiate each entry of A with respect to z to obtain the matrix A'. Furthermore, for all $1 \leq i \leq n$, we differentiate each entry of eigenvectors e_i and the eigenvalue λ_i to obtain e_i' and λ_i', respectively. Specifically, it follows from (A1) that

$$A'e_i + Ae_i' = \lambda_i' e_i + \lambda_i e_i' \text{ for all } i = 1, 2, \cdots, n. \tag{A2}$$

Then, the following procedure computes both λ_1 and λ_1'.

Power Iteration I.
INPUT: Irreducible nonnegative diagonalizable matrix A
OUTPUT: Estimates of λ_1 and λ_1'

(1) Initialize $q^{(0)}$ such that all its entries are strictly positive.
  - Fix a tolerance value ϵ.
  - While $|q^{(k)} - q^{(k-1)}| > \epsilon$,
    - Set

$$\lambda^{(k)} = ||Aq^{(k-1)}||,$$

$$q^{(k)} = \frac{Aq^{(k-1)}}{\lambda^{(k)}},$$

$$\mu^{(k)} = \|\boldsymbol{A}'\boldsymbol{q}^{(k-1)} + \boldsymbol{A}\boldsymbol{r}^{(k-1)} - \lambda^{(k)}\boldsymbol{r}^{(k-1)}\|,$$
$$\boldsymbol{r}^{(k)} = \frac{\boldsymbol{A}\boldsymbol{r}^{(k-1)} + \boldsymbol{A}'\boldsymbol{q}^{(k-1)} - \mu^{(k)}\boldsymbol{q}^{(k-1)}}{\lambda^{(k)}}.$$

- Increment k by one.

(2) Set $\lambda_1 \leftarrow \lambda^{(k)}$ and $\lambda_1' \leftarrow \mu^{(k)}$.

Theorem A1. *If $\boldsymbol{A}$ is an irreducible nonnegative diagonalizable matrix and $\boldsymbol{q}^{(0)}$ has positive components with unit norm, then, as $k \to \infty$, we have*

$$\lambda^{(k)} \to \lambda_1,\ \boldsymbol{q}^{(k)} \to \boldsymbol{e}_1,\ \mu^{(k)} \to \lambda_1'.$$

Here, $\boldsymbol{q}^{(k)} \to \boldsymbol{e}_1$ means that $\left\|\boldsymbol{q}^{(k)} - \boldsymbol{e}_1\right\| \to 0$ as $k \to \infty$.

Before we present the proof of Theorem A1, we remark that the usual power iteration method computes only $\lambda^{(k)}$ and $\boldsymbol{q}^{(k)}$. Then, it is well-known (see, for example, [22]) that $\lambda^{(k)}$ and $\boldsymbol{q}^{(k)}$ tend to λ_1 and $\boldsymbol{e}_1$, respectively.

Now, since $\boldsymbol{e}_i$ spans $\mathbb{R}^n$, we can write $\boldsymbol{q}^{(0)} = \sum_{i=1}^n \alpha_i \boldsymbol{e}_i$ for any initial vector $\boldsymbol{q}^{(0)}$. The next technical lemma provides closed formulas for $\lambda^{(k)}$, $\boldsymbol{q}^{(k)}$, $\mu^{(k)}$, and $\boldsymbol{r}^{(k)}$ in terms of λ_i, $\boldsymbol{e}_i$ and α_i.

Lemma A1. *Let $\boldsymbol{q}^{(0)} = \sum_{i=1}^n \alpha_i \boldsymbol{e}_i$. Then,*

$$\boldsymbol{q}^{(k)} = \frac{\sum_{i=1}^n \alpha_i \lambda_i^k \boldsymbol{e}_i}{\|\sum_{i=1}^n \alpha_i \lambda_i^k \boldsymbol{e}_i\|}, \tag{A3}$$

$$\lambda^{(k)} = \frac{\|\sum_{i=1}^n \alpha_i \lambda_i^k \boldsymbol{e}_i\|}{\|\sum_{i=1}^n \alpha_i \lambda_i^{k-1} \boldsymbol{e}_i\|}, \tag{A4}$$

$$\boldsymbol{r}^{(k)} = \frac{\sum_{i=1}^n (\alpha_i \boldsymbol{e}_i' + \alpha_i' \boldsymbol{e}_i)\lambda_i^k + (k\lambda_i' - \sum_{j=1}^k \mu^{(j)})\alpha_i \lambda_i^{k-1} \boldsymbol{e}_i}{\|\sum_{i=1}^n \alpha_i \lambda_i^k \boldsymbol{e}_i\|}, \tag{A5}$$

$$\mu^{(k)} = \frac{\left\|\sum_{i=1}^n (\alpha_i \boldsymbol{e}_i' + \alpha_i' \boldsymbol{e}_i)\lambda_i^{k-1}(\lambda_i - \lambda^{(k)}) + \alpha_i \lambda_i^{k-1}\lambda_i' \boldsymbol{e}_i + ((k-1)\lambda_i' - \sum_{j=1}^{k-1} \mu^{(j)})\alpha_i \lambda_i^{k-2}(\lambda_i - \lambda^{(k)})\boldsymbol{e}_i\right\|}{\|\sum_{i=1}^n \alpha_i \lambda_i^{k-1} \boldsymbol{e}_i\|}. \tag{A6}$$

Proof. Since $\boldsymbol{q}^{(k)}$ is defined recursively as $\boldsymbol{q}^{(k)} = \frac{\boldsymbol{A}\boldsymbol{q}^{(k-1)}}{\lambda^{(k)}} = \frac{\boldsymbol{A}\boldsymbol{q}^{(k-1)}}{\|\boldsymbol{A}\boldsymbol{q}^{(k-1)}\|}$, we have that

$$\boldsymbol{q}^{(k)} = \frac{\boldsymbol{A}^k \boldsymbol{q}^{(0)}}{\|\boldsymbol{A}^k \boldsymbol{q}^{(0)}\|}.$$

Then, it follows from Equation (A1) that

$$\boldsymbol{A}^k \boldsymbol{q}^{(0)} = \boldsymbol{A}^k \sum_{i=1}^n \alpha_i \boldsymbol{e}_i = \sum_{i=1}^n \alpha_i (\boldsymbol{A}^k \boldsymbol{e}_i) = \sum_{i=1}^n \alpha_i \lambda_i^k \boldsymbol{e}_i, \tag{A7}$$

and, so, we obtain (A3). Similarly, from (A1), we have that

$$\lambda^{(k)} = \|\boldsymbol{A}\boldsymbol{q}^{(k-1)}\| = \frac{\|\boldsymbol{A}^k \boldsymbol{q}^{(0)}\|}{\|\boldsymbol{A}^{k-1}\boldsymbol{q}^{(0)}\|} = \frac{\|\sum_{i=1}^n \alpha_i \lambda_i^k \boldsymbol{e}_i\|}{\|\sum_{i=1}^n \alpha_i \lambda_i^{k-1} \boldsymbol{e}_i\|},$$

as required for (A4).

Next, we note that $r^{(0)} = \sum_{i=1}^{n} \alpha_i e_i' + \sum_{i=1}^{n} \alpha_i' e_i$. Then, using the recursive definition of $r^{(k)}$, we have

$$r^{(k)} = \frac{A^k r^{(0)} + \sum_{j=0}^{k-1} A^j A' A^{k-j-1} q^{(0)} - (\sum_{j=1}^{k} \mu^{(j)}) A^{k-1} q^{(0)}}{\|A^k q^{(0)}\|}. \tag{A8}$$

Then, from (A1), we have

$$A^k r^{(0)} = A^k \left(\sum_{i=1}^{n} \alpha_i e_i' + \sum_{i=1}^{n} \alpha_i' e_i \right) = \sum_{i=1}^{n} \alpha_i (A^k e_i') + \sum_{i=1}^{n} \alpha_i' \lambda_i^k e_i. \tag{A9}$$

and, from (A2),

$$A' \sum_{i=1}^{n} \alpha_i \lambda_i^{k-j-1} e_i = \sum_{i=1}^{n} \alpha_i \lambda_i^{k-j-1} (A' e_i) = \sum_{i=1}^{n} \alpha_i \lambda_i^{k-j-1} (\lambda_i' e_i + \lambda_i e_i' - A e_i').$$

Therefore, using (A1) again,

$$\begin{aligned} \sum_{j=0}^{k-1} A^j A' \sum_{i=1}^{n} \alpha_i \lambda_i^{k-j-1} e_i &= \sum_{j=0}^{k-1} A^j \sum_{i=1}^{n} \alpha_i \lambda_i^{k-j-1} (\lambda_i' e_i + \lambda_i e_i' - A e_i') \\ &= k \sum_{i=1}^{n} \alpha_i \lambda_i^{k-1} \lambda_i' e_i + \sum_{i=1}^{n} \alpha_i \lambda_i^k e_i' - \sum_{i=1}^{n} \alpha_i (A^k e_i'). \end{aligned}$$

Therefore, we obtain (A5).

Finally, we recall that $\mu^{(k)}$ is defined as

$$\mu^{(k)} = \|A' q^{(k-1)} + A r^{(k-1)} - \lambda^{(k)} r^{(k-1)}\|.$$

Then, by replacing $r^{(k-1)}$ and $q^{(k-1)}$ from (A5) and (A3), respectively, and then using Equation (A2), we obtain (A6). □

Finally, we are ready to demonstrate the correctness of Power Iteration I.

Proof of Theorem A1. Since A is an irreducible nonnegative diagonalizable matrix, λ_1 is real positive and there exists $0 < \epsilon < 1$ such that $\frac{|\lambda_i|}{\lambda_1} < \epsilon$ for all $i = 2, 3, \cdots, n$ (see, for example, [11]). For purposes of brevity, we write

$$\Phi_k = \sum_{i=1}^{n} \alpha_i \lambda_i^k e_i \tag{A10}$$

and, so, we can rewrite (A3) as

$$q^{(k)} = \frac{\Phi_k}{\|\Phi_k\|} = \frac{\lambda_1^k}{\|\Phi_k\|} \frac{\Phi_k}{\lambda_1^k} = \frac{\lambda_1^k}{\|\Phi_k\|} \left(\alpha_1 e_1 + \sum_{i=2}^{n} \alpha_i \frac{\lambda_i^k}{\lambda_1^k} e_i \right).$$

Now, since $\lambda_i^k / \lambda_1^k \le \epsilon^k$ for all $i = 2, \ldots, n$, we have that

$$\left\| \frac{\Phi_k}{\lambda_1^k} - \alpha_1 e_1 \right\| \le C_1 \epsilon^k \text{ for some constant } C_1. \tag{A11}$$

Then, using the triangle inequality, we have that as $k \to \infty$, $\left| \frac{\|\Phi_k\|}{\lambda_1^k} - \alpha_1 \right| \to 0$ and, thus, $\frac{\lambda_1^k}{\|\Phi_k\|} \to \frac{1}{\alpha_1}$. Therefore, $\|q^{(k)} - e_1\| \to 0$ as required.

It should be noted that since $\frac{\lambda_1^k}{||\Phi_k||}$ tends to a finite limit, we have that $\frac{\lambda_1^k}{||\Phi_k||}$ is bounded above by some constant. In other words, we have that

$$\frac{\lambda_1^k}{||\Phi_k||} \leq C_2 \text{ for some constant } C_2. \tag{A12}$$

Next, we show the following inequality:

$$|\lambda^{(k)} - \lambda_1| \leq C_3 \epsilon^{k-1} \text{ for some constant } C_3. \tag{A13}$$

Using (A4), we have that

$$\frac{||\Phi_k - \lambda_1 \Phi_{k-1}||}{||\Phi_{k-1}||} = \frac{\lambda_1^{k-1}}{||\Phi_{k-1}||} \frac{\sum_{i=1}^n \alpha_i \lambda_i^k e_i - \alpha_i \lambda_1 \lambda_i^{k-1} e_i}{\lambda_1^{k-1}} = \left(\frac{\lambda_1^{k-1}}{||\Phi_{k-1}||}\right) \cdot \lambda_1 \cdot \sum_{i=2}^n \alpha_i \left(\frac{\lambda_i^k}{\lambda_1^k} - \frac{\lambda_i^{k-1}}{\lambda_1^{k-1}}\right) e_i .$$

Now, observe that $\left(\frac{\lambda_i^k}{\lambda_1^k} - \frac{\lambda_i^{k-1}}{\lambda_1^{k-1}}\right) \leq 2\epsilon^{k-1}$ for $i = 2, \ldots, n$. Since $\frac{\lambda_1^{k-1}}{||\Phi_{k-1}||} \leq C_2$, we have (A13) after applying the triangle inequality.

Again, to reduce clutter, we introduce the following abbreviations:

$$\begin{aligned}
D_k &= \sum_{i=1}^n (\alpha_i e_i' + \alpha_i' e_i) \lambda_i^{k-1} (\lambda_i - \lambda^{(k)}), \\
E_k &= \sum_{i=1}^n \alpha_i \lambda_i^{k-1} \lambda_i' e_i, \\
F_k &= \sum_{i=1}^n \left((k-1)\lambda_i' - \sum_{j=1}^{k-1} \mu^{(j)} \right) \alpha_i \lambda_i^{k-2} (\lambda_i - \lambda^{(k)}) e_i.
\end{aligned}$$

Thus, we can rewrite (A6) as

$$\mu^{(k)} = \frac{||D_k + E_k + F_k||}{||\Phi_{k-1}||} \leq \lambda_1' + \frac{||D_k||}{||\Phi_{k-1}||} + \frac{||E_k - \lambda_1' \Phi_{k-1}||}{||\Phi_{k-1}||} + \frac{||F_k||}{||\Phi_{k-1}||} .$$

Next, we bound each of the summands on the right-hand side. Specifically, we show the following inequalities:

$$\frac{||D_k||}{||\Phi_{k-1}||} + \frac{||E_k - \lambda_1' \Phi_{k-1}||}{||\Phi_{k-1}||} \leq C_4 \epsilon^{k-1} \text{ for some constant } C_4, \tag{A14}$$

$$\frac{||F_k||}{||\Phi_{k-1}||} \leq C_5 (k-1) \epsilon^{k-1} + C_5 \left(\sum_{j=1}^{k-1} \mu^{(k)} \right) \epsilon^{k-1} \text{ for some constant } C_5. \tag{A15}$$

To demonstrate (A14), we consider

$$\frac{||D_k||}{\lambda_1^{k-1}} = \left\| \sum_{i=1}^n (\alpha_i e_i' + \alpha_i' e_i) \frac{\lambda_i^{k-1}}{\lambda_1^{k-1}} (\lambda_i - \lambda^{(k)}) \right\| \leq ||\alpha_1 e_1' + \alpha_1' e_1|| |\lambda_1 - \lambda^{(k)}| + \epsilon^{k-1} \sum_{i=2}^n ||\alpha_i e_i' + \alpha_i' e_i|| |\lambda_i - \lambda^{(k)}|.$$

We use (A13) to bound the first summand by some constant multiple of ϵ^{k-1}. On the other hand, we have $|\lambda_i - \lambda^{(k)}| \leq |\lambda_i - \lambda_1| + |\lambda_1 - \lambda^{(k)}| \leq \max\{|\lambda_i - \lambda_1| : 2 \leq i \leq n\} + C_3 \epsilon^{k-1}$ for $2 \leq i \leq n$. In other words, the second summand is also bounded by some constant multiple of ϵ^{k-1}. Next, we consider

$$\frac{||E_k - \lambda_1' \Phi_{k-1}||}{\lambda_1^{k-1}} = \left\| \sum_{i=1}^n \alpha_i \frac{\lambda_i^{k-1}}{\lambda_1^{k-1}} (\lambda_i' - \lambda_1') e_i \right\| \leq \epsilon^{k-1} \sum_{i=2}^n |\alpha_i (\lambda_i' - \lambda_1')|.$$

and, so, $\frac{\|E_k-\lambda_1'\Phi_{k-1}\|}{\lambda_1^{k-1}}$ is also bounded by a multiple of ϵ^{k-1}. Therefore, since $\frac{\lambda_1^{k-1}}{\|\Phi_{k-1}\|} \le C_2$, we have (A14). Using similar methods, we can establish (A15).

Next, we apply (A14) and then recursively apply (A15) until the right-hand side is free of $\mu^{(i)}$s. Then, it follows that

$$\mu^{(k)} \le \lambda_1' + C_4\epsilon^{k-1} + C_5(k-1)\epsilon^{k-1} + \prod_{j=2}^{k-1}(1+C_5\epsilon^{k-j}) + C_5\epsilon^{k-1}\sum_{i=1}^{k-1}(\lambda_1' + C_4\epsilon^{k-i-1}C_5(k-i-1)\epsilon^{k-i-1})\prod_{j=2}^{i}(1+C_5\epsilon^{k-j})). \quad \text{(A16)}$$

Furthermore, since $i \le k-1$, $\prod_{j=2}^{i}(1+C_5\epsilon^{k-j}) \le \prod_{j=2}^{k-1}(1+C_5\epsilon^{k-j})$, we can rewrite (A16) as

$$\mu^{(k)} \le \lambda_1' + C_4\epsilon^{k-1} + C_5(k-1)\epsilon^{k-1} + \prod_{j=2}^{k-1}(1+C_5\epsilon^{k-j})\left(1 + C_5\epsilon^{k-1}\sum_{i=1}^{k-1}(\lambda_1' + C_4\epsilon^{k-i-1}C_5(k-i-1)\epsilon^{k-i-1})\right). \quad \text{(A17)}$$

Next, it follows from standard calculus that $\prod_{j=2}^{k-1}(1+C_5\epsilon^{k-j}) < e^{\frac{C_5}{1-\epsilon}}$. Furthermore, since $\epsilon < 1$, we have $\sum_{i=0}^{k-2}\epsilon^j < \frac{1}{1-\epsilon}$ and $\sum_{i=0}^{k-2} j\epsilon^j < \frac{1}{(1-\epsilon)^2}$. Putting everything together, we have

$$\mu^{(k)} \le \lambda_1' + C_4\epsilon^{k-1} + C_5(k-1)\epsilon^{k-1} + C_5\epsilon^{k-1}e^{\frac{C_5}{1-\epsilon}}\left(1 + (k-1)\lambda_1' + \frac{C_4}{1-\epsilon} + \frac{C_5}{(1-\epsilon)^2}\right). \quad \text{(A18)}$$

As $k \to \infty$, since $\epsilon < 1$, we have $\epsilon^k \to 0$ and $k\epsilon^k \to 0$. Therefore, $\lim_{k\to\infty}\mu^{(k)} \le \lambda_1'$. Using similar methods, we have that $\lim_{k\to\infty}\mu^{(k)} \ge \lambda_1'$ and, so, $\lim_{k\to\infty}\mu^{(k)} = \lambda_1'$, as required. □

Next, we modify Power Iteration I so as to compute the higher order derivatives. We omit a detailed proof as it is similar to the proof of Theorem A1.

Power Iteration II.

INPUT: Irreducible nonnegative diagonalizable matrix A

OUTPUT: Estimates of λ_1, λ_1', and λ_1''

(1) Initialize $q^{(0)}$ such that all its entries are strictly positive.
- Fix a tolerance value ϵ.
- While $|q_{(k)} - q_{(k-1)}| > \epsilon$,
  - Set
$$\begin{aligned}
\lambda^{(k)} &= \|Aq^{(k-1)}\|,\\
q^{(k)} &= \frac{Aq^{(k-1)}}{\lambda^{(k)}},\\
\mu^{(k)} &= \|A'q^{(k-1)} + Ar^{(k-1)} - \lambda^{(k)}r^{(k-1)}\|,\\
r^{(k)} &= \frac{Ar^{(k-1)} + A'q^{(k-1)} - \mu^{(k)}q^{(k-1)}}{\lambda^{(k)}},\\
\nu^{(k)} &= \|A''q^{(k-1)} + 2A'r^{(k-1)} + As^{(k-1)} - \lambda^{(k)}s^{(k-1)} - 2\mu^{(k)}r^{(k-1)}\|,\\
s^{(k)} &= \frac{A''q^{(k-1)} + 2A'r^{(k-1)} + As^{(k-1)} - 2\mu^{(k)}r^{(k-1)} - \nu^{(k)}q^{(k-1)}}{\lambda^{(k)}}.
\end{aligned}$$
  - Increment k by one.

(2) Set $\lambda_1 \leftarrow \lambda^{(k)}$, $\lambda_1' \leftarrow \mu^{(k)}$ and $\lambda_1'' \leftarrow \nu^{(k)}$.

Theorem A2. *If A is an irreducible nonnegative diagonalizable matrix and $q^{(0)}$ has positive components with unit norm, then, as $k \to \infty$, we have*

$$\lambda^{(k)} \to \lambda_1,\ q^{(k)} \to e_1,\ \mu^{(k)} \to \lambda_1',\ \nu^{(k)} \to \lambda_1''.$$

Finally, we end this appendix with a power iteration method that computes the partial derivatives when the elements of the given matrix are bivariate functions.

Power Iteration III.

INPUT: Irreducible nonnegative diagonalizable matrix $\boldsymbol{A}$

OUTPUT: Estimates of λ_1, $(\lambda_1)_x$, $(\lambda_1)_y$, $(\lambda_1)_{xx}$, $(\lambda_1)_{yy}$, and $(\lambda_1)_{xy}$

(1) Initialize $\boldsymbol{q}^{(0)}$ such that all its entries are strictly positive.

- Fix a tolerance value ϵ.
- While $|\boldsymbol{q}^{(k)} - \boldsymbol{q}^{(k-1)}| > \epsilon$,
  - Set

$$
\begin{aligned}
\lambda^{(k)} &= \|\boldsymbol{A}q^{(k-1)}\|,\\
q^{(k)} &= \frac{\boldsymbol{A}q^{(k-1)}}{\lambda^{(k)}},\\
\lambda_x^{(k)} &= \|\boldsymbol{A}_x\boldsymbol{q}^{(k-1)} + \boldsymbol{A}\boldsymbol{q}_x^{(k-1)} - \lambda\boldsymbol{q}_x^{(k-1)}\|,\\
\boldsymbol{q}_x^{(k)} &= \frac{\boldsymbol{A}_x\boldsymbol{q}^{(k-1)} + \boldsymbol{A}\boldsymbol{q}_x^{(k-1)} - \lambda_x^{(k-1)}\boldsymbol{q}^{(k-1)}}{\lambda^{(k)}},\\
\lambda_y^{(k)} &= \|\boldsymbol{A}_y\boldsymbol{q}^{(k-1)} + \boldsymbol{A}\boldsymbol{q}_y^{(k-1)} - \lambda\boldsymbol{q}_y^{(k-1)}\|,\\
\boldsymbol{q}_y^{(k)} &= \frac{\boldsymbol{A}_y\boldsymbol{q}^{(k-1)} + \boldsymbol{A}\boldsymbol{q}_y^{(k-1)} - \lambda_y^{(k-1)}\boldsymbol{q}^{(k-1)}}{\lambda^{(k)}},\\
\lambda_{xx}^{(k)} &= \|\boldsymbol{A}_{xx}\boldsymbol{q}^{(k-1)} + 2\boldsymbol{A}_x\boldsymbol{q}_x^{(k-1)} + \boldsymbol{A}\boldsymbol{q}_{xx}^{(k-1)} - \lambda^{(k-1)}\boldsymbol{q}_{xx}^{(k-1)} - 2\lambda_x^{(k-1)}\boldsymbol{q}_x^{(k-1)}\|,\\
\boldsymbol{q}_{xx}^{(k)} &= \frac{\boldsymbol{A}_{xx}\boldsymbol{q}^{(k-1)} + 2\boldsymbol{A}_x\boldsymbol{q}_x^{(k-1)} + \boldsymbol{A}\boldsymbol{q}_{xx}^{(k-1)} - 2\lambda_x^{(k-1)}\boldsymbol{q}_x^{(k-1)} - \lambda_{xx}^{(k-1)}\boldsymbol{q}^{(k-1)}}{\lambda^{(k)}}\\
\lambda_{yy}^{(k)} &= \|\boldsymbol{A}_{yy}\boldsymbol{q}^{(k-1)} + 2\boldsymbol{A}_y\boldsymbol{q}_y^{(k-1)} + \boldsymbol{A}\boldsymbol{q}_{yy}^{(k-1)} - \lambda^{(k-1)}\boldsymbol{q}_{yy}^{(k-1)} - 2\lambda_y^{(k-1)}\boldsymbol{q}_y^{(k-1)}\|,\\
\boldsymbol{q}_{yy}^{(k)} &= \frac{\boldsymbol{A}_{yy}\boldsymbol{q}^{(k-1)} + 2\boldsymbol{A}_y\boldsymbol{q}_y^{(k-1)} + \boldsymbol{A}\boldsymbol{q}_{yy}^{(k-1)} - 2\lambda_y^{(k-1)}\boldsymbol{q}_y^{(k-1)} - \lambda_{yy}^{(k-1)}\boldsymbol{q}^{(k-1)}}{\lambda^{(k)}}\\
\lambda_{xy}^{(k)} &= \|\boldsymbol{A}_{xy}\boldsymbol{q}^{(k-1)} + \boldsymbol{A}_x\boldsymbol{q}_y^{(k-1)} + \boldsymbol{A}_y\boldsymbol{q}_x^{(k-1)} + \boldsymbol{A}\boldsymbol{q}_{xy}^{(k-1)} - \lambda^{(k-1)}\boldsymbol{q}_{xy}^{(k-1)} - \lambda_x^{(k-1)}\boldsymbol{q}_y^{(k-1)} - \lambda_y^{(k-1)}\boldsymbol{q}_x^{(k-1)}\|,\\
\boldsymbol{q}_{xy}^{(k)} &= \frac{\boldsymbol{A}_{xy}\boldsymbol{q}^{(k-1)} + \boldsymbol{A}_x\boldsymbol{q}_y^{(k-1)} + \boldsymbol{A}_y\boldsymbol{q}_x^{(k-1)} + \boldsymbol{A}\boldsymbol{q}_{xy}^{(k-1)} - \lambda_{xy}^{(k-1)}\boldsymbol{q}^{(k-1)} - \lambda_x^{(k-1)}\boldsymbol{q}_y^{(k-1)} - \lambda_y^{(k-1)}\boldsymbol{q}_x^{(k-1)}}{\lambda^{(k)}}.
\end{aligned}
$$

  - Increment k by one.
- Set $\lambda^{(k)} \leftarrow \lambda_1$, $\lambda_x^{(k)} \leftarrow (\lambda_1)_x$, $\lambda_y^{(k)} \leftarrow (\lambda_1)_y$, $\lambda_{xx}^{(k)} \leftarrow (\lambda_1)_{xx}$, $\lambda_{yy}^{(k)} \leftarrow (\lambda_1)_{yy}$, $\lambda_{xy}^{(k)} \leftarrow (\lambda_1)_{xy}$.

Theorem A3. *If $\boldsymbol{A}$ is an irreducible nonnegative diagonalizable matrix and $\boldsymbol{q}^{(0)}$ has positive components with unit norm, then, as $k \to \infty$, we have $\lambda_{xx}^{(k)} \to (\lambda_1)_{xx}$, $\lambda_{yy}^{(k)} \to (\lambda_1)_{yy}$, $\lambda_{xy}^{(k)} \to (\lambda_1)_{xy}$.*

References

1. Yazdi, S.M.H.T.; Kiah, H.M.; Garcia-Ruiz, E.; Ma, J.; Zhao, H.; Milenkovic, O. DNA-Based Storage: Trends and Methods. *IEEE Trans. Mol. Biol. Multi-Scale Commun.* **2015**, *1*, 230–248. [CrossRef]
2. Immink, K.A.S.; Cai, K. Efficient balanced and maximum homopolymer-run restricted block codes for DNA-based data storage. *IEEE Commun. Lett.* **2019**, *23*, 1676–1679. [CrossRef]
3. Nguyen, T.T.; Cai, K.; Immink, K.A.S.; Kiah, H.M. Capacity-Approaching Constrained Codes with Error Correction for DNA-Based Data Storage. *IEEE Trans. Inf. Theory* **2021**, *67*, 5602–5613. [CrossRef]
4. Kovačević, M.;Vukobratović, D. Asymptotic Behavior and Typicality Properties of Runlength-Limited Sequences. *IEEE Trans. Inf. Theory* **2022**, 68, 1638–1650. [CrossRef]
5. Popovski, P.; Fouladgar, A.M.; Simeone, O. Interactive joint transfer of energy and information. *IEEE Trans. Commun.* **2013**, *61*, 2086–2097. [CrossRef]
6. Fouladgar, A.M.; Simeone, O.; Erkip, E. Constrained codes for joint energy and information transfer. *IEEE Trans. Commun.* **2014**, *62*, 2121–2131. [CrossRef]

7. Tandon, A.; Motani, M.; Varshney, L.R. Subblock-constrained codes for real-time simultaneously energy and information transfer. *IEEE Trans. Inf. Theory* **2016**, *62*, 4212–4227. [CrossRef]
8. Immink, K.A.S.; Cai, K. Block Codes for Energy-Harvesting Sliding- Window Constrained Channels. *IEEE Commun. Lett.* **2020**, *24*, 2383–2386. [CrossRef]
9. Immink, K.A.S.; Cai, K. Properties and Constructions of Energy-Harvesting Sliding-Window Constrained Codes. *IEEE Commun. Lett.* **2020**, *24*, 1890–1893. [CrossRef]
10. Wu, T.Y.; Tandon, A.; Varshney, L.R.; Motani, M. Skip-sliding window codes. *IEEE Trans. Commun.* **2021**, *69*, 2824–2836. [CrossRef]
11. Marcus, B.H.; Roth, R.M.; Siegel, P.H. *An Introduction to Coding for Constrained Systems*; Lecture Notes; 2001. Available online: https://ronny.cswp.cs.technion.ac.il/wp-content/uploads/sites/54/2016/05/chapters1-9.pdf (accessed on 1 October 2020).
12. Kolesnik, V.D.; Krachkovsky, V.Y. Generating functions and lower bounds on rates for limiting error-correcting codes. *IEEE Trans. Inf. Theory* **1991**, *37*, 778–788. [CrossRef]
13. Gu, J.; Fuja, T. A generalized Gilbert-Varshamov bound derived via analysis of a code-search algorithm. *IEEE Trans. Inf. Theory* **1993**, *39*, 1089–1093. [CrossRef]
14. Marcus, B.H.; Roth, R.M. Improved Gilbert-Varshamov bound for constrained systems. *IEEE Trans. Inf. Theory* **1992**, *38*, 1213–1221. [CrossRef]
15. Winick, K.A.; Yang, S.H. Upper bounds on the size of error-correcting runlength-limited codes. *Eur. Trans. Telecommun.* **1996**, *37*, 273–283. [CrossRef]
16. Goyal, K.; Kiah, H.M. Evaluating the Gilbert-Varshamov Bound for Constrained Systems. In Proceedings of the 2022 IEEE International Symposium on Information Theory (ISIT), Espoo, Finland, 26 Jun–1 July 2022; pp. 1348–1353.
17. Tolhuizen, L.M.G.M. The generalized Gilbert-Varshamov bound is implied by Turan's theorem. *IEEE Trans. Inf. Theory* **1997**, *43*, 1605–1606. [CrossRef]
18. Luenberger, D.G. *Introduction to Linear and Nonlinear Programming*; Addison-Wesley: Reading, MA, USA, 1973.
19. Rockafellar, T. *Convex Analysis*; Princeton University: Pressrinceton, NJ, USA, 1970.
20. Kashyap, N.; Roth, R.M.; Siegel, P.H. The Capacity of Count-Constrained ICI-Free Systems. In Proceedings of the 2019 IEEE International Symposium on Information Theory (ISIT), Paris, France, 7–12 July 2019; pp. 1592–1596.
21. Tandon, A.; Kiah, H.M.; Motani, M. Bounds on the size and asymptotic rate of subblock-constrained codes. *IEEE Trans. Inf. Theory* **2018**, *64*, 6604–6619. [CrossRef]
22. Stewart, G.W. *Introduction to Matrix Computations*; Computer Science and Applied Mathematics; Academic Press: New York, NY, USA, 1973.

entropy

Article

Optimal Quaternary Hermitian LCD Codes

Liangdong Lu *, Ruihu Li and Yuezhen Ren

Fundamentals Department, Air Force Engineering University, Xi'an 710051, China; liruihu@aliyun.com (R.L.); renyzlw@163.com (Y.R.)
* Correspondence: kelinglv@163.com

Abstract: Linear complementary dual (LCD) codes, which are a class of linear codes introduced by Massey, have been extensively studied in the literature recently. It has been shown that LCD codes play a role in measures to counter passive and active side-channel analyses on embedded cryptosystems. In this paper, tables are presented of good quaternary Hermitian LCD codes and they are used in the construction of puncturing, shortening and combination codes. The results of this, including three tables of the best-known quaternary Hermitian LCD codes of any length $n \leq 25$ with corresponding dimension k, are presented. In addition, many of these quaternary Hermitian LCD codes given in this paper are optimal and saturate the lower or upper bound of Grassl's code table, and some of them are nearly optimal.

Keywords: quaternary code; Hermitian; linear complementary dual; linear code; optimal

1. Introduction

Let q be a power of a prime p, $\mathbb{F}_q$ be a finite field with q elements, and $\mathbb{F}_q^n$ be an n-dimensional vector space over $\mathbb{F}_q$. A q-ary $[n,k,d]_q$ linear code over $\mathbb{F}_q$ is a k-dimensional subspace of $\mathbb{F}_q^n$ with Hamming distance d. For a given $[n,k]_q$ linear code, the code $\mathcal{C}^{\perp} = \{x | x \cdot c = 0, c \in \mathcal{C}\}$ is called the dual code of $\mathcal{C}$. A q-ary linear code $\mathcal{C}$ is called a linear complementary dual (LCD) code if it meets its dual trivially, that is, $\mathcal{C} \cap \mathcal{C}^{\perp} = \{0\}$, which was given by Massey [1,2]. In addition to their applications in data storage, communication systems, and consumer electronics, LCD codes have recently been employed in cryptography and quantum error correcting. Carlet and Guilley in ref. [3] showed that LCD codes play an important role in armoring implementations against side-channel attacks and presented several constructions of LCD codes.

In [4], according to finite geometry theory, Lu et al. proposed the *radical codes* $\mathcal{R}(\mathcal{C})$ of $\mathcal{C}$ and $\mathcal{C}^{\perp}$, which are $\mathcal{R}(\mathcal{C}) = \mathcal{C} \cap \mathcal{C}^{\perp}$. If $\mathcal{R}(\mathcal{C}) = \mathcal{C} \cap \mathcal{C}^{\perp} = \{0\}$, then $\mathcal{C}$ is called a zero radical code, which is the same as the LCD code presented in [2]. Using these zero radical codes, they constructed families of maximal entanglement entanglement-assisted quantum error-correcting codes, which can help to engineer more reliable quantum communication schemes and quantum computers. Furthermore, constructions of Hermitian zero radical BCH codes were discussed in [5], which are also called reversible codes in [1] or LCD cyclic codes in [6]. Güneri et al. studied quasi-cyclic LCD codes and introduced Hermitian LCD codes [7]. Moreover, for the Euclidean case, the question of when cyclic codes are LCD codes is answered affirmatively by Yang and Massey in [8]. Ding et al. investigated LCD cyclic codes in [6], in which several families of LCD cyclic codes were constructed. It is shown that some LCD cyclic codes are optimal linear codes or have the best possible parameters for cyclic codes. Shi et al. constructed a lot of good LCD codes [9–12]. Moreover, many works have focused on the construction of LCD codes with good parameters, see [13–21].

Recently, Carlet, Mesnager, Tang, Qi and Pellikaan in [22] have shown that any $[n,k,d]$-linear code over $\mathbb{F}_{q^2}$ is equivalent to an $[n,k,d]$-linear Hermitian LCD code over $\mathbb{F}_{q^2}$ for $q > 2$. Araya, Harada and Saito in [23] gave some conditions for the nonexistence of quaternary Hermitian linear complementary dual codes with large minimum weights.

Inspired by these works and extending our previous work in [4], we study constructions of linear Hermitian LCD codes over $\mathbb{F}_4$. Then, some families of linear Hermitian LCD codes with good parameters are constructed from the known optimal codes via puncturing, extending, shortening and the combination method. Compared with the tables of best known linear codes (referred to as the *Database* later) maintained by Markus Grassl in [24], some of our codes presented in this paper saturate the lower bound of Grassl's code table.

In this paper, an optimal quaternary Hermitian LCD code $[18,7,9]$ is given, which improves the minimal distance of the codes in [4,25,26]. According to classification codes in [27], there exist some optimal quaternary Hermitian LCD codes $[15,4,8]$, $[16,4,9]$, $[17,4,10]$, $[19,4,13]$, $[23,5,14]$ and $[15,6,7]$. According to [24], the following quaternary Hermitian LCD codes we give in this section are also optimal linear codes: $[n,k,d]$ for $21 \leq n \leq 25$ and $16 \leq k \leq 18$; $[n-i, 15-i, d]$ for $21 \leq n \leq 24$ and $0 \leq i \leq 2$; and $[23,4,15]$, $[24,5,15]$, $[21,6,12]$, $[22,6,12]$, $[23,6,13]$, $[24,6,14]$, and $[25,8,12]$.

This paper is organized as follows. In Section 2, we provide some required basic knowledge on Hermitian LCD codes. We derive constructions of Hermitian LCD codes in Section 3. In Section 4, we discuss Hermitian LCD codes with good parameters.

2. Preliminary

In this section, we introduce some basic concepts on quaternary linear codes. Let $\mathbb{F}_4 = \{0, 1, \omega, \varpi\}$ be the Galois field with four elements, with $\varpi = 1 + \omega = \omega^2, \omega^3 = 1$. Denote the n-dimensional space over $\mathbb{F}_4$ by $\mathbb{F}_4^n$; we call a k-dimensional subspace C of $\mathbb{F}_4^n$ a k-dimensional linear code of length n and denote it as $C = [n,k]$. A matrix G whose rows form the basis of C is called a generator matrix of C. If the minimum distance of C is d, then C can be denoted as $C = [n,k,d]$. A code $C = [n,k,d]$ is an *optimal* code if there is no $[n,k,d+1]$ code. An *optimal* code is denoted $[n,k,d_o(n,k)]$ in this paper. For a given code $[n,k,d]$, if d is the largest value present known, then C is called the *best-known code and also denoted as* $[n,k,d_o(n,k)]$. Denote $d_l(n,k) = max\{d| \text{ as an } [n,k,d] \text{ LCD code}\}$. If a $C = [n,k,d_l(n,k)]$ LCD code saturates the lower or upper bound of Grassl's code table [24], we call C an optimal LCD code and can say $d_l(n,k) = d_o(n,k)$. If $d_l(n,k) = d_o(n,k) - 1$, we call C a nearly optimal LCD code.

Define the Hermitian inner product of u, $v \in \mathbb{F}_4^n$ as

$$(u,v)_h = uv^2 = u_1\bar{v}_1 + u_2\bar{v}_2 + \cdots + u_n\bar{v}_n.$$

The Hermitian dual code of $C = [n,k]$ is $C^{\perp h} = \{x \mid (x,y)_h = 0, \forall y \in C\}$, and $C^{\perp h} = [n, n-k]$. A generator matrix $H = H_{(n-k)\times n}$ of $C^{\perp h}$ is called a parity check matrix of C. If $C \subseteq C^{\perp h}$, C is called a *weakly self-orthogonal* code. If C is a self-orthogonal code, then each generator matrix G of C must satisfy rank$(GG^\dagger) = 0$, where $G^\dagger$ is the conjugate transpose of G.

If $C \cap C^{\perp h} = \{0\}$, then C (or $C^{\perp h}$) is called a *quaternary Hermitian LCD* code, and each generator matrix G of C must satisfy $k = $ rank$(GG^\dagger)$, see refs. [2,4].

In the following sections, we will discuss the construction of Hermitian quaternary LCD code $C = [n,k,d]$, where d is as large as possible for a given n and $k \leq 5$. Firstly, we present some notation for later use.

Let $\mathbf{1_n} = (1,1,...,1)_{1\times n}$ and $\mathbf{0_n} = (0,0,...,0)_{1\times n}$ denote an all-one vector and an all-zero vector of length n, respectively.

Construct

$$S_2 = \begin{pmatrix} 0 & 1 & 1 & 1 & 1 \\ 1 & 0 & 1 & \omega & \varpi \end{pmatrix} = (\alpha_1, ..., \alpha_5),$$

$$S_3 = \begin{pmatrix} S_2 & \mathbf{0}_{2\times 1} & S_2 & S_2 & S_2 \\ \mathbf{0}_5 & 1 & \mathbf{1}_5 & \omega\mathbf{1}_5 & \varpi\mathbf{1}_5 \end{pmatrix} = (\beta_1, \beta_2, \cdots, \beta_{21}),$$

$$S_4 = \begin{pmatrix} S_3 & \mathbf{0}_{3\times 1} & S_3 & S_3 & S_3 \\ \mathbf{0}_{21} & 1 & \mathbf{1}_{21} & \omega\mathbf{1}_{21} & \varpi\mathbf{1}_{21} \end{pmatrix} = (\gamma_1, \gamma_2, \cdots, \gamma_{85}).$$

$$S_5 = \begin{pmatrix} S_4 & \mathbf{0}_{4\times 1} & S_4 & S_4 & S_4 \\ \mathbf{0}_{85} & 1 & \mathbf{1}_{85} & \omega\mathbf{1}_{85} & \varpi\mathbf{1}_{85} \end{pmatrix} = (\zeta_1, \zeta_2, \cdots, \zeta_{341}).$$

$$\vdots$$

$$S_k = \begin{pmatrix} S_{k-1} & \mathbf{0}_{k-1\times 1} & S_{k-1} & S_{k-1} & S_{k-1} \\ \mathbf{0}_{\frac{4(k-1)}{3}} & 1 & \mathbf{1}_{\frac{4(k-1)}{3}} & \omega\mathbf{1}_{\frac{4(k-1)}{3}} & \varpi\mathbf{1}_{\frac{4(k-1)}{3}} \end{pmatrix}$$

It is well known that the matrix S_2 generates the $[5,2,4]$ simplex code with weight polynomial $1+15y^4$. S_3 generates the $[21,3,16]$ simplex code with weight polynomial $1+63y^{16}$. S_4 generates the $[85,4,64]$ simplex code with weight polynomial $1+255y^{64}$, S_5 generates the $[341,5,256]$ simplex code with weight polynomial $1+1023y^{256}$, and $S_k S_k^\dagger = 0$ for $k = 2,3,4,5,\cdots$, see ref. [28].

Notation

In the following sections, the conjugation is defined by $\bar{x} = x^2$ for $x \in \mathbf{F}_4$. We use 2 and 3 to represent ω and ϖ in each generator matrix of linear codes, respectively. An $[n,k,d]_4$ code is denoted as $[n,k,d]$ for short.

3. Hermitian LCD Linear Codes over $\mathbb{F}_4$

In this subsection, we discuss the construction of $[n,k]$ optimal Hermitian quaternary LCD codes. For $k \geq 5$ and $n \leq 20$, there are some Hermitian quaternary LCD codes in [21, 23, 26, 28]. For $20 \leq n \leq 25$, there is no systematic discussion in the literature. The discussion is presented in four cases for $n \leq 25$.

Lemma 1 ([4,29]). *If $21 \leq n \leq 25$ and $1 \leq k \leq 5$, then $d_l(2,24) = 18$, $d_l(2,25) = 19$, $d_l(3,21) = 15$, $d_l(3,22) = 15$, $d_l(4,22) = 14$, $d_l(4,23) = 15$, $d_l(5,24) = 15$. All the other Hermitian quaternary LCD codes saturate the lower bound of Grassl's code table [24].*

Proof. Refs. [4,29] proved this lemma. □

Lemma 2 ([30]). *There exist $[n,n-2,2]$ and $[n,n-3,2]$ quaternary Hermitian LCD codes.*

Proof. (1) For when n is even, let $G = \left[I_2 \middle| \frac{\mathbf{1}_{1\times n}}{\mathbf{0}_{1\times n}} \right]$. If G is a check matrix of C with generator matrix H, then $C = [n,n-2,2]$ and $rank(HH^h) = n-2$. For when n is even, let $G = \left[I_2 \begin{pmatrix} \varpi \\ \varpi \end{pmatrix} \middle| \frac{\mathbf{1}_{1\times n}}{{}_{1\times n}} \right]$. If G is a check matrix of C with generator matrix H, then $C = [n,n-2,2]$ and $rank(HH^h) = n-2$.

(2) For when n is odd, let $G = \left[I_3 \middle| \frac{\mathbf{1}_{1\times n}}{\mathbf{0}_{2\times n}} \right]$. If G is a check matrix of C with generator matrix H, then $C = [n,n-3,2]$ and $rank(HH^h) = n-3$. For when n is even, let $G = \left[I_3 \begin{pmatrix} \varpi \\ \varpi \\ 0 \end{pmatrix} \middle| \frac{\mathbf{1}_{1\times n}}{\mathbf{0}_{2\times n}} \right]$. If G is a check matrix of C with generator matrix H, then $C = [n,n-3,2]$ and $rank(HH^h) = n-3$. □

Theorem 1. *If $21 \leq n \leq 25$ and $13 \leq k \leq 18$, then there exist 29 optimal quaternary Hermitian LCD codes saturating the lower bound of Grassl's code table [24], as in Table 1.*

Table 1. **Optimal quaternary Hermitian LCD codes with** $21 \le n \le 25$ **and** $13 \le k \le 19$**.**

$n\backslash k$	13	14	15	16	17	18	19
21	6	5	5	4	3	2	2
22	6	6	5	4	4	3	2
23		6	6	5	4	4	3
24			6	6	5	4	4
25				6	6	5	4

Proof. For $21 \le n \le 25$, calculating by Magma, one can obtain nine optimal LCD codes as follows: $[21,14,5]$, $[21,15,5]$, $[21,16,4]$, $[22,16,4]$, $[24,16,6]$, $[22,18,3]$, $[23,18,4]$, $[25,18,5]$, $[23,19,3]$.

And then, calculating by Magma, one can obtain another five optimal codes, $[27,19,6]$, $[26,21,4]$, $[25,18,5]$, $[26,20,4]$, $[33,24,6]$, which are not all quaternary Hermitian LCD codes.

Case 1. Construction of quaternary Hermitian LCD codes via puncturing. Puncturing $\mathcal{C} = [23,15,6]$ on coordinate sets $\{16\}$, $\{1,19\}$, one can obtain $[22,15,5]$ and $[21,17,3]$ Hermitian quaternary LCD codes. Puncturing $\mathcal{C} = [24,17,5]$ on coordinate sets $\{1,18\}$, one can obtain the $[22,17,4]$ Hermitian quaternary LCD code. Puncturing $\mathcal{C} = [24,19,4]$on coordinate sets $\{1,4,8\}$, one can obtain the $[21,19,2]$ quaternary Hermitian LCD code.

Case 2. Construction of LCD codes via shortening. Shortening $\mathcal{C} = [27,19,6]$ on coordinate sets $\{1,4\}$, $\{1,2,3,8\}$, $\{1,2,3,4,7\}$, $\{1,2,3,4,7,8\}$, one can obtain the $[25,17,6]$, $[23,15,6]$, $[22,14,6]$, $[21,13,6]$ Hermitian quaternary LCD codes, respectively. Shortening $\mathcal{D} = [26,21,4]$ on coordinate sets $\{1\}$, $\{1,2\}$ obtain $[25,20,4]$ and $[24,19,4]$ Hermitian quaternary LCD codes, respectively. Shortening $\mathcal{D} = [25,18,5]$ on coordinate sets $\{4\}$ and $\{1,4\}$, one can obtain the $[24,17,5]$, $[23,16,5]$ Hermitian quaternary LCD codes. Shortening $\mathcal{D} = [26,20,4]$ on coordinate sets $\{1\}$, $\{1,2\}$, $\{1,2,4\}$, one can obtain the $[25,19,4]$, $[24,18,4]$, $[23,17,4]$ Hermitian quaternary LCD codes. Shortening $\mathcal{D} = [33,24,6]$ on coordinate sets $\{1,2,3,4,5,6,7,8\}$ and $\{1,2,3,4,5,6,7,8,9\}$, one can obtain the $[25,16,6]$ and $[24,15,6]$ Hermitian quaternary LCD codes. Shortening $\mathcal{D} = [33,24,6]$ on coordinate sets $\{1,2,3,4,5,6,7,8,9,10\}$ and $\{1,2,3,4,5,6,7,8,9,10,14\}$, one can obtain the $\mathcal{C} = [23,14,6]$ and $[22,13,6]$ Hermitian quaternary LCD codes. □

Remark 1. *In Theorem 2, all of the codes are optimal quaternary Hermitian LCD codes. Since* $[21,3,16]$ *is a simplex code, there is no* $[21,18,3]$ *quaternary Hermitian LCD code. Hence,* $[21,18,2]$ *is an optimal quaternary Hermitian LCD code. By shortening* $\mathcal{D} = [33,24,6]$ *on coordinate sets* $\{1,2,3,4,5,6,7,8,9,10,11,12\}$*, we can obtain* $\mathcal{C} = [21,12,6]$*. This is a nearly optimal quaternary Hermitian LCD code with weight enumerator* $1 + 279z^6 + 1116z^7 + 5739z^8 + 22023z^9 + 79815z^{10} + \ldots$*.*

Theorem 2. *If* $21 \le n \le 25$ *and* $6 \le k \le 8$*, then* $d_l(6,21) = 12$*,* $d_l(6,22) = 12$*,* $d_l(6,23) = 13$*,* $d_l(6,24) = 14$*,* $d_l(8,25) = 12$*,* $d_l(7,20) = 10$*. All these codes are quaternary Hermitian LCD codes saturating the lower or upper bound of Grassl's code table.*

Proof. A constacyclic code $\mathcal{C} = [21,15,5]$ is given in [21], where its generator polynomial is $x^6 + \overline{\omega}x^5 + x^4 + \overline{\omega}x^2 + x + \overline{\omega}$. The dual code of $\mathcal{C}$ is the code $\mathcal{D} = [21,6,12]$ with a generator matrix $G_{6,21}$, and both $\mathcal{C}$ and $\mathcal{D}$ are quaternary Hermitian LCD codes.

Let

$$G_{6,21} = \begin{pmatrix} 211210221102122100000 \\ 303201310313021010000 \\ 221130310133220001000 \\ 022113031013322000100 \\ 320131031302101000010 \\ 223203322032332000001 \end{pmatrix},$$

$$G_{6,24} = \begin{pmatrix} 100000111120112310122020 \\ 010000011112011231012202 \\ 001000201111101123201220 \\ 000100120111310112020122 \\ 000010112011231011202012 \\ 000001111201123101220201 \end{pmatrix},$$

$$G_{7,20} = \begin{pmatrix} 11011111101000000011 \\ 11120323003110000012 \\ 30132223011030000020 \\ 11202023001001100001 \\ 11000132002013010001 \\ 30220233000013001003 \\ 30313002003012000101 \end{pmatrix},$$

$$G_{8,25} = \begin{pmatrix} 1000000010012123213103310 \\ 0100000031322111123203311 \\ 0010000012120332303223021 \\ 0001000021122001100022303 \\ 0000100013332221330202233 \\ 0000010010113203310220220 \\ 0000001001011320330022022 \\ 0000000112200212232000033 \end{pmatrix},$$

There exists a quaternary Hermitian LCD code $[24, 6, 14]$ with generator matrix $G_{6,24}$. Its weight enumerator is $1 + 207z^{14} + 378z^{15} + 630z^{16} + 360z^{17} + 495z^{18} + 1062z^{19} + 585z^{20} + 180z^{21} + 162z^{22} + 36z^{23}$. Puncturing $\mathcal{C} = [24, 6, 14]$ on coordinate sets $\{7\}$, $\{1,3\}$, we can obtain two quaternary Hermitian LCD codes: $[23, 6, 13]$, $[22, 6, 12]$.

There exists a quaternary Hermitian LCD code $[20, 7, 10]$ with generator matrix $G_{7,20}$. Its weight enumerator is $1 + 210z^{10} + 594z^{11} + 969z^{12} + 1647z^{13} + 2703z^{14} + 3519z^{15} + 3060z^{16} + 2205z^{17} + 1107z^{18} + 291z^{19} + 78z^{20}$.

There exists a quaternary Hermitian LCD code $[25, 8, 12]$ with generator matrix $G_{8,25}$. Its weight enumerator is $1 + 177z^{12} + 540z^{13} + 1365z^{14} + 2721z^{15} + 4836z^{16} + 8283z^{17} + 10938z^{18} + 11694z^{19} + 10983z^{20} + 7734z^{21} + 4185z^{22} + 1617z^{23} + 411z^{24} + 25z^{25}$.

Shortening the $[25, 8, 12]$ quaternary Hermitian LCD code on coordinate sets $\{2\}$, one can obtain $[24, 7, 12]$. Its weight enumerator is $1 + 102z^{12} + 267z^{13} + 561z^{14} + 1086z^{15} + 1764z^{16} + 2628z^{17} + 3144z^{18} + 2730z^{19} + 2226z^{20} + 1233z^{21} + 495z^{22} + 120z^{23} + 27z^{24}$. We can deduce a submatrix $G_{7,25}$ from $G_{8,25}$. Setting $G_{7,25}$ as a generator matrix, one can obtain $[25, 7, 12]$. □

Theorem 3. *If $21 \leq n \leq 25$ and $8 \leq k \leq 15$, then there exist 27 quaternary Hermitian LCD codes, as in Table 2.*

Table 2. **Optimal quaternary Hermitian LCD codes with** $21 \leq n \leq 25$ **and** $8 \leq k \leq 15$.

$n \backslash k$	8	9	10	11	12	13	14	15
21	9	8	7	6				
22	10	8	8	7	6			
23	11	9	8	8	7	6		
24	11	10	9	8	8	7	6	
25		11	10	9	8	7	7	6

Proof. Let

$$A_{12}^{\top} = \begin{pmatrix} 300201200120300312 \\ 330322220222130112 \\ 133330122212313132 \\ 213031312011331230 \\ 002033213230313123 \\ 021303131201133123 \\ 300300221033231123 \\ 330133122213123323 \\ 033110212131112103 \\ 203212121103311021 \\ 020120012030031210 \\ 002012001203003121 \end{pmatrix},$$

$$A_{11}^{\top} = \begin{pmatrix} 1232130030332100 \\ 3202331131102132 \\ 1100132302320200 \\ 1321332231223320 \\ 0013213203303002 \\ 0131021110330323 \\ 1322322221212333 \\ 2203012112300132 \\ 3122131011102120 \\ 0002212120320222 \\ 3223331032121221 \end{pmatrix}.$$

There exists a code $[30, 18, 8]$ with generator matrix $G_{18,30} = \left[I_{18} \middle| A_{12} \right]$. It is not a quaternary Hermitian LCD code. Shortening $\mathcal{C} = [30, 18, 8]$ on coordinate sets $\{1, 3, 6, 12, 13, 17\}$, $\{1, 2, 3, 4, 5, 6, 8\}$, $\{1, 2, 3, 4, 5, 6, 7, 8\}$ and $\{1, 2, 3, 4, 5, 6, 7, 8, 10\}$, one can obtain quaternary Hermitian LCD codes $[24, 12, 8]$, $[23, 11, 8]$, $[22, 10, 8]$ and $[21, 9, 8]$, respectively.

There exists a code $[27, 16, 7]$ with generator matrix $G_{16,27} = \left[I_{16} \middle| A_{11} \right]$. Shortening $\mathcal{C} = [27, 16, 7]$ on coordinate sets $\{1, 2\}, \{1, 2, 3\}, \{1, 2, 3, 4\}$, $\{1, 2, 3, 4, 5\}$ and $\{1, 2, 3, 4, 5, 6\}$, one can obtain quaternary Hermitian LCD codes $[25, 14, 7]$, $[24, 13, 7]$, $[23, 12, 7]$, $[22, 11, 7]$ and $[21, 10, 7]$, respectively.

$$\text{Let } A_{10}^{\top} = \begin{pmatrix} 11121122120230323210 \\ 00000000000000000000 \\ 12103313201003102111 \\ 11331313032000112032 \\ 21133320003300003220 \\ 01030322203233222121 \\ 32210120113300112032 \\ 00331212201211230320 \\ 11321302013232210003 \\ 11010110212023020323 \end{pmatrix},$$

$$B_{16} = \begin{pmatrix} 0331200330200 \\ 0033102033020 \\ 2330330112100 \\ 0233003311210 \\ 1201303302020 \\ 2213122121000 \\ 0221321212100 \\ 0022113221210 \\ 1220202211020 \\ 2211033130300 \\ 0221130313030 \\ 3133123113000 \\ 0313331211300 \\ 0031313321130 \\ 3112111310210 \\ 1133222202120 \end{pmatrix},$$

There exists a code $[30, 20, 6]$ with generator matrix $G_{20,30} = \left[I_{20} \middle| A_{10} \right]$. Shortening $\mathcal{C} = [30, 20, 6]$ on coordinate sets $\{1, 2, 3, 4, 5\}, \{1, 2, 3, 4, 5, 6\}, \{1, 2, 3, 5, 6, 7, 13\}$, $\{1, 2, 3, 4, 5, 6, 7, 8, 9\}$ and $\{1, 2, 3, 4, 5, 6, 7, 8\}$, one can obtain quaternary Hermitian LCD codes $[25, 15, 6]$, $[24, 14, 6]$, $[23, 13, 6]$, $[22, 12, 6]$ and $[21, 11, 6]$, respectively.

There exists a code $[29, 16, 8]$ with generator matrix $G_{16,29} = \left[I_{16} \middle| B_{16} \right]$. It is not a quaternary Hermitian LCD code. Shortening $\mathcal{C} = [29, 16, 8]$ on coordinate sets $\{1, 2, 3, 4\}$, $\{1, 2, 3, 4, 6\}$, $\{1, 2, 3, 4, 5, 6\}$, $\{1, 2, 3, 4, 5, 6, 8\}$, $\{1, 2, 3, 4, 5, 6, 7, 8\}$, one can obtain quaternary Hermitian LCD codes $[25, 12, 8]$, $[24, 11, 8]$, $[23, 10, 8]$, $[22, 9, 8]$ and $[21, 8, 8]$, respectively.

$$\text{Let } A_{14} = \begin{pmatrix} 13000123002211 \\ 10211103211330 \\ 01021110321133 \\ 33231222301220 \\ 03323122230122 \\ 22110130001230 \\ 02211013000123 \\ 33112232033321 \\ 12200332312223 \\ 32113300102111 \\ 12300221101300 \\ 01230022110130 \\ 00123002211013 \\ 33321033112232 \\ 21110321133001 \\ 11111111111111 \end{pmatrix},$$

$$A_{15} = \begin{pmatrix} 102333010301203 \\ 210033301030123 \\ 122000202121223 \\ 013221122033211 \\ 202131213310100 \\ 220013121331010 \\ 223330023223223 \\ 123212100103011 \\ 113310121300022 \\ 212032120112232 \\ 322220031221030 \\ 033023210111210 \\ 000220311212022 \\ 000312113202231 \\ 000121022211230 \\ 000102331310131 \end{pmatrix},$$

$$A_{12} = \begin{pmatrix} 333231302012 \\ 122021230233 \\ 012231331333 \\ 110121333101 \\ 322213123331 \\ 123133323323 \\ 321131111021 \\ 301331322211 \\ 212033023133 \\ 021232013200 \\ 113202212020 \\ 000012102221 \\ 000001110222 \end{pmatrix},$$

There exists a code $[30,16,9]$ with generator matrix $G_{16,30} = \left[I_{16} \middle| A_{14}\right]$. It is not a quaternary Hermitian LCD code. Shortening $\mathcal{C} = [30,16,9]$ on coordinate sets $\{1,2,3,4,5\}$, $\{1,2,3,4,5,11\}$, $\{1,2,3,4,5,6,11\}$ and $\{1,2,3,4,5,6,11\}$, one can obtain quaternary Hermitian LCD codes $[25,11,9]$, $[24,10,9]$, $[23,9,9]$ and $[22,8,9]$, respectively.

There exists a code $[31,16,10]$ with generator matrix $G_{16,31} = \left[I_{16} \middle| A_{15}\right]$. It is not a quaternary Hermitian LCD code. Shortening $\mathcal{C} = [31,16,10]$ on coordinate sets $\{8,9,10,11,16\}$, $\{1,6,9,10,12,15\}$, $\{2,4,5,9,10,13,15\}$ and $\{3,4,7,8,11,12,13,15\}$, one can obtain quaternary Hermitian LCD codes $[26,11,10]$, $[25,10,10]$, $[24,9,10]$ and $[23,8,11]$, respectively. Puncturing $\mathcal{C} = [23,8,11]$ on coordinate sets $\{2\}$ and $\{1,2\}$, one can obtain quaternary Hermitian LCD codes $[22,8,10]$ and $[21,8,9]$, respectively.

There exists a quaternary Hermitian LCD code $[25,13,7]$ with generator matrix $G_{13,25} = \left[I_{13} \middle| A_{12}\right]$. □

Theorem 4. *$d_l(7,21) = 10$, $d_l(7,22) = 11, d_l(7,22) = 11$, $d_l(7,23) = 12$, $d_l(7,25) = 13$, $d_l(6,25) = 14$, $d_l(12,25) = 8$, $d_l(13,25) = 7$, $d_l(7,18) = 9$ and $d_l(7,19) = 9$ are Hermitian quaternary LCD codes.*

Proof. Let

$$G_{7,24} = \begin{pmatrix} 022312110003211100000321 \\ 102231211000321110000032 \\ 110223121100032121000003 \\ 211022311110003232100000 \\ 121102232111000303210000 \\ 312110223211100000321000 \\ 231211020321110000032100 \end{pmatrix},$$

$$G_{7,25} = \begin{pmatrix} 1100000032031300131303121 \\ 0010000003203130213130311 \\ 0001000003123223332223321 \\ 0000100033111212020312021 \\ 0000010020112011011101111 \\ 0000001011212331312020201 \\ 0000000112322303222332331 \end{pmatrix},$$

$$G_{7,19} = \begin{pmatrix} 1130121231010000000 \\ 0133203320031200000 \\ 0303332320310100000 \\ 0131030320010011000 \\ 0130001110020230300 \\ 0301202120000230010 \\ 0302110010030220003 \end{pmatrix},$$

$$G_{6,25} = \begin{pmatrix} 3111201330100001230133122 \\ 1111110133030000122013312 \\ 2311100013323000012201331 \\ 1131131001312300001220133 \\ 1213130100101230003122013 \\ 1121313010000123003312201 \end{pmatrix}$$

There exists a code $[24,7,13]$ with generator matrix $G_{7,24}$. Its weight enumerator is $1+384z^{13}+744z^{14}+888z^{15}+1746z^{16}+2544z^{17}+3156z^{18}+2928z^{19}+2118z^{20}+1200z^{21}+540z^{22}+120z^{23}+15z^{24}$. It is not a quaternary Hermitian LCD code. Puncturing $\mathcal{C}_1$ on coordinate sets $\{1\}$, $\{1,3\}$, $\{1,2,7\}$, we can obtain $[23,7,12]$, $[22,7,11]$, $[21,7,10]$ quaternary Hermitian LCD codes.

There exists a quaternary Hermitian LCD code $[25,7,13]$ with generator matrix $G_{7,25}$. Its weight enumerator is $1+189z^{13}+495z^{14}+750z^{15}+1179z^{16}+1908z^{17}+2577z^{18}+2967z^{19}+2667z^{20}+1932z^{21}+1092z^{22}+495z^{23}+117z^{24}+15z^{25}$.

There exists a quaternary Hermitian LCD code $[25,6,14]$ with generator matrix $G_{6,25}$. Its weight enumerator is $1+48z^{14}+240z^{15}+432z^{16}+534z^{17}+573z^{18}+648z^{19}+657z^{20}+510z^{21}+363z^{22}+84z^{23}+6z^{24}$.

There exists an optimal quaternary Hermitian LCD code $[19,7,9]$ with generator matrix $G_{7,19}$. Its weight enumerator is $1+195z^{9}+483z^{10}+888z^{11}+1479z^{12}+2361z^{13}+3165z^{14}+3327z^{15}+2508z^{16}+1368z^{17}+492z^{18}+117z^{19}$. Puncturing the quaternary Hermitian LCD code $[19,7,9]$ on coordinate sets $\{1\}$, one can obtain the optimal quaternary Hermitian LCD code $[18,7,9]$ with weight enumerator $1+393z^{9}+666z^{10}+1245z^{11}+2193z^{12}+3315z^{13}+3597z^{14}+2799z^{15}+1554z^{16}+504z^{17}+117z^{18}$. □

4. Discussion and Conclusions

This paper is dedicated to the construction of quaternary Hermitian LCD codes. For $k \le n$ and $n \le 25$, each $[n,k]$ quaternary Hermitian LCD code is constructed. Some of these quaternary Hermitian LCD codes constructed in this paper are optimal codes which saturate the bound of the minimum distance of the code table in [24], and some of them are nearly optimal codes. According to weight enumerators for classification codes in [27], there exist some optimal codes, $[15,4,9]$, $[16,4,10]$, $[17,4,11]$, $[19,4,14]$, and $[23,5,15]$, which are not LCD codes. In addition, the number of these five optimal codes is one.

Thus, the $[15,4,8]$, $[16,4,9]$, $[17,4,10]$, $[19,4,13]$, and $[23,5,14]$ quaternary Hermitian LCD codes in this paper are optimal. In [27], all of the codes with parameters of $[15,6,8]$ are self-orthogonal. Thus, the quaternary Hermitian LCD code in this paper, $[15,6,7]$, is also optimal. We emphasize that there are three quaternary Hermitian LCD codes, $[18,7,9]$, $[19,7,9]$ and $[20,7,10]$, which are optimal.

According to ref. [24], the following quaternary Hermitian LCD codes constructed in this paper are also optimal codes with parameters of $[n,k,d]$ for $21 \leq n \leq 25$ and $16 \leq k \leq 18$; $[n-i, 15-i, d]$ for $21 \leq n \leq 24$ and $0 \leq i \leq 2$: $[23,4,15]$, $[24,5,15]$, $[21,6,12]$, $[22,6,12]$, $[23,6,13]$, $[24,6,14]$, $[25,8,12]$ and $[20,7,10]$. Except for these codes mentioned above, the quaternary Hermitian LCD codes constructed in this paper do not reach the known upper or lower bounds of the minimum distance of a linear code. Nonetheless, the minimum distances of these codes appears to be the best possible. These codes are the best possible among those obtainable by our approach.

Combining the results in the previous subsections, we improved the table of lower and upper bounds on the minimum distance of quaternary Hermitian LCD codes for $n \leq 20$ [4,25,30] in Table 3. In addition, many lower and upper bounds of the minimal distance of Hermitian LCD codes with a length of $n \leq 25$ are listed. To make the bounds in Table 3 tighter, we need to choose other quaternary Hermitian LCD codes better than those given in this paper and investigate other code constructions to raise the lower bounds. We also plan to explore the construction of Hermitian LCD codes from a geometric aspect to decrease the upper bounds.

In [4,20,25], it has been shown that if there exists a quaternary Hermitian $[n,k,d]$ code over F_{q^2}, then there exists a maximal entanglement entanglement-assisted quantum error correcting code (EAQECC) over F_q with parameters $[[n, 2k-n+c, d; c]]$, where c is the rank of the product of the parity check matrix and its conjugate. Moreover, a maximal entanglement EAQECC derived from an LCD code has the same minimum distance as the underlying classical code. Hence, all of the optimal quaternary Hermitian LCD codes can be used to construct optimal binary maximal entanglement EAQECCs. In addition, from the three quaternary Hermitian LCD codes $[18,7,9]$ given in this paper, a maximal entanglement EAQECC $[[18,7,9;11]]$ can be constructed, which improves the minimal distance of the codes in [4,25]. The maximal entanglement EAQECCs $[[19,7,9;12]]$ and $[[20,7,10;12]]$ are optimal and are different to the codes constructed in [30].

Table 3. Lower and upper bounds on the minimum distance of quaternary Hermitian LCD codes. The bold entries represent improvements over prior work. The superscript * represents the codes that achieve bounds given in the Grassl table.

$n\backslash k$	1	2	3	4	5	6	7	8	9	10	11	12
3	3 *	2 *										
4	3 *	2	1									
5	5 *	3	2	2 *								
6	5 *	4 *	3	2 *	1							
7	7 *	5 *	4 *	3 *	2 *	2 *						
8	7 *	6 *	5 *	4 *	3 *	2 *	1					
9	9 *	6	6 *	5 *	4 *	3 *	2 *	2 *				
10	9 *	7	6 *	6 *	5 *	4 *	3 *	2 *	1	1		
11	11 *	8 *	7 *	6 *	6 *	5 *	4 *	3 *	2 *	2 *	1	
12	11 *	9 *	8 *	7 *	6 *	5	4 *	4 *	3 *	2 *	2 *	1
13	13 *	10 *	9 *	8 *	7 *	6 *	5 *	4 *	4 *	3 *	2 *	2 *
14	13 *	10	9	8	7–8	7 *	6 *	5 *	4 *	4 *	3 *	2 *
15	15 *	11	10	9	8 *	7	7 *	6 *	5 *	4 *	4 *	3 *
16	15 *	12 *	11	10	9 *	8 *	7–8	6–7	6 *	5 *	4 *	4 *
17	17 *	13 *	12 *	11	10 *	9 *	7–8	7–8	6–7	6 *	5 *	4 *
18	17 *	14 *	13 *	11–12	10 *	9–10	**9** *	8 *	7–8	6 *	5–6	5 *

Table 3. *Cont.*

$n\backslash k$	1	2	3	4	5	6	7	8	9	10	11	12
19	19 *	14	13	12 *–13	11 *	10 *	9 *	8 *–9	8 *	7 *	6 *	5–6
20	19 *	15	14	13 *	12 *	11 *	10 *	9 *	8 *–9	7–8	6–7	6 *
21	21 *	16 *	15	14 *	12	12 *	10–11	9–10	8–9	7–9	6–8	6–7
22	22 *	17 *	15	14	13	12 *–13	11–12	**10**	8–10	8–9	7–9	6–8
23	23 *	18 *	16 *	15	14	13 *	12 *–13	11	9–11	8–10	8–9	7–9
24	24 *	18	17 *	16 *	15	14 *	12–13	11–13	10–12	9–11	8–10	8–9
25	25 *	19	18 *	17 *	15	14–15	13–14	12 *–13	11–13	10–12	9–11	8–10
$n\backslash k$	13	14	15	16	17	18	19	20	21	22	23	24
14	1											
15	2 *	2 *										
16	3 *	2 *	1									
17	3–4	3 *	2 *	2 *								
18	4 *	3 *	3 *	2 *	1							
19	5 *	4 *	3 *	3 *	2 *	2 *						
20	5–6	5 *	4 *	3 *	2	2 *	1	1				
21	6 *	5 *–6	5 *	4 *	3 *	2	2 *	2 *	1			
22	6 *–7	6 *	5 *–6	4 *–5	4 *	3 *	2 *	2 *	2	1		
23	6–8	6 *–7	6 *	5 *–6	4 *–5	4 *	2 *	2 *	2 *	2 *	1 *	
24	7–9	6–8	6 *–7	6 *	5 *–6	4 *–5	3 *	3 *	2 *	2 *	2 *	1 *
25	7–9	7–9	6–8	6 *–7	6 *	5 *–6	4 *	4 *	3 *	2 *	2 *	2 *

Author Contributions: L.L. completed research design, data analysis, and the leading of writing of the article; R.L. provided important guidance in solving difficult or complex problems in the manuscript; Y.R. proofread all drafts. All authors contributed to the writing and revision of the article, providing constructive suggestions and improvements to ensure that the article accurately expresses complex research findings. All authors have read and agreed to the published version of the manuscript.

Funding: This research was funded by National Natural Science Foundation of China: U21A20428; Natural Science Foundation of Shaanxi: 2023-JC-YB-003 and 2023-JC-QN-0033.

Data Availability Statement: The authors confirm that the data supporting the findings of this study are available within the manuscript.

Conflicts of Interest: The authors declare no conflicts of interest.

References

1. Massey, J.L. Reversible codes. *Inf. Control* **1964**, *7*, 369–380. [CrossRef]
2. Massey, J.L. Linear codes with complementary duals. *Discret. Math.* **1992**, *106–107*, 337–342. [CrossRef]
3. Carlet, C.; Guilley, S. Complementary dual codes for counter-measures to side-channel attacks. *Adv. Math. Commun.* **2016**, *10*, 131–150. [CrossRef]
4. Lu, L.; Li, R.; Guo, L.; Fu, Q. Maximal entanglement entanglement-assisted quantum codes constructed from linear codes. *Quantum Inf. Process.* **2015**, *14*, 165–182. [CrossRef]
5. Lv, L.; Li, R.; Fu, Q.; Li, X. Maximal entanglement entanglement-assisted quantum codes constructed from quaternary BCH codes. In Proceedings of the IEEE Advanced Information Technology, Electronic and Automation Control Conference, Chongqing, China, 19–20 December 2015.
6. Ding, C.; Li, C.; Li, S. LCD cyclic codes over finite fields. *IEEE Trans. Inf. Theory* **2018**, *63*, 4344–4356.
7. Güneri, C.; Özkaya, B.; Solé, P. Quasi-cyclic complementary dual codes. *Finite Fields Their Appl.* **2016**, *42*, 67–80. [CrossRef]
8. Yang, X.; Massey, J.L. The necessary and sufficient condition for a cyclic code to have a complementary dual. *Discret. Math.* **1994**, *126*, 391–393. [CrossRef]
9. Shi, M.; Özbudak, F.; Xu, L.; Solé, P. LCD codes from tridiagonal Toeplitz matrices. *Finite Fields Their Appl.* **2021**, *75*, 101892. [CrossRef]
10. Shi, M.; Huang, D.; Sok, L.; Solé, P. Double circulant LCD codes over Z_4. *Finite Fields Their Appl.* **2019**, *58*, 133–144. [CrossRef]

11. Sok, L.; Shi, M.; Solé, P. Construction of optimal LCD codes over large finite fields. *Finite Fields Their Appl.* **2018**, *50*, 138–153. [CrossRef]
12. Shi, M.; Li, S.; Kim, J.; Solé, P. LCD and ACD codes over a noncommutative non-unital ring with four elements. *Cryptogr. Commun.* **2022**, *14*, 627–640. [CrossRef]
13. Hou, X.; Oggier, F. On LCD codes and lattices. In Proceedings of the IEEE International Symposium on Information Theory (ISIT), Barcelona, Spain, 10–15 July 2016; pp. 1501–1505. [CrossRef]
14. Lina, E.R.L.; Nocon, E.G. On the construction of some LCD codes over finite fields. *Manila J. Sci.* **2016**, *9*, 67–82.
15. Zhu, S.; Pang, B.; Sun, Z. The reversible negacyclic codes over finite fields. *arXiv* **2016**, arXiv:1610.08206v1.
16. Galvez, L.; Kim, J.; Lee, N.; Roe, Y.; Won, B. Some bounds on binary LCD codes. *Cryptogr. Commun.* **2018**, *10*, 719–728. [CrossRef]
17. Araya, M.; Harada, M. On the classification of linear complementary dual codes. *Discret. Math.* **2019**, *342*, 270–278. [CrossRef]
18. Araya, M.; Harada, M. On the minimum weights of binary linear complementary dual codes. *Cryptogr. Commun.* **2019**, *12*, 285–300. [CrossRef]
19. Fu, Q.; Li, R.; Fu, F.; Rao, Y. On the Construction of Binary Optimal LCD Codes with Short Length. *Int. J. Found. Comput. Sci.* **2019**, *30*, 1237–1245. [CrossRef]
20. Lai, C.; Brun, T.; Wilde, M. Duality in Entanglement-assisted quantum error correction. *IEEE Trans. Inf. Theory* **2013**, *59*, 4020–4024. [CrossRef]
21. Dougherty, S.T.; Kim, J.-L.; Ozkaya, B.; Sok, L.; Solé, P. The combinatorics of LCD codes: Linear Programming bound and orthogonal matrices. *Int. J. Inf. Coding Theory* **2017**, *4*, 116–128. [CrossRef]
22. Carlet, C.; Mesnager, S.; Tang, C.; Qi, Y.; Pellikaan, R. Linear Codes Over F_q Are Equivalent to LCD Codes for $q > 3$. *IEEE Trans. Inf. Theory* **2018**, *64*, 3010–3017. [CrossRef]
23. Araya, M.; Harada, M.; Saito, K. Quaternary Hermitian linear complementary dual codes. *IEEE Trans. Inf. Theory* **2020**, *66*, 2751–2759. [CrossRef]
24. Grassl, M. Bounds on the Minimum Distance of Linear Codes. 2024. Available online: http://www.codetables.de (accessed on 28 February 2024).
25. Lai, C.; Ashikhmin, A. Linear Programming Bounds for Entanglement-Assisted Quantum Error-Correcting Codes by Split Weight Enumerators. *IEEE Trans. Inf. Theory* **2018**, *64*, 622–639. [CrossRef]
26. Kschischang, F.; Pasupathy, S. Some ternary and quantum codes and associated sphere pachings. *IEEE Trans. Inform. Theory* **1992**, *38*, 227–246. [CrossRef]
27. Bouyukliev, L.; Grassl, M.; Varbanov, Z. New bounds for $n_4(k,d)$ and classification of some optimal codes over $GF(4)$. *Discret. Math.* **2004**, *281*, 43–66. [CrossRef]
28. Li, R. Research on Additive Quantum Error Correcting Codes. Ph.D. Thesis, Northwest Poly-Technical University, Xi'an, China, 2004.
29. Lu, L.; Li, R.; Guo, L. Entanglement-assisted quantum codes from quaternary codes of dimension five. *Int. J. Quantum Inf.* **2017**, *14*, 1750017. [CrossRef]
30. Harada, M. Some optimal entanglement-assisted quantum codes constructed from quaternary Hermitian linear complementary dual codes. *Int. Quantum Inf.* **2019**, *17*, 1950053. [CrossRef]

entropy

MDPI

Article

On the Dimensions of Hermitian Subfield Subcodes from Higher-Degree Places

Sabira El Khalfaoui [1,†] and Gábor P. Nagy [2,3,*,†]

1 Institut de Recherche Mathématique de Rennes-IRMAR-UMR 6625, University Rennes, F-35000 Rennes, France; sabiraelkhalfaoui@gmail.com
2 Bolyai Institute, University of Szeged, Aradi Vértanúk tere 1, H-6720 Szeged, Hungary
3 HUN-REN-ELTE Geometric and Algebraic Combinatorics Research Group, Pázmány Péter Sétány 1/C, H-1117 Budapest, Hungary
* Correspondence: nagyg@math.u-szeged.hu
† These authors contributed equally to this work.

Abstract: The focus of our research is the examination of Hermitian curves over finite fields, specifically concentrating on places of degree three and their role in constructing Hermitian codes. We begin by studying the structure of the Riemann–Roch space associated with these degree-three places, aiming to determine essential characteristics such as the basis. The investigation then turns to Hermitian codes, where we analyze both functional and differential codes of degree-three places, focusing on their parameters and automorphisms. In addition, we explore the study of subfield subcodes and trace codes, determining their structure by giving lower bounds for their dimensions. This presents a complex problem in coding theory. Based on numerical experiments, we formulate a conjecture for the dimension of some subfield subcodes of Hermitian codes. Our comprehensive exploration seeks to deepen the understanding of Hermitian codes and their associated subfield subcodes related to degree-three places, thus contributing to the advancement of algebraic coding theory and code-based cryptography.

Keywords: Hermitian curves; degree-three places; Riemann–Roch space; Hermitian codes; subfield subcodes; automorphisms of Hermitian codes

1. Introduction

The advent of quantum computers presents significant threats to classical cryptographic schemes, requiring the development of post-quantum cryptographic primitives that resist quantum attacks. In this regard, algebraic geometry (AG) codes have gained considerable attention due to their error-correcting capabilities and potential applications in secure communication and cryptographic protocols. Among various classes of AG codes, subfield subcodes stand out against structural attacks, making them good candidates for deployment in post-quantum cryptography.

Within linear codes over finite field extensions, the process of generating subfield subcodes, commonly referred to as restriction, entails converting a given linear code C over a large field extension $\mathbb{F}_{q^n}$ into a code that is defined over a subfield $\mathbb{F}_{q^m}$, where m divides n. This strategic approach restricts the codewords of C to elements found within the smaller field $\mathbb{F}_{q^m}$, effectively concealing the details about the structure inherent in C. A classic example of this concept is the Reed–Solomon codes, which are algebraic geometry (AG) codes constructed over a projective line. They are widely used in practical applications, with their subfield subcodes represented by Goppa codes. In particular, in cryptography, especially within a McEliece cryptosystem, subfield subcodes play a crucial role in hiding the code structure, thus enhancing its resilience against distinguishing attacks [1,2]. The long-lasting security of the McEliece cryptosystem based on Goppa codes [3] emphasizes its effectiveness in preventing such attacks. Despite subsequent proposals exploring Reed–Solomon codes [4], AG codes, and their subcodes [5], all have been susceptible to structural attacks. By imposing restrictions, cryptographic systems can enhance their security by minimizing the risk of potential attacks aimed at distinguishing the chosen subfield subcode. With growing interest in AG codes, particularly Hermitian codes, they are being evaluated as feasible alternatives to Reed–Solomon codes in specific applications [6]. Hermitian codes have been extensively studied in prior research [7–12], particularly those associated with the point at infinity of the Hermitian curve. However, in [13,14], the authors introduced an alternative construction of Hermitian codes associated with higher-degree places on the Hermitian curve.

Our contribution involves conducting further research on Hermitian codes associated with degree-three places, deriving additional properties, and establishing explicit bases for the corresponding Riemann–Roch spaces; additionally, this should align with previous findings in [13]. The stabilizer of a degree-three place has order $3(q^2 - q + 1)$; the action of this group and the associated quotient curve has been studied by Cossidente, Korchmáros, and Torres [15]. We make heavy use of their approach which relates the Hermitian curve with the curve projective curve $XY^q + YZ^q + ZX^q = 0$. Beelen, Montanucci, and Vicino [16] studied another class of Hermitian quotient curves, which are obtained by automorphisms stabilizing a degree-three place of the Hermitian curve.

One-point Hermitians of degree-three places have improved minimum distances, as shown by the Matthews–Michel bound [14], and have been further strengthened by Korchmáros and Nagy in [13]. Moreover, we explore the properties of their subfield subcodes, with a particular focus on determining their true dimensions through explicit constructions. This investigation aims to provide a precise understanding of the codes' capabilities for our future work. Since the family of subfield subcodes of Hermitian codes associated with degree-three places holds promise for the construction of an improved and secure McEliece cryptosystem, the aforementioned investigation will enable a comparison of these parameters with those of other existing codes (see [12], Table 1), such as Goppa codes, to assess the potential improvement in the key size of the McEliece cryptosystem. This suggests that such a proposal could reduce the key size and meet the security level required by NIST [17]. Using bounds on the dimensions offers only an estimate of the code's performance, which means that this will not help us accurately decide whether these codes can achieve the required security level with an improved key size.

The paper is structured as follows. In Section 2, we introduce the essential background of AG codes constructed from a Hermitian curve, including Hermitian curves, divisors, and the Riemann–Roch space. In Section 3, we provide some facts on the geometry of degree 3 places of the Hermitian curve, and the unitary transformations which stabilize the given degree-three place. Our main tool is the Hermitian sesquilinear form $\langle u, v\rangle = u_1 v_1^q - u_2 v_3^q - u_3 v_2^q$ and the Frobenius map Fr_{q^2}. Section 4 deals with their corresponding Riemann–Roch spaces. We explore their structure and give explicit and practical bases over $\mathbb{F}_{q^6}$, and a decomposition into invariant subspaces over $\mathbb{F}_{q^2}$ (Theorem 3). In Section 5, we study the functional and differential Hermitian codes of a degree 3 place, where we explicitly give the monomial equivalence between them (Theorem 4). In Section 6, we give the main result on the dimensions of the subfield subcodes of degree 3 place Hermitian codes (Theorem 5). This result consists of a theorem that provides a lower bound on the dimensions of the underlying codes, while the conjecture suggests a possible equality based on numerical experiments.

The computational results were obtained using the HERMITIAN package [18] within the GAP [19] computer algebra system. This involved implementing higher-degree places of Hermitian curves, their divisors and the associated Hermitian codes. This package employs a generic method for computing the bases of Riemann–Roch spaces, independent of the results presented in this paper. Specifically, we acquired computational evidence supporting Conjecture 1 without relying on the theoretical findings of this work.

2. Algebraic Geometry (AG) Codes

2.1. Hermitian Curves and Their Divisors

For more details, we refer the reader to [15,20,21]. The Hermitian curve, denoted as $\mathscr{H}_q$, over the finite field $\mathbb{F}_{q^2}$ in affine coordinates is given by the equation:

$$\mathscr{H}_q : Y^q + Y = X^{q+1}.$$

This curve has a genus $g = \frac{q(q-1)}{2}$, classifying it as a maximal curve because it achieves the maximum number of $\mathbb{F}_{q^2}$-rational points, which is $\#\mathscr{H}_q(\mathbb{F}_{q^2}) = q^3 + 1$. Furthermore, $\mathscr{H}_q$ has a unique point at infinity, denoted Q_∞.

A divisor on $\mathscr{H}_q$ is a formal sum $D = n_1Q_1 + \cdots + n_kQ_k$, where $n_1, \cdots, n_k$ are integers and $Q_1, \cdots, Q_k$ are points on $\mathscr{H}_q$. The degree of the divisor D is defined as $\deg(D) = \sum_{i=1}^{k} n_i$. The valuation of D at a point Q_i is $v_{Q_i}(D) = n_i$, and the support of D is the set $\{Q_i \mid n_i \neq 0\}$.

The Frobenius automorphism, denoted as Fr_{q^2}, is defined over the algebraic closure $\overline{\mathbb{F}}_{q^2}$ and acts on elements as follows:

$$\mathrm{Fr}_{q^2} : \overline{\mathbb{F}}_{q^2} \to \overline{\mathbb{F}}_{q^2}, \quad x \mapsto x^{q^2}.$$

It acts on the points of $\mathscr{H}_q$ by applying Fr_{q^2} to their coordinates. A point Q on $\mathscr{H}_q$ is $\mathbb{F}_{q^2}$-rational if and only if it is fixed by $\mathrm{Fr}_{q^2}(Q)$. Over $\overline{\mathbb{F}}_{q^2}$, the points in $\mathscr{H}_q$ correspond one-to-one to the places in the function field $\overline{\mathbb{F}}_{q^2}(\mathscr{H}_q)$.

For a divisor D, its Frobenius image is given by

$$\mathrm{Fr}_{q^2}(D) = n_1\mathrm{Fr}_{q^2}(Q_1) + \cdots + n_k\mathrm{Fr}_{q^2}(Q_k).$$

and D is $\mathbb{F}_{q^2}$-rational if $D = \mathrm{Fr}_{q^2}(D)$. In particular, if all points $Q_1, \ldots, Q_k$ are in $\mathscr{H}_q(\mathbb{F}_{q^2})$, then D is inherently $\mathbb{F}_{q^2}$-rational.

2.2. Riemann–Roch Spaces

For a non-zero function g in the function field $\overline{\mathbb{F}}_{q^2}$ and a place P, $v_P(g)$ stands for the order of g at P. If $v_P(g) > 0$, then P is a zero of g, while if $v_P(g) < 0$, then P is a pole of g with multiplicity $-v_P(g)$. The principal divisor of a non-zero function g is $(g) = \sum_P v_P(g)P$.

The *Riemann–Roch space* associated with an $\mathbb{F}_{q^2}$-rational divisor G is the $\mathbb{F}_{q^2}$ vector space

$$\mathscr{L}(G) := \{g \in \mathbb{F}_{q^2}(\mathscr{H}_q) \mid (g) + G \geq 0\} \cup 0.$$

From ([20], Riemann's Theorem 1.4.17), we have

$$\dim \mathscr{L}(G) \geq \deg(G) + 1 - \mathfrak{g},$$

with equality if $\deg(G) \geq 2\mathfrak{g} - 1$.

In this work, our primary focus is on an $\mathbb{F}_{q^2}$-rational divisor G of the form sP, where P is a degree r place in $\mathbb{F}_{q^2}(\mathscr{H}_q)$ and s is a positive integer. In the extended constant field $\mathbb{F}_{q^6}(\mathscr{H}_q)$ of $\mathbb{F}_{q^2}(\mathscr{H}_q)$ with degree r, let $P_1, P_2, \cdots, P_r$ be the extensions of P. These points are degree-one places in $\mathbb{F}_{q^{2r}}(\mathscr{H}_q)$, and, after appropriately labeling the indices, $P_i = \mathrm{Fr}^i_{q^2}(P_1)$, where the indices are considered modulo r.

2.3. Hermitian Codes

Here, we outline the construction of an AG code from the Hermitian curve.

In algebraic coding theory, Hermitian codes stand out as a significant class of algebraic geometry (AG) codes, renowned for their distinctive properties. These codes are constructed from Hermitian curves defined over finite fields. These codes are typically viewed as functional AG codes, denoted by $C_{\mathcal{L}}(D,G)$. In this standard approach, the divisor G is usually a multiple of a single place of degree one. The set $\mathcal{P}$, which encompasses all the rational points in $\mathscr{H}_q$, is listed as $\{Q_1,\ldots,Q_n\}$. This approach gives rise to a structure known as a one-point code. However, it is important to note that recent research in the field suggests that the use of a more varied selection for the divisor G can result in the creation of better AG codes [13,14].

Consider a divisor $D = Q_1 + Q_2 + \cdots + Q_n$, where all Q_i are distinct rational points, and an $\mathbb{F}_{q^2}$-rational divisor G such that $\mathrm{Supp}(G) \cap \mathrm{Supp}(D) = \emptyset$. By numbering the places in the support of D, we define an evaluation map ev_D such that $\mathrm{ev}_D(g) = (g(Q_1),\ldots,g(Q_n))$ for $g \in \mathscr{L}(G)$.

The functional AG code associated with the divisor G is

$$C_{\mathcal{L}}(D,G) := \{(g(Q_1), g(Q_2), \cdots, g(Q_n)) \mid g \in \mathscr{L}(G)\} = \mathrm{ev}_D(\mathscr{L}(G)),$$

Theorem 1 ([20], Theorem 2.2.2)**.** *$C_{\mathcal{L}}(D,G)$ is an $[n,k,d]$ code with parameters*

$$k = \dim \mathscr{L}(G) - \dim \mathscr{L}(G-D) \quad \textit{and} \quad d \geq n - \deg G.$$

The dual of an AG code can be described as a residue code (see [20] for more details), i.e.,

$$C_{\mathcal{L}}(D,G)^{\perp} = C_{\Omega}(D,G).$$

Furthermore, the differential code $C_{\Omega}(D,G)$ is monomially equivalent to the functional code

$$C_{\mathcal{L}}(D, W + D - G),$$

where W represents a canonical divisor of $\overline{\mathbb{F}}_{q^2}(\mathscr{H}_q)$. The notion of monomial equivalence of codes is defined as follows. Let $C \leq \mathbb{F}_q^n$ be linear subspaces and $\boldsymbol{\mu} = (\mu_1,\ldots,\mu_n) \in (\mathbb{F}_q^*)^n$ with non-zero entries. We define the Schur product

$$\boldsymbol{\mu} \star C = \{(\mu_1 x_1,\ldots,\mu_n x_n) \mid (x_1,\ldots,x_n) \in C\}.$$

The vector $\boldsymbol{\mu}$ is also called a multiplier. Clearly, $\boldsymbol{\mu} \star C \leq \mathbb{F}_q^n$. Two linear codes $C_1, C_2 \leq \mathbb{F}_q^n$ are monomially equivalent if $C_2 = \boldsymbol{\mu} \star C_1$ for some multiplier $\boldsymbol{\mu}$. Monomially equivalent codes share identical dimensions and minimum distances; however, this correspondence does not preserve all crucial properties of the code.

2.4. Subfield Subcodes and Trace Codes

For the efficient construction of codes over $\mathbb{F}_q$, one approach involves working with codes originally defined over an extension field $\mathbb{F}_{q^m}$. When considering a code $\mathcal{C}$ within $\mathbb{F}_{q^m}^n$, a subfield subcode of $\mathcal{C}$ is its restriction to the field $\mathbb{F}_q$. This process, often employed in the definition of codes such as BCH codes, Goppa codes, and alternant codes, plays a fundamental role.

Let q be a prime power and m be a positive integer. Let C denote a linear code of parameters $[n,k]$ defined over the finite field $\mathbb{F}_{q^m}$. The *subfield subcode* of C over $\mathbb{F}_q$, represented as $C|_{\mathbb{F}_q}$, is the set

$$C|_{\mathbb{F}_q} = C \cap \mathbb{F}_q^n,$$

which consists of all codewords in C that have their components in $\mathbb{F}_q$.

The subfield subcode $C|_{\mathbb{F}_q}$ is a linear code over $\mathbb{F}_q$ with parameters $[n,k_0,d_0]$, satisfying the inequalities $d \leq d_0 \leq n$ and $n-k \leq n-k_0 \leq m(n-k)$. Moreover, a parity check matrix for C over $\mathbb{F}_q$ provides up to $m(n-k)$ linearly independent parity check equations over $\mathbb{F}_q$ for the subfield subcode $C|_{\mathbb{F}_q}$. Typically, the minimum distance d_0 of the subfield subcode exceeds that of the original code C.

Let $\mathrm{Tr}_{\mathbb{F}_{q^m}/\mathbb{F}_q}$ denote the trace function from $\mathbb{F}_{q^m}$ down to $\mathbb{F}_q$, expressed as

$$\mathrm{Tr}_{\mathbb{F}_{q^m}/\mathbb{F}_q}(x) = x + x^q + x^{q^2} + \ldots + x^{q^{m-1}}.$$

For any vector $c = (c_1, c_2, \ldots, c_n) \in \mathbb{F}_q^n$, we define

$$\mathrm{Tr}_{\mathbb{F}_{q^m}/\mathbb{F}_q}(c) = \Big(\mathrm{Tr}_{\mathbb{F}_{q^m}/\mathbb{F}_q}(c_1), \mathrm{Tr}_{\mathbb{F}_{q^m}/\mathbb{F}_q}(c_2), \ldots, \mathrm{Tr}_{\mathbb{F}_{q^m}/\mathbb{F}_q}(c_n)\Big).$$

Furthermore, for a linear code C of length n and dimension k over $\mathbb{F}_{q^m}$, the code

$$\mathrm{Tr}_{\mathbb{F}_{q^m}/\mathbb{F}_q}(C) = \{\mathrm{Tr}_{\mathbb{F}_{q^m}/\mathbb{F}_q}(c) \mid c \in C\}$$

is a linear code of length n and dimension k_1 over $\mathbb{F}_q$.

A seminal result by Delsarte connects subfield subcodes with trace codes:

Theorem 2 ([22]). *Let C be an $[n,k]$ linear code over $\mathbb{F}_q$. Then, the dual of the subfield subcode of C is the trace code of the dual code of C, i.e.,*

$$(C|_{\mathbb{F}_q})^{\perp} = \mathrm{Tr}_{\mathbb{F}_{q^m}/\mathbb{F}_q}(C^{\perp}).$$

Finding the exact dimension of a subfield subcode of a linear code is typically a hard problem. However, a basic estimation can be obtained by applying Delsarte's theorem [22]:

$$\dim C|_{\mathbb{F}_q} \geq n - m(n-k). \tag{1}$$

In [20] (Chapter 9), various results are discussed with respect to the subfield subcodes and trace codes of AG codes. This motivated us to formulate the following propositions on the dimension of the subfield subcodes of AG codes, which are useful for the case $G = sP$ with a place P of higher degree.

Proposition 1. *Let G_1 be a positive divisor of the Hermitian curve $\mathscr{H}_q$ and $D = Q_1 + \cdots + Q_n$ be the sum of $\mathbb{F}_{q^2}$-rational places such that* $\mathrm{Supp}(G) \cap \mathrm{Supp}(D) = \emptyset$. *Assume that* $\deg G_1 < n/q$. *Then,*

$$\dim C_{\mathcal{L}}(D, G_1)\mid_{\mathbb{F}_q} = 1.$$

Proof. Let f be a function in $\mathscr{L}(G_1)$ such that $f(Q_i) \in \mathbb{F}_q$ for $i = 1, \cdots, n$. Then, $f^q - f \in \mathscr{L}(qG_1)$ (since $\mathscr{L}(G_1)^q \subseteq \mathscr{L}(qG_1)$), and hence $f^q - f \in \mathscr{L}(qG_1 - D)$, where

$$\mathscr{L}(qG_1 - D) = \ker(\mathrm{ev}_D) = \{x \in \mathscr{L}(qG_1) \mid v_{P_i}(x) > 0 \text{ for } i = 1, \ldots, n\}.$$

Since $\deg(qG_1 - D) < 0$, it follows that $\mathscr{L}(qG_1 - D) = 0$ and $f^q - f = 0$, which implies that $f \in \mathbb{F}_q$. Consequently, $\dim C_{\mathcal{L}}(D, G_1)|_{\mathbb{F}_q} = 1$. □

3. The Geometry of Hermitian Degree-Three Places

In this section, we collect useful facts on degree-three places of the Hermitian curve, their stabilizer subgroups, and Riemann–Roch spaces.

3.1. The Hermitian Sesquilinear Form

The Hermitian curve $\mathscr{H}_q$ has the affine equation $X^{q+1} = Y + Y^q$. The Hermitian function field $\overline{\mathbb{F}}_{q^2}(\mathscr{H}_q)$ is generated by x, y so that $x^{q+1} = y + y^q$ holds. The Frobenius field automorphism $\mathrm{Fr}_{q^2} : x \mapsto x^{q^2}$ of the algebraic closure $\overline{\mathbb{F}}_{q^2}$ includes an action on rational functions, places, divisors, and curve automorphisms. For this action, we continue to use the notation Fr_{q^2} in the exponent: $P^{\mathrm{Fr}_{q^2}}, f^{\mathrm{Fr}_{q^2}}, D^{\mathrm{Fr}_{q^2}}$, etc.

Let K be a field extension of $\mathbb{F}_{q^2}$. An affine point is a pair $(a,b) \in K^2$. A projective point $(a:b:c)$ is a one-dimensional subspace $\{(at,bt,ct) \mid t \in K\}$ of K^3. If $c \neq 0$, then the projective point $(a:b:c)$ is identified with the affine point $(a/c, b/c)$. For $u = (u_1, u_2, u_3)$, $v = (v_1, v_2, v_3) \in K^3$, we define the Hermitian form

$$\langle u, v\rangle = u_1 v_1^q - u_2 v_3^q - u_3 v_2^q.$$

Clearly, $\langle u, v\rangle$ is additive in u and v, $\langle \alpha u, \beta v\rangle = \alpha\beta^q\langle u, v\rangle$, and

$$\langle u, v\rangle^q = \langle v^{\mathrm{Fr}_{q^2}}, u\rangle.$$

The point u is self-conjugate if

$$0 = \langle u, u\rangle = u_1^{q+1} - u_2 u_3^q - u_2^q u_3.$$

This is the projective equation $X^{q+1} - YZ^q - Y^q Z = 0$ of the Hermitian curve $\mathscr{H}_q$. Let $u = (u_1 : u_2 : u_3)$ be a projective point. The polar line of u has equation

$$u^\perp : \langle (X_1, X_2, X_3), u\rangle = u_1^q X_1 - u_3^q X_2 - u_2^q X_3 = 0.$$

If u is on $\mathscr{H}_q$, then $u^\perp$ is the tangent line at u. More precisely, $u^\perp$ intersects $\mathscr{H}_q$ at u and $u^{\mathrm{Fr}_{q^2}}$ with multiplicities q and 1, respectively. If u is $\mathbb{F}_{q^2}$-rational, then $u = u^{\mathrm{Fr}_{q^2}}$, and the intersection multiplicity is $q+1$.

3.2. Unitary Transformations and Curve Automorphism

Let A be a 3×3 matrix. The linear map $u \mapsto uA$ will also be denoted by A. If A is invertible, then it induces a projective linear transformation, denoted by $\hat{A} : (u_1 : u_2 : u_3) \mapsto (u_1' : u_2' : u_3') = (u_1 : u_2 : u_3)^{\hat{A}}$, where

$$\begin{aligned} u_1' &= a_{11}u_1 + a_{21}u_2 + a_{31}u_3, \\ u_2' &= a_{12}u_1 + a_{22}u_2 + a_{32}u_3, \\ u_3' &= a_{13}u_1 + a_{23}u_2 + a_{33}u_3. \end{aligned}$$

We use the same notation $\hat{A} : (X, Y) \mapsto (X', Y') = (X, Y)^{\hat{A}}$ for the partial affine map:

$$(X, Y) \mapsto (X', Y') = \left(\frac{a_{11}X + a_{21}Y + a_{31}}{a_{13}X + a_{23}Y + a_{33}}, \frac{a_{12}X + a_{22}Y + a_{32}}{a_{13}X + a_{23}Y + a_{33}}\right).$$

The action $f(X, Y) \mapsto f((X, Y)^{\hat{A}^{-1}})$ of $\hat{A}$ on rational functions will be indicated by A^*. The following lemma is straightforward.

Lemma 1. *Let $f(X, Y)$ be a polynomial of total degree n. Define the degree n homogeneous polynomial $F(X, Y, Z) = Z^n f(X/Z, Y/Z)$. Then,*

$$f^{A^*}(X, Y) = \frac{F((X, Y, 1)A^{-1})}{(a_{13}X + a_{23}Y + a_{33})^n}.$$

We remark that the line $a_{13}X + a_{23}Y + a_{33} = 0$ can be seen as the pre-image of the line at infinity under $\hat{A}$.

The linear transformation A is unitary if

$$\langle uA, vA\rangle = \langle u, v\rangle$$

holds for all u, v. Since $\langle ., .\rangle$ is non-degenerate, unitary transformations are invertible. Moreover, for all u, v, one has

$$\begin{aligned}\langle (v^{\mathrm{Fr}_{q^2}})A, uA\rangle &= \langle v^{\mathrm{Fr}_{q^2}}, u\rangle \\ &= \langle u, v\rangle^q \\ &= \langle uA, vA\rangle^q \\ &= \langle (vA)^{\mathrm{Fr}_{q^2}}, uA\rangle.\end{aligned}$$

This implies $(v^{\mathrm{Fr}_{q^2}})A = (vA)^{\mathrm{Fr}_{q^2}}$ for all v, that is, A and Fr_{q^2} commute. This shows that unitary transformations are defined over $\mathbb{F}_{q^2}$. They form a group which is denoted by $GU(3,q)$. A useful fact is that if b_1, b_2, b_3 is a basis and

$$\langle b_i A, b_j A\rangle = \langle b_i, b_j\rangle$$

for all $i, j \in \{1,2,3\}$, then A is unitary.

Let $A \in GU(3,q)$. If (x,y) is a generic point of $\mathscr{H}_q$, then $(x', y') = (x,y)^{\hat{A}}$ satisfies

$$(x')^{q+1} - y' - (y')^q = \langle x', y'\rangle = \langle x, y\rangle = 0.$$

Therefore, (x', y') is a generic point of $\mathscr{H}_q$, and A^* induces an automorphism of the function field $\overline{\mathbb{F}}_{q^2}(\mathscr{H}_q)$. If A is defined over $\mathbb{F}_{q^2}$, then A^* is an automorphism of $\mathbb{F}_{q^2}(\mathscr{H}_q)$.

3.3. Places of Degree Three and Their Lines

Let $a_1, b_1 \in \mathbb{F}_{q^6} \setminus \mathbb{F}_{q^2}$ be scalars such that $a_1^{q+1} = b_1 + b_1^q$. In other words, (a_1, b_1) is an affine point of $\mathscr{H}_q : X^{q+1} = Y + Y^q$, defined over $\mathbb{F}_{q^6}$. Write $a_2 = a_1^{q^2}$, $b_2 = b_1^{q^2}$, $a_3 = a_2^{q^2}$, $b_3 = b_2^{q^2}$, and $p_i = (a_i, b_i, 1)$. Then, $p_{i+1} = p_i^{\mathrm{Fr}_{q^2}}$, $\langle p_i, p_i\rangle = 0$, and

$$0 = \langle p_i, p_i\rangle^q = \langle p_i^{\mathrm{Fr}_{q^2}}, p_i\rangle = \langle p_{i+1}, p_i\rangle$$

hold for $i = 1,2,3$, with the indices taking modulo three. Since $\langle .,.\rangle$ is non-trivial, $\gamma_i = \langle p_i, p_{i+1}\rangle \in \mathbb{F}_{q^6} \setminus \{0\}$. More precisely,

$$\gamma_1^{q^3} = \langle p_1, p_2\rangle^{q^3} = \langle p_2^{\mathrm{Fr}_{q^2}}, p_1\rangle^{q^2} = \langle p_2^{(\mathrm{Fr}_{q^2})^2}, p_1^{\mathrm{Fr}_{q^2}}\rangle = \langle p_1, p_2\rangle = \gamma_1,$$

which shows $\gamma_i \in \mathbb{F}_{q^3} \setminus \{0\}$. Clearly, $\gamma_{i+1} = \gamma_i^{q^2}$ and $\gamma_{i+2} = \gamma_i^q$. By $\gamma_i \neq 0$, the vectors p_1, p_2, p_3 are linearly independent over $\mathbb{F}_{q^6}$.

Let K be a field containing $\mathbb{F}_{q^6}$. Since p_1, p_2, p_3 is a basis in K^3, any $u \in K^3$ can be written as

$$u = x_1 p_1 + x_2 p_2 + x_3 p_3,$$

with $x_i \in K$. Computing

$$\langle u, p_{i+1}\rangle = \langle x_1 p_1 + x_2 p_2 + x_3 p_3, p_{i+1}\rangle = x_i \langle p_i, p_{i+1}\rangle,$$

we obtain $x_i = \langle u, p_{i+1}\rangle / \gamma_i$. In the basis p_1, p_2, p_3, the Hermitian form has the shape

$$\begin{aligned}\langle u, v\rangle &= \langle x_1 p_1 + x_2 p_2 + x_3 p_3, y_1 p_1 + y_2 p_2 + y_3 p_3\rangle \\ &= x_1 y_2^q \langle p_1, p_2\rangle + x_2 y_3^q \langle p_2, p_3\rangle + x_3 y_1^q \langle p_3, p_1\rangle \\ &= \gamma_1 x_1 y_2^q + \gamma_1^{q^2} x_2 y_3^q + \gamma_1^{q^4} x_3 y_1^q.\end{aligned}$$

In this coordinate frame, the Hermitian curve has projective equation

$$\gamma_1 X_1 X_2^q + \gamma_1^{q^2} X_2 X_3^q + \gamma_1^{q^4} X_3 X_1^q = 0.$$

Let x, y be the generators of the function field $\overline{\mathbb{F}}_{q^2}(\mathscr{H}_q)$ such that $x^{q+1} = y + y^q$. Write

$$\ell_i = \langle (x, y, 1), p_i \rangle = a_i^q x - y - b_i^q.$$

Then,

$$(x, y, 1) = \frac{\ell_2}{\gamma_1} p_1 + \frac{\ell_3}{\gamma_2} p_2 + \frac{\ell_1}{\gamma_3} p_3$$

and

$$0 = x^{q+1} - y - y^q = \langle (x, y, 1), (x, y, 1) \rangle = \frac{\ell_1 \ell_2^q}{\gamma_1^q} + \frac{\ell_2 \ell_3^q}{\gamma_2^q} + \frac{\ell_3 \ell_1^q}{\gamma_3^q}. \tag{2}$$

The Hermitian curve $\mathscr{H}_q$ is non-singular, the places of $\overline{\mathbb{F}}_{q^2}(\mathscr{H}_q)$ correspond to the projective points over the algebraic closure $\overline{\mathbb{F}}_{q^2}$. Let P_i denote the place corresponding to $(a_i : b_i : 1)$. P_i is defined over $\mathbb{F}_{q^6}$, $P_{i+1} = P_i^{\mathrm{Fr}_{q^2}}$, and

$$P = P_1 + P_2 + P_3$$

is an $\mathbb{F}_{q^2}$-rational place of degree three.

The line $a_i^q X - Y - b_i^q = 0$ is tangent to $\mathscr{H}_q$ at p_i; the intersection multiplicities are q and 1 at p_i and p_{i+1}, respectively. This implies that the zero divisor $(\ell_i)_0$ is $qP_i + P_{i+1}$, and the principal divisor of ℓ_i is

$$(\ell_i) = qP_i + P_{i+1} - (q+1)Q_\infty. \tag{3}$$

3.4. The Stabilizer of a Degree-Three Place

Let $\beta_1 \in \mathbb{F}_{q^6}$ be an element such that $\beta_1^{q^3+1} = 1$. Define $\beta_2 = \beta_1^{q^2}$, $\beta_3 = \beta_2^{q^2}$. Then,

$$\beta_i \beta_{i+1}^q = \beta_i^{q^3+1} = 1.$$

For $p_i' = \beta_i p_i$, this implies that

$$\langle p_i', p_{i+1}' \rangle = \beta_i \beta_{i+1}^q \langle p_i, p_{i+1} \rangle = \langle p_i, p_{i+1} \rangle.$$

Hence, for all $i, j \in \{1, 2, 3\}$,

$$\langle p_i', p_j' \rangle = \langle p_i, p_j \rangle.$$

This shows that we can extend the map $p_i \mapsto p_i'$ to a unitary linear map $B = B(\beta_1) : u \mapsto u'$ in the following way. Write

$$u = x_1 p_1 + x_2 p_2 + x_3 p_3,$$

with $x_i = \langle u, p_{i+1} \rangle / \gamma_i$, and define

$$u' = x_1 p_1' + x_2 p_2' + x_3 p_3' = x_1 \beta_1 p_1 + x_2 \beta_2 p_2 + x_3 \beta_3 p_3. \tag{4}$$

The extension B is a unique unitary transformation. As we have seen in Section 3.2, this implies that $B = B(\beta_1)$ is a well-defined element of the general unitary group $GU(3,q)$. The set

$$\mathcal{B} = \{B(\beta_1) \mid \beta_1 \in \mathbb{F}_{q^6}, \beta_1^{q^3+1} = 1\}$$

is a cyclic subgroup of $GU(3,q)$, whose order is $|\mathcal{B}| = q^3 + 1$.

In the projective plane, B induces a projective linear transformation $\hat{B}$. $\hat{B}$ is trivial if and only if $\beta_1 = \beta_2 = \beta_1^{q^2}$, that is, if and only if $\beta_i \in \mathbb{F}_{q^2}$. As $\gcd(q^3+1, q^2-1) = q+1$, $\hat{B}$ is trivial if and only if $\beta_1^{q+1} = 1$. The set $\hat{\mathcal{B}} = \{\hat{B} \mid B \in \mathcal{B}\}$ is a cyclic group of unitary projective linear transformations, whose order is $|\hat{\mathcal{B}}| = q^2 - q + 1$.

In a similar way, we fix the elements

$$\delta_i = \gamma_i^{\frac{q^3-q}{2}}.$$

since $\gamma_1 \in \mathbb{F}_{q^3}$, $\delta_i \in \mathbb{F}_{q^3}$. Moreover,

$$\delta_i^{q^3+1} = \delta_i^2 = \gamma_i^{q^3-q} = \gamma_i^{1-q}.$$

As before, the map

$$\Delta : p_i \mapsto p_i'' = \delta_i p_{i-1}$$

preserves the Hermitian form:

$$\langle p_i'', p_{i+1}'' \rangle = \langle \delta_i p_{i-1}, \delta_{i+1} p_i \rangle = \delta_i^{q^3+1} \langle p_{i-1}, p_i \rangle = \gamma_i^{1-q} \gamma_{i-1} = \gamma_i.$$

Hence, Δ extends to a unitary linear map, which commutes with Fr_{q^2} and normalizes $\mathcal{B}$. Indeed,

$$p_i^{\Delta^{-1}B\Delta} = (\delta_{i+1}^{-1} p_{i+1})^{B\Delta} = (\delta_{i+1}^{-1} \beta_{i+1} p_{i+1})^{\Delta} = \beta_{i+1} p_i,$$

and hence, $\Delta^{-1} B \Delta = B^{q^2}$. Δ^3 maps p_i to $\delta_1\delta_2\delta_3 p_i$, and

$$\delta_1\delta_2\delta_3 = \delta_1^{1+q+q^2} = \left(\gamma_1^{\frac{q^3-q}{2}}\right)^{1+q+q^2} = \left(\gamma_1^{q^3-1}\right)^{\frac{(q+1)q}{2}} = 1.$$

Therefore, Δ has order 3.

As introduced in Section 3.2, the unitary transformations B and Δ induce automorphisms B^* and Δ^* of the function field.

Proposition 2. *The group $\mathcal{B}^* = \{B^* \mid B \in \mathcal{B}\}$ of curve automorphisms has order $q^2 - q + 1$, and Δ^* normalizes $\mathcal{B}^*$ by*

$$(\Delta^*)^{-1} B^* \Delta^* = (B^*)^{q^2} = (B^*)^{q-1}.$$

Both $\mathcal{B}^*$ and Δ^* stabilize the degree-three place P.

Proposition 3. *Let $\beta_1 \in \mathbb{F}_{q^6}$ be an element such that $\beta_1^{q^3+1} = 1$. Define $\beta_2 = \beta_1^{q^2}$, $\beta_3 = \beta_2^{q^2}$, and the unitary map $B = B(\beta_1) \in \mathcal{B}$. Then,*

$$\left(\frac{\ell_i}{\ell_{i+1}}\right)^{B^*} = \beta_i^{q+1} \left(\frac{\ell_i}{\ell_{i+1}}\right).$$

Proof. By Lemma 1,

$$\begin{aligned}\ell_i^{B^*} &= \frac{\langle (x,y,1)B^{-1}, p_i\rangle}{w} \\ &= \frac{\langle (x,y,1), p_iB\rangle}{w} \\ &= \frac{\langle (x,y,1), \beta_i p_i\rangle}{w} \\ &= \frac{\beta_i^q \ell_i}{w},\end{aligned}$$

where the linear $w = w_1x + w_2y + w_3$ over $\mathbb{F}_{q^2}$ depends only on B. Therefore,

$$\left(\frac{\ell_i}{\ell_{i+1}}\right)^{B^*} = \frac{\beta_i^q}{\beta_{i+1}^q}\left(\frac{\ell_i}{\ell_{i+1}}\right) = \beta_i^{q-q^3}\left(\frac{\ell_i}{\ell_{i+1}}\right) = \beta_i^{q+1}\left(\frac{\ell_i}{\ell_{i+1}}\right). \quad \square$$

4. Riemann–Roch Spaces Associated with a Degree-Three Place

In this section, we keep using the notation of the previous section: P_i is a degree-one place of $\mathbb{F}_{q^6}(\mathscr{H}_q)$ associated with the projective point $(a_i : b_i : 1)$. $P_i^{\mathrm{Fr}_{q^2}} = P_{i+1}$; the index $i = 1,2,3$ always takes modulo three. $P = P_1 + P_2 + P_3$ is an $\mathbb{F}_{q^2}$-rational place of degree three of $\mathbb{F}_{q^2}(\mathscr{H}_q)$. The generators x, y of $\overline{\mathbb{F}}_{q^2}(\mathscr{H}_q)$ satisfy $x^{q+1} = y + y^q$. The rational function $\ell_i = a_i^q x - y - b_i^q$ is obtained from the tangent line of $\mathscr{H}_q$ at P_i.

4.1. Basis and Decomposition of the Riemann–Roch Space

Let s, u, v be positive integers such that $v \leq q$ and $s = u(q+1) - v$. Clearly, u, v are uniquely defined by s. In [13], the Riemann–Roch space associated with the divisor sP is given as

$$\mathscr{L}(sP) = \left\{\frac{f}{(\ell_1\ell_2\ell_3)^u} \mid f \in \mathbb{F}_{q^2}[X,Y],\ \deg f \leq 3u,\ v_{P_i}(f) \geq v\right\} \cup \{0\}.$$

The Weierstrass semigroup $H(P)$ consists of the integers $s \geq 0$ such that the pole divisor $(f)_\infty = sP$ for some $f \in \mathbb{F}_{q^2}(\mathscr{H}_q)$, see [20] (Section 6.5) and [16]. If $s \notin H(P)$, then it is called a Weierstrass gap; the set of Weierstrass gaps is denoted by $G(P)$. By [13] (Theorem 3.1), we have

$$G(P) = \{u(q+1) - v \mid 0 \leq v \leq q,\ 0 < 3u \leq v\}.$$

By the Weierstrass Gap Theorem ([20], Theorem 1.6.8), $|G(P)| = \mathfrak{g}$ for a place of degree one. In our case, P has degree three and the situation is slightly more complicated.

Lemma 2.

$$3|G(P)| = \begin{cases}\mathfrak{g} & \text{if } q \equiv 0,1 \pmod 3,\\ \mathfrak{g}-1 & \text{if } q \equiv 2 \pmod 3.\end{cases}$$

Proof. The lemma follows from

$$\begin{aligned}|G(P)| &= \sum_{1\leq u\leq q/3} |\{3u, \ldots, q\}| \\ &= \sum_{i=1}^{\lfloor q/3\rfloor} q+1-3u \\ &= \frac{\lfloor q/3\rfloor(2q-1-3\lfloor q/3\rfloor)}{2}. \quad \square\end{aligned}$$

The following proposition gives an explicit basis for the Riemann–Roch space $\mathscr{L}(sP)$ over the extension field $\mathbb{F}_{q^6}$.

Proposition 4. *Let t, u, v be positive integers such that $v \leq q$ and $t = u(q+1) - v$. Define the rational functions*

$$U_{t,i} = \ell_i^{2u-v} \ell_{i+1}^{v-u} \ell_{i+2}^{-u} = \left(\frac{\ell_i}{\ell_{i+2}}\right)^u \left(\frac{\ell_{i+1}}{\ell_i}\right)^{v-u}, \qquad i = 1, 2, 3.$$

Define $U_{0,i} = 1$ as the constant function for $i = 1, 2, 3$. Then, the following holds:

(i) $(U_{t,i})^{\mathrm{Fr}_{q^2}} = U_{t,i+1}$.

(ii) *The principal divisor of $U_{t,i}$ is*

$$(U_{t,i}) = -tP + \big((3u - v - 1)q + (q - v)\big)P_i + \big(v(q-2) + 3u\big)P_{i+1}.$$

In particular, if $3u \geq v + 1$, then $(U_{t,i}) \geq -tP$.

(iii) *The elements $U_{t,i}$, $t \geq 0$, $i = 1, 2, 3$ are linearly independent with the following exception: $q \equiv 2 \pmod 3$, $t = (q^2 - q + 1)/3$,*

$$\frac{U_{t,1}}{\gamma_1^q} + \frac{U_{t,2}}{\gamma_2^q} + \frac{U_{t,3}}{\gamma_3^q} = 0. \tag{5}$$

(iv) *The set*

$$\mathcal{U}(s) = \{U_{t,i} \mid t \in H(P),\ t \leq s,\ i = 1, 2, 3,\ (3t, i) \neq (q^2 - q + 1, 3)\}$$

of rational functions is a basis of $\mathscr{L}(sP)$ over $\mathbb{F}_{q^6}$.

Proof. Note first that u, v are uniquely defined by t; therefore, $U_{t,i}$ is well defined. (i) is trivial and (ii) is straightforward from (3). To show (iii), let us write a linear combination in the form

$$\alpha_1 U_{t,1} + \alpha_2 U_{t,2} + \alpha_3 U_{t,3} = \sum_{\substack{r<t \\ i=1,2,3}} \lambda_{r,i} U_{r,i} \tag{6}$$

such that $(\alpha_1, \alpha_2, \alpha_3) \neq (0, 0, 0)$. The right-hand side has a valuation of at least $-t + 1$ at P_1, P_2, P_3. If $t \neq (q^2 - q + 1)/3$ and $\alpha_i \neq 0$, then the right-hand side has valuation $-t$ at P_{i+2}. Hence, $\alpha_i = 0$ for all $i = 1, 2, 3$, a contradiction. Assume $t = (q^2 - q + 1)/3$. Then,

$$U_{t,i} = \frac{\ell_i \ell_{i+1}^q}{(\ell_1 \ell_2 \ell_3)^{\frac{q+1}{3}}},$$

and (5) follows from (2). We can use (5) to eliminate $U_{t,3}$ from (6); that is, we can assume $\alpha_3 = 0$. Then, again, the only term that has a valuation $-t$ at P_{i+2} is $\alpha_i U_{t,i}$ with $\alpha_i \neq 0$. Since the left- and right-hand sides of (6) must have the same valuations at P_1, P_3, $\alpha_1 = \alpha_2 = 0$ must hold, a contradiction.

(iv) By (iii), $\mathcal{U}(s)$ consists of linearly independent elements. To show that it is a basis of $\mathscr{L}(sP)$, it suffices to show that $|\mathcal{U}(s)| = \dim(\mathscr{L}(sP))$ for $3s \geq 2\mathfrak{g} - 2$. On the one hand, in this case, $\dim(\mathscr{L}(sP)) = 3s + 1 - \mathfrak{g}$. On the other hand,

$$|\mathcal{U}(s)| = 1 + 3(s - |G(P)|) - \varepsilon = 3s + 1 - (3|G(P)| + \varepsilon),$$

where $\varepsilon = 0$ if $q \equiv 0, 1 \pmod 3$, and $\varepsilon = 1$ if $q \equiv 2 \pmod 3$. By Lemma 2, $3|G(P)| + \varepsilon = \mathfrak{g}$, and the claim follows. □

It is useful to have a decomposition of $\mathscr{L}(sP)$ over $\mathbb{F}_{q^2}$.

Theorem 3. *For a $t \geq 0$ integer and $\alpha \in \mathbb{F}_{q^6}$, define the $\mathbb{F}_{q^2}$-rational function*

$$W_{t,\alpha} = \alpha U_{t,1} + \alpha^{q^2} U_{t,2} + \alpha^{q^4} U_{t,3}$$

and the $\mathbb{F}_{q^2}$-linear space

$$\mathcal{W}_t = \{W_{t,\alpha} \mid \alpha \in \mathbb{F}_{q^6}\}.$$

For $t \in H(P)$, we have

$$\dim(\mathcal{W}_t) = \begin{cases} 1 & \text{if } t = 0, \\ 2 & \text{if } q \equiv 2 \pmod 3 \text{ and } t = (q^2 - q + 1)/3, \\ 3 & \text{otherwise.} \end{cases}$$

The $\mathbb{F}_{q^2}$-rational Riemann–Roch space $\mathscr{L}(sP)$ has the direct sum decomposition

$$\mathscr{L}(sP) = \bigoplus_{t \in H(P),\, t \leq s} \mathcal{W}_t. \tag{7}$$

Proof. For $t \in H(P)$, $\mathcal{W}_t$ is the set of $\mathbb{F}_{q^2}$-rational functions in the space spanned by $U_{t,1}, U_{t,2}, U_{t,3}$. The claims follow from Proposition 4. □

4.2. Invariant Subspaces of $\mathscr{L}(sP)$

Lemma 3. *Let $b \in \mathbb{F}_{q^6}$ such that $b^{q^3+1} = 1$. Then, $(b^{q+1})^{q^2} = (b^{q+1})^{q-1}$ and $(b^{q+1})^{q^4} = (b^{q+1})^{-q}$.*

Proof. By assumption, b^{q+1} has order $q^2 - q + 1$. The claim follows from the facts that $q^2 - (q-1)$ and $q^4 - q$ are divisible by $q^2 - q + 1$. □

The following lemma shows that the basis elements in $\mathcal{U}(s)$ are eigenvectors of $\mathcal{B}^*$.

Lemma 4. *Let $\beta_1 \in \mathbb{F}_{q^6}$ be an element such that $\beta_1^{q^3+1} = 1$. Define $\beta_2 = \beta_1^{q^2}$, $\beta_3 = \beta_2^{q^2}$, and the unitary map $B = B(\beta_1) \in \mathcal{B}$. Then,*

$$(U_{t,i})^{B^*} = \beta_i^{t(q+1)} U_{t,i}.$$

Proof. Proposition 3 implies

$$\left(\frac{\ell_i}{\ell_{i+2}}\right)^{B^*} = \frac{1}{\beta_{i+2}^{q+1}} \left(\frac{\ell_i}{\ell_{i+2}}\right)$$

and

$$\left(\frac{\ell_{i+1}}{\ell_i}\right)^{B^*} = \frac{1}{\beta_i^{q+1}} \left(\frac{\ell_{i+1}}{\ell_i}\right).$$

By Lemma 3, $\frac{1}{\beta_{i+2}^{q+1}} = (\beta_i^{q+1})^{-q^4} = (\beta_i^{q+1})^q$. Write $t = u(q+1) - v$ with $0 \leq v \leq q$. Then,

$$B^* : \left(\frac{\ell_i}{\ell_{i+2}}\right)^u \left(\frac{\ell_{i+1}}{\ell_i}\right)^{v-u} \mapsto (\beta_i^{q+1})^{qu} \left(\frac{\ell_i}{\ell_{i+2}}\right)^u (\beta_i^{q+1})^{-v+u} \left(\frac{\ell_{i+1}}{\ell_i}\right)^{v-u}$$

The result follows from the definition of u and v. □

Proposition 5.

(i) Let $\beta_1 \in \mathbb{F}_{q^6}$ be an element such that $\beta_1^{q^3+1} = 1$, and $B = B(\beta_1) \in \mathcal{B}$. Then,

$$(W_{t,\alpha})^{B^*} = W_{t,\beta_1^{t(q+1)}\alpha}.$$

(ii) The subspaces $\mathcal{W}_t$, $t \in H(P)$ are $\mathcal{B}^*$-invariant.

(iii) The $\mathbb{F}_{q^2}\mathcal{B}^*$-modules $\mathcal{W}_t$ and $\mathcal{W}_s$ are isomorphic if and only if one of the following holds:

- *(a)* $s \equiv t \pmod{q^2 - q + 1}$;
- *(b)* $s \equiv (q-1)t \pmod{q^2 - q + 1}$;
- *(c)* $s \equiv -qt \pmod{q^2 - q + 1}$.

Proof. (i) and (ii) follow from Lemma 4. (iii) Let $\Phi : \mathcal{W}_t \to \mathcal{W}_s$ be an $\mathbb{F}_{q^2}\mathcal{B}^*$-module isomorphism between $\mathcal{W}_t$ and $\mathcal{W}_s$. It can be written as

$$(W_{t,\alpha})^{\Phi} = W_{t,\alpha\varphi},$$

where $\varphi : \mathbb{F}_{q^6} \to \mathbb{F}_{q^6}$ is an $\mathbb{F}_{q^2}$-linear bijection. Moreover,

$$\begin{aligned}(W_{t,\alpha})^{B^*\Phi} &= (W_{t,\beta_1^{t(q+1)}\alpha})^{\Phi} = W_{s,(\beta_1^{t(q+1)}\alpha)\varphi},\\ (W_{t,\alpha})^{\Phi B^*} &= (W_{s,\alpha\varphi})^{B^*} = W_{s,\beta_1^{s(q+1)}(\alpha\varphi)}.\end{aligned}$$

Since $b = \beta_1^{q+1}$ satisfies $b^{q^2-q+1} = 1$, this means that for any $\alpha, b \in \mathbb{F}_{q^6}$, $b^{q^2-q+1} = 1$, we have

$$(b^t\alpha)\varphi = b^s(\alpha\varphi).$$

Let b be an element of order $q^2 - q + 1$ in $\mathbb{F}_{q^6}$. If b^t or b^s is in $\mathbb{F}_{q^2}$, then $b^t = b^s$ and a) hold. Assume that neither b^t nor b^s is in $\mathbb{F}_{q^2}$. Then, $\mathbb{F}_{q^6} = \mathbb{F}_{q^2}(b^t) = \mathbb{F}_{q^2}(b^s)$, and over $\mathbb{F}_{q^2}$, the minimal polynomial of b^t has the degree three. Assume $b^{3t} + c_1b^{2t} + c_2b^t + c_3 = 0$ with $c_0, c_1, c_2 \in \mathbb{F}_{q^2}$. Then,

$$\begin{aligned}0 &= (b^{3t} + c_1b^{2t} + c_2b^t + c_3)\varphi\\ &= (b^{3t}\varphi) + c_1(b^{2t}\varphi) + c_2(b^t\varphi) + c_3(1\varphi)\\ &= (b^{3s} + c_1b^{2s} + c_2b^s + c_3)(1\varphi).\end{aligned}$$

As φ is bijective, $1\varphi \neq 0$, $0 = b^{3s} + c_1b^{2s} + c_2b^s + c_3$ follows. This means that b^s has the same minimal polynomial and $b^t \to b^s$ extends to a field automorphism of $\mathbb{F}_{q^6}$ over $\mathbb{F}_{q^2}$. This implies $b^s = b^t$, $b^s = (b^t)^{q^2}$ or $b^s = (b^t)^{q^4}$, and the claim follows. □

5. Hermitian Codes of Degree-Three Places and Their Duals

In this section, we explore the one-point Hermitian codes of degree-three places and their dual codes. Let P be a degree-three place on the Hermitian curve $\mathcal{H}_q$; $Q_1, \ldots, Q_n, Q_\infty$ are its $\mathbb{F}_{q^2}$-rational places, where $n = q^3$. We define the divisors $D = Q_1 + Q_2 + \cdots + Q_n$, $\widetilde{D} = D + Q_\infty$, and $G = sP$ for a positive integer s.

5.1. Functional Hermitian Codes of Degree-Three Places

Given a divisor D and G, we define the degree-three place functional Hermitian code $C_{\mathcal{L}}(D, sP)$ as:

$$C_{\mathcal{L}}(D,G) := \{(g(Q_1), g(Q_2), \cdots, g(Q_n)) \mid g \in \mathcal{L}(G)\},$$

This code forms an $[n,k]$ AG code, where $k \geq 3s - \mathfrak{g} + 1$, achieving equality when $\lfloor \frac{2\mathfrak{g}-2}{3} \rfloor < s < n/3$. Furthermore, the code has a minimum distance $d \geq d^* = q^3 - 3s$, where d^* is the designed minimum distance.

Furthermore, another degree-three place functional Hermitian code associated with G, denoted by $C_{\mathcal{L}}(\widetilde{D}, G)$, is constructed by evaluating the functions in $\mathscr{L}(G)$ at all rational points $Q_1, Q_2, \cdots, Q_n$ and the point at infinity Q_∞ as follows:

$$C_{\mathcal{L}}(\widetilde{D}, G) := \{(g(Q_1), g(Q_2), \cdots, g(Q_n), g(Q_\infty)) \mid g \in \mathscr{L}(G)\},$$

Clearly, $C_{\mathcal{L}}(\widetilde{D}, G)$ has a length of $n+1$. Concerning the dimensions, we have the following result.

Proposition 6. *If $s < q^3/3$, then $\mathscr{L}(sP)$, $C_{\mathcal{L}}(D, G)$ and $C_{\mathcal{L}}(\widetilde{D}, G)$ have the same dimensions.*

Proof. If $f \in \ker \mathrm{ev}_D$, then $f \in \mathscr{L}(sP - D)$, which is trivial if $s < q^3/3$. In this case, $\ker \mathrm{ev}_{\widetilde{D}}$ is also trivial. □

Remark 1. *Numerical experiments show that $\mathscr{L}(sP)$, $C_{\mathcal{L}}(D, G)$ and $C_{\mathcal{L}}(\widetilde{D}, G)$ have the same dimension if $s < (q^3+1)/3 + q - 1$.*

In the study of the divisors D and $\widetilde{D}$, we make use of the polynomial

$$R(X, Y) = X \prod_{\substack{c \in \mathbb{F}_{q^2} \\ c^q + c \neq 0}} (Y - c).$$

As shown in [13] (Section 2), the principal divisor of $R(x, y) \in \mathbb{F}_{q^2}(\mathscr{H}_q)$ is

$$(R(x, y)) = D - q^3 Q_\infty. \tag{8}$$

Further properties of $R(x, y)$ are given in the following proposition.

Proposition 7. *In the function field, we have*

$$x^q R(x, y) = y^{q^2} - y \qquad \text{and} \qquad R(x, y) = x^{q^2} - x.$$

The differential of $R(x, y)$ is

$$d(R(x, y)) = -dx.$$

Proof. Clearly,

$$\prod_{\substack{c \in \mathbb{F}_{q^2} \\ c^q + c = 0}} (Y - c) = Y^q + Y,$$

and

$$\prod_{\substack{c \in \mathbb{F}_{q^2} \\ c^q + c \neq 0}} (Y - c) = \frac{\prod_{c \in \mathbb{F}_{q^2}} (Y - c)}{\prod_{\substack{c \in \mathbb{F}_{q^2} \\ c^q + c = 0}} (Y - c)} = \frac{Y^{q^2} - Y}{Y^q + Y}.$$

Hence, by $x^{q+1} = y + y^q$,

$$x^q R(x, y) = x^{q+1} \prod_{\substack{c \in \mathbb{F}_{q^2} \\ c^q + c \neq 0}} (y - c) = x^{q+1} \frac{y^{q^2} - y}{y^q + y} = y^{q^2} - y.$$

Using this, we obtain

$$x^q(x^{q^2} - x) = (x^{q+1})^q - x^{q+1} = y^q + y^{q^2} - (y + y^q) = y^{q^2} - y = x^q R(x, y).$$

Canceling by x^q, we get $R(x, y) = x^{q^2} - x$, and $d(R(x, y)) = -dx$ follows immediately. □

5.2. Differential Hermitian Codes of Degree-Three Places

Differential Hermitian codes of degree-three places are essential counterparts to functional codes on the Hermitian curve $\mathscr{H}_q$. The dual code $C_\Omega(D, G)$ of $C_\mathcal{L}(D, G)$ is called the differential code. It constitutes an $[n, \ell(G - D) - \ell(G) + \deg D, d^\perp]$ code, where $d^\perp \le \deg(G) - (2\mathfrak{g} - 2)$, with $\deg(G) - (2\mathfrak{g} - 2)$ being its designed distance.

Ref. [20] (Proposition 8.1.2) provides an explicit description of the differential code as a functional code

$$C_\Omega(D, G) = C_\mathscr{L}(D - G + (dt) - (t)),$$

where t is an element of $\mathbb{F}_{q^2}(\mathscr{H}_q)$ such that $v_{Q_i}(t) = 1$ for all $i \in \{1, \ldots, q^3, \infty\}$. If $G = sP$ and $D = Q_1 + \cdots + Q_{q^3}$, then $t = R(x, y)$ is a good choice, with

$$(dt) = (-dx) = (2\mathfrak{g} - 2)Q_\infty = (q - 2)(q + 1)Q_\infty,$$

see [20] (Lemma 6.4.4). Then, (8) implies the following proposition:

Proposition 8.

$$C_\Omega(D, sP) = C_\mathscr{L}(D, (q^3 + q^2 - q - 2)Q_\infty - sP). \quad \square$$

The computation of $C_\Omega(\widetilde{D}, sP)$ is more complicated. We claim the next results for the prime powers $q \equiv 2 \pmod 3$, since the proofs are rather transparent in this case. We are certain that they hold for $q \equiv 1 \pmod 3$ as well. Our opinion is supported by numerical experiments with $q \le 8$.

Lemma 5. *Assume $q \equiv 2 \pmod 3$ and define the $\mathbb{F}_{q^2}$-rational function*

$$T = \frac{1}{3}\left(\frac{\ell_1^{q^2}}{\ell_2} + \frac{\ell_2^{q^2}}{\ell_3} + \frac{\ell_3^{q^2}}{\ell_1}\right).$$

Then,

$$d\left(\frac{R}{(\ell_1\ell_2\ell_3)^{\frac{q^2-q+1}{3}}}\right) = -\left(\frac{T}{(\ell_1\ell_2\ell_3)^{\frac{q^2-q+1}{3}}}\right)dx.$$

Proof. We have $d\ell_i = (a_i - x)^q dx$, and

$$\begin{aligned} \ell_i^{q^2} - \ell_{i+1} &= a_i^{q^3} x^{q^2} - y^{q^2} - b_i^{q^3} - (a_{i+1}^q x - y - b_{i+1}^q) \\ &= a_{i+1}^q (x^{q^2} - x) - (y^{q^2} - y) \\ &= a_{i+1}^q R(x, y) - x^q R(x, y) \\ &= (a_{i+1} - x)^q R(x, y). \end{aligned}$$

In one line,

$$\frac{(a_{i+1} - x))^q}{\ell_{i+1}} = \frac{\ell_1^{q^2}/\ell_2 - 1}{R(x, y)}. \tag{9}$$

Hence,

$$\begin{aligned} d(\ell_1\ell_2\ell_3) &= \ell_1\ell_2\ell_3 \cdot \left(\frac{(a_1-x)^q}{\ell_1} + \frac{(a_2-x)^q}{\ell_2} + \frac{(a_3-x)^q}{\ell_3} \right) dx \\ &= \ell_1\ell_2\ell_3 \cdot \left(\frac{\ell_1^{q^2}/\ell_2 - 1}{R} + \frac{\ell_2^{q^2}/\ell_3 - 1}{R} + \frac{\ell_3^{q^2}/\ell_1 - 1}{R} \right) dx \\ &= \frac{\ell_1\ell_2\ell_3}{R}(3T-3)dx. \end{aligned}$$

This implies

$$d\left(R(\ell_1\ell_2\ell_3)^{\frac{-q^2+q-1}{3}} \right) = \left(-(\ell_1\ell_2\ell_3)^{\frac{-q^2+q-1}{3}} \right) dx + \\ R\left(-\frac{1}{3}(\ell_1\ell_2\ell_3)^{\frac{-q^2+q-4}{3}} \right) \frac{\ell_1\ell_2\ell_3}{R}(3T-3)dx.$$

By easy cancellation

$$\begin{aligned} d\left(R(\ell_1\ell_2\ell_3)^{\frac{-q^2+q-1}{3}} \right) &= \left(-(\ell_1\ell_2\ell_3)^{\frac{-q^2+q-1}{3}} \right) dx + -\frac{1}{3}(\ell_1\ell_2\ell_3)^{\frac{-q^2+q-1}{3}}(3T-3)dx \\ &= -\left(\frac{T}{(\ell_1\ell_2\ell_3)^{\frac{q^2-q+1}{3}}} \right) dx. \quad \square \end{aligned}$$

Lemma 6. *Assume $q \equiv 2 \pmod 3$ and define the $\mathbb{F}_{q^2}$-rational functions*

$$T = \frac{1}{3}\left(\frac{\ell_1^{q^2}}{\ell_2} + \frac{\ell_2^{q^2}}{\ell_3} + \frac{\ell_3^{q^2}}{\ell_1} \right) \qquad \text{and} \qquad R_1 = \frac{R}{(\ell_1\ell_2\ell_3)^{\frac{q^2-q+1}{3}}}.$$

Let G be a divisor of $\mathbb{F}_{q^2}(\mathcal{H}_q)$ whose support is disjoint from the support of $\widetilde{D}$. Then,

$$\mathcal{L}(\widetilde{D} - G + (dR_1) - (R_1)) = \mathcal{L}\left(\frac{(q^2-1)(q+1)}{3}P - G \right) \cdot \frac{(\ell_1\ell_2\ell_3)^{\frac{q^2-1}{3}}}{T}.$$

Proof. We have

$$\begin{aligned} \widetilde{D} - G + (dR_1) - (R_1) &= \widetilde{D} - G + (T) - \frac{q^2-q+1}{3}(\ell_1\ell_2\ell_3) + (dx) \\ &\quad - (R) + \frac{q^2-q+1}{3}(\ell_1\ell_2\ell_3) \\ &= \widetilde{D} - G + (T) + (dx) - (R) \\ &= Q_\infty + q^3 Q_\infty + (2\mathfrak{g}-2)Q_\infty - G + (T) \\ &= (q^2-1)(q+1)Q_\infty - G + (T) \\ &= \frac{(q^2-1)(q+1)}{3}P - \left((\ell_1\ell_2\ell_3)^{\frac{q^2-1}{3}} \right) - G + (T). \end{aligned}$$

For Riemann–Roch spaces, the results follow. □

Lemma 7. *For any $i, j \in \{1,2,3\}$, we have*

$$\left(\frac{\ell_i}{\ell_j} \right)(Q_\infty) = 1.$$

Proof. We use the local expansion $\tau(t) = (t : 1 : t^{q+1} + \cdots)$ of $\mathscr{H}_q$ at Q_∞. The dots represent terms of a higher degree.

$$\left(\frac{\ell_i}{\ell_j}\right)(\tau(t)) = \frac{a_i^q t - 1 - b_i^q (t^{q+1} + \cdots)}{a_j^q t - 1 - b_j^q (t^{q+1} + \cdots)},$$

which implies

$$\left(\frac{\ell_i}{\ell_j}\right)(Q_\infty) = \left(\frac{\ell_i}{\ell_j}\right)(\tau(0)) = 1. \quad \square$$

Lemma 8. *Assume $q \not\equiv 0 \pmod 3$ and define the $\mathbb{F}_{q^2}$-rational functions*

$$T = \frac{1}{3}\left(\frac{\ell_1^{q^2}}{\ell_2} + \frac{\ell_2^{q^2}}{\ell_3} + \frac{\ell_3^{q^2}}{\ell_1}\right) \quad \text{and} \quad T_1 = \frac{(\ell_1\ell_2\ell_3)^{\frac{q^2-1}{3}}}{T}.$$

Then, $T_1(Q_\infty) = 1$.

Proof. Since

$$\frac{\ell_i^{q^2}}{\ell_{i+1}(\ell_1\ell_2\ell_3)^{\frac{q^2-1}{3}}}$$

is the product of terms such as ℓ_i/ℓ_j, it takes the value of 1 at Q_∞. This implies $(1/T_1)(Q_\infty) = 1$. $\square$

Before stating our main result on differential codes, we remind the reader that two linear codes C_1, C_2 are monomially equivalent if $C_2 = \boldsymbol{\mu} \star C_1$ for some multiplier vector $\boldsymbol{\mu}$.

Theorem 4. *Assume $q \equiv 2 \pmod 3$ and define the $\mathbb{F}_{q^2}$-rational functions*

$$T = \frac{1}{3}\left(\frac{\ell_1^{q^2}}{\ell_2} + \frac{\ell_2^{q^2}}{\ell_3} + \frac{\ell_3^{q^2}}{\ell_1}\right) \quad \text{and} \quad T_1 = \frac{(\ell_1\ell_2\ell_3)^{\frac{q^2-1}{3}}}{T}.$$

Let G be a divisor of $\mathbb{F}_{q^2}(\mathscr{H}_q)$, whose support is disjoint from the support of $\widetilde{D}$. Define $\mu_i = T_1(Q_i)$ for $i \in \{1, \ldots, q^3, \infty\}$ and write $\boldsymbol{\mu} = (\mu_i)$. Then, all entries $\mu_i \in \mathbb{F}_{q^2}^*$, and

$$C_\Omega(\widetilde{D}, G) = \boldsymbol{\mu} \star C_{\mathscr{L}}(\widetilde{D}, \frac{(q^2-1)(q+1)}{3} P - G).$$

Proof. If $i \in \{1, \ldots, q^3\}$, then $\ell_i^{q^2}(Q_i) = \ell_{i+1}(Q_i)$. Therefore, $T(Q_i) = 1$ and $T_1(Q_i)$ is a well-defined non-zero element in $\mathbb{F}_q$. Lemma 8 implies $T_1(Q_\infty) = 1$. The theorem follows from Lemma 6. $\square$

Corollary 1.

$$C_\Omega(\widetilde{D}, sP) = \boldsymbol{\mu} \star C_{\mathcal{L}}\left(\widetilde{D}, \left(\frac{(q^2-1)(q+1)}{3} - s\right)P\right).$$

6. Hermitian Subfield Subcodes from Degree-Three Places

In this section, we study the subfield subcodes of $C_{\mathcal{L}}(D, sP)$. As before, q is a prime power, $s \geq 0$ integer, and P is a place of degree three of the Hermitian curve $\mathscr{H}_q$. The divisor $D = Q_1 + \cdots + Q_n$, $n = q^3$, is defined as the sum of the $\mathbb{F}_{q^2}$-rational affine places of $\mathscr{H}_q$. The rational place at infinity is Q_∞ and $\widetilde{D} = D + Q_\infty$.

6.1. Trace Maps of Hermitian Functions and Hermitian Codes

We collect properties of the maps $z \mapsto z^q + z$ and $z \mapsto z^q - z$, where z is either a field element, a function, or a vector. We refer to $z^q + z$ as the trace of z, and to the map itself as the trace map $\mathrm{Tr} = \mathrm{Tr}_{\mathbb{F}_{q^2}/\mathbb{F}_q}$. Clearly, Tr is linear over $\mathbb{F}_q$.

Lemma 9. *Consider a positive divisor G_1. The trace map satisfies the following properties:*

(i) *For any function $f \in \mathscr{L}(G_1)$, its trace lies within $\mathscr{L}(qG_1)$, implying $\mathrm{Tr}(\mathscr{L}(G_1)) \subseteq \mathscr{L}(qG_1)$.*
(ii) *Similarly, for any codeword $c \in C_{\mathcal{L}}(D, G_1)$, its trace resides in $C_{\mathcal{L}}(D, qG_1)$.*
(iii) *$\mathrm{Tr}(C_{\mathcal{L}}(D, G_1))$ is an $\mathbb{F}_q$-linear subspace of $C_{\mathcal{L}}(D, qG_1) \cap \mathbb{F}_q^n$.*

Proof. Since $G_1 \geq 0$, we have $\mathscr{L}(G_1), \mathscr{L}(G_1)^q \leq \mathscr{L}(qG_1)$; hence, (i) holds. Then, (i) implies (ii), and (iii) follows trivially. □

Proposition 9. *Let G_1 be a positive divisor that satisfies $\deg G_1 < n/q$. Then, $\mathrm{Tr}(C_{\mathcal{L}}(D, G_1))$ is an $\mathbb{F}_q$-linear subfield subcode of $C_{\mathcal{L}}(D, qG_1)$. Its dimension is*

$$\dim_{\mathbb{F}_q}(\mathrm{Tr}(C_{\mathcal{L}}(D, G_1))) = 2\dim_{\mathbb{F}_{q^2}}(\mathscr{L}(G_1)) - 1.$$

Proof. $\mathrm{Tr}(C_{\mathcal{L}}(D, G_1))$ is an $\mathbb{F}_q$-linear subfield subcode by Lemma 9. The trace map Tr and the evaluation map ev_D commute, and by $\deg(G_1) < n$, ev_D is injective. Define the $\mathbb{F}_q$-linear map

$$\tau : \mathscr{L}(G_1) \to C_{\mathcal{L}}(D, qG_1) \cap \mathbb{F}_q^n, \qquad f \mapsto \mathrm{ev}_D(\mathrm{Tr}(f)).$$

On the one hand,

$$\dim_{\mathbb{F}_q}(\mathscr{L}(G_1)) = 2\dim_{\mathbb{F}_{q^2}}(\mathscr{L}(G_1)) = \dim \mathrm{Im}(\tau) + \dim \ker(\tau).$$

We have to show that $\ker(\tau) = 1$. Define $\varepsilon \in \mathbb{F}_{q^2}$ such that $\varepsilon = 1$ if q is even and $\varepsilon = g^{(q+1)/2}$ if q is odd and g is a primitive element in $\mathbb{F}_{q^2}$. Then, $\varepsilon^{q-1} = -1$. For the rational function $f \in \mathbb{F}_{q^2}(\mathscr{H}(q))$, we have

$$\begin{aligned} f \in \ker(\tau) &\Rightarrow f^q + f = 0 \\ &\Rightarrow (\varepsilon f)^q = \varepsilon f \\ &\Rightarrow \varepsilon f \in \mathbb{F}_q \\ &\Rightarrow f \in \varepsilon^{-1}\mathbb{F}_q. \end{aligned}$$

This finishes the proof. □

6.2. An Explicit Subfield Subcode

In this subsection, we study a subfield subcode of $C_{\mathcal{L}}(D, (q^2 - q + 1)P)$. As $q^2 - q + 1 = (q-1)(q+1) - (q-1)$, one has

$$U_{q^2-q+1,i} = \frac{\ell_i^q \ell_{i+2}}{\ell_{i+1}\ell_{i+2}^q}.$$

The vector space $W_{q^2-q+1} \leq \mathscr{L}((q^2 - q + 1)P)$ consists of the functions

$$W_{q^2-q+1,\alpha} = \alpha\frac{\ell_1^q \ell_3}{\ell_2 \ell_3^q} + \alpha^{q^2}\frac{\ell_2^q \ell_1}{\ell_3 \ell_1^q} + \alpha^{q^4}\frac{\ell_3^q \ell_2}{\ell_1 \ell_2^q}, \qquad \alpha \in \mathbb{F}_{q^6}.$$

For rational functions $f, g \in \mathbb{F}_{q^6}(\mathscr{H}_q)$, we introduce the relation

$$f \approx g \Longleftrightarrow f(Q_i) = g(Q_i) \quad \text{for all } i \in \{1, \ldots, q^3, \infty\}.$$

This is clearly an equivalence relation, which can be also written in terms of the principal divisor

$$f \approx g \Longleftrightarrow (f - g) \geq \widetilde{D},$$

or in terms of the evaluation map

$$f \approx g \Longleftrightarrow \mathrm{ev}_{\widetilde{D}}(f) = \mathrm{ev}_{\widetilde{D}}(g).$$

Lemma 10.

(i) $(U_{q^2-q+1,i})^q \approx U_{q^2-q+1,i+2}$.

(ii) $(W_{q^2-q+1,\alpha})^q \approx W_{q^2-q+1,\alpha^{q^3}}$.

Proof. Lemma 7 implies $U_{q^2-q+1,i}(Q_\infty) = 1$. In the proof of Lemma 5, we have seen that $\ell_i^{q^2} - \ell_{i+1} = (a_{i+1} - x)^q R(x, y)$. Therefore, $(\ell_i^{q^2} - \ell_{i+1})(Q_i) = 0$ for all $i \in \{1, \ldots, q^3\}$. This shows

$$\begin{aligned}
(U_{q^2-q+1,i})^q(Q_i) &= \left(\frac{\ell_i^{q^2} \ell_{i+2}^q}{\ell_{i+1}^q \ell_{i+2}^{q^2}} \right)(Q_i) \\
&= \left(\frac{\ell_{i+1} \ell_{i+2}^q}{\ell_{i+1}^q \ell_i} \right)(Q_i) \\
&= U_{q^2-q+1,i+2}(Q_i)
\end{aligned}$$

This proves (i). For (ii):

$$\begin{aligned}
(W_{q^2-q+1,\alpha})^q &= (\alpha U_{q^2-q+1,1} + \alpha^{q^2} U_{q^2-q+1,2} + \alpha^{q^4} U_{q^2-q+1,3})^q \\
&\approx \alpha^q U_{q^2-q+1,3} + \alpha^{q^3} U_{q^2-q+1,1} + \alpha^{q^5} U_{q^2-q+1,2} \\
&= \alpha^{q^3} U_{q^2-q+1,1} + (\alpha^{q^3})^{q^2} U_{q^2-q+1,2} + (\alpha^{q^3})^{q^4} U_{q^2-q+1,3} \\
&= W_{q^2-q+1,\alpha^{q^3}}. \quad \square
\end{aligned}$$

Proposition 10. *The set*

$$\widetilde{\mathcal{W}} = \{\mathrm{ev}_D(W_{q^2-q+1,\alpha}) \mid \alpha \in \mathbb{F}_{q^3}\}$$

is a three-dimensional $\mathbb{F}_q$-linear subfield subcode of $C_{\mathcal{L}}(D, (q^2 - q + 1)P)$.

Proof. Lemma 10(ii) implies that $\mathrm{ev}_D(W_{q^2-q+1,\alpha})$ has $\mathbb{F}_q$-entries if and only if $\alpha^{q^3} = \alpha$. $\square$

6.3. Main Result and a Conjecture

Theorem 5. *Let $q \geq 3$ be a prime power, $n = q^3$, $D = Q_1 + \cdots + Q_n$ be the sum of rational affine places of $\mathbb{F}_{q^2}(\mathscr{H}_q)$, and P be a place of degree three. The dimension of the subfield subcode of the one-point Hermitian code is*

$$\dim C_{\mathcal{L}}(D, sP)|_{\mathbb{F}_q} \geq \begin{cases} 7 & \text{for } s = 2\mathfrak{g} = q(q-1), \\ 10 & \text{for } s = 2\mathfrak{g} + 1 = q^2 - q + 1. \end{cases}$$

Proof. Set $G_1 = (q - 1)P$. By Proposition 9,

$$\mathcal{T} = \mathrm{ev}_D(\mathrm{Tr}(\mathscr{L}(G_1)))$$

is an $\mathbb{F}_q$-linear subspace in $C_{\mathcal{L}}(D, q(q-1)P)|_{\mathbb{F}_q}$. Since $\dim(\mathscr{L}((q-1)P)) = 4$, $\mathcal{T}$ has dimension seven. This proves $\dim C_{\mathcal{L}}(D, q(q-1)P)|_{\mathbb{F}_q} \geq 7$.

Let $\widetilde{\mathcal{W}}$ be the three-dimensional $\mathbb{F}_q$-linear subfield subcode of $C_{\mathcal{L}}(D, (q^2-q+1)P)$ given in Proposition 10. We show that $\mathcal{T} \cap \widetilde{\mathcal{W}} = \{0\}$; the inequality $\dim C_{\mathcal{L}}(D, (q^2-q+1)P)|_{\mathbb{F}_q} \geq 10$ will follow. On the one hand,

$$\widetilde{\mathcal{W}} \leq \mathrm{ev}_D(\mathcal{W}_{q^2-q+1}).$$

On the other hand, using Theorem 3, we have

$$\mathcal{T} \leq \mathrm{ev}_D(\mathscr{L}(q(q-1)P)) = \mathrm{ev}_D\left(\bigoplus_{t \in H(P), t \leq q(q-1)} \mathcal{W}_t\right).$$

As ev_D is injective on $\mathscr{L}((q^2-q+1)P)$, and

$$\left(\bigoplus_{t \in H(P), t \leq q(q-1)} \mathcal{W}_t\right) \cap \mathcal{W}_{q^2-q+1} = \{0\},$$

we obtain $\mathcal{T} \cap \widetilde{\mathcal{W}} = \{0\}$. This completes the proof. □

Our proof was constructive, we used the subfield subcodes given explicitly in the previous subsections. Based on computer calculations for small q, we have the following conjecture.

Conjecture 1. *If $q \geq 4$, then equalities hold in Theorem 5.*

The claim of the conjecture has some equivalent formulations.

Proposition 11. *The following are equivalent.*

(i) $\dim C_{\mathcal{L}}(D, (q^2-q)P)|_{\mathbb{F}_q} = 7$.

(ii) $\dim C_{\mathcal{L}}(D, (q^2-q-1)P)|_{\mathbb{F}_q} = 1$.

(iii) $\dim C_{\mathcal{L}}(D, sP)|_{\mathbb{F}_q} = 1$ *for all* $0 \leq s \leq 2\mathfrak{g} - 1 = q^2 - q - 1$.

Proof. We use the notation of the proof of Theorem 5. Assume (i). We have $\mathscr{L}((q-1)P) = \mathcal{W}_0 \oplus \mathcal{W}_{q-1}$. Moreover, $\mathcal{T}$ is an $\mathbb{F}_q\mathcal{B}$-module that decomposes into the direct sum of a one-dimensional submodule and a six-dimensional submodule. Note that any non-trivial irreducible $\mathbb{F}_q\mathcal{B}$-module has dimension six. Since $\mathcal{T} \cap C_{\mathcal{L}}(D, (q^2-q-1)P)$ is a proper submodule, the only possibility is that it is one-dimensional over $\mathbb{F}_q$. (ii) follows. Trivially, (ii) implies (iii). Let us now assume (iii).

$$\dim_{\mathbb{F}_q} C_{\mathcal{L}}(D, (q^2-q)P)/C_{\mathcal{L}}(D, (q^2-q-1)P) = 6,$$

and therefore,

$$\dim_{\mathbb{F}_q} C_{\mathcal{L}}(D, (q^2-q)P)|_{\mathbb{F}_q}/C_{\mathcal{L}}(D, (q^2-q-1)P)|_{\mathbb{F}_q} \leq 6.$$

This implies $\dim C_{\mathcal{L}}(D, (q^2-q)P)|_{\mathbb{F}_q} \leq 7$. Together with Theorem 5, we have (i). □

We have a partial result related to case (iii) of Proposition 11.

Proposition 12. $\dim C_{\mathcal{L}}(D, sP)|_{\mathbb{F}_q} = 1$ *for all* $0 \leq s \leq \frac{2}{3}\mathfrak{g}$.

Proof. Fix an arbitrary integer s in the range $0 \leq s < \frac{2}{3}\mathfrak{g}$ and consider a generic element $(c_1, \ldots, c_{q^3}) \in C_q(s)$. This corresponds to a function g in $\mathscr{L}(sP)$ such that $c_i = g(Q_i)$ is an element of $\mathbb{F}_q$ for each $i = 1, \ldots, q^3$. We note that there exists a $\gamma \in \mathbb{F}_q$ such that at least q^2 of the c_i values is equal to γ. In other words, the function $g - \gamma$ is in $\mathscr{L}(sP)$ and has at least q^2 zeros on $\mathscr{H}_q$. However, a non-zero function in $\mathscr{L}(sP)$ cannot have more than $\deg(G) \leq 2\mathfrak{g} = q(q-1)$ zeros, leading us to conclude that $g - \gamma$ must be the zero function. This implies that every c_i is equal to γ, and hence $C_{\mathcal{L}}(D, sP)|_{\mathbb{F}_q}$ consists of constant vectors. This completes the proof. □

7. Conclusions

In summary, our research has uncovered important properties of the family of Hermitian subfield subcodes associated with degree-three places. We achieved this by precisely determining the dimension of these codes for certain parameters and providing explicit bases for the corresponding Riemann–Roch spaces. Moreover, we conducted experiments aimed at calculating the exact dimension of the underlying family of codes across a broad spectrum of parameters. This process has contributed to the reformulation of certain conjectures, with some being proven. Additionally, we have established lower bounds on the dimension of Hermitian subfield subcodes associated with the divisor sP, where P is a degree-three Hermitian place, for specific cases such as $0 \leq s \leq \frac{2}{3}\mathfrak{g}$, $s = 2\mathfrak{g}$, and $s = 2\mathfrak{g} + 1$, utilizing the bases of the underlying family of codes. Our motivation to explore the properties of Hermitian subfield subcodes stems from their potential as a family of AG codes for post-quantum cryptography use. In our future work, we anticipate using the parameters of subfield subcodes of degree-three Hermitian codes to enhance and secure the McEliece cryptosystem.

Author Contributions: Software, S.E.K. and G.P.N.; Investigation, S.E.K. and G.P.N.; Writing—original draft, S.E.K. and G.P.N. All authors have read and agreed to the published version of the manuscript.

Funding: This research was funded by French National Research Agency grant number ANR Barracuda (ANR-21-CE39-0009), French government Investissements d'Avenir program grant number ANR-11-LABX-0020-01, Quantum Information National Laboratory of Hungary grant umber 2022-2.1.1-NL-2022-00004, and National Research, Development and Innovation Office grant number SNN 132625.

Institutional Review Board Statement: Not applicable.

Data Availability Statement: No relevant new data were created in this research.

Conflicts of Interest: The authors declare no conflicts of interest.

References

1. Sendrier, N. On the security of the McEliece public-key cryptosystem. In *Information, Coding and Mathematics: Proceedings of Workshop Honoring Prof. Bob McEliece on His 60th Birthday*; Springer: Berlin/Heidelberg, Germany, 2002; pp. 141–163.
2. Faugere, J.C.; Gauthier-Umana, V.; Otmani, A.; Perret, L.; Tillich, J.P. A distinguisher for high-rate McEliece cryptosystems. *IEEE Trans. Inf. Theory* **2013**, *59*, 6830–6844. [CrossRef]
3. McEliece, R.J. A public-key cryptosystem based on algebraic. *Coding Thv.* **1978**, *4244*, 114–116.
4. Couvreur, A.; Gaborit, P.; Gauthier-Umaña, V.; Otmani, A.; Tillich, J.P. Distinguisher-based attacks on public-key cryptosystems using Reed–Solomon codes. *Des. Codes Cryptogr.* **2014**, *73*, 641–666. [CrossRef]
5. Couvreur, A.; Márquez-Corbella, I.; Pellikaan, R. Cryptanalysis of McEliece cryptosystem based on algebraic geometry codes and their subcodes. *IEEE Trans. Inf. Theory* **2017**, *63*, 5404–5418. [CrossRef]
6. Macdonald, T.G.; Pursley, M.B. Hermitian codes for frequency-hop spread-spectrum packet radio networks. *IEEE Trans. Wirel. Commun.* **2003**, *2*, 529–536. [CrossRef]
7. Stichtenoth, H. A note on Hermitian codes over GF (q/sup 2/). *IEEE Trans. Inf. Theory* **1988**, *34*, 1345–1348. [CrossRef]
8. Little, J.; Saints, K.; Heegard, C. On the structure of Hermitian codes. *J. Pure Appl. Algebra* **1997**, *121*, 293–314. [CrossRef]
9. Yang, K.; Kumar, P.V. On the true minimum distance of Hermitian codes. In Proceedings of the Coding Theory and Algebraic Geometry: Proceedings of the International Workshop, Luminy, France, 17–21 June 1991; Springer: Berlin/Heidelberg, Germany, 1992; pp. 99–107.
10. Korchmáros, G.; Nagy, G.P.; Timpanella, M. Codes and gap sequences of Hermitian curves. *IEEE Trans. Inf. Theory* **2019**, *66*, 3547–3554. [CrossRef]
11. Ren, J. On the structure of Hermitian codes and decoding for burst errors. *IEEE Trans. Inf. Theory* **2004**, *50*, 2850–2854. [CrossRef]

12. Lhotel, M.; Khalfaoui, S.E.; Nardi, J. Goppa-like AG codes from $C\_\{a, b\}$ curves and their behaviour under squaring their dual *arXiv* **2023**, arXiv:2303.08687.
13. Korchmáros, G.; Nagy, G.P. Hermitian codes from higher degree places. *J. Pure Appl. Algebra* **2013**, *217*, 2371–2381. [CrossRef]
14. Matthews, G.L.; Michel, T.W. One-point codes using places of higher degree. *IEEE Trans. Inf. Theory* **2005**, *51*, 1590–1593 [CrossRef]
15. Cossidente, A.; Korchmáros, G.; Torres, F. On curves covered by the Hermitian curve. *J. Algebra* **1999**, *216*, 56–76. [CrossRef]
16. Beelen, P.; Montanucci, M.; Vicino, L. Weierstrass semigroups and automorphism group of a maximal curve with the third largest genus. *arXiv* **2023**, arXiv:2303.00376.
17. Post-Quantum Cryptography. Available online: http://csrc.nist.gov/projects/post-quantum-cryptography (accessed on 6 February 2024).
18. Nagy, G.P.; El Khalfaoui, S. HERmitian, HERmitian/Computing with Divisors, Riemann-Roch Spaces and AG-Odes of Hermitian Curves, Version 0.3. 2024. GAP Package. Available online: https://github.com/nagygp/Hermitian (accessed on 11 March 2024).
19. GAP—Groups, Algorithms, and Programming, Version 4.12.2pre. Available online: https://www.gap-system.org (accessed on 11 March 2024).
20. Stichtenoth, H. *Algebraic Function Fields and Codes*; Springer Science & Business Media: Berlin/Heidelberg, Germany, 2009; Volume 254.
21. Stepanov, S.A. *Codes on Algebraic Curves*; Springer Science & Business Media: Berlin/Heidelberg, Germany, 2012.
22. Delsarte, P. On subfield subcodes of modified Reed-Solomon codes. *IEEE Trans. Inf. Theory* **1975**, *21*, 575–576. [CrossRef]

entropy

MDPI

Article

Construction of Optimal Two-Dimensional Optical Orthogonal Codes with at Most One Pulse per Wavelength

Minfeng Shao * and Xianhua Niu

School of Computer and Software Engineering, Xihua University, Chengdu 610097, China; rurustef1212@gmail.com
* Correspondence: shaomf@mail.xhu.edu.cn

Abstract: Two-dimensional optical orthogonal codes have important applications in optical code division multiple access networks. In this paper, a generic construction of two-dimensional optical orthogonal codes with at most one pulse per wavelength (AM-OPPW 2D OOCs) is proposed. As a result, some optimal AM-OPPW 2D OOCs with new parameters can be yielded. The new AM-OPPW 2D OOC may support more subscribers and heavier asynchronous traffic compared with known constructions.

Keywords: two-dimensional optical orthogonal code (2D OOC); optical orthogonal code (OOC); optical code division multiple access network

1. Introduction

With the advantage of combining the large transmission bandwidth of fiber-optic media and the flexibility of code division multiple access (CDMA) techniques, the optical code division access system (OCDMA) has been extensively studied since the 1980s. In this system, unipolar $\{0,1\}$ optical orthogonal codes (OOCs [1]) are employed as spreading codes. However, this multiple-access scheme has a drawback in that the effect of multiple-access interference (MAI) cannot be completely eliminated as in directly spreading CDMA systems. Thus, one of the key points for the OCDMA system is to design OOCs with low cross-correlation and off-peak autocorrelation. In the meantime, to enlarge the discrimination between the correct codeword and interfering codewords, we also need a large peak autocorrelation value, i.e., the weight of the OOCs. Finally, since the number of users in the system is less than or equal to the code size of OOCs, it is beneficial to design OOCs with large code sizes. However, as the volume of codewords or the weight of the code increases rapidly, the code length increases rapidly. Thus, optimal solutions, i.e., optimal OOCs, were proposed with respect to the tradeoff of those parameters (see, e.g., [2–10]).

In the meantime, two-dimensional optical orthogonal codes (2D OOCs) that spread in both time and wavelength were introduced for the OCDMA system to overcome this drawback. Similarly, to minimize multiple-access interference, we have to minimize the cross-correlation and off-peak autocorrelation of 2D OOCs; to support a large number of users, we need a large set of 2D OOCs. Moreover, to simplify the practical implementations, restrictions, such as at most one pulse per wavelength (AM-OPPW) and at most one pulse per time slot (AM-OPPTS), are often imposed on 2D OOCs [11]. However, these parameters are not independent of each other. They suffer some theoretic bounds, for instance, the Johnson bound [4] and the bound for 2D OOCs with the AM-OPPW restriction [11]. So far, various works have addressed optimal 2D OOCs with respect to these bounds [11–27].

The main idea of this paper is to generate new optimal AM-OPPW 2D OOCs based on known OOCs and 2D OOCs. In [16,17,19], OOCs were used to construct 2D OOCs by spreading them in the time domain, i.e., the OOCs form rows of 2D OOCs. In our construction, the OOCs are utilized to determine which rows of 2D OOCs are not all-zero vectors. In this way, new AM-OPPW 2D OOCs can be yielded with large sizes, some of which are optimal with respect to the theoretic bound proposed in [11]. Further, we also analyze the performances of the new 2D OOCs under the chip-synchronous and chip-asynchronous assumptions, respectively.

The remainder of this paper is organized as follows. Section 2 reviews some necessary preliminaries. Section 3 introduces the new construction of AM-OPPW 2D OOCs. Section 4 conducts the performances of the new AM-OPPW 2D OOCs under the chip-synchronous and chip-asynchronous assumptions, respectively. Section 5 concludes this paper.

2. Preliminaries

Let Λ, T, w, and λ be positive integers, and $\langle a\rangle_b$ be the least non-negative residue of a modulo b for positive integers a and b. A $(\Lambda \times T, w, \lambda)$ *two-dimensional optical orthogonal code* (2D OOC) $\mathcal{C}$ is a family of $\{0,1\}$ arrays of order $\Lambda \times T$ with constant weight w satisfying the following two properties:

(1) The autocorrelation property

$$R_{X,X}(\tau) = \sum_{k=0}^{\Lambda-1}\sum_{t=0}^{T-1} X_{k,t}X_{k,\langle t+\tau\rangle_T} \leq \lambda,\ 0 < \tau \leq T-1, \tag{1}$$

(2) The cross-correlation property

$$R_{X,Y}(\tau) = \sum_{k=0}^{\Lambda-1}\sum_{t=0}^{T-1} X_{k,t}Y_{k,\langle t+\tau\rangle_T} \leq \lambda,\ 0 \leq \tau \leq T-1, \tag{2}$$

where $X = (X_{k,t})_{0\leq k<\Lambda, 0\leq t<T} \in \mathcal{C}$, $Y = (Y_{k,t})_{0\leq k<\Lambda, 0\leq t<T} \in \mathcal{C}$ and $X \neq Y$.

If λ is the smallest integer such that (1) and (2) hold, then we say that λ is the *maximum collision parameter* (MCP) of $\mathcal{C}$. If $\Lambda = 1$, then $\mathcal{C}$ is exactly an *optical orthogonal code* (OOC) [1].

The following restrictions on the placement of pulse within an array are often proposed for 2D OOCs to simplify the practical implementations [11]:

- Arrays with one pulse per wavelength (OPPW): For any array X in $\mathcal{C}$, the element 1 appears exactly once in each row of X.
- Arrays with at most one pulse per wavelength (AM-OPPW): For any array X in $\mathcal{C}$, the element 1 appears at most once in each row of X.
- Arrays with one pulse per time slot (OPPTS): For any array X in $\mathcal{C}$, the element 1 appears exactly once in each column of X.
- Arrays with at most one pulse per time slot (AM-OPPTS): For any array X in $\mathcal{C}$, the element 1 appears at most once in each column of X.

Obviously, OPPW (OPPTS resp.) is a special case of AM-OPPW (AM-OPPTS resp.).

In the following, we briefly review the theoretic bounds on the code size of OOCs and 2D OOCs with AM-OPPW.

Lemma 1 ([4]). *The maximum possible size $\Phi(1 \times T, w, \lambda)$ of an OOC with parameters $(1 \times T, w, \lambda)$ is bounded by*

$$\Phi(1\times T, w, \lambda) \leq \left\lfloor \frac{1}{w}\left\lfloor \frac{T-1}{w-1}\left\lfloor \frac{T-2}{w-2}\cdots\left\lfloor \frac{T-\lambda}{w-\lambda}\right\rfloor\cdots\right\rfloor\right\rfloor\right\rfloor.$$

Lemma 2 ([11]). *The maximum possible size $\Phi(\Lambda \times T, w, \lambda)$ of a $(\Lambda \times T, w, \lambda)$ 2D OOC with AM-OPPW is bounded by*

$$\Phi(\Lambda\times T, w, \lambda) \leq \left\lfloor \frac{\Lambda}{w}\left\lfloor \frac{T(\Lambda-1)}{w-1}\left\lfloor \frac{T(\Lambda-2)}{w-2}\cdots\left\lfloor \frac{T(\Lambda-\lambda)}{w-\lambda}\right\rfloor\cdots\right\rfloor\right\rfloor\right\rfloor.$$

In particular, for the 2D OOC with OPPW,

$$\Phi(\Lambda \times T, w, \lambda) \leq T^{\lambda}.$$

An OOC (a 2D OOC with AM-OPPW resp.) is called *optimal* if the number of codewords achieves the theoretic bound in Lemma 1 (Lemma 2 resp.).

3. Optimal AM-OPPW 2D OOCs via Known AM-OPPW 2D OOCs and OOCs

In this section we introduce a general construction of AM-OPPW 2D OOCs based on known OOCs and AM-OPPW 2D OOCs.

Let $\mathcal{C} = \{C^0, C^1, \cdots, C^{M-1}\}$ be an AM-OPPW 2D OOC with parameters $(\Lambda \times T, \Lambda, \lambda_1)$. For $0 \leq i < M$, C^i is defined by

$$C^i = ({C_0^i}^\top, {C_1^i}^\top, \cdots, {C_{\Lambda-1}^i}^\top)^\top = \begin{pmatrix} c^i_{0,0}, & c^i_{0,1}, & \cdots, c^i_{0,T-1} \\ c^i_{1,0}, & c^i_{1,1}, & \cdots, c^i_{1,T-1} \\ \vdots & \vdots & \vdots \\ c^i_{\Lambda-1,0}, & c^i_{\Lambda-1,1}, & \cdots, c^i_{\Lambda-1,T-1} \end{pmatrix},$$

where $\top$ is the transpose operation, and the T-dimensional vector $C^i_j = \left(c^i_{j,0}, c^i_{j,1}, \cdots, c^i_{j,T-1}\right)$ is the $(j+1)$-th row of the array C^i, $0 \leq j < \Lambda$. Let $\mathcal{S} = \{S^0, \cdots, S^{N-1}\}$ be an OOC with parameters (n, Λ, λ_2), where $S^r = (s^r_0, \cdots, s^r_{n-1})$ for $0 \leq r < N$.

With the above preparation, we can construct an AM-OPPW 2D OOC $\mathcal{X} = \{X^{(C^i,S^r,j)} \mid C^i \in \mathcal{C}, S^r \in \mathcal{S}, 0 \leq i < M, 0 \leq r < N, 0 \leq j < n\}$ as follows.

Construction A: For each three-tuple (i, r, j), $0 \leq i < M$, $0 \leq r < N$, $0 \leq j < n$, run the following Algorithm 1 to generate a new $n \times T$ array $X^{(C^i,S^r,j)}$:

Algorithm 1 Generate the new array

Input: C^i, S^r, j.
  Initiate: $\tau = 0, t = 0$;
  while $0 \leq k < n$ **do**
    if $s^r_{k+j} = 1$ **then**
      $X_k^{(C^i,S^r,j)} = C^i_\tau$;
      $\tau = \tau + 1$;
    else
      $X_k^{(C^i,S^r,j)} = \mathbf{0}$; // $\mathbf{0}$ is the all-zero T-dimensional vector
    end if
    $k = k + 1$;
  end while
  return $X^{(C^i,S^r,j)} = \left(X_0^{(S^r,C^i,j)}, X_1^{(S^r,C^i,j)}, \cdots, X_{n-1}^{(S^r,C^i,j)}\right)^\top$.

Theorem 1. *The 2D OOC $\mathcal{X}$ generated by Construction A is an AM-OPPW 2D OOC with parameters $(n \times T, w, \lambda)$, code size nNM, and $\lambda \leq \max\{\lambda_1, \lambda_2\}$.*

Proof. We first show that the MCP of $\mathcal{X}$ is less than or equal to $\max\{\lambda_1, \lambda_2\}$. By (1) and (2), it is sufficient to investigate

$$R_{X^{(C^{i_1},S^{r_1},j_1)}, X^{(C^{i_2},S^{r_2},j_2)}}(\tau) = \sum_{k=0}^{\Lambda-1} \sum_{t=0}^{T-1} X_{k,t}^{(C^{i_1},S^{r_1},j_1)} X_{k,\langle t+\tau\rangle_T}^{(C^{i_2},S^{r_2},j_2)},$$

which is divided into two cases according to the values of i, r, and j.

Case I: $(r_1, j_1) \neq (r_2, j_2)$. By Algorithm 1, the rows $X_k^{(C^{i_1}, S^{r_1}, j_1)} \neq \mathbf{0}$ and $X_k^{(C^{i_2}, S^{r_2}, j_2)} \neq \mathbf{0}$ if and only if $s^{r_1}_{k+j_1} = 1$ and $s^{r_2}_{k+j_2} = 1$, where $0 \leq k < n$. Note that both $X_k^{(C^{i_1}, S^{r_1}, j_1)} \neq \mathbf{0}$ and $X_k^{(C^{i_2}, S^{r_2}, j_2)} \neq \mathbf{0}$ contain at most one element 1. Thus, the cross-correlation value $R_{X^{(C^{i_1}, S^{r_1}, j_1)}, X^{(C^{i_2}, S^{r_2}, j_2)}}(\tau)$ is less than or equal to the correlation of S^{r_1} and S^{r_2} at time shift $j_2 - j_1$, i.e., $\leq \lambda_2$.

Case II: $(r_1, j_1) = (r_2, j_2)$. By Algorithm 1, $X_k^{(C^{i_1}, S^{r_1}, j_1)} \neq \mathbf{0}$ and $X_k^{(C^{i_2}, S^{r_1}, j_1)} \neq \mathbf{0}$ are rows of C^{i_1} and C^{i_2}, respectively. Hence, the correlation value $R_{X^{(C^{i_1}, S^{r_1}, j_1)}, X^{(C^{i_2}, S^{r_1}, j_1)}}(\tau)$ is less than or equal to the correlation of C^{i_1} and C^{i_2} at time shift τ. Then, the nontrivial correlation value $R_{X^{(C^{i_1}, S^{r_1}, j_1)}, X^{(C^{i_1}, S^{r_1}, j_1)}}(\tau)$, i.e., $i_1 \neq i_2$ or ($i_1 = i_2$ and $\tau \not\equiv 0 \pmod T$)), is less than or equal to λ_1.

In addition, it is easy to check that $|\mathcal{X}| = nNM$. Therefore, the AM-OPPW 2D OOC $\mathcal{X}$ has parameters $(n \times T, \Lambda, \lambda)$ and size nNM, where $\lambda \leq \max\{\lambda_1, \lambda_2\}$. □

In what follows, we present some results obtained by Construction A for specific cases of $\lambda = 1, 2$. Firstly, for $\lambda = 1$, we have the following result:

Corollary 1. *If C is an optimal OPPW 2D OOC with parameters $(\Lambda \times T, \Lambda, 1)$ and $\mathcal{S}$ is an optimal OOC with parameters $(n, \Lambda, 1)$, then the AM-OPPW 2D OOC $\mathcal{X}$ generated by Construction A with parameters $(n \times T, \Lambda, 1)$ is optimal for $T \geq \Lambda$ and $\Lambda(\Lambda - 1) \mid (n-1)$.*

Proof. Because of the optimality of both the OOC $\mathcal{S}$ and the OPPW 2D OOC $\mathcal{C}$, the code size of $\mathcal{S}$ and $\mathcal{C}$ are, respectively, $M = T$ and $N = \left\lfloor \frac{1}{\Lambda} \left\lfloor \frac{n-1}{\Lambda-1} \right\rfloor \right\rfloor$ by Lemmas 1 and 2. Thus, applying Theorem 1, we obtain that $\mathcal{X}$ is an AM-OPPW 2D OOC with parameters $(n \times T, \Lambda, 1)$ and the code size $nNM = nT\left\lfloor \frac{1}{\Lambda} \left\lfloor \frac{n-1}{\Lambda-1} \right\rfloor \right\rfloor$. On the one hand, the fact $\Lambda(\Lambda-1) \mid (n-1)$ implies that $nT\left\lfloor \frac{1}{\Lambda} \left\lfloor \frac{n-1}{\Lambda-1} \right\rfloor \right\rfloor = nT\frac{n-1}{\Lambda(\Lambda-1)}$, i.e., the code size of $\mathcal{X}$ is $nT\frac{n-1}{\Lambda(\Lambda-1)}$. On the other hand, it follows from Lemma 2 that

$$|\mathcal{X}| \leq \left\lfloor \frac{n}{\Lambda} \left\lfloor \frac{T(n-1)}{\Lambda - 1} \right\rfloor \right\rfloor = nT\frac{n-1}{\Lambda(\Lambda-1)},$$

where the last equality holds for $\Lambda(\Lambda-1) \mid (n-1)$. Thus, $\mathcal{X}$ is optimal with respect to the bound in Lemma 2. This finishes the proof. □

In Table 1, we list some known optimal OOCs with parameters $(n, \Lambda, 1)$ satisfying $\Lambda(\Lambda-1)|(n-1)$, where p is a prime and q is a prime power.

Table 1. Some known optimal OOCs with $\Lambda(\Lambda-1)|(n-1)$.

Parameters	Code Size	Constraint	Ref.
$(q^2+q+1, q+1, 1)$	1		[4,28]
$\left(\frac{q^{d+1}-1}{q-1}, q+1, 1\right)$	$\frac{q^d-1}{q^2-1}$	d even	[4]
$(n, 3, 1)$	$\frac{n-1}{6}$	$n \equiv 1 \pmod 6$	[4]
$(p, w, 1)$	r	$p = w(w-1)r+1$	[29]

As an application of Corollary 1, in Table 2, we provide some optimal AM-OPPW 2D OOCs by means of the optimal OPPW 2D OOCs in [19] and optimal OOCs in Table 1.

Table 2. Some new optimal AM-OPPW 2D OOCs from Corollary 1.

Parameters	Code Size	Constraint
$((q^2+q+1)\times T, q+1, 1)$	$(q^2+q+1)T$	$T = p_k p_{k-1}\cdots p_1$ with $p_k \geq p_{k-1} \geq p_1 \geq q+1$
$\left(\frac{q^{d+1}-1}{q-1}\times T, q+1, 1\right)$	$\frac{T(q^{d+1}-1)(q^d-1)}{(q-1)(q^2-1)}$	$T = p_k p_{k-1}\cdots p_1$ with $p_k \geq p_{k-1} \geq p_1 \geq q+1$
$(n\times T, 3, 1)$	$\frac{Tn(n-1)}{6}$	$T = p_k p_{k-1}\cdots p_1$ with $p_k \geq p_{k-1} \geq p_1 \geq 3$ $n \equiv 1 \bmod 6$
$(p\times T, w, 1)$	rpT	$p = w(w-1)r+1$ $T = p_k p_{k-1}\cdots p_1$ with $p_k \geq p_{k-1} \geq p_1 \geq w$

Next, for $\lambda = 2$, we have the following corollary.

Corollary 2. *Let $\mathcal{C}$ be an optimal OPPW 2D OOC with parameters $(\Lambda\times T, \Lambda, 2)$ and $\mathcal{S}$ be an optimal OOC with parameters $(n, \Lambda, 2)$. Then, the AM-OPPW 2D OOC $\mathcal{X}$ generated by Construction A with parameters $(n\times T, \Lambda, 2)$ is optimal if $\Lambda(\Lambda-1)(\Lambda-2)|(n-2)$ or $(\Lambda-2)|(n-2)$ and $\Lambda(\Lambda-1)|\frac{(n-1)(n-2)}{\Lambda-2}$.*

Proof. The proof is similar to that of Corollary 1. □

It was shown in [30] that there exist optimal OOCs with parameters $(n, 4, 2)$ for $n \in \{10, 26, 34, 50, 74, 98\}$. Note that $(4\times 3)\times 2|(n-2)$ or $2|(n-2)$ and $(4\times 3)|\frac{(n-1)(n-2)}{2}$ for $n \in \{10, 26, 34, 50, 74, 98\}$. Associated with the optimal OPPW 2D OOC of parameters $(\Lambda\times p, \Lambda, 2)$ in [11], where p is a prime and $2 < \Lambda \leq p$, the following result can be directly obtained from Corollary 2.

Corollary 3. *Let $\mathcal{C}$ be the optimal OPPW 2D OOC with parameters $(4\times p, 4, 2)$ and $\mathcal{S}$ be the optimal OOC with parameters $(n, 4, 2)$, where $p \geq 4$ is a prime and $n \in \{10, 26, 34, 50, 74, 98\}$. Then, AM-OPPW 2D OOC generated from Construction A is optimal with parameters $(n\times p, 4, 2)$.*

Remark 1. *Compared with 2D OOCs, the AM-OPPW 2D OOC may have a lower code rate because the AM-OPPW condition is indeed a constraint from the perspective of code construction. The reader may refer to [12] for a more detailed comparison.*

4. Performance Analysis of the New Optimal AM-OPPW 2D OOCs

Let $\mathcal{X}$ be the optimal AM-OPPW 2D OOC with parameters $(n\times T, \Lambda, 1)$ and code size nMN generated from Corollary 1 based on a known AM-OPPW 2D OOC with parameters $(\Lambda\times T, \Lambda, 1)$ and code size M together with a known OOC with parameters $(n, \Lambda, 1)$ and code size N. From now on, we examine its performances under the chip-synchronous and chip-asynchronous assumptions, respectively.

In an OCDMA using on–off keying (OOK), "1" and "0" are sent with equal probability but only bit "1" is encoded by the 2D OOC. Following the simple protocol in [1], we analyze the performance of the OCMDA in an ideal case where performance deterioration is only due to multiple-access interference (MAI) so that the effects of physical noises, such as thermal noise, shot noise, and beat noise are ignored [31]. That is, a decision error occurs only when the accumulative MAI reaches over a decision threshold and a data bit zero is transmitted. In addition, before correlation is performed, a hard-limiter is often placed at the front end of a receiver for reducing the effects of MAI [32]. Thus, throughout this section we discuss the performances of the new 2D OOC in the ideal case with a hard-limiter.

4.1. Performance Analysis under the Chip-Synchronous Assumption

Without loss of generality, let $X^{(C^0,S^0,0)}$ be the desired codeword. Let q_l be the probability of l hits in a time slot when it cross-correlates with all the other codewords $X^{(C^{i_1},S^{r_1},j_1)}$, where $0 \leq l \leq 1, 0 \leq i_1 < M, 0 \leq r_1 < N, 0 \leq j_1 < n$, and $(i,r,j) \neq (0,0,0)$.

For the chip-synchronous case, the hard-limiting error probability of the new AM-OPPW 2D OOCs with parameters $(n \times T, \Lambda, \lambda)$ in on–off keying (OOK) data modulation is [33]

$$P_{syn} = \frac{1}{2}\sum_{j=\Delta}^{\Lambda}\binom{\Lambda}{j}\sum_{i=0}^{j}(-1)^{j-i}\binom{j}{i}\left(\sum_{m=0}^{\lambda}\frac{\binom{m}{i}}{\binom{m}{\Lambda}}q_m\right)^{K-1}, \tag{3}$$

where K denotes the number of simultaneous users and Δ is the decision threshold. Hence, for the case $\lambda = 1$, to derive the error probability of the new AM-OPPW 2D OOCs we only need to calculate the probabilities q_0 and q_1.

Firstly, we count the number of the hits between arrays $X^{(C^0,S^0,j0)}$ and $X^{(C^{i_1},S^{r_1},j_1)}$ to compute q_1. Recall from Algorithm 1 that their k-th rows $X_k^{(C^0,S^0,0)} \neq \mathbf{0}$ and $X_k^{(C^{i_1},S^{r_1},j_1)} \neq \mathbf{0}$ if and only if

$$s_k^0 = s_{k+j_1}^{r_1} = 1, \quad 0 \leq k < n. \tag{4}$$

When $s_{k+0}^0 = s_{k+j_1}^{r_1} = 1$, one hit occurs exactly once as τ running through all the possible time delays, i.e., $0 \leq \tau < T$, since the two rows $X_k^{(C^0,S^0,0)}$ and $X_k^{(C^{i_1},S^{r_1},j_1)}$ contain exactly one element 1, respectively. Note that the OOCs S^0 and S^{r_1} have weight Λ. According to the proof of Theorem 1, the following are true:

- When $r_1 \neq 0$, (4) happens exactly Λ^2 times as j_1 ranges from 0 to $n-1$. Then, there are $M(N-1)\Lambda^2$ hits since i_1 and r_1, respectively, have M and $N-1$ possible choices;
- When $r_1 = 0$ and $j_1 \neq 0$, (4) happens exactly $\Lambda^2 - \Lambda$ times as j_1 ranges from 1 to $n-1$. Then, there are $M(\Lambda^2 - \Lambda)$ hits since i_1 has M possible choices;
- When $r_1 = 0$ and $j_1 = 0$, (4) happens exactly Λ times. Then, there are $(M-1)\Lambda$ hits since i_1 has $M-1$ possible choices.

Therefore, there are $\Lambda^2 NM - \Lambda$ hits in total. Then, we have

$$q_1 = \frac{\Lambda^2 NM - \Lambda}{2T(nMN-1)}, \tag{5}$$

where the factor $1/2$ comes from the assumptions that the error occurs only if a data bit zero is transmitted and the element 0 is sent with probability $1/2$. $(nMN-1)$ denotes the number of codewords except for $X^{(C^0,S^0,0)}$, and T is the number of all the time slots. Secondly, the fact $q_0 + q_1 = 1$ implies

$$q_0 = 1 - \frac{\Lambda^2 NM - \Lambda}{2T(nMN-1)}. \tag{6}$$

In the sequel, we present some simulation results acquired by MATLAB r2023b as an example.

Example 1. *Let C be the optimal OPPW 2D OOC with parameters $(5 \times 25, 5, 1)$ and code size $M = 25$ [19] and $\mathcal{S}$ be the optimal OOC with parameters $(41, 5, 1)$ and code size $N = 2$ [5]. Then, we can construct a new optimal AM-OPPW 2D OOC with parameters $(41 \times 25, 5, 1)$ and code size $nMN = 41 \times 25 \times 2 = 2050$ using Construction A. In this case, using (5) and (6) we obtain $q_1 = 0.0122$ and $q_0 = 0.9878$. Then, we can calculate the hard-limited chip-*

synchronous error probability by means of (3), *which is plotted against K simultaneous users with threshold* $\Delta = \Lambda = 5$ *in Figure 1. Similarly, based on the OPPW 2D OOC with parameters* $(5 \times 35, 5, 1)$ *[19], an optimal AM-OPPW 2D OOC with parameters* $(41 \times 35, 5, 1)$ *and code size* $nMN = 41 \times 35 \times 2 = 2870$ *can also be yielded by Construction A.*

In [34], the multi-wavelength optical orthogonal codes (MWOOCs) with parameters $(41 \times 31, 5, 1)$ *and code size* 1681 *can be generated. As a comparison, we plot the hard-limited chip-synchronous error probability of the MWOOCs with parameters* $(41 \times 31, 5, 1)$ *and our new 2D OOCs with parameters* $(41 \times 25, 5, 1)$ *and* $(41 \times 35, 5, 1)$ *together in Figure 1.*

Further, simulation for the new 2D OOCs with parameters $(41 \times 25, 5, 1)$ *(*$(41 \times 35, 5, 1)$ *resp.) is performed by choosing K codewords for K simultaneous users randomly from the* 2050 *(2870 resp.) codewords. Particularly, the transmission time delay of each codeword is chosen from a random integer in [0,25) to simulate the chip-synchronous condition. In order to attain the error probability, the simulation is iterated* 10^4 *times for* $K \in \{350, 400, 450, 500, 550\}$.

As shown in Figure 1, the new 2D OOC with parameters $(41 \times 35, 5, 1)$ *has better performance than the MWOOC with parameters* $(41 \times 31, 5, 1)$*, while the MWOOC performs better than the new 2D OOC parameters* $(41 \times 25, 5, 1)$*. However, the code size of the new 2D OOCs, even for the case with parameters* $(41 \times 25, 5, 1)$*, are larger than that of the MWOOCs. This is desirable. On the one hand, the larger the code size, the more the users in the OCDMA systems. On the other hand, new 2D OOCs with large size may support multicode keying in OCDMA systems [35].*

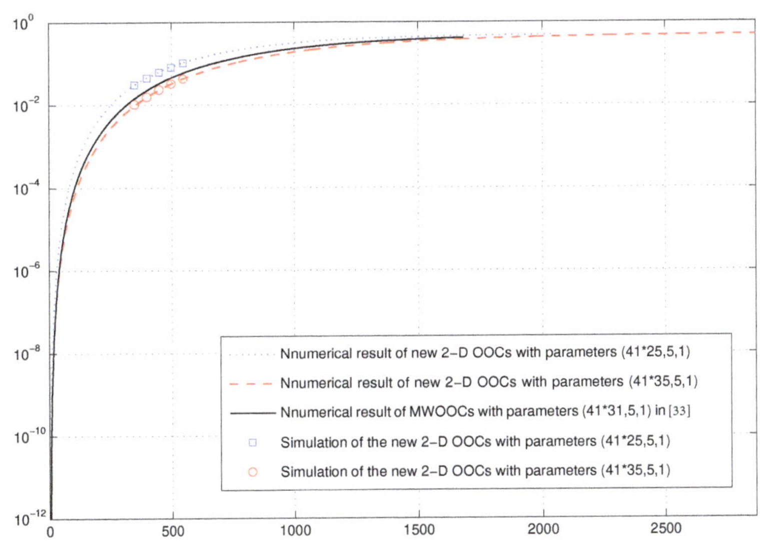

Figure 1. Error probabilities versus the numbers of simultaneous users under the chip-synchronous assumptions [33].

4.2. Performance Analysis under the Chip-Asynchronous Assumption

It is known that the chip-synchronous assumption provides pessimistic upper bounds on the performance of the system, whereas the chip-asynchronous assumption assures a more accurate performance [32]. In this subsection, we study the hard-limiting performance of the new AM-OPPW 2D OOCs under the chip-asynchronous assumption.

For the chip-asynchronous case, the hard-limiting error probability of the new AM-OPPW 2D OOCs with parameters $(n \times T, \Lambda, \lambda)$ in on–off keying (OOK) data modulation is [17,33]

$$P_{asyn} = \frac{1}{2} \sum_{r=\Delta}^{\Lambda} \binom{\Lambda}{r} \sum_{j=0}^{\Lambda-r} \binom{\Lambda - r}{j} 2^j \cdot \sum_{i=0}^{2r+j} (-1)^{2r+j-i} \binom{2r+j}{i} \cdot \left[\sum_{k=0}^{\lambda} \sum_{l=0}^{\lambda} q_{k,l} \frac{\binom{i}{k+l}}{\binom{2\Lambda}{k+l}} \right]^{K-1},$$

where K denotes the number of simultaneous users, $q_{i,j}$ denotes the probability of the cross-correlation value in the preceding time slot equal to $0 \leq i \leq \lambda$ (the present time slot $1 \leq j \leq \lambda$, respectively), and Δ is the decision threshold. In particular, for the new AM-OPPW 2D OOCs with parameters $(n \times T, \Lambda, 1)$, we then have

$$P_{asyn} = \frac{1}{2}\sum_{r=\Delta}^{\Lambda}\binom{\Lambda}{r}\sum_{j=0}^{\Lambda-r}\binom{\Lambda-r}{j}2^{j}\cdot\sum_{i=0}^{2r+j}(-1)^{2r+j-i}\binom{2r+j}{i}\cdot\left[q_{0,0}+\frac{(q_{0,1}+q_{1,0})i}{2w}+\frac{q_{1,1}\binom{i}{2}}{\binom{2\Lambda}{2}}\right]^{K-1}. \tag{7}$$

That is, it is sufficient to determine $q_{i,j}$, $i, j \in \{0,1\}$ for computing P_{asyn}.

According to [36], the 2D OOCs with $\lambda = 1$ satisfy that

$$q_{1,0} = q_{0,1}, \tag{8}$$

$$q_{1,1} = q_1 - q_{0,1}, \tag{9}$$

$$q_{0,0} = 1 - q_{1,1} - q_{1,0} - q_{0,1}. \tag{10}$$

To derive $q_{1,1}$, we need to count the total number of two consecutive hits, i.e., two hits occurring firstly at the preceding time slot and subsequently the present time slot, when the desired code array correlates with all the other arrays in the code set. Without loss of generality, assume that $X^{(C^0,S^0,0)}$ is the desired array.

Firstly, we discuss the arrays from the set $\{X^{(C,S,j)} \mid C \in \mathcal{C} \text{ and } (S \neq S^0 \text{ or } j \neq 0)\}$. Assume that there exists a hit at the time slot τ, i.e., $R_{X^{(C^0,S^0,0)},X^{(C,S,j)}}(\tau) = 1$. Note that for $S \neq S^0$ or $j \neq 0$, there exists at most one integer k, $0 \leq k < n$, such that $s_{k+j} = s^0_k = 1$ since their non-trivial correlation value is no more than 1. Then, by Algorithm 1, for any $C \in \mathcal{C}$ and any $0 \leq j \leq n-1$, both $X_k^{(C,S,j)} \neq \mathbf{0}$ and $X_k^{(C^0,S^0,0)} \neq \mathbf{0}$ occur at most once for all the integers $0 \leq k < n$, which indicates that $X^{(C,S,j)}$ and $X^{(C^0,S^0,0)}$ have at most one hit for all the time slots. This is to say, no other hits happen except for the one at time slot τ.

Secondly, we investigate the arrays based on the same OOC S^0 and $j = 0$, i.e., $\left\{X^{(C,S^0,0)} \mid C \in \mathcal{C}\right\}$. Suppose that there is a hit at the time slot τ, i.e., $R_{X^{(C^0,S^0,0)},X^{(C,S^0,0)}}(\tau) = 1$. In the OOC S^0, there are Λ elements $s^0_k = 1$ where $0 \leq k < n$. If $s^0_k = 1$, the rows $X_k^{(C,S^0,0)}$ and $X_k^{(C^0,S^0,0)}$ contain exactly one element 1 otherwise they are all-zero vectors according to Algorithm 1. Then, there are Λ possible time slots τ such that $R_{X^{(C^0,S^0,0)},X^{(C,S^0,0)}}(\tau) = 1$ and $\Lambda - 1$ times τ' such that $R_{X^{(C^0,S^0,0)},X^{(C,S^0,0)}}(\tau') = 1$ when τ' varies over $\{0,1,\cdots,T-1\} \setminus \{\tau\}$ for a given τ. Thus, in total, $\Lambda(\Lambda-1)(M-1)$ hits happen as C ranging over the set $\mathcal{C} \setminus \{C^0\}$. This to say, there are $\frac{\Lambda(\Lambda-1)(M-1)}{T-1}$ consecutive hits on average.

Based on the above analysis, we have

$$q_{1,1} = \frac{\Lambda(\Lambda-1)(M-1)}{2T(nMN-1)(T-1)}, \tag{11}$$

where the factor $1/2$ comes from the assumptions that the error occurs only if a data bit zero is transmitted and the element 0 is sent with probability $1/2$, $(nMN-1)$ is the number of codewords except $X^{(C^0,S^0,0)}$, and T is the number of all the time slots.

Then, by (8), (9), and (10), we get

$$q_{1,0} = q_{0,1} = q_1 - q_{1,1} = \frac{\Lambda^2 NM - \Lambda}{2T(nMN-1)} - \frac{\Lambda(\Lambda-1)(M-1)}{2T(nMN-1)(T-1)}, \tag{12}$$

and

$$q_{0,0} = 1 - q_{1,1} - q_{1,0} - q_{0,1} = 1 - \frac{\Lambda^2 NM - \Lambda}{T(nMN-1)} + \frac{\Lambda(\Lambda-1)(M-1)}{2T(nMN-1)(T-1)}. \tag{13}$$

Finally, we present some simulation results obtained using MATLAB as an example.

Example 2. *Analyzing the new 2D OOCs with parameters* $(41 \times 25, 5, 1)$ *and* $(41 \times 35, 5, 1)$ *generated in Example 1, using* (11), (13), *and* (12), *we can calculate that* $q_{11} = 0.0002$, $q_{00} = 0.9759$ *and* $q_{10} = 0.0120$ *(*$q_{11} = 0.0001$, $q_{00} = 0.9827$ *and* $q_{10} = 0.0086$ *resp.). Substituting them into* (7), *we derive the hard-limited chip-asynchronous error probability, which is plotted against K simultaneous users in Figure 2, where* $\Delta = \Lambda = 5$. *As a comparison, we also plot the hard-limited chip-asynchronous error probability of the MWOOCs with parameters* $(41 \times 31, 5, 1)$ *together with our new 2D OOCs with parameters* $(41 \times 25, 5, 1)$ *and* $(41 \times 35, 5, 1)$ *in Figure 2.*

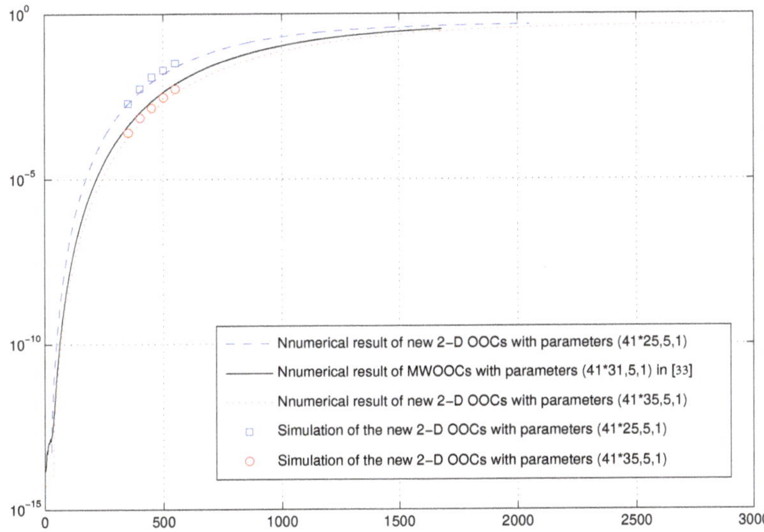

Figure 2. Error probabilities versus the numbers of simultaneous users under chip-asynchronous assumptions [33].

Simulations are conducted by choosing K codewords for K simultaneous users randomly from 2050 *(*2870 *resp.) codewords. Specifically, the transmission time of each codeword is chosen from a random real number between 0 and 25 to simulate the chip asynchronous condition. In order to acquire an error probability, the simulations are iterated* 10^4 *times for* $K \in \{350, 400, 450, 500, 550\}$. *As shown in Figure 2, the simulation result is very close to the chip-asynchronous curves given by* (7).

In addition, we compare the performance of the new optimal AM-OPPW 2D *OOC with parameters* $(41 \times 25, 5, 1)$ *under the hard-limited chip asynchronous and hard-limited chip synchronous conditions in Figure 3. It is seen that the performance of the hard-limited chip asynchronous is better than the hard-limited chip synchronous case, which is consistent with the result in [32].*

In Figure 4, we plot the performance of the new 2D *OOC with parameters* $(41 \times 25, 5, 1)$ *under hard-limited chip-asynchronous conditions for the decision threshold* Δ *with the value varying from* 3 *to* 5. *It was firstly pointed out in [32] that the higher the threshold level, the better system performance since multiple users will become less probable to occupy a particular chip above the level of the threshold. Clearly, our simulation result reveals this fact.*

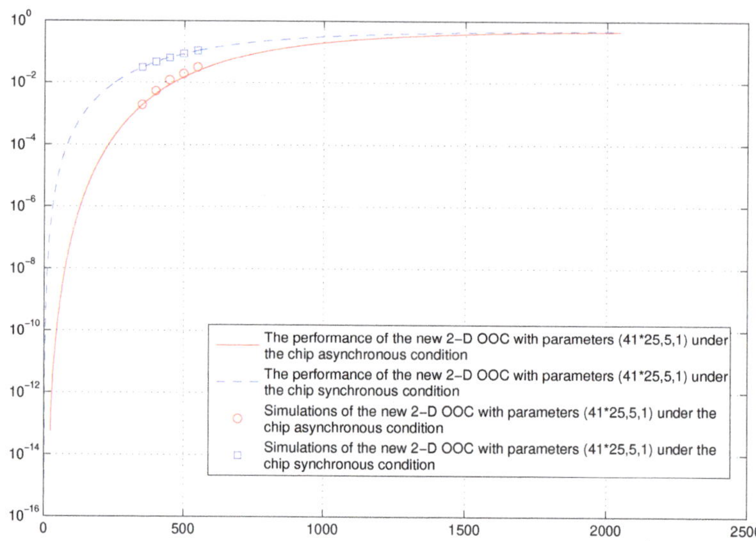

Figure 3. Error probabilities of the new optimal AM-OPPW 2D OOC under hard-limited chip-asynchronous and hard-limited chip synchronous conditions.

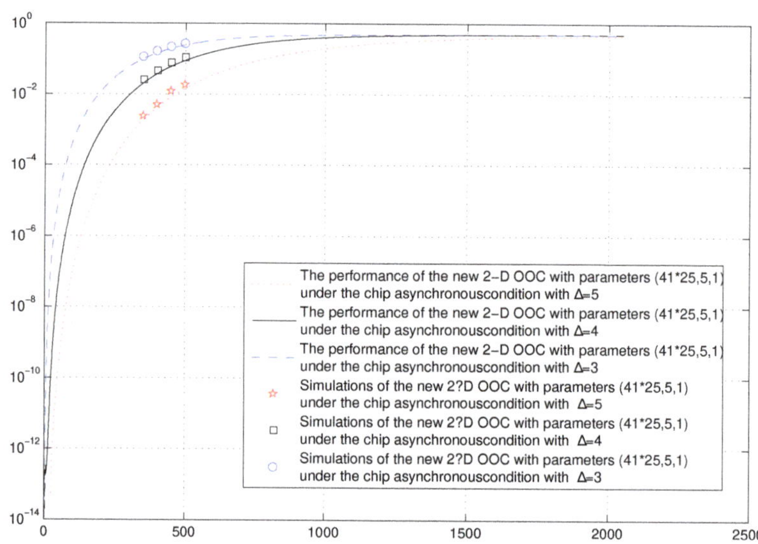

Figure 4. Error probabilities of the new optimal AM-OPPW 2D OOC under the hard-limited chip asynchronous with different decision threshold Δ.

5. Conclusions

In this paper, a new generic construction of AM-OPPW 2D OOCs was proposed. By restricting the OOCs and OPPW 2D OOCs to optimal ones, optimal AM-OPPW 2D OOCs and asymptotically optimal 2D OOCs with new parameters were obtained. Additionally, the performance of the new AM-OPPW 2D OOCs was demonstrated under both chip-synchronous and chip-asynchronous assumptions.

However, in general, the known parameters of AM-OPPW 2D OOCs are quite limited, and the performance of AM-OPPW 2D OOCs in real-world scenarios remains an open question.

Author Contributions: Investigation, M.S.; Writing—original draft, M.S.; Writing—review & editing, X.N. All authors have read and agreed to the published version of the manuscript.

Funding: This research was funded by Sichuan Provincial Natural Science Foundation Innovative Research Group under Grant 2024NSFTD0008.

Institutional Review Board Statement: Not applicable.

Data Availability Statement: The original contributions presented in the study are included in the article, further inquiries can be directed to the corresponding author.

Conflicts of Interest: The authors declare no conflict of interest.

References

1. Salehi, J.A. Code division multiple-access techniques in optical fiber networks-part I: Fundamental principles. *IEEE Trans. Commun.* **1989**, *37*, 824–833. [CrossRef]
2. Chang, Y.; Fuji-Hara, R.; Miao, Y. Combinatorial construcions of optimal optical orthogonal codes with weight 4. *IEEE Trans. Inf. Theory* **2003**, *49*, 1283–1292. [CrossRef]
3. Chu, W.; Golomb, S.W. A new recursive construction for optical orthogonal codes. *IEEE Trans. Inf. Theory* **2003**, *49*, 3072–3076.
4. Chung, F.R.K.; Salehi, J.A.; Wei, V.K. Optical orthogonal codes: Design, analysis, and applications. *IEEE Trans. Inf. Theory* **1989**, *35*, 595–604. [CrossRef]
5. Chung, J.-H.; Yang, K. Asymptotically optimal optical orthogonal codes with new parameters. *IEEE Trans. Inf. Theory* **2013**, *59*, 3999–4005. [CrossRef]
6. Ding, C.; Xing, C. Cyclotomic optical orthogonal codes of composite lengths. *IEEE Trans. Commun.* **2004**, *52*, 263–268. [CrossRef]
7. Ge, G.; Yin, J. Constructions for optimal $(v, 4, 1)$ optical orthogonal codes. *IEEE Trans. Inf. Theory* **2001**, *47*, 2998–3004. [CrossRef]
8. Fuji-Hara, R.; Miao, Y. Optical orthogonal codes: Their bounds and new optimal constructions. *IEEE Trans. Inf. Theory* **2000**, *46*, 2396–2406.
9. Moreno, O.; Omrani, R.; Kumar, P.V.; Lu, H. A generalized Bose-Chowla family of optical orthogonal codes and distinct differnece sets. *IEEE Trans. Inf. Theory* **2007**, *53*, 1907–1910. [CrossRef]
10. Yin, J. Some combinatorial constructions for optical orthogonal codes. *Discr. Math.* **1998**, *185*, 201–219. [CrossRef]
11. Omrani, R.; Garg, G.; Kumar, P.V.; Elia, P.; Bhambhani, P. Large families of asymptotically optimal two-dimensional optical orthogonal codes. *IEEE Trans. Inf. Theory* **2012**, *58*, 1163–1185. [CrossRef]
12. Cai, H.; Liang, H.B.; Tang, X.H. Constructions of optimal 2-D optical orthogonal codes via generalized cyclotomic classes. *IEEE Trans. Inf. Theory* **2015**, *61*, 688–695. [CrossRef]
13. Cao, H.; Wei, R. Combinatorial constructions for optimal two-dimensional optical orthogonal codes. *IEEE Trans. Inf. Theory* **2009**, *55*, 1387–1394. [CrossRef]
14. Feng, T.; Chang, Y. Combinatorial constructions for optimal two-dimensional optical orthogonal codes with $\lambda = 2$. *IEEE Trans. Inf. Theory* **2011**, *57*, 6796–6819. [CrossRef]
15. Shivaleela, E.S.; Sivarajan, K.N.; Selvarajan, A. Design of a new family of two-dimensional codes for fiber-optic CDMA networks. *J. Lightw. Technol.* **1998**, *16*, 501–508. [CrossRef]
16. Sun, S.; Yin, H.; Wang, Z.; Xu, A. A new family of 2-D optical orthogonal codes and analysis of its performance in optical CDMA access networks. *J. Lightw. Technol.* **2006**, *24*, 1646–1653.
17. Wang, T.-C.; Yang, G.-C.; Chang, C.Y.; Kwong, W.C. A new family of 2-D codes for fiber-optic CDMA systems with and without the chip-synchronous assumption. *J. Lightw. Technol.* **2009**, *27*, 2612–2620. [CrossRef]
18. Wang, J.; Yin, J. Two-dimensional optical orthogonal codes and semicyclic group divisible designs. *IEEE Trans. Inf. Theory* **2010**, *56*, 2177–2187. [CrossRef]
19. Yang, G.-C.; Kwong, W.C. Performance comparison of multiwavelength CDMA and WDMA+ CDMA for fiber-optic networks. *IEEE Trans. Commun.* **1997**, *45*, 1426–1434. [CrossRef]
20. Yang, Y.; Tang, X.H.; Udaya, P.; Peng, D.Y. New bound on frequency hopping sequence sets and its optimal constructions. *IEEE Trans. Inf. Theory* **2011**, *57*, 7605–7613. [CrossRef]
21. Alderson, T.L.; Mellinger, K.E. Optical orthogonal codes from singer groups. In *Coding Theory and Cryptology*; World Scientific: Hackensack, NJ, USA, 2007; Volume 3, pp. 51–70.
22. Cai, H.; Zhou, Z.C.; Yang, Y.; Tang, X.H. A new construction of frequency-hopping sequences with optimal partial hamming correlation. *IEEE Trans. Inf. Theory* **2014**, *60*, 1139–1141.
23. Chen, J.-J.; Yang, G.-C. CDMA fiber-optic systems with optical hard limiters. *J. Lightw. Technol.* **2001**, *19*, 950–958. [CrossRef]
24. Gu, F.R.; Wu, J. Construction of two-dimensional wavelength/time optical orthogonal codes using difference family. *J. Lightw. Technol.* **2005**, *23*, 3642–3652. [CrossRef]

25. Shivaleela, E.S.; Selvarajan, A.; Srinivas, T. Two-dimensional optical orthogonal codes for fiber-optic CDMA networks. *J. Lightw. Technol.* **2005**, *23*, 647–654. [CrossRef]
26. Wang, X.; Chang, Y.; Feng, T. Optimal 2-D $(n \times m, 3, 2, 1)$-optical Orthogonal Codes. *IEEE Trans. Inf. Theory* **2013**, *59*, 710–725 [CrossRef]
27. Yin, J. A general construction for optimal cyclic packing designs. *J. Combin. Theory Ser. A* **2002**, *97*, 272–284. [CrossRef]
28. Lee, S.; Seo, S. New construction of multiwavelength optical orthogonal codes. *IEEE Trans. Commun.* **2002**, *50*, 2003–2008.
29. Chung, H.; Kumar, P.V. Optical orthogonal codes-new bounds and an optimal construction. *IEEE Trans. Inf. Theory* **1990**, *36*, 866–873. [CrossRef]
30. Feng, T.; Chang, Y.; Ji, L. Constructions for strictly cyclic 3-designs and applications to optimal OOCs with $\lambda = 2$. *J. Combin. Theory Ser. A* **2008**, *115*, 1527–1551. [CrossRef]
31. Tancevski, L.; Rusch, L.A. Impart of the beat noise on the performance of 2-D optimal CDMA systems. *IEEE Commun. Lett.* **2000**, *4*, 264–266. [CrossRef]
32. Salehi, J.A.; Brackett, C.A. Code division multiple-access techniques in optical fiber networks-part II: Systems performance analysis. *IEEE Trans. Commun.* **1989**, *37*, 834–850. [CrossRef]
33. Hus, C.-C.; Chang, Y.-C.; Yang, G.-C.; Chang, C.-L.; Kwong, W.C. Performance analysis of 2-D O-CDMA codes without the chip-synchronous assumption. *IEEE J. Sel. Areas Commun.* **2007**, *25*, 135–143.
34. Kwong, W.C.; Yang, G.-C.; Baby, V.; Brés, C.-S.; Prucnal, P.R. Multiple-wavelength optical orthogonal codes under prime-sequence permutations for optical CDMA. *IEEE Trans. Commun.* **2005**, *53*, 117–123. [CrossRef]
35. Narimanov, E.; Kwong, W.C.; Yang, G.-C.; Prucnal, P.R. Shifted carrier-hopping prime codes for multicode keying in wavelength-time O-CDMA. *IEEE Trans. Commun.* **2005**, *53*, 2150–2156. [CrossRef]
36. Hsu, C.-H.; Yang, G.-C.; Kwong, W.C. Hard-limiting performance analysis of 2-D optical codes under the chip-asynchronous assumption. *IEEE Trans. Commun.* **2008**, *56*, 762–768. [CrossRef]

entropy

MDPI

Article

On Algebraic Properties of Primitive Eisenstein Integers with Applications in Coding Theory

Abdul Hadi [1,2], Uha Isnaini [1], Indah Emilia Wijayanti [1] and Martianus Frederic Ezerman [3,*]

1 Department of Mathematics, Universitas Gadjah Mada, Sekip Utara Bulaksumur 21, Yogyakarta 55281, Indonesia; abdulhadi1989@mail.ugm.ac.id or abdulhadi@lecturer.unri.ac.id (A.H.); isnainiuha@ugm.ac.id (U.I.); ind_wijayanti@ugm.ac.id (I.E.W.)
2 Department of Mathematics, Universitas Riau, Tampan, Pekanbaru 28293, Indonesia
3 School of Physical and Mathematical Sciences, Nanyang Technological University, 21 Nanyang Link, Singapore 637371, Singapore
* Correspondence: fredezerman@ntu.edu.sg

Abstract: An even Eisenstein integer is a multiple of an Eisenstein prime of the least norm. Otherwise, an Eisenstein integer is called odd. An Eisenstein integer that is not an integer multiple of another one is said to be primitive. Such integers can be used to construct signal constellations and complex-valued codes over Eisenstein integers via a carefully designed modulo function. In this work, we establish algebraic properties of even, odd, and primitive Eisenstein integers. We investigate conditions for the set of all units in a given quotient ring of Eisenstein integers to form a cyclic group. We perform set partitioning based on the multiplicative group of the set. This generalizes the known partitioning of size a prime number congruent to 1 modulo 3 based on the multiplicative group of the Eisenstein field in the literature.

Keywords: Eisenstein integers; unit group; set partitioning; signal constellation

1. Introduction

Eisenstein integers, named after the mathematician Ferdinand Gotthold Max Eisenstein, are complex numbers that can be expressed as $\alpha := a + b\rho$, where a and b are integers and $\rho = e^{2\pi i/3} = \frac{-1}{2} + \frac{\sqrt{3}}{2}i$ such that $\rho^3 = 1$ in $\mathbb{C}$ and $i^2 = -1$. The integers a and b are the *real part* and the *rho part*, respectively. Since the set of all Eisenstein integers, denoted by $\mathbb{Z}[\rho]$, forms a commutative ring with identity, it is commonly referred to as *the ring of Eisenstein integers* [1]. Occasionally, it is also called *the ring of Eisenstein–Jacobi integers*. The integers possess remarkable geometric properties. They form a hexagonal lattice in the complex plane, making them particularly useful in coding theory, cryptography, and signal processing. They allow for optimal packing and minimal energy configurations in various practical setups. The ring $\mathbb{Z}[\rho]$ is a Euclidean domain and, hence, is also a principal ideal domain and a unique factorization domain. Inspired by the algebraic properties of Gaussian integers discussed in, e.g., [2,3], many researchers have discovered properties of $\mathbb{Z}[\rho]$ by generalizing important properties of the ring of integers $\mathbb{Z}$ and the ring of Gaussian integers $\mathbb{Z}[i]$. We know of fundamental concepts such as the factor ring, the unit structure of the factor ring, and the Euler-Totient function on Eisenstein integers from results presented in [4–7].

Gullerud and Mbirika in [7] introduced the notion of even and odd numbers in $\mathbb{Z}[\rho]$. Revisiting their motivation, the prime number 2 has the least norm, in this case defined as the absolute value, in $\mathbb{Z}$. The quotient by the ideal generated by the even prime 2 has two cosets that partition $\mathbb{Z}$ into even and odd integers. Since $1 - \rho$ and its *associates* are primes

https://doi.org/10.3390/e27040337

with the least norm, to be formally defined below, in $\mathbb{Z}[\rho]$, we can pick $1-\rho$ to play the role of an even prime in $\mathbb{Z}[\rho]$, just like 2 in $\mathbb{Z}$. Unlike in $\mathbb{Z}$, however, the quotient by the ideal generated by $1-\rho$ is the set whose elements partition $\mathbb{Z}[\rho]$ into three sets, which we call *even*, *odd of Type 1*, and *odd of Type 2* sets. Some of their properties were investigated based on the norm and the sum of the real and the rho parts in [7].

In $\mathbb{Z}[\rho]$, an Eisenstein integer that is not an integer multiple of another is called *primitive*. Such an integer can be used to construct signal constellations and complex-valued codes over Eisenstein integers. These codes are obtained through a modulo function. Complex-valued codes are mathematical representations of coded symbols in communication systems, where codewords are constructed from complex numbers rather than real-valued symbols. These codes are particularly useful in digital communication for efficient modulation and error correction. We have provided a necessary and sufficient condition for an Eisenstein integer to be primitive in [8]. In that same work, we also constructed signal constellations for codes over $\mathbb{Z}[\rho]$ by studying primitive and non-primitive Eisenstein integers. In communication systems, a *signal constellation* is a physical diagram that depicts all possible symbols used by a signaling system to transmit data better. Mathematically, a signal constellation is a set of the residual class rings obtained by taking some modulo. Eisenstein integers have been used in designing denser and more efficient patterns in signal transmission. Such patterns have been shown to be beneficial in modern approaches, such as multiple input multiple output (MIMO) in [9], physical-layer network coding in [10–13], and compute and forward in [14].

Primitive Eisenstein integers exhibit excellent algebraic and number theoretic properties for applications in cryptography and error-correcting codes. There is an isomorphism between $\mathbb{Z}[\rho]$ modulo a primitive Eisenstein integer and $\mathbb{Z}$ modulo an integer, based on Theorem 8 below. In this work, we focus on discovering further algebraic properties of primitive Eisenstein integers as well as even and odd Eisenstein integers.

The multiplicative group of units in the quotient ring of Eisenstein integers has applications in coding theory. It has been used as QAM signals in [15,16], for enhanced spatial modulation in [17], and as a tool for set partitioning and multilevel-coded modulation in [18]. The set partitioning method leverages on the cyclic group structure of the units in the Eisenstein field $\mathbb{Z}[\rho]/\langle\psi\rangle$ such that the norm of ψ is a prime integer $q \equiv 1 \pmod 3$.

Constructions of codes over a number of other rings based on their primitive elements have been proposed in the literature. They utilize an isomorphism between a quotient ring induced by a primitive element and the ring of integers modulo the norm of a primitive element. The isomorphism sends a one-dimensional signal to a higher-dimensional signal. This general approach has been successfully performed to obtain codes. Examples include codes over $\mathbb{Z}[i]$ built based on primitive Gaussian integers in [19], codes over Lipschitz integers based on primitive Lipschitz integers in [20], and codes over Hurwitz integers, again using the primitive Lipschitz integers in [21–23]. The properties of primitive Lipschitz integers that are beneficial for encoding can be found in [24].

Li, Gan, and Ling in [25] provided a necessary and sufficient condition for two Eisenstein integers to be relatively prime.

Theorem 1 ([25]). *Two arbitrary Eisenstein integers α and θ are relatively prime if and only if*

$$\gcd\left(N_\rho(\alpha), N_\rho(\theta), \frac{2}{\sqrt{3}}\,\mathrm{Im}(\alpha\bar{\theta})\right) = 1,$$

with $\bar{\theta}$ being the conjugate of θ, or, equivalently,

$$\gcd\left(N_\rho(\alpha), N_\rho(\theta), \mathrm{Re}(\alpha\bar{\theta}) - \frac{1}{\sqrt{3}}\,\mathrm{Im}(\alpha\bar{\theta})\right) = 1.$$

We also know, this time from [26] that, if a Gaussian integer α and its conjugate $\bar{\alpha}$ are relatively prime, then $\alpha^{-1} \pmod{\bar{\alpha}}$ is an integer. This fact is useful in constructing multi-channel modulo samplers from Gaussian integers. It seems that no one has checked if the analogue of the fact and its application work over $\mathbb{Z}[\rho]$.

Freudenberger and Shavgulidze in [18] considered finite sets of Eisenstein integers $\mathcal{E}_\eta = \{\mu_\eta(\alpha) : \alpha \in \mathbb{Z}_{N_\rho(\eta)}\}$. They paid special attention to the case of $\eta = \psi$, which is a primitive and prime Eisenstein integer whose norm is a prime $q \equiv 1 \pmod 3$, as a two-dimensional signal constellation. Computing $\mu_\psi(\alpha)$ according to (2) below, the set of all units in $\mathcal{E}_\eta$, denoted by $(\mathcal{E}_\psi)^*$, can then be considered as a signal constellation for the general spatial modulation. In general, $\mathcal{E}_\eta$ is a representation of the quotient ring of Eisenstein integers only when η is primitive. In such a case, we can then partition $(\mathcal{E}_\psi)^*$ into $n = \frac{\varphi(\psi)}{6}$ subsets, indexed by $j \in \{0, 1, \ldots, n-1\}$, as

$$(\mathcal{E}_\psi)^*_{(j)} = \{\alpha^{n+j}, \alpha^{2n+j}, \alpha^{3n+j}, \alpha^{4n+j}, \alpha^{5n+j}, \alpha^{6n+j}\} = \{\pm\alpha^j, \pm\rho\alpha^j, \pm(1+\rho)\alpha^j\},$$

with α being a generator of the cyclic group $(\mathcal{E}_\psi)^*$ that corresponds to the generator of the cyclic group $(\mathbb{Z}[\rho]/\langle\psi\rangle)^*$. We can perform set partitioning on $(\mathcal{E}_\psi)^*_{(j)}$ according to the following theorem to obtain a larger minimum distance in each subset.

Theorem 2 (Proposition 1 in [18]). *Let $j \in \{0, 1, \ldots, n-1\}$. The minimum Euclidean distance in $(\mathcal{E}_\psi)^*_{(j)}$ is $\|\alpha^j\|$. We can partition $(\mathcal{E}_\psi)^*_{(j)}$ further into three subsets*

$$(\mathcal{E}_\psi)^*_{(j)} = \{\pm\alpha^j\} \cup \{\pm\rho\alpha^j\} \cup \{\pm(1+\rho)\alpha^j\},$$

each with minimum Euclidean distance $2\|\alpha^j\|$. We can also partition $(\mathcal{E}_\psi)^*_{(j)}$ into two subsets

$$(\mathcal{E}_\psi)^*_{(j)} = \{\alpha^j, \rho\alpha^j, -(1+\rho)\alpha^j\} \cup \{-\alpha^j, -\rho\alpha^j, (1+\rho)\alpha^j\},$$

each with minimum Euclidean distance $\sqrt{3}\|\alpha^j\|$.

In this paper, we gladly report the following contributions.

1. We establish further algebraic properties of primitive, even, and odd Eisenstein integers. We then answer Question 6.1 in [7]. Let ψ be an Eisenstein prime such that $N_\rho(\psi) = q$ is a prime integer and $q \equiv 1 \pmod 3$.
   a. Are the (non-associate) distinct pairs of primes ψ and $\overline{\psi}$ always of the same odd class? The answer is *yes, they are*.
   b. Does the corresponding q predict the odd class of ψ and $\overline{\psi}$? The answer is *no, it does not*.
2. Taking advantage of Theorem 1, our Theorem 22 confirms that, if Eisenstein integers α and $\bar{\alpha}$ are relatively prime, then $\alpha^{-1} \pmod{\bar{\alpha}}$ is in $\mathbb{Z}$. This result leads to a construction of multi-channel modulo samplers.
3. We prove important properties of the set of all units in a quotient ring of $\mathbb{Z}[\rho]$ when the set forms a cyclic group. The multiplicative group of the set leads to a nice set partitioning that generalizes Theorem 2 by using the modulo function in (1), which differs from the original modulo function in (2).

In terms of organization, Section 2 reviews known properties of Eisenstein integers. Section 3 presents our new results. We establish the algebraic properties of Eisenstein integers related to their being even, odd, or primitive. We look into the cyclic groups in the quotient ring. Set partitioning based on the multiplicative group of units in the quotient ring is the focus of Section 4. Section 5 highlights the role of primitive Eisenstein integers in the relevant code constructions. Section 6 contains a summary and several concluding remarks.

2. Preliminaries

This section recalls known properties of Eisenstein integers related to their being prime, primitive, odd or even. We also recall useful results on the quotient rings and and the unit group in a quotient ring.

2.1. Ring of Eisenstein Integers

Since $\rho = \frac{-1}{2} + \frac{\sqrt{3}}{2}i$ is a complex primitive third root of unity, we have $\rho^3 = 1$ and $(\rho - 1)(\rho^2 + \rho + 1) = 0$ implies $\rho^2 + \rho + 1 = 0$. Addition and multiplication in $\mathbb{Z}[\rho]$ are defined, respectively, by

$$(a + b\rho) + (c + d\rho) = (a + c) + (b + d)\rho$$
$$(a + b\rho) \cdot (c + d\rho) = (ac - bd) + (ad + bc - bd)\rho.$$

The *conjugate* and *norm* of $\alpha = a + b\rho \in \mathbb{Z}[\rho]$ for $a, b \in \mathbb{Z}$ are defined, respectively, as

$$\bar{\alpha} = (a - b) - b\rho \text{ and } N_\rho(\alpha) = N_\rho(\bar{\alpha}) = \alpha\,\bar{\alpha} = a^2 + b^2 - ab \in \mathbb{Z}.$$

By definition, $N_\rho(\alpha) = \|\alpha\|^2$, where $\|\cdot\|$ denotes the Euclidean distance, and the norm is multiplicative since $N_\rho(\alpha\theta) = N_\rho(\alpha)\, N_\rho(\theta)$ for all $\alpha, \theta \in \mathbb{Z}[\rho]$.

The division algorithm works over $\mathbb{Z}[\rho]$, i.e., for $\alpha, \eta \neq 0 \in \mathbb{Z}[\rho]$, there exists a unique quotient θ and a remainder δ in $\mathbb{Z}[\rho]$ such that $\alpha = \theta\eta + \delta$ and $N_\rho(\delta) < N_\rho(\eta)$. Since $\mathbb{Z}[\rho]$ is a Euclidean domain (ED), it is a principal ideal domain (PID) and a unique factorization domain (UFD).

In $\mathbb{Z}[\rho]$, an element η divides α, denoted by $\eta \mid \alpha$, if there exists $\theta \in \mathbb{Z}[\rho]$ such that $\alpha = \theta\eta$. We say that α is a *unit* in $\mathbb{Z}[\rho]$ if $\alpha\lambda = 1$ for some $\lambda \in \mathbb{Z}[\rho]$. A unit has a unique multiplicative inverse. It is known that α is a unit if and only if $N_\rho(\alpha) = 1$ and that $\mathbb{Z}[\rho]$ has 6 units. These are $\pm 1, \pm\rho$, and $\pm(1 + \rho)$. We say that α and β are *associates*, denoted by $\alpha \sim \eta$, if $\alpha = \theta\, \eta$ for some unit $\theta \in \mathbb{Z}[\rho]$. The associates of $\alpha = a + b\rho$ are $\pm\alpha$, $\pm\rho\alpha$, and $\pm(1 + \rho)\alpha$, with $\rho\alpha = -b + (a - b)\,\rho$ and $(1 + \rho)\alpha = (a - b) + a\,\rho$.

The *greatest common divisor* (GCD) ω of $\alpha, \theta \in \mathbb{Z}[\rho]$, denoted by $\omega := \gcd(\alpha, \theta)$, is the largest Eisenstein integer in terms of modulus, up to multiplication by any unit, that divides *both* α and θ. Every common divisor of α and θ divides ω.

Let $Q(\cdot)$ denote the quantization to the closest Eisenstein integer in as [27,28]. Fixing a nonzero $\eta \in \mathbb{Z}[\rho]$, we can define a *modulo function* $\mu_\eta(\cdot)$ as

$$\mu_\eta(\alpha) := \alpha \pmod{\eta} = \alpha - Q(\tfrac{\alpha}{\eta}) \cdot \eta. \tag{1}$$

Algorithm 1, which computes a remainder $\mu_\eta(\alpha)$ when α is divided by η, is a slight adaptation of the version in [11,27].

We highlight that the modulo function μ_η in (1) is different from the modulo function

$$\mu_\eta(\alpha) = \alpha - \lfloor \tfrac{\alpha}{\eta} \rceil \eta, \tag{2}$$

with $\lfloor\cdot\rceil$ denoting the rounding to the nearest integer as defined in [29]. For avoidance of doubt, we choose to define $\lfloor x \rceil := \lfloor x + 0.5 \rfloor$ for all $x \in \mathbb{R}$ in this paper. Our choice is somewhat arbitrary. If so desired, one can define $\lfloor x \rceil := \lceil x - 0.5 \rceil$ for all $x \in \mathbb{R}$.

Algorithm 1: Finding a remainder $\delta := \alpha \pmod{\eta}$ on input a given α and a fixed η.

1. $z \leftarrow \frac{\alpha}{\eta} = \mathrm{Re}(z) + \mathrm{Im}(z)i$ and $z - \rho \leftarrow \mathrm{Re}(z-\rho) + \mathrm{Im}(z-\rho)i$.
2. The nearest Eisenstein integers $\theta_1 \in \mathbb{Z}[\sqrt{3}i]$ and $\theta_2 \in \rho + \mathbb{Z}[\sqrt{3}i]$ are

$$\theta_1 \leftarrow \lfloor \mathrm{Re}(z) \rceil + \left\lfloor \frac{\mathrm{Im}(z)}{\sqrt{3}} \right\rceil \sqrt{3}i$$
$$\theta_2 \leftarrow \lfloor \mathrm{Re}(z-\rho) \rceil + \left\lfloor \frac{\mathrm{Im}(z-\rho)}{\sqrt{3}} \right\rceil \sqrt{3}i + \rho.$$

3. $\delta_1 \leftarrow \alpha - \theta_1\, \eta$ and $\delta_2 \leftarrow \alpha - \theta_2\, \eta$.
4. Output $\delta := \alpha \pmod{\eta}$ based on

$$\delta \leftarrow \delta_1, \text{ if } N_\rho(\delta_1) < N_\rho(\delta_2), \text{ or } N_\rho(\delta_1) = N_\rho(\delta_2) \text{ and } \mathrm{Re}(\theta_1) < \mathrm{Re}(\theta_2),$$
$$\delta \leftarrow \delta_2, \text{ otherwise.}$$

We use the modulo function in (1) because it gives us $N_\rho(\mu_\eta(\alpha)) = N_\rho(\delta) \leq N_\rho(\alpha)$ for every $\alpha \in \mathbb{Z}[\rho]$. In contrast, using (2) over $\mathbb{Z}[\rho]$ implies the existence of $\eta \in \mathbb{Z}[\rho]$ such that $N_\rho(\mu_\eta(\alpha)) > N_\rho(\alpha)$ for some $\alpha \in \mathbb{Z}[\rho]$.

Example 1. *Let $\eta = -6 + 5\rho$ and $\alpha = 5$. Since*

$$\frac{5}{-6+5\rho} = \frac{5(-11-5\rho)}{(-6+5\rho)(-11-5\rho)} = \frac{-55}{91} + \frac{-25}{91}\rho,$$

we have

$$\left\lfloor \frac{5}{-6+5\rho} \right\rceil = \left\lfloor \frac{-55}{91} \right\rceil + \left\lfloor \frac{-25}{91} \right\rceil \rho = -1 + 0\rho = -1.$$

Applying (2)*, we obtain*

$$\mu_\eta(5) = 5 - (-1)(-6+5\rho) = -1 + 5\rho \text{ and}$$
$$N_\rho(\mu_\eta(5)) = N_\rho(-1+5\rho) = 31 > 25 = N_\rho(5).$$

2.2. Prime and Primitive Eisenstein Integers

An $\alpha \in \mathbb{Z}[\rho]$ is called *(Eisenstein) prime* if α cannot be expressed as $\alpha = \theta\eta$ where θ and η are not units in $\mathbb{Z}[\rho]$. In other words, α is Eisenstein prime if *all* of its divisors are of the form $u\,\alpha$ with $u \in \{\pm 1, \pm\rho, \pm(1+\rho)\}$. Otherwise, α is *(Eisenstein) composite.* An $\alpha = a + b\rho$ is primitive if $\gcd(a, b) = 1$.

Eisenstein primes are classified as follows:

1. The prime $1 - \rho$ and its associates.
2. The prime $c + d\,\rho$, with $N_\rho(c + d\,\rho) = q$ such that q is a prime in $\mathbb{Z}$, with $q \equiv 1 \pmod 3$, and its associates.
3. The prime $p \in \mathbb{Z}$ such that $p \equiv 2 \pmod 3$ and its associates.

For the rest of this paper, let $\beta := 1 - \rho$ and let p and q be prime integers such that $p \equiv 2 \pmod 3$ and $q = \psi\,\overline{\psi} \equiv 1 \pmod 3$, where ψ and $\overline{\psi}$ are non-associate Eisenstein primes. We denote a generic Eisenstein prime by γ.

Remark 1. *Units as well as Eisenstein primes β and ψ up to associates are primitive Eisenstein integers. Any prime integer $p \equiv 2 \pmod 3$ and its associates are* not *primitive Eisenstein integers. We note that $5 + 4\rho$ is primitive but not an Eisenstein prime since $5 + 4\rho = (1-\rho)(2+3\rho)$.*

Theorem 3 ([30]). *If γ_1 and γ_2 are Eisenstein primes such that $N_\rho(\gamma_1) = N_\rho(\gamma_2)$, then $\gamma_1 \sim \gamma_2$ or $\gamma_1 \sim \overline{\gamma_2}$. If $N_\rho(\gamma_1) = 3$, then $\gamma_1 \sim \beta$. If $N_\rho(\gamma_1) = p^2$, with $p \equiv 2 \pmod 3$, then $\gamma_1 \sim \overline{\gamma_1}$. Lastly, if q is a prime integer such that $N_\rho(\gamma_1) = q \equiv 1 \pmod 3$, then $\gamma_1 \not\sim \overline{\gamma_1}$.*

Theorem 4 ([8]). *Given any two elements $\alpha, \theta \in \mathbb{Z}[\rho]$, we have $N_\rho(\alpha) = N_\rho(\theta) \in \mathbb{Z}$ if and only if $\alpha \sim \theta$ or $\alpha \sim \bar{\theta}$.*

Gullerud and Mbirika stated in Theorem 5.8 of [7] that any power of an Eisenstein prime ψ is a primitive element. To prove this valid claim, they had assumed that if the norms of two Eisenstein integers are the same, then they are associates. This *assumption is invalid*. Theorem 4 states that it does *not* hold in general. We reproduce the original theorem and supply a proof in Appendix A. Our proof uses Theorem 4.

Theorem 5 (Theorem 5.8 in [7]). *Let $\psi = x + y\rho$ be a prime in $\mathbb{Z}[\rho]$. If $N_\rho(\psi) = q \equiv 1 \pmod 3$ be such that q is a prime in $\mathbb{Z}$, then ψ^n is a primitive Eisenstein integer for all $n \in \mathbb{N}$.*

Proof. See Appendix A. □

In another recent work, we have established a necessary and sufficient condition for an Eisenstein integer to be primitive.

Theorem 6 ([8]). *An Eisenstein integer η is primitive if and only if $\eta \sim \beta^r \psi_1^{r_1} \cdots \psi_m^{r_m}$, with*

- *$r \in \{0, 1\}$, m, and r_i are nonnegative integers,*
- *$N_\rho(\psi_i) = q_i \in \mathbb{Z}$ is a prime such that $q_i \equiv 1 \pmod 3$ for $0 \le i \le m$,*
- *$q_i \ne q_j$ for $i, j \in \{0, 1, \ldots, m\}$ such that $i \ne j$.*

2.3. On the Quotient Ring of Eisenstein Integers

Since $\mathbb{Z}[\rho]$ is a PID, any ideal is of the form $\langle \eta \rangle$ for some $\eta \in \mathbb{Z}[\rho]$. A congruence in $\mathbb{Z}[\rho]$ modulo $\langle \eta \rangle$ can then be defined. For any $\alpha, \theta \in \mathbb{Z}[\rho]$, we have $\alpha \equiv \theta \pmod \eta$ if and only if $\alpha - \theta \in \langle \eta \rangle$. For any $\alpha \in \mathbb{Z}[\rho]$, the *equivalence class* of α with respect to η, denoted by $[\alpha]_\eta$, is defined to be

$$[\alpha]_\eta = \{\theta \in \mathbb{Z}[\rho] \,:\, \theta \equiv \alpha \pmod \eta\}.$$

The set $\{[\alpha]_\eta \,:\, \alpha \in \mathbb{Z}[\rho]\}$ forms the *quotient ring* $\mathbb{Z}[\rho]/\langle \eta \rangle$.

We will soon make use of three results from [4].

Theorem 7 ([4]). *If $\eta \in \mathbb{Z}[\rho] \setminus \{0\}$ is such that $\eta = a + b\rho = t(m + n\rho)$, with $\gcd(a, b) = t$ and $\gcd(m, n) = 1$, then the complete residue system is*

$$\mathbb{Z}[\rho]/\langle \eta \rangle = \{[x + y\rho]_\eta \,:\, 0 \le x < tN_\rho(m + n\rho),\ 0 \le y < t\},$$

with $[x + y\rho]_\eta := x + y\rho + \langle \eta \rangle$.

Theorem 8 ([4]). *If η is a primitive Eisenstein integer, then $\mathbb{Z}[\rho]/\langle \eta \rangle \cong \mathbb{Z}_{N_\rho(\eta)}$.*

Theorem 9 ([4]). *If $n \in \mathbb{N}$, then $\mathbb{Z}[\rho]/\langle n \rangle \cong \mathbb{Z}_n[\rho]$.*

The ring $\mathbb{Z}_n[\rho]$ is known as *the ring of Eisenstein integers modulo n*.

2.4. Even and Odd Eisenstein Integers

By Theorem 7, for $\beta = 1-\rho \in \mathbb{Z}[\rho]$, we have $\mathbb{Z}[\rho]/\langle\beta\rangle = \{[0]_\beta,\ [1]_\beta,\ [2]_\beta\}$, with

$$[0]_\beta = \{x+y\rho \in \mathbb{Z}[\rho] \ : \ x+y\rho \equiv 0 \ (\text{mod } \beta)\},$$
$$[1]_\beta = \{x+y\rho \in \mathbb{Z}[\rho] \ : \ x+y\rho \equiv 1 \ (\text{mod } \beta)\},$$
$$[2]_\beta = \{x+y\rho \in \mathbb{Z}[\rho] \ : \ x+y\rho \equiv 2 \ (\text{mod } \beta)\}.$$

An Eisenstein integer α is *even* if $\alpha \in [0]_\beta$. An Eisenstein integer α is *odd* if α is in $[1]_\beta \cup [2]_\beta$. More precisely, α is *odd of Type-1* if $\alpha \in [1]_\beta$. It is *odd of Type-2* if $\alpha \in [2]_\beta$. We denote the respective sets of all even, odd Type-1, and odd Type-2 Eisenstein integers by E, O_1, and O_2.

Remark 2. *By Theorem 6, an Eisenstein integer of the form $(1+\rho)^\ell \beta \psi_1^{r_1} \cdots \psi_m^{r_m}$ is even primitive and an Eisenstein integer of the form $(1+\rho)^\ell \psi_1^{r_1} \cdots \psi_m^{r_m}$ is odd primitive.*

We have a simple characterization based on the sum of the real and the rho parts.

Theorem 10 ([7]). *For any $x+y\rho \in \mathbb{Z}[\rho]$, we have*

i. $x+y\rho \in E$ *if and only if* $x+y \equiv 0 \ (\text{mod } 3)$ *if and only if* $N_\rho(x+y\rho) \equiv 0 \ (\text{mod } 3)$.
ii. $x+y\rho \in O_1$ *if and only if* $x+y \equiv 1 \ (\text{mod } 3)$, *which implies* $N_\rho(x+y\rho) \equiv 1 \ (\text{mod } 3)$.
iii. $x+y\rho \in O_2$ *if and only if* $x+y \equiv 2 \ (\text{mod } 3)$, *which implies* $N_\rho(x+y\rho) \equiv 1 \ (\text{mod } 3)$.

Example 2. *A prime β, its associates and multiples are even Eisenstein integers. The other primes are odd Eisenstein integers. The prime $\psi_1 = 2+3\rho$ is an odd Eisenstein integer of Type-2. The prime $\psi_2 = 3+4\rho$ is an odd Eisenstein integer of Type-1. Any prime integer $p \equiv 2 \ (\text{mod } 3)$ is an odd Eisenstein integer of Type-2.*

Theorem 11 ([7]). *If α, θ, τ, τ', σ, and σ' are in $\mathbb{Z}[\rho]$ such that $\theta \in E$, $\tau, \tau' \in O_1$, and $\sigma, \sigma' \in O_2$, then*

$$\alpha \cdot \theta \in E, \quad \tau \cdot \sigma \in O_2, \quad \tau \cdot \tau' \text{ and } \sigma \cdot \sigma' \in O_1.$$

2.5. Unit Group in the Quotient Ring of Eisenstein Integers

The set of all units in $\mathbb{Z}[\rho]/\langle\eta\rangle$, formally defined to be

$$(\mathbb{Z}[\rho]/\langle\eta\rangle))^* = \{[\alpha]_\eta \in \mathbb{Z}[\rho]/\langle\eta\rangle \ : \ \gcd(\alpha,\eta) = 1\},$$

is a group under multiplication. The Euler-Totient function with respect to $\eta \in \mathbb{Z}[\rho]$ is the order of unit group $(\mathbb{Z}[\rho]/\langle\eta\rangle)^*$,

$$\varphi_\rho(\eta) = |(\mathbb{Z}[\rho]/\langle\eta\rangle)^*|.$$

If η and 1 are associates, then $\varphi_\rho(\eta) = 1$.

Recall that γ denotes a generic Eisenstein prime. We have the following easy way to determine the units in $\mathbb{Z}[\rho]/\langle\gamma^n\rangle$.

Theorem 12 ([4]). *The set of all units in $\mathbb{Z}[\rho]/\langle\gamma^n\rangle$ are*

$$(\mathbb{Z}[\rho]/\langle\beta^n\rangle)^* = \{[x+y\rho]_{\beta^n} \in \mathbb{Z}[\rho]/\langle\beta^n\rangle \ : \ x+y \not\equiv 0 \ (\text{mod } 3)\},$$
$$(\mathbb{Z}[\rho]/\langle\psi^n\rangle)^* = \{[x]_{\psi^n} \in \mathbb{Z}[\rho]/\langle\psi^n\rangle \ : \ \gcd(x,q) = 1\},$$
$$(\mathbb{Z}[\rho]/\langle p^n\rangle)^* = \{[x+y\rho]_{p^n} \in \mathbb{Z}[\rho]/\langle p^n\rangle \ : \ \gcd(x,p) = 1 \text{ or } \gcd(y,p) = 1\}.$$

The unit group $\mathbb{Z}_n^*$ in $\mathbb{Z}$ is cyclic if and only if $n \in \{2, 4, p^k, 2p^k\}$, where p is an odd prime and k is a positive integer. A necessary and sufficient condition for the unit group $(\mathbb{Z}[\rho]/\langle\eta\rangle)^*$ to be cyclic is known.

Theorem 13 ([31,32]). *A unit group $(\mathbb{Z}[\rho]/\langle\eta\rangle)^*$ is cyclic if and only if*

$$\eta \text{ is an element or an associate of an element in } \{\beta, \beta^2, 2\beta, \psi^k, p\},$$

where $k \in \mathbb{N}$, ψ is an Eisenstein prime such that $N_\rho(\psi) = q \equiv 1 \pmod 3$, and p is a prime integer such that $p \equiv 2 \pmod 3$.

Theorem 14 ([7]). *If $\eta \in \mathbb{Z}[\rho] \setminus \{0\}$, then $\varphi_\rho(\eta)$ is even, except when η is a unit, or η and 2 are associates.*

Theorem 15 ([33]). *Let $\eta \in \mathbb{Z}[\rho] \setminus \{0\}$ be such that η is not a unit. If $\beta \not\sim \eta \not\sim 2$, then $6 \mid \varphi_\rho(\eta)$.*

Theorem 16 ([33]). *If $\eta \sim n$ for an $n \in \mathbb{Z}$, then $\varphi(n) \mid \varphi_\rho(\eta)$ and $\varphi(\varphi(n)) \leq \varphi(\varphi_\rho(\eta))$. In particular, for any positive integer k,*

$$\varphi_\rho(\eta) = \begin{cases} \varphi(n), & \text{if } n = 1, \\ n\varphi(n), & \text{if } n = 3^k, \\ (\varphi(n))^2, & \text{if } n = q^k, \text{ with } q \equiv 1 \pmod 3 \text{ being a prime integer}, \\ \left(n + \frac{n}{p}\right)\varphi(n), & \text{if } n = p^k, \text{ with } p \equiv 2 \pmod 3 \text{ being a prime integer}. \end{cases}$$

3. Further Properties of Eisenstein Integers

We discuss further properties of primitive, even, and odd Eisenstein integers in the first subsection. The second subsection centers on the cyclic group of units in the quotient rings of Eisenstein integers.

3.1. On Even, Odd, and Primitive Eisenstein Integers

Theorem 17. *Let $\alpha, \theta \in \mathbb{Z}[\rho]$. The following statements hold:*

i. *If $\alpha, \theta \in E$, then $\alpha + \theta \in E$.*
ii. *If $\alpha, \theta \in O_1$, then $\alpha + \theta \in O_2$.*
iii. *If $\alpha, \theta \in O_2$, then $\alpha + \theta \in O_1$.*
iv. *If $\alpha \in O_1$ and $\theta \in O_2$, then $\alpha + \theta \in E$.*
v. *If $\alpha \in E$ and $\theta \in O_1$, then $\alpha + \theta \in O_1$.*
vi. *If $\alpha \in E$ and $\theta \in O_2$, then $\alpha + \theta \in O_2$.*

Proof. A straightforward application of Theorem 10 confirms the assertions. □

Theorem 18. *Let $\alpha, \theta \in \mathbb{Z}[\rho]$.*

i. *If $\alpha \in E$ and $\alpha \sim \theta$, then $\theta, \bar{\alpha} \in E$.*
ii. *If $\alpha \in O_1$ and $\alpha \sim \theta$, then $\theta = \alpha, \rho\alpha, -(1+\rho)\alpha \in O_1$, and $-\theta \in O_2$.*
iii. *If $\alpha \in O_2$ and $\alpha \sim \theta$, then $\theta = \alpha, \rho\alpha, -(1+\rho)\alpha \in O_2$, and $-\theta \in O_1$.*
iv. *If $\alpha \in O_1$, then $\bar{\alpha} \in O_1$.*
v. *If $\alpha \in O_2$, then $\bar{\alpha} \in O_2$.*

Proof. We proceed by items as listed.

i. Let $\alpha = a + b\rho \in E$ and $\theta \sim \alpha$. By Theorems 4 and 10, $N_\rho(\alpha) \equiv 0 \pmod 3$ and $N_\rho(\theta) = N_\rho(\alpha) = N_\rho(\bar{\alpha}) \equiv 0 \pmod 3$, affirming $\theta, \bar{\alpha} \in E$.

ii. Assuming $\alpha = a + b\rho \in O_1$ and $\alpha \sim \theta$, Theorem 10 yields $(a+b) \equiv 1 \pmod 3$. Hence,

$$\begin{aligned}
-\alpha &= -a - b \equiv 2(a+b) \equiv 2 \pmod 3,\\
\rho\alpha &= -b + (a-b) \equiv a - 2b \equiv a + b \equiv 1 \pmod 3,\\
-\rho\alpha &= b + (b-a) \equiv 2b - a \equiv 2b + 2a \equiv 2(a+b) \equiv 2 \pmod 3,\\
-(1+\rho)\alpha &= (-a+b) - a \equiv b - 2a \equiv b + a \equiv 1 \pmod 3,\\
(1+\rho)\alpha &= a - b + a \equiv 2a - b \equiv 2(a+b) \equiv 2 \pmod 3.
\end{aligned}$$

Thus, $\theta \in O_1$ and $-\theta \in O_2$ whenever $\theta \in \{\alpha, \rho\alpha, -(1+\rho)\alpha\}$.

iii. Assuming $\alpha = a + b\rho \in O_2$ and $\alpha \sim \theta$, Theorem 10 yields $(a+b) \equiv 2 \pmod 3$. Hence,

$$\begin{aligned}
-\alpha &= -a - b \equiv 2(a+b) \equiv 4 \equiv 1 \pmod 3,\\
\rho\alpha &= -b + (a-b) \equiv a - 2b \equiv a + b \equiv 2 \pmod 3,\\
-\rho\alpha &= b + (b-a) \equiv 2b - a \equiv 2b + 2a \equiv 2(a+b) \equiv 4 \equiv 1 \pmod 3,\\
-(1+\rho)\alpha &= (-a+b) - a \equiv b - 2a \equiv b + a \equiv 2 \pmod 3,\\
(1+\rho)\alpha &= a - b + a \equiv 2a - b \equiv 2(a+b) \equiv 4 \equiv 1 \pmod 3.
\end{aligned}$$

Thus, $\theta \in O_2$ and $-\theta \in O_1$ whenever $\theta \in \{\alpha, \rho\alpha, -(1+\rho)\alpha\}$.

iv. Assuming $\alpha = a + b\rho \in O_1$, Theorem 10 gives us $a + b \equiv 1 \pmod 3$. Hence, $a - b - b \equiv a - 2b \equiv a + b \equiv 1 \pmod 3$, ensuring $\bar{\alpha} \in O_1$

v. Assuming $\alpha = a + b\rho \in O_2$, we obtain $a + b \equiv 2 \pmod 3$ by Theorem 10. Hence, $a - b - b \equiv a - 2b \equiv a + b \equiv 2 \pmod 3$ and $-a - b \equiv 2(a+b) \equiv 4 \equiv 1 \pmod 3$, which means $\bar{\alpha} \in O_2$.

□

We can now answer Question 6.1 in [7].

- By Theorem 18 iv. and v., we conclude that distinct primes ψ and $\overline{\psi}$ which are non-associates always belong to the the same odd class. Both are in O_1 or both are in O_2.
- Any prime $q \equiv 1 \pmod 3$ is always in O_1. By Theorem 11, however, both ψ and $\overline{\psi}$ are in O_1 or both are in O_2. We note, for example, that both $\psi_1 = 2 + 3\rho$ and $\overline{\psi_1} = -1 - 3\rho$ are in O_2. Both $\psi_2 = 3 + \rho$ and $\overline{\psi_2} = 2 - \rho$ are in O_1, with $q = N_\rho(\psi_1) = N_\rho(\psi_2) = 7 \equiv 1 \pmod 3$ being in O_1. Without further investigation, the q that corresponds to a given ψ does not automatically identify which odd class both ψ and $\overline{\psi}$ belong to.

The next result is a corollary to Theorem 11.

Corollary 1. *Given an odd Eisenstein integer*

$$\eta = \prod_{\psi_i \in O_1} \psi_i^{r_i} \prod_{\psi_j \in O_2} \psi_j^{s_j} \prod_{p_k \in O_2} p_k^{t_k},$$

if $(\sum s_j + \sum t_k) \equiv 0 \pmod 2$, *then* $\eta \in O_1$. *Otherwise,* $\eta \in O_2$.

Proof. By Theorem 11, if $(\sum s_j + \sum t_k) \equiv 0 \pmod 2$, then

$$\prod_{\psi_i \in O_1} \psi_i^{r_i} \in O_1 \text{ and } \prod_{\psi_j \in O_2} \psi_j^{s_j} \prod_{p_k \in O_2} p_k^{t_k} \in O_1,$$

ensuring $\eta \in O_1$. If $(\sum s_j + \sum t_k) \equiv 1 \pmod 2$, then $\prod_{\psi_j \in O_2} \psi_j^{s_j} \prod_{p_k \in O_2} p_k^{t_k} \in O_2$. Since $\prod_{\psi_i \in O_1} \psi_i^{r_i} \in O_1$, we confirm that $\eta \in O_2$. □

Theorem 19. *The associates and conjugates of a primitive Eisenstein integer are also primitive Eisenstein integers.*

Proof. If $\eta = a + b\rho$ such that $\gcd(a, b) = 1$, then

$$\gcd(a-b,-b) = \gcd(b-a,b) = \gcd(-a,-b) = \gcd(a-b,a) = \gcd(b-a,-a) = 1.$$

Hence, its conjugate $\overline{\eta} = a - b - b\rho$ and associates $\pm\alpha, \pm\rho\alpha$ and $\pm(1+\rho)\alpha$, with $\rho\alpha = -b + (a-b)\rho$ and $(1+\rho)\alpha = (a-b) + a\rho$, are primitives. □

We know from Corollary 3 in [34] that an Eisenstein integer $\alpha = a + b\rho$ and its conjugate $\overline{\alpha}$ are relatively prime if and only if $\gcd(a-b, b) = 1$ and $\gcd(a-2b, 3) = 1$. Since $\gcd(a-b, b) = 1$ is equivalent to $\gcd(a, b) = 1$, and $\gcd(a-2b, 3) = 1$ is equivalent to $a + b \equiv \pm 1 \pmod 3$, we can use the following equivalent expression of the corollary.

Proposition 1. *An Eisenstein integer $\alpha = a + b\rho$ and its conjugate $\overline{\alpha}$ are relatively prime if and only if $\gcd(a, b) = 1$ and $a + b \equiv \pm 1 \pmod 3$. In short, an Eisenstein integer and its conjugate are relatively prime if and only if the Eisenstein integer is odd and primitive.*

The next result is a direct consequence of Proposition 1.

Corollary 2. *If an odd primitive Eisenstein integer η is not a unit, then η and $\overline{\eta}$ are not associates.*

Proof. Let η be an odd primitive Eisenstein integer such that η is not a unit. If η and $\overline{\eta}$ are associates, then $\gcd(\eta, \overline{\eta}) = \eta$, which contradicts Proposition 1. □

Theorem 20. *Let $\eta = \prod_{\psi_i \in O_1} \psi_i^{r_i} \prod_{\psi_j \in O_2} \psi_j^{s_j}$ be an odd primitive Eisenstein integer. If $\sum s_j \equiv 0 \pmod 2$, then $\eta \in O_1$. Otherwise, $\eta \in O_2$.*

Proof. By Theorem 11, if $\sum s_j \equiv 0 \pmod 2$, then

$$\prod_{\psi_i \in O_1} \psi_i^{r_i} \in O_1 \text{ and } \prod_{\psi_j \in O_2} \psi_j^{s_j} \in O_1,$$

implying $\eta \in O_1$. On the other hand, if $\sum s_j \equiv 1 \pmod 2$, then $\prod_{\psi_j \in O_2} \psi_j^{s_j} \in O_2$. Since $\prod_{\psi_i \in O_1} \psi_i^{r_i} \in O_1$, it is clear that $\eta \in O_2$. □

Theorem 21. *Let η be a non-unit primitive Eisenstein integer.*

i. *If η is even, then $\gcd(\eta, \overline{\eta}) = \beta$.*

ii. *If η and β are not associates, then η and $\overline{\eta}$ are also not associates.*

Proof. We prove the assertions according to their order of appearance.

i. Let $u \in \mathbb{Z}[\rho]$ be a unit and let $\eta = u\beta\psi_1^{r_1} \cdots \psi_k^{r_k}$. Since $\overline{\beta} = (1+\rho)\beta$, we have

$$\overline{\eta} = (1+\rho)u\beta\overline{\psi_1^{r_1}} \cdots \overline{\psi_k^{r_k}}.$$

By Proposition 1, we have $\gcd(\psi_1^{r_1} \cdots \psi_k^{r_k}, \overline{\psi_1^{r_1}} \cdots \overline{\psi_k^{r_k}}) = 1$. Thus, $\gcd(\eta, \overline{\eta}) = \beta$.

ii. For a contradiction, let us assume that η and $\overline{\eta}$ are associates. Let $u \in \mathbb{Z}[\rho]$ be a unit such that $\eta = u\psi_1^{r_1} \cdots \psi_k^{r_k}$. Then,

$$\psi_1^{r_1} \cdots \psi_k^{r_k} \sim \overline{\psi_1}^{r_1} \cdots \overline{\psi_k}^{r_k}, \text{ contradicting Corollary 2.}$$

If $\eta = u\beta\psi_1^{r_1}\cdots\psi_k^{r_k}$ for some unit $u \in \mathbb{Z}[\rho]$, then

$$\begin{aligned}\beta\psi_1^{r_1}\cdots\psi_k^{r_k} &\sim \bar{\beta}\overline{\psi_1}^{r_1}\cdots\overline{\psi_k}^{r_k},\\ \beta\psi_1^{r_1}\cdots\psi_k^{r_k} &\sim (1+\rho)\beta\overline{\psi_1}^{r_1}\cdots\overline{\psi_k}^{r_k},\\ \psi_1^{r_1}\cdots\psi_k^{r_k} &\sim \overline{\psi_1}^{r_1}\cdots\overline{\psi_k}^{r_k}, \text{ contradicting Corollary 2.}\end{aligned}$$

□

Theorem 22. *If an Eisenstein integer $\alpha = a + b\rho$ and its conjugate $\bar{\alpha}$ are relatively prime, then the modular multiplicative inverse $c \equiv \alpha^{-1} \pmod{\bar{\alpha}}$ is an integer.*

Proof. By Theorem 1 and recalling that $N_\rho(\alpha) = N_\rho(\bar{\alpha})$, we have

$$\begin{aligned}1 &= \gcd\left(N_\rho(\alpha), \frac{2}{\sqrt{3}}\operatorname{Im}(\alpha^2)\right) = \gcd(a^2+b^2-ab, b(2a-b))\\ &= \gcd(a^2+b^2-ab, b) = \gcd(a^2+b^2-ab, 2a-b).\end{aligned}$$

Hence, there are integers c and d such that

$$c(2a-b) + d(a^2+b^2-ab) = c(\alpha+\bar{\alpha}) + d\alpha\bar{\alpha} = 1.$$

We verify that $c\alpha \equiv 1 \pmod{\bar{\alpha}}$ and confirm that $c \equiv \alpha^{-1} \pmod{\bar{\alpha}}$. □

Corollary 3. *If η is an odd primitive Eisenstein integer, then the modular multiplicative inverse $c \equiv \eta^{-1} \pmod{\bar{\eta}}$ is an integer.*

Proof. By Proposition 1, $\gcd(\eta, \bar{\eta}) = 1$. Applying Theorem 22 settles the claim. □

Theorem 23. *An Eisenstein integer α is an associate of $\bar{\alpha}$ if and only if α is an associate of n or $k\beta$ for some $n, k \in \mathbb{Z}$.*

Proof. If $\alpha \sim n$ then $\bar{\alpha} \sim \bar{n}$ and $n \sim \alpha$. If $\alpha \sim k\beta$ for some $k \in \mathbb{Z}$, then $\bar{\alpha} \sim k\bar{\beta} \sim k\beta \sim \alpha$. Conversely, if $\alpha = a + b\rho$ and $\alpha \sim \bar{\alpha}$, then $\alpha = u\bar{\alpha}$ for some unit u in $\mathbb{Z}[\rho]$.

- If $u = 1$, then $a + b\rho = (a-b) - b\rho$. In this case, $b = 0$, which implies $\alpha = a$.
- If $u = \rho$, then $a + b\rho = b + a\rho$. Hence, $a = b$, implying $\alpha = a + a\rho = a(1+\rho)$.
- If $u = -(1+\rho)$, then $a + b\rho = -a + (b-a)\rho$. Hence, $a = 0$, which yields $\alpha = b\rho$.
- If $u = -1$, then $a + b\rho = (b-a) + b\rho$. We obtain $b = 2a$ and, hence, $\alpha = a + 2a\rho = a(1+2\rho)$.
- If $u = -\rho$, then $a + b\rho = -b - a\rho$. We obtain $b = -a$ and, therefore, $\alpha = a - a\rho = a(1-\rho)$.
- If $u = 1+\rho$, then $a + b\rho = a + (a-b)\rho$. We have $a = 2b$, which means $\alpha = 2b + b\rho = b(2+\rho)$.

Having covered all cases, we confirm that α is an associate of n or $k\beta$ for some $n, k \in \mathbb{Z}$. □

Recalling Theorem 3, we know that $\psi \not\sim \overline{\psi}$ whenever ψ is an Eisenstein prime.

Corollary 4. *If α is a primitive Eisenstein integer such that α is not a unit and α is neither β nor any of its associates, then α and $\bar{\alpha}$ are not associates.*

Proof. Given the conditions on α, it is neither an associate of any $n \in \mathbb{Z}$ nor a multiple $k\beta$ of β with $k \in \mathbb{Z}$. The conclusion follows by Theorem 23. □

3.2. The Group of Units as a Cyclic Group

If α is a generator element of a cyclic group G of order n, then α^i is also a generator of G if and only if $\gcd(i,n) = 1$. The number of generators of such a G is $\varphi(n)$. Moreover, an $\alpha \in G$ is a generator of G if and only if $\alpha^{\frac{n}{q}} \neq 1$ for each prime divisor q of n.

The cyclic group $(\mathbb{Z}[\rho]/\langle\eta\rangle)^*$ of order $\varphi_\rho(\eta)$ have $\varphi(\varphi_\rho(\eta))$ generators. Our next result shows that the probability of successfully selecting one generator in the cyclic group $(\mathbb{Z}[\rho]/\langle\eta\rangle)^*$ at random is smaller than doing so in the cyclic group $\mathbb{Z}_n^*$.

Theorem 24. *If η is an associate of some $n \in \mathbb{N}$, then* $\dfrac{\varphi(\varphi_\rho(\eta))}{\varphi_\rho(\eta)} \leq \dfrac{\varphi(\varphi(n))}{\varphi(n)}$.

Proof. By Theorem 16, we know that $\varphi(n) \mid \varphi_\rho(\eta)$ whenever η and $n \in \mathbb{N}$ are associates. For $a, b \in \mathbb{N}$, it is well known that, if $a \mid b$, then $\frac{\varphi(b)}{\varphi(a)} \leq \frac{b}{a}$. Hence, we have

$$\frac{\varphi(\varphi_\rho(\eta))}{\varphi(\varphi(n))} \leq \frac{\varphi_\rho(\eta)}{\varphi(n)}, \text{ which implies} \frac{\varphi(\varphi_\rho(\eta))}{\varphi_\rho(\eta)} \leq \frac{\varphi(\varphi(n))}{\varphi(n)}.$$

□

Example 3. *For the Eisenstein prime $p = 5$, the order of the cyclic group $(\mathbb{Z}[\rho]/\langle 5\rangle)^* \cong (\mathbb{Z}_5[\rho])^*$ is $\varphi_\rho(5) = 5^2 - 1 = 24$ whose prime factorization is $\varphi_\rho(5) = 2^3 \cdot 3$. Let α be a generator of $(\mathbb{Z}_5[\rho])^*$. It suffices to show that*

$$\alpha^{\frac{\varphi_\rho(5)}{3}} = \alpha^8 \neq 1 \pmod 5 \text{ and } \alpha^{\frac{\varphi_\rho(5)}{2}} = \alpha^{12} \neq 1 \pmod 5.$$

We can select $\alpha := 2 + \rho$ to generate $(\mathbb{Z}_5[\rho])^*$, since $\alpha^8 = 4 + 4\rho \pmod 5$ and $\alpha^{12} = 4 \pmod 5$. The other seven generators are

$$\alpha^5 = 1 + 4\rho, \quad \alpha^7 = 1 + 3\rho, \quad \alpha^{11} = 3 + 2\rho, \quad \alpha^{13} = 3 + 4\rho,$$
$$\alpha^{17} = 4 + \rho, \quad \alpha^{19} = 4 + 2\rho, \quad \alpha^{23} = 2 + 3\rho.$$

The group $\mathbb{Z}_5^*$ has $\varphi(\varphi(5)) = \varphi(4) = 2$ generators, namely, 2 and 3. It is clear that

$$\frac{\varphi(\varphi_\rho(5))}{\varphi_\rho(5)} = \frac{8}{24} < \frac{2}{4} = \frac{\varphi(\varphi(5))}{\varphi(5)}.$$

Theorem 25. *If $(\mathbb{Z}[\rho]/\langle\eta\rangle)^*$ is a cyclic group, then*

$$\prod_{\alpha \in (\mathbb{Z}[\rho]/\langle\eta\rangle)^*} \alpha \equiv -1 \pmod \eta.$$

Proof. Let $(\mathbb{Z}[\rho]/\langle\eta\rangle)^*$ be a cyclic group. By Theorem 13, η is an element in the set $\{\beta, \beta^2, 2\beta, \psi^k\}$, a prime $p \equiv 2 \pmod 3$, or any of their associates. We investigate by the values that η takes.

If $\gamma = \beta$, then, by Theorem 12, we get $(\mathbb{Z}[\rho]/\langle\beta\rangle)^* = \{[1]_\beta, [2]_\beta\}$. Hence,

$$\prod_{\alpha \in (\mathbb{Z}[\rho]/\langle\beta\rangle)^*} \alpha \equiv 1 \cdot 2 \equiv 2 \equiv -1 \pmod \beta.$$

If $\gamma = 2$, then $(\mathbb{Z}[\rho]/\langle 2\rangle)^*$ is a cyclic group of order $\varphi_\rho(2) = 3$. Letting θ be a generator,

$$\prod_{\alpha \in (\mathbb{Z}[\rho]/\langle 2\rangle)^*} \alpha \equiv \prod_{0 \leq t \leq 2} \theta^t \equiv \theta^3 \pmod 2.$$

Since the generators of $(\mathbb{Z}[\rho]/\langle 2\rangle)^*$ are ρ and $1+\rho$, we have $\theta^3 \equiv 1 \equiv -1 \pmod 2$.

If $\gamma \in \{\beta^2, 2\beta, \psi^k\}$ or $\gamma = p \equiv 2 \pmod 3$ such that $p \neq 2$, then $\varphi_\rho(\gamma)$ is an even number, by Theorem 14. Letting θ be a generator of $(\mathbb{Z}[\rho]/\langle\gamma\rangle)^*$,

$$\prod_{\alpha\in(\mathbb{Z}[\rho]/\langle\gamma\rangle)^*} \alpha \equiv \prod_{0\le t\le\varphi_\rho(\gamma)-1} \theta^t \equiv \theta^{\frac{\varphi_\rho(\gamma)(\varphi_\rho(\gamma)-1)}{2}} \pmod{\gamma}.$$

The order of θ is an even number $\varphi_\rho(\gamma)$. Hence, $\theta^{\frac{\varphi_\rho(\gamma)}{2}} \in (\mathbb{Z}[\rho]/\langle\gamma\rangle)^*$ must be -1 because -1 is the only element of order 2 in $(\mathbb{Z}[\rho]/\langle\gamma\rangle)^*$. Since $\varphi_\rho(\gamma)-1$ is an odd number,

$$\theta^{\frac{\varphi_\rho(\gamma)(\varphi_\rho(\gamma)-1)}{2}} = \left(\theta^{\frac{\varphi_\rho(\gamma)}{2}}\right)^{\varphi_\rho(\gamma)-1} \pmod{\gamma} = (-1)^{\varphi_\rho(\gamma)-1} \pmod{\gamma} = -1 \pmod{\eta}.$$

□

The Wilson Theorem over $\mathbb{Z}$ had been generalized to Gaussian integers in [35], but not to Eisenstein integers in the prior literature. We highlight that we have achieved this as a special case of Theorem 25.

Theorem 26 (Wilson Theorem for Eisenstein Integers). *If $\gamma \in \mathbb{Z}[\rho]$ is an Eisenstein prime, then*

$$\prod_{\alpha\in(\mathbb{Z}[\rho]/\langle\gamma\rangle)^*} \alpha \equiv -1 \pmod{\gamma}.$$

4. Set Partitioning Based on the Multiplicative Group

In a recent work [8], we proposed a number of Eisenstein constellations $\mathcal{E}_\eta$ as two-dimensional signal constellations by using the modulo function in (1). The setup, given a suitable η, has

$$\begin{aligned} \mathcal{E}_\eta &= \{\mu_\eta(\alpha) : \alpha \in \mathcal{R}_\eta\} \text{ with} \\ \mathcal{R}_\eta &= \{x + y\rho : 0 \le x < tN_\rho(m+n\rho) \text{ and } 0 \le y < t\}. \end{aligned} \tag{3}$$

In that work, we also introduced set partitioning of Eisenstein integers based on *additive* subgroups. In this section, we focus on set partitioning based on the *multiplicative* group.

We now propose Eisenstein constellations $(\mathcal{E}_\eta)^*$, corresponding to the cyclic group $(\mathbb{Z}[\rho]/\langle\eta\rangle)^*$, with $\eta \in \{\beta^2, 2\beta, \psi^k : k \in \mathbb{N}\}$ or η being an odd prime integer $p \equiv 2 \pmod 3$. In doing this, we generalize Proposition 1 in [18], which covers the case of $\eta = \psi$. Our set partitioning technique for signal constellation $(\mathcal{E}_\eta)^*$ benefits from the facts that $(\mathbb{Z}[\rho]/\langle\eta\rangle)^*$ is a cyclic group of order $\varphi_\rho(\eta)$, by Theorem 13, and $\varphi_\rho(\eta) \equiv 0 \pmod 6$, by Theorem 15. The elements of $(\mathcal{E}_\eta)^*$ can be expressed as powers of a generator α as

$$(\mathcal{E}_\eta)^* = \left\{\alpha^0, \alpha^1, \ldots, \alpha^{\varphi_\rho(\eta)-1}\right\}.$$

Letting $n := \frac{\varphi_\rho(\eta)}{6}$, the set of all unit (see [29] for $\eta = \psi$) is

$$\{\alpha^n, \alpha^{2n}, \alpha^{3n}, \alpha^{4n}, \alpha^{5n}, \alpha^{6n}\} = \{\pm 1, \pm\rho, \pm(1+\rho)\}.$$

We can then partition $(\mathcal{E}_\eta)^*$ into n subsets, indexed by $j \in \{0, 1, \ldots, n-1\}$, as

$$(\mathcal{E}_\eta)^*_{(j)} = \{\alpha^{n+j}, \alpha^{2n+j}, \alpha^{3n+j}, \alpha^{4n+j}, \alpha^{5n+j}, \alpha^{6n+j}\} = \{\pm\alpha^j, \pm\rho\alpha^j, \pm(1+\rho)\alpha^j\}.$$

All elements of $(\mathcal{E}_\eta)^*$ can be found by calculating α^j for $j \in \{0, 1, \ldots, n-1\}$ using the modulo function in (1), followed by multiplying each α^j by the units.

Our next result extends Theorem 2 to the cases $\eta \in \{2\beta, \beta^2, \psi^k : k \in \mathbb{N}\}$ or η being an odd prime integer $p \equiv 2 \pmod 3$.

Theorem 27. *Let $\eta \in \{2\beta, \beta^2, \psi^k : k \in \mathbb{N}\}$ or $\eta = p$, with $p \equiv 2 \pmod 3$ being an odd prime. If α is a generator of $(\mathcal{E})^*_\eta$, then the minimum Euclidean distance in the subset $(\mathcal{E}_\eta)^*_{(j)}$ is $\|\alpha^j\|$. Furthermore, $(\mathcal{E}_\eta)^*_{(j)}$ can be partitioned into three subsets*

$$(\mathcal{E}_\eta)^*_{(j)} = \{\pm\alpha^j\} \cup \{\pm\rho\alpha^j\} \cup \{\pm(1+\rho)\alpha^j\},$$

each with minimum Euclidean distance $2\|\alpha^j\|$. We also can partition $(\mathcal{E}_\eta)^*_{(j)}$ into two subsets

$$(\mathcal{E}_\eta)^*_{(j)} = \{\alpha^j, \rho\alpha^j, -(1+\rho)\alpha^j\} \cup \{-\alpha^j, -\rho\alpha^j, (1+\rho)\alpha^j\},$$

each with minimum Euclidean distance $\sqrt{3}\|\alpha^j\|$.

Proof. Two neighboring points in $(\mathcal{E}_\eta)^*_{(j)}$ have a phase difference of $\pi/3$. Hence, the pair together with the origin form an equilateral triangle whose sides are of length $\|\alpha^j\|$, confirming that the minimum Euclidean distance is $\|\alpha^j\|$.

The sets $\{\pm\alpha^j\}, \{\pm\rho\alpha^j\}$ and $\{\pm(1+\rho)\alpha^j\}$ contain points whose pairwise phase difference is π, ensuring the minimum distance $2\|\alpha^j\|$. The sets $\{\alpha^j, \rho\alpha^j, -(1+\rho)\alpha^j\}$ and $\{-\alpha^j, -\rho\alpha^j, (1+\rho)\alpha^j\}$ contain points whose pairwise phase difference is $2\pi/3$, yielding the minimum distance of $\sqrt{3}\|\alpha^j\|$. □

Example 4. *(Primitive but not prime) Given a primitive Eisenstein $\psi^2 = -5 + 3\rho$, with $\psi = 2 + 3\rho$, we have the cyclic group $(\mathbb{Z}[\rho]/\langle -5+3\rho \rangle)^* \cong (\mathcal{E}_{-5+3\rho})^*$ generated by $\alpha = 3$. Since $\varphi_\rho(\psi^2) = 42$, we can partition $(\mathcal{E}_{\psi^2})^*$ into 7 subsets defined as*

$$(\mathcal{E}_{\psi^2})^*_{(j)} = \{\pm\alpha^j, \pm\rho\alpha^j, \pm(1+\rho)\alpha^j\} \text{ with } j \in \{0,1,2,3,4,5,6\}.$$

Since $\alpha = 3$, by using the modulo function (1), *we have*

$$\alpha^2 = -4 - 2\rho, \quad \alpha^3 = -4 - \rho, \quad \alpha^4 = 1 - \rho, \quad \alpha^5 = -2, \quad \alpha^6 = -1 - 3\rho.$$

We rely on Theorem 27 to partition $(\mathcal{E}_{\psi^2})^*_{(j)}$ into three subsets and two subsets, each with respective minimum Euclidean distances $2\|\alpha^j\|$ and $\sqrt{3}\|\alpha^j\|$ for $j \in \{0,1,2,3,4,5,6\}$ as follows:

$$\begin{aligned}
(\mathcal{E}_{\psi^2})^*_{(0)} &= \{1,\ \rho,\ 1+\rho,\ -1, -\rho,\ -1-\rho\},\\
&= \{1,\ -1\} \cup \{\rho,\ -\rho\} \cup \{-1-\rho,\ 1+\rho\},\\
&= \{1,\ \rho,\ -1-\rho\} \cup \{-1, -\rho, 1+\rho\},\\
(\mathcal{E}_{\psi^2})^*_{(1)} &= \{3,\ 3+3\rho,\ 3\rho,\ -3,\ -3-3\rho,\ -3\rho\},\\
&= \{3,\ -3\} \cup \{3\rho,\ -3\rho\} \cup \{-3-3\rho,\ 3+3\rho\},\\
&= \{3,\ 3\rho,\ -3-3\rho\} \cup \{-3,\ -3\rho,\ 3+3\rho\},\\
(\mathcal{E}_{\psi^2})^*_{(2)} &= \{4+2\rho,\ 2+4\rho,\ -2+2\rho,\ -4-2\rho,\ -2-4\rho,\ 2-2\rho\},\\
&= \{4+2\rho,\ -4-2\rho\} \cup \{2+4\rho,\ -2-4\rho\} \cup \{-2+2\rho,\ 2-2\rho\},\\
&= \{4+2\rho,\ -2-4\rho\ \ -2+2\rho\} \cup \{\ -4-2\rho,\ 2+4\rho,\ 2-2\rho\},
\end{aligned}$$

$$\begin{aligned}
(\mathcal{E}_{\psi^2})^*_{(3)} &= \{4+\rho,\ 3+4\rho,\ -1+3\rho,\ -4-\rho,\ -3-4\rho,\ 1-3\rho\},\\
&= \{4+\rho,\ -4-\rho\} \cup \{3+4\rho,\ -3-4\rho\} \cup \{-1+3\rho,\ 1-3\rho\},\\
&= \{4+\rho,\ -1+3\rho,\ -3-4\rho\} \cup \{-4-\rho,,\ 1-3\rho,\ 3+4\rho\},\\
(\mathcal{E}_{\psi^2})^*_{(4)} &= \{2+\rho,\ 1+2\rho,\ -1+\rho,\ -2-\rho,\ -1-2\rho,\ 1-\rho\},\\
&= \{2+\rho,\ -2-\rho\} \cup \{-1+\rho,\ 1-\rho\} \cup \{-1-2\rho,\ 1+2\rho\},\\
&= \{2+\rho,\ -1-2\rho,\ -1+\rho\} \cup \{-2-\rho,\ 1+2\rho,\ 1-\rho\},\\
(\mathcal{E}_{\psi^2})^*_{(5)} &= \{2,\ 2+2\rho,\ 2\rho,\ -2,\ -2-2\rho,\ -2\rho\},\\
&= \{2,\ -2\} \cup \{2\rho,\ -2\rho\} \cup \{-2-2\rho,\ 2+2\rho\},\\
&= \{2,\ 2\rho,\ -2-2\rho,\} \cup \{-2,\ 2+2\rho,\ -2\rho\},\\
(\mathcal{E}_{\psi^2})^*_{(6)} &= \{3+2\rho,\ 1+3\rho,\ -2+\rho,\ -3-2\rho,\ -1-3\rho,\ 2-\rho\},\\
&= \{3+2\rho, -3-2\rho\} \cup \{1+3\rho,\ -1-3\rho\} \cup \{-2+\rho,\ 2-\rho\},\\
&= \{3+2\rho,\ -1-3\rho,\ -2+\rho\} \cup \{-3-2\rho,\ 1+3\rho,\ 2-\rho\}.
\end{aligned}$$

Figures 1–3 visualize the Eisenstein constellations $(\mathcal{E}_{\psi^2})^*$ and its signal partitions in $\mathbb{C}$.

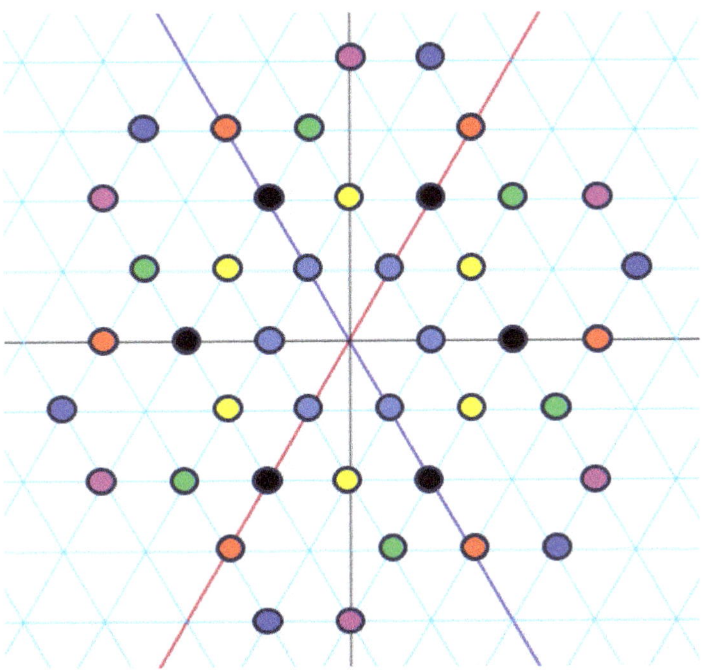

Figure 1. Set partitioning of $(\mathcal{E}_{\psi^2})^*$ into seven subsets. Circles represent the integers, with colours corresponding to indices.

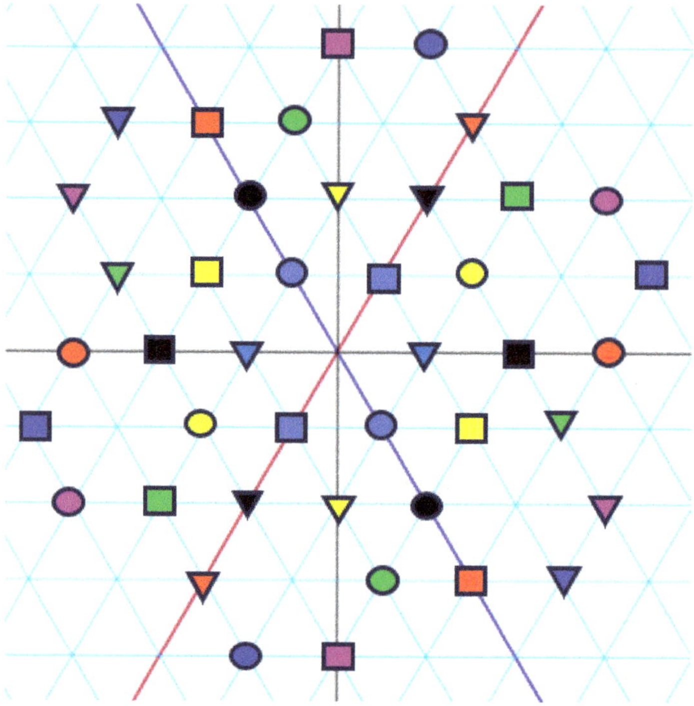

Figure 2. Set partitioning of $(\mathcal{E}_{\psi^2})^*_{(j)}$ into three subsets. Colours correspond to indices. Forms (circle, square, and triangle) correspond to subsets.

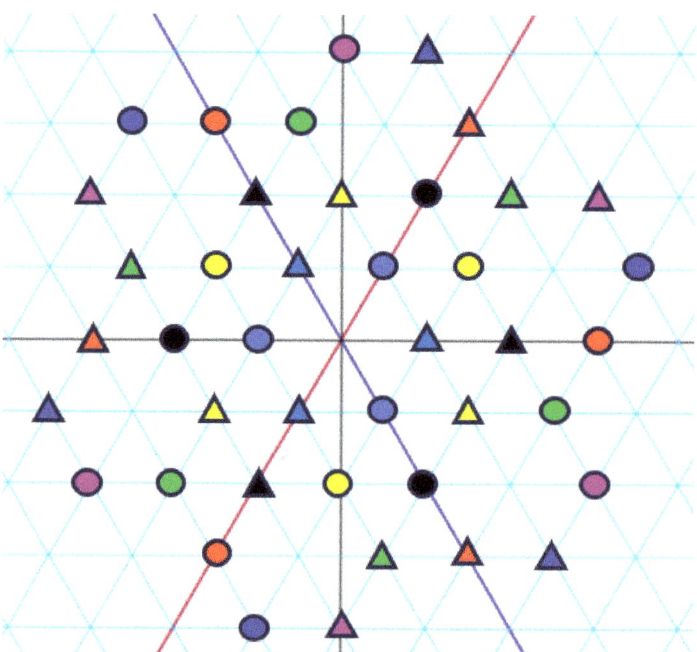

Figure 3. Set partitioning of $(\mathcal{E}_{\psi^2})^*_{(j)}$ into two subsets. Colours correspond to indices. Forms (circle and triangle) correspond to subsets.

Example 5. *(Prime but not primitive) Given an Eisenstein prime $p = 5$, we have the cyclic group $(\mathbb{Z}[\rho]/\langle 5\rangle)^* \cong (\mathcal{E}_5)^*$ generated by $\alpha = 2+\rho$. Since $\varphi_\rho(5) = 24$, we can partition $(\mathcal{E}_5)^*$ into 4 subsets as*

$$(\mathcal{E}_5)^*_{(j)} = \{\pm\alpha^j, \pm\rho\alpha^j, \pm(1+\rho)\alpha^j\}, \text{ with } j \in \{0,1,2,3\}.$$

Since $\alpha = 2+\rho$, the modulo function in (1) *gives us $\alpha^2 = -2-2\rho$ and $\alpha^3 = -2+\rho$. By Theorem 27, we partition $(\mathcal{E}_5)^*_{(j)}$ into three and two subsets each with respective minimum Euclidean distances $2\|\alpha^j\|$ and $\sqrt{3}\|\alpha^j\|$ for $j \in \{0,1,2,3\}$ as follows:*

$$\begin{aligned}
(\mathcal{E}_5)^*_{(0)} &= \{1,\ \rho,\ 1+\rho,\ -1, -\rho,\ -1-\rho\},\\
&= \{1,\ -1\} \cup \{\rho,\ -\rho\} \cup \{-1-\rho,\ 1+\rho\},\\
&= \{1,\ \rho,\ -1-\rho\} \cup \{-1, -\rho, 1+\rho\},\\
(\mathcal{E}_5)^*_{(1)} &= \{2+\rho,\ 1+2\rho,\ -1+\rho,\ -2-\rho,\ -1-2\rho,\ 1-\rho\},\\
&= \{2+\rho,\ -2-\rho\} \cup \{-1+\rho,\ 1-\rho\} \cup \{-1-2\rho,\ 1+2\rho\},\\
&= \{2+\rho,\ -1-2\rho,\ -1+\rho\} \cup \{-2-\rho,\ 1+2\rho,\ 1-\rho\},\\
(\mathcal{E}_5)^*_{(2)} &= \{2,\ 2+2\rho,\ 2\rho,\ -2,\ -2-2\rho,\ -2\rho\},\\
&= \{2,\ -2\} \cup \{2\rho,\ -2\rho\} \cup \{-2-2\rho,\ 2+2\rho\},\\
&= \{2,\ -2-2\rho,\ 2\rho\} \cup \{-2,\ 2+2\rho,\ -2\rho\},\\
(\mathcal{E}_5)^*_{(3)} &= \{3+2\rho,\ -3-2\rho,\ -2+\rho,\ 2-\rho,\ -1-3\rho,\ 1+3\rho\},\\
&= \{3+2\rho,\ -3-2\rho\} \cup \{-2+\rho,\ 2-\rho\} \cup \{-1-3\rho,\ 1+3\rho\},\\
&= \{3+2\rho,\ -1-3\rho,\ -2+\rho\} \cup \{-3-2\rho,\ 2-\rho,\ 1+3\rho\}.
\end{aligned}$$

Figures 4–6 visualize the constellation $(\mathcal{E}_5)^*$ and its signal partitions in $\mathbb{C}$.

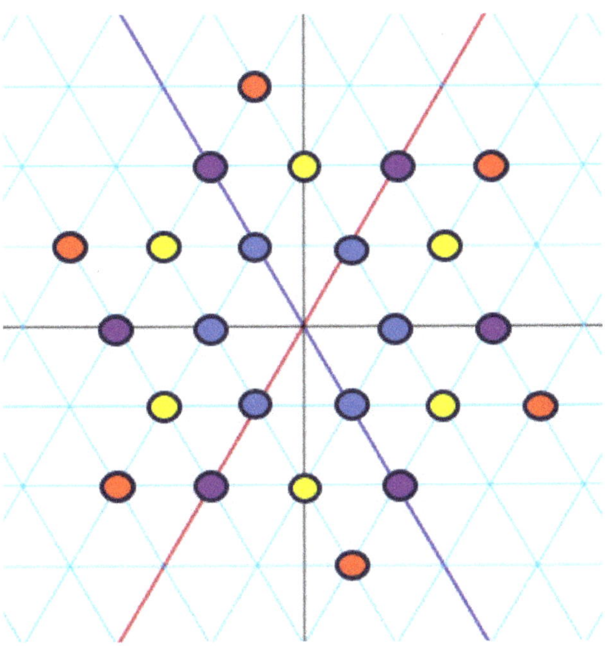

Figure 4. Set partitioning of $(\mathcal{E}_5)^*$ into four subsets. Circles represent the integers, with colours corresponding to indices.

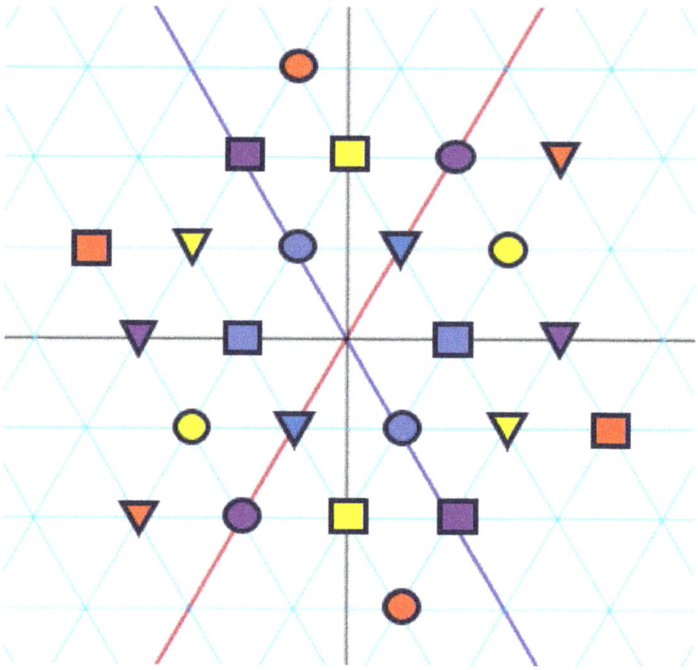

Figure 5. Set partitioning of $(\mathcal{E}_5)^*_{(j)}$ into three subsets. Forms (circle, square, and triangle) correspond to subsets. Colours correspond to indices.

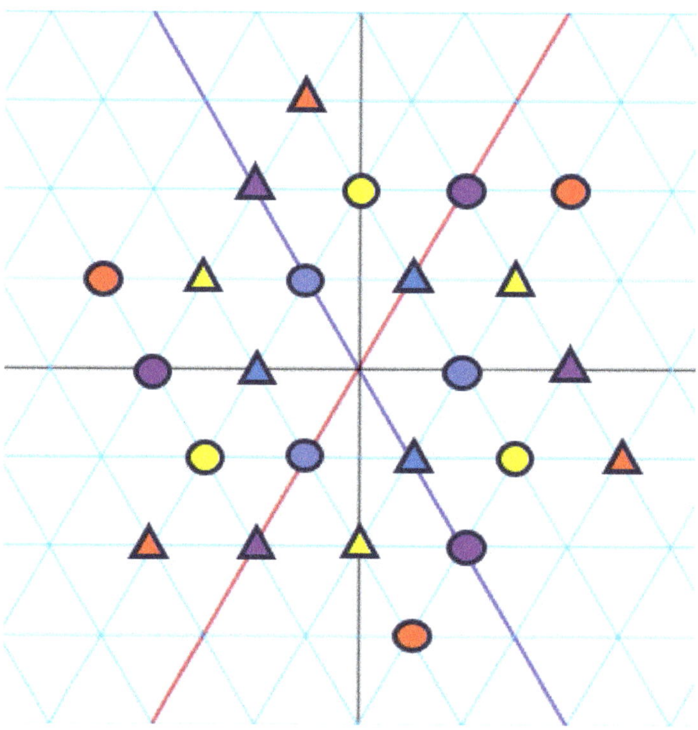

Figure 6. Set partitioning of $(\mathcal{E}_5)^*_{(j)}$ into two subsets. Form (circle and triangle) correspond to subsets. Colours correspond to indices.

5. Discussion

We can use a primitive Eisenstein integer η to construct signal constellations and complex-valued codes over Eisenstein integers. We consider the sets $\mathcal{R}_\eta$ and $\mathcal{E}_\eta$ in (3) as code alphabets, where $\mathcal{E}_\eta$ is obtained through the modulo function in (1), based on an isomorphism between $\mathbb{Z}[\rho]$ modulo a primitive Eisenstein integer η and $\mathbb{Z}$ modulo a norm of the primitive Eisenstein as in Theorem 8. Codes over Eisenstein integers whose alphabet set $\mathcal{E}_\psi$ is an Eisenstein field of cardinality a prime $q \equiv 1 \pmod 3$ were investigated in [29] and [36]. The Eisenstein field corresponds to a quotient ring of Eisenstein integers over an ideal generated by a prime and a primitive Eisenstein integer ψ. More generally, a recent code construction via a quotient ring of Eisenstein integers induced by an ideal generated by a primitive but not a prime Eisenstein integer can be found in [8]. Table 1 provides an example. The alphabet set $\mathcal{E}_{\psi^2}$ is obtained from the quotient ring $\mathbb{Z}[\rho]/\langle\psi^2\rangle$ with primitive Eisenstein $\psi^2 = -5+3\rho$ and $\psi = 2+3\rho$ via the modulo function in (1).

Table 1. Elements in $Z[\rho]/\langle\psi^2\rangle \cong \mathbb{Z}_{49}$ and $\mathcal{E}_{\psi^2}$.

$\mathbb{Z}[\rho]/\langle\psi^2\rangle$	$\mathcal{E}_{\psi^2}$	$\mathbb{Z}[\rho]/\langle\psi^2\rangle$	$\mathcal{E}_{\psi^2}$	$\mathbb{Z}[\rho]/\langle\psi^2\rangle$	$\mathcal{E}_{\psi^2}$
$[0]_{\psi^2}$	0	$[17]_{\psi^2}$	$-1+\rho$	$[34]_{\psi^2}$	$-2+2\rho$
$[1]_{\psi^2}$	1	$[18]_{\psi^2}$	ρ	$[35]_{\psi^2}$	$-1+2\rho$
$[2]_{\psi^2}$	2	$[19]_{\psi^2}$	$1+\rho$	$[36]_{\psi^2}$	2ρ
$[3]_{\psi^2}$	3	$[20]_{\psi^2}$	$2+\rho$	$[37]_{\psi^2}$	$1+2\rho$
$[4]_{\psi^2}$	$-1+3\rho$	$[21]_{\psi^2}$	$3+\rho$	$[38]_{\psi^2}$	$2+2\rho$
$[5]_{\psi^2}$	3ρ	$[22]_{\psi^2}$	$4+\rho$	$[39]_{\psi^2}$	$3+2\rho$
$[6]_{\psi^2}$	$1+3\rho$	$[23]_{\psi^2}$	$-3-4\rho$	$[40]_{\psi^2}$	$4+2\rho$
$[7]_{\psi^2}$	$2+3\rho$	$[24]_{\psi^2}$	$-2-4\rho$	$[41]_{\psi^2}$	$-3-3\rho$
$[8]_{\psi^2}$	$3+3\rho$	$[25]_{\psi^2}$	$2+4\rho$	$[42]_{\psi^2}$	$-2-3\rho$
$[9]_{\psi^2}$	$-4-2\rho$	$[26]_{\psi^2}$	$3+4\rho$	$[43]_{\psi^2}$	$-1-3\rho$
$[10]_{\psi^2}$	$-3-2\rho$	$[27]_{\psi^2}$	$-4-\rho$	$[44]_{\psi^2}$	-3ρ
$[11]_{\psi^2}$	$-2-2\rho$	$[28]_{\psi^2}$	$-3-\rho$	$[45]_{\psi^2}$	$1-3\rho$
$[12]_{\psi^2}$	$-1-2\rho$	$[29]_{\psi^2}$	$-2-\rho$	$[46]_{\psi^2}$	-3
$[13]_{\psi^2}$	-2ρ	$[30]_{\psi^2}$	$-1-\rho$	$[47]_{\psi^2}$	-2
$[14]_{\psi^2}$	$1-2\rho$	$[31]_{\psi^2}$	$-\rho$	$[48]_{\psi^2}$	-1
$[15]_{\psi^2}$	$2-2\rho$	$[32]_{\psi^2}$	$1-\rho$		
$[16]_{\psi^2}$	$-2+\rho$	$[33]_{\psi^2}$	$2-\rho$		

A *code* is a nonempty subset $C \subseteq \mathcal{E}_\eta^n$ whose elements are called *codewords*. A *linear code* C of length n over $\mathcal{E}_\eta$ is a submodule of $\mathcal{E}_\eta^n$. Since $\mathcal{E}_\eta$ and $\mathcal{E}_\eta^n$ are abelian groups, we say that C is a *group code* if it is a subgroup of $\mathcal{E}_\eta^n$. When $\mathcal{E}_\eta$ is a finite field, that is, $\mathcal{E}_\eta^n$ is a vector space of dimension n over $\mathcal{E}_\eta$, a linear code C is a subspace of $\mathcal{E}_\eta^n$. We call C an (n,k) code if C has exactly $|\mathcal{E}_\eta|^k$ codewords.

By Corollaries 2 and 4, odd primitives η and $\bar{\eta}$ are not associates. Hence, $\langle\eta\rangle \neq \langle\bar{\eta}\rangle$ and, therefore, $\mathbb{Z}[\rho]/\langle\eta\rangle \neq \mathbb{Z}[\rho]/\langle\bar{\eta}\rangle$. By Proposition 1, odd primitives $\psi_1^{r_1}\cdots\psi_k^{r_k}$ and $\overline{\psi_1^{r_1}\cdots\psi_k^{r_k}}$ are relatively prime. By the Chinese Remainder Theorem (CRT) with $N_\rho(\psi_i) = q_i$ being a prime integer such that $q_i \equiv 1 \pmod 3$, we have

$$\mathbb{Z}[\rho]/\langle q_1^{r_1}\cdots q_k^{r_k}\rangle \cong \mathbb{Z}[\rho]/\langle\psi_1^{r_1}\cdots\psi_k^{r_k}\rangle \times \mathbb{Z}[\rho]/\langle\overline{\psi_1^{r_1}\cdots\psi_k^{r_k}}\rangle.$$

For an even primitive Eisenstein integer η, however, the CRT does not hold. Hence,

$$\mathbb{Z}[\rho]/\langle n\rangle \ncong \mathbb{Z}[\rho]/\langle\eta\rangle \times \mathbb{Z}[\rho]/\langle\bar{\eta}\rangle \text{ with } N_\rho(\eta) = n.$$

Set partitioning based on an *additive* subgroup is structurally *not feasible* on the Eisenstein field $\mathcal{E}_\psi$ due to its cardinality being a prime integer. Hence, set partitioning based on a *multiplicative* group of the Eisenstein field $\mathcal{E}_{\psi}$ was proposed in [18]. The investigation leveraged on the fact that a multiplicative group of the Eisenstein field is cyclic to perform set partitioning. Theorem 27 is an insightful generalization. It extends set partitioning to a multiplicative group of a quotient ring of Eisenstein integers when the group is designed to be cyclic.

Given a primitive Eisenstein integer η, the quotient ring $\mathbb{Z}[\rho]/\langle\eta\rangle \cong \mathbb{Z}_{N_\rho(\eta)}$ defines a finite set of representative elements that form the signal constellation

$$\mathcal{E}_\eta = \{\mu_\eta(\alpha) : \alpha \in \mathbb{Z}_{N_\rho(\eta)}\}.$$

This constitutes a special case of (3), where $\mu_\eta(\alpha)$ denotes the modulo function in (1) applied to an Eisenstein integer α. Such a structure is fundamental in designing multidimensional lattice codes. It enables efficient encoding and decoding procedures. By integrating Eisenstein constellations into coding theory, we establish a direct link between complex-valued codes and structured lattice-based signal constellations. The resulting codes benefit from increased minimum Euclidean distances, enhancing signal robustness in noisy communication channels.

6. Summary and Concluding Remarks

We have just reported properties of primitive, even, or odd Eisenstein integers. For the odd ones, we investigated whether they are of Type 1 or 2 and their implied properties according to the type.

Given an Eisenstein prime ψ such that $N_\rho(\psi) = q$ is a prime integer equivalent to $1 \pmod 3$, we settled the question posed as Question 6.1 in [7]. If ψ and $\overline{\psi}$ are distinct Eisenstein primes which are not associates, then they belong to the same odd class. If one of them is of Type 1, then the other is also of Type 1. The same goes for Type 2. The corresponding q, however, is insufficient to conclude which odd class ψ and $\overline{\psi}$ belong to.

We have confirmed that, if Eisenstein integers α and $\bar{\alpha}$ are relatively prime, then $\alpha^{-1} \pmod{\bar{\alpha}}$ is in $\mathbb{Z}$. We also managed to prove that the multiplicative group of the set of all units in a quotient ring of $\mathbb{Z}[\rho]$ forms a cyclic group. This leads to a nice set partitioning, allowing us to propose Eisenstein signal constellations. Some examples were given to further illustrate the insights.

Many algebraic signal constellations have been known to enhance the performance of communication systems. Studying use cases and measuring the optimality of certain families of constellations form an important topic in modern communications. Constructing good constellations and benchmarking their performance against previously best-known ones, either in general or for specific setups, are interesting directions to consider.

Author Contributions: Conceptualization, A.H.; investigation—mostly A.H., helped by U.I., I.E.W., and M.F.E.; validation, A.H., U.I., I.E.W., and M.F.E.; writing—original draft, A.H.; writing—review and editing, M.F.E.; visualization, A.H.; supervision, U.I. and I.E.W. All authors have read and agreed to the submitted version of the manuscript.

Funding: This research received no external funding.

Institutional Review Board Statement: Not applicable.

Data Availability Statement: The data is contained within the article.

Acknowledgments: A. Hadi is supported by the Indonesian Education Scholarship (BPI), provided by the Center for Higher Education Funding and Assessment of the Indonesian Ministry of Higher Education, Science, and Technology, No. 00082/J5.2.3./BPI.06/9/2022. His studies benefit from the Indonesia Endowment Fund for Education (LPDP).

Conflicts of Interest: The authors declare no conflicts of interest.

Appendix A. Proof of Theorem 5

We prove by induction. Starting with $n = 1$, we have

$$\psi^n = \psi = x + y\rho \text{ and } N_\rho(\psi) = q = x^2 + y^2 - xy.$$

Let us assume that $\gcd(x, y) = r \geq 1$. Hence, $r \mid x$ and $r \mid y$, implying $r \mid (x^2 + y^2 - xy)$, that is $r \mid q$. Since q is prime integer, $r = 1$ or $r = q$. If $r = q$, then $x = rs = qs$ and $y = rt = qt$ for some $s, t \in \mathbb{Z}$. Observing that

$$q = x^2 + y^2 - xy = q^2 N_\rho(s + t\rho),$$

we obtain $1 = q\, N_\rho(s + t\rho)$, which is impossible since q is a prime integer. Thus, we conclude that $r = \gcd(x, y) = 1$.

Next, we assume $\psi^k = c + d\rho$, where $\gcd(c, d) = 1$ for some $k \geq 1$. We have

$$\begin{aligned} \psi^{k+1} &= (x + y\rho)^{k+1} = (x + y\rho)^k (x + y\rho) \\ &= (c + d\rho)(x + y\rho) = (xc - yd) + (xd + yc - yd)\rho. \end{aligned} \tag{A1}$$

Letting $A = xc - yd$ and $B = xd + yc - yd$, it now suffices to show that $\gcd(A, B) = 1$. For a contradiction, suppose that $\gcd(A, B) = r > 1$. We have $r \mid A$ and $r \mid B$. Since $q^{k+1} = N_\rho(\psi^{k+1}) = A^2 + B^2 - AB$, we are sure that $r \mid (A^2 + B^2 - AB)$, implying $r \mid q^{k+1}$. Since q is a prime integer, $r = 1$ or $r = q^m$ for some $m \in \{1, \ldots, k+1\}$. We show that having $r = q^m$ is impossible. Again, since $r \mid A$ and $r \mid B$, we can write $A = q^m s$ and $B = q^m t$ for some $s, t \in \mathbb{Z}$. Using the expression

$$q^{k+1} = A^2 + B^2 - AB = q^{2m} N_\rho(s + t\rho), \tag{A2}$$

we consider three cases, namely, $2m > k + 1$, $2m = k + 1$, and $2m < k + 1$.

Case A1. If $2m > k + 1$, then $q^{2m-(k+1)} \geq q > 1$. Hence, $q^{2m-(k+1)} N_\rho(s + t\rho) > 1$, which contradicts (A2).

Case A2. If $2m < k + 1$, then $N_\rho(s + t\rho) = q^{k+1-2m} = N_\rho(\psi^{k+1-2m})$. By Theorem 4,

$$s + t\rho \sim \psi^{k+1-2m} \text{ or } s + t\rho \sim \overline{\psi}^{k+1-2m}.$$

If $s + t\rho \sim \psi^{k+1-2m}$, then

$$A + B\rho = q^m (s + t\rho) \sim q^m \psi^{k+1-2m}.$$

Since $\psi^{k+1} = A + B\rho$ by Equation (A1), we obtain $\psi^{2m} \sim q^m = \psi^m \overline{\psi}^m$, which means that $\psi \sim \overline{\psi}$. This contradicts Theorem 3, in which $\psi \nsim \overline{\psi}$. Similarly, if $s + t\rho \sim \overline{\psi}^{k+1-2m}$, then $\psi \sim \overline{\psi}$, which is a contradiction.

Case A3. If $2m = k + 1$, then, by Equation (A2), $N_\rho(s + t\rho) = 1$, meaning $s + t\rho$ is a unit in $\mathbb{Z}[\rho]$. Since $\psi^{k+1} = A + B\rho = q^m(s + t\rho)$, we know that $\psi^{k+1} = \psi^{2m} \sim q^m = \psi^m \overline{\psi}^m$ and, hence, $\psi \sim \overline{\psi}$, which is a contradiction.

Thus, $\gcd(A, B) = r = 1$ and the proof is now complete.

References

1. Ireland, K.; Rosen, M.I.; Rosen, M. *A Classical Introduction to Modern Number Theory*, 2nd ed.; Springer Science & Business Media: New York, NY, USA, 1990; ISBN 978-1-4757-2103-4.

2. Cross, J.T. The Euler φ-function in the Gaussian Integers. *Am. Math. Mon.* **1983**, *90*, 518–528. [CrossRef]
3. Dresden, G.; Dymacek, W.M. Finding factors of factor rings over the Gaussian integers. *Am. Math. Mon.* **2005**, *112*, 602–611. [CrossRef]
4. Ozkan, E.; Ozturk, R.; Aydogdu, A. On the factor rings of Eisenstein integers. *Erzincan Univ. J. Sci. Technol.* **2013**, *6*, 165–174.
5. Misaghian, M. Factor rings and their decompositions in the Eisenstein integers ring $\mathbb{Z}[\omega]$. *Armen. J. Math.* **2013**, *5*, 58–68.
6. Bucaj, V. Finding factors of factor rings over Eisenstein integers. *Int. Math. Forum* **2013**, *9*, 1521–1537. [CrossRef]
7. Gullerud, E.; Mbirika, A. An Euler phi function for the Eisenstein integers and some applications. *Integers* **2020** Art. No. A20. Available online: https://math.colgate.edu/~integers/u20/u20.pdf (accessed on 26 February 2025).
8. Hadi, A.; Isnaini, U.; Wijayanti, I.E.; Ezerman, M.F. On codes over Eisenstein integers. *arXiv* **2024**. [CrossRef]
9. Stern, S.; Rohweder, D.; Freudenberger, J.; Fischer, R.F.H. Binary multilevel coding over Eisenstein integers for MIMO broadcast transmission. In Proceedings of the International ITG Workshop Smart Antennas (WSA 2019), Vienna, Austria, 24–26 April 2019; pp. 1–8.
10. Feng, C.; Silva, D.; Kschischang, F.R. An algebraic approach to physical-layer network coding. *IEEE Trans. Inf. Theory* **2013**, *59*, 7576–7596.
11. Sun, Q.T.; Yuan, J.; Huang, T.; Shum, K.W. Lattice network codes based on Eisenstein integers. *IEEE Trans. Commun.* **2013**, *61*, 2713–2725. [CrossRef]
12. Sun, Q. T.; Yuan, J.; Huang, T. On lattice-partition-based physical-layer network coding over GF(4). *IEEE Commun. Lett.* **2013**, *17*, 1988–1991.
13. Fang, D.; Burr, A.; Wang, Y. Eisenstein integer based multi-dimensional coded modulation for physical-layer network coding over $\mathbb{F}_4$ in the two-way relay channels. In Proceedings of the European Conference on Networks and Communications (EuCNC 2014), Bologna, Italy, 23–26 June 2014; pp. 1–5.
14. Tunali, N.E.; Huang, Y.C.; Boutros, J.J.; Narayanan, K.R. Lattices over Eisenstein integers for compute-and-forward. *IEEE Trans. Inf. Theory* **2015**, *61*, 5306–5321.
15. Dong, X.; Soh, C.B.; Gunawan, E.; Tang, L. Groups of algebraic integers used for coding QAM signals. *IEEE Trans. Inf. Theory* **1998**, *44*, 1848–1860. [CrossRef]
16. Dong, X.; Soh, C.B.; Gunawan, E. Multiplicative groups used for coding QAM signals. *IMA J. Math. Control Inform.* **2002**, *19*, 229–243. [CrossRef]
17. Goutham Simha, G.D.; Raghavendra M.A.N.S.; Shriharsha, K.; Acharya, U.S. Signal constellations employing multiplicative groups of Gaussian and Eisenstein integers for enhanced spatial modulation. *Phys. Commun.* **2017**, *25*, 546–554.
18. Freudenberger, J.; Shavgulidze, S. Signal constellations based on Eisenstein integers for generalized spatial modulation. *IEEE Commun. Lett.* **2017**, *21*, 556–559. [CrossRef]
19. Freudenberger, J.; Ghaboussi, F.; Shavgulidze, S. New coding techniques for codes over Gaussian integers. *IEEE Trans. Commun.* **2013**, *61*, 3114–3124. [CrossRef]
20. Freudenberger, J.; Ghaboussi, F.; Shavgulidze, S. New four-dimensional signal constellations from Lipschitz integers for transmission over the Gaussian channel. *IEEE Trans. Commun.* **2015**, *63*, 2420–2427.
21. Rohweder, D.; Stern, S.; Fischer, R.F.; Shavgulidze, S.; Freudenberger, J. Four-dimensional Hurwitz signal constellations, set partitioning, detection, and multilevel coding. *IEEE Trans. Commun.* **2021**, *69*, 5079–5090.
22. Güzeltepe, M. On some perfect codes over Hurwitz integers. *Math. Adv. Pure Appl. Sci.* **2018**, *1*, 39–45.
23. Duran, R.; Guzeltepe, M. An algebraic construction technique for codes over Hurwitz integers. *Hacet. J. Math. Stat.* **2023**, *52*, 652–672. [CrossRef]
24. Duran, R.; Guzeltepe, M. Encoder Lipschitz integers: The Lipschitz integers that have the "division with small remainder" property. In *Rendiconti del Circolo Matematico di Palermo Series 2*; Springer: Berlin/Heidelberg, Germany, 2024; Volume 73, pp. 1–15.
25. Li, C.; Gan, L.; Ling, C. Coprime sensing via Chinese remaindering over quadratic fields—Part II: Generalizations and applications. *IEEE Trans. Signal Process.* **2019**, *67*, 2911–2922. [CrossRef]
26. Gong, Y.; Gan, L.; Liu, H. Multi-channel modulo samplers constructed from Gaussian integers. *IEEE Signal Process. Lett.* **2021**, *28*, 1828–1832. [CrossRef]
27. Jarvis, K.; Nevins, M. ETRU: NTRU over the Eisenstein integers. *Des. Codes Cryptog.* **2013**, *74*, 219–242.
28. Conway, J.H.; Sloane, N.J.A. *Sphere Packings, Lattices and Groups*, 3rd ed.; Springer: New York, NY, USA, 2019, ISBN 9780387985855.
29. Huber, K. Codes over Eisenstein-Jacobi integers. *AMS. Contemp. Math.* **1994**, *168*, 165–179.
30. Löfgren, S. *The Eisenstein Integers and Cubic Reciprocity*; Technical Report; Uppsala University: Uppsala, Sweden, 2022.
31. Vargas, J.D. Recillas, H.T. *La función de Euler en Los Enteros de Eisenstein-Jacobi*; Reportes de Investigación; Departamento de Matemáticas, Universidad Autónoma Metropolitana-Iztapalapa: Mexico City, Mexico, 1989.
32. Vargas, J.D.; Barrios, C.J.R.; Recillas, H.T. The Euler totient function on quadratic fields. *JP J. Algebra Number Theory Appl.* **2021**, *52*, 17–94.

33. Hadi, A.; Isnaini, U.; Wahyudi, E.E.; Wijayanti, I.E.; Ezerman, M.F. RSA-like schemes over Eisenstein integers, 2024, *under review*.
34. Li, C.; Gan, L.; Ling, C. Coprime sensing via Chinese remaindering over quadratic fields—Part I: Array designs. *IEEE Trans. Signal Process.* **2019**, *67*, 2898–2910.
35. Awad, Y.; El-Kassar, A.N.; Kadri, T. Rabin public-key cryptosystem in the domain of Gaussian integers. In Proceedings of the 2018 International Conference on Computer and Applications (ICCA), Beirut, Lebanon, 25–26 August 2018; pp. 336–340.
36. da Nobrega Neto, T.P.; Interlando, J.C.; Favareto, O.M.; Elia, M.; Palazzo, R. Lattice constellations and codes from quadratic number fields. *IEEE Trans. Inf. Theory* **2001**, *47*, 1514–1527.

entropy

MDPI

Article

A Family of Optimal Linear Functional-Repair Regenerating Storage Codes

Henk D. L. Hollmann

Institute of Computer Science, University of Tartu, Tartu 50409, Estonia; henk.hollmann@ut.ee

Abstract: We construct a family of linear optimal functional-repair regenerating storage codes with parameters $\{m, (n,k), (r, \alpha, \beta)\} = \{(2r - \alpha + 1)\alpha/2, (r+1, r), (r, \alpha, 1)\}$ for any integers r, α with $1 \leq \alpha \leq r$, over any field when $\alpha \in \{1, r-1, r\}$, and over any finite field $\mathbb{F}_q$ with $q \geq r-1$ otherwise. These storage codes are Minimum-Storage Regenerating (MSR) when $\alpha = 1$, Minimum-Bandwidth Regenerating (MBR) when $\alpha = r$, and represents extremal points of the (convex) attainable cut-set region different from the MSR and MBR points in all other cases. It is known that when $2 \leq \alpha \leq r-1$, these parameters cannot be realized by exact-repair storage codes. Each of these codes come with an explicit and relatively simple repair method, and repair can even be realized as help-by-transfer (HBT) if desired. The coding states of codes from this family can be described geometrically as configurations of $r+1$ subspaces of dimension α in an m-dimensional vector space with restricted sub-span dimensions. A few "small" codes with these parameters are known: one for $(r, \alpha) = (3, 2)$ dating from 2013 and one for $(r, \alpha) = (4, 3)$ dating from 2024. Apart from these, our codes are the first examples of explicit, relatively simple, optimal functional-repair storage codes over a small finite field, with an explicit repair method and with parameters representing an extremal point of the attainable cut-set region distinct from the MSR and MBR points.

Keywords: distributed storage; storage codes; functional repair; cut-set bound; MDS codes

1. Introduction

The amount of data in need of storage continues to grow at an astonishing rate. The International Data Corporation (IDC) predicts that the Global Datasphere (the total amount of data created, captured, copied, and consumed globally) will grow from 149 zettabytes in 2024 [1], to 181 zettabytes by the end of 2025 [2,3], and to an estimated 394 zettabytes in 2028 [4] (a zettabyte equals 10^{21} bytes). These developments may even be accelerated by the advancement of generative AI models. In view of these developments, the importance of efficient data storage management can hardly be underestimated. A major challenge is to devise storage technologies that are capable of handling these huge amounts of data in an efficient, reliable, and economically feasible way.

1.1. Distributed Storage Systems and Storage Codes

In modern storage systems, data storage is handled by a *Distributed Storage System* (DSS). A DSS stores data across potentially unreliable storage units commonly referred to as *storage nodes*, which are typically located in servers in data centers in widely different locations. Efficient update and repair mechanisms are critical for maintaining stability, especially during node failures [5]. To handle the occasional loss of a storage node, the DSS employs *redundancy*, in the form of a *storage code* [6,7]. Often, a DSS simply employs *replication*, where the storage code takes the form of a *repetition code*. But nowadays, many storage systems such as Amazon S3 [8]; Goole File System [9] and its successor Colossus [10]; Microsoft's Azure [11–13]; and Facebook's storage systems [14,15], offer a storage mode involving a (non-trivial) erasure code. Especially for *cold data* (data that remains unchanged, for example for archiving), but also for warm data (data that needs to be updated only occasionally), non-trivial erasure codes such as Reed–Solomon (RS) codes, Locally Repairable Codes (LRCs) or Regenerating Codes (RGCs) are considered or already applied [7,16]. For example, Microsoft Azure employs a Reed–Solomon code for archiving purposes [11]. Hadoop implements various Reed–Solomon (RS) codes [17,18], and the implementation of other codes such as HTEC has been proposed, see, e.g., [19]. The Redundant Array of Independent Disks (RAID) standard RAID-6 specifies the use of two-parity erasure codes, see, e.g., [20]. Huawei OceanStor Dorado [21,22] employs Elastic EC, offering choice between replication and EC, for example RAID-TP (triple parity), and IBM Ceph also offers a choice of EC profiles [23,24] (see also [25]). Several good overviews of modern storage codes and their performance are available, see for example [16,26–29]. For a general and recent reference on storage systems, see [30], and for an overview of Big–Data management, see [31].

1.2. Node Repair

In the case of a lost node, the DSS uses the storage code to repair the damage. During repair, the DSS introduces a *replacement node* (sometimes called a *newcomer* node) into the system and downloads a small amount of data from some of the remaining nodes, referred to as the *helper* nodes; the data obtained is then used to compute a block of replacement data that is to be placed on the replacement node. This process, commonly referred to as *node repair*, comes in two variations. In the simplest repair mode, referred to as *exact repair* (ER) [32,33], the data stored on the newcomer node is an *exact* copy of the data stored on the lost node. A more subtle repair mode, first considered in [6], is *functional repair* (FR), where the replacement data need not be an exact copy of the lost data, but is designed to maintain the possibility of recovering the data that was originally stored, as well as to maintain the possibility for future repairs. An ER storage code can be thought of as an *erasure code* that enables efficient repair. In contrast, an FR storage code can be seen as a *family* of codes, all having the same parameters, where an erasure in a codeword from a code in the family is corrected into a codeword from possibly another code in the family [29] (Section 3.1.1). We define and discuss *linear* FR storage codes in detail in Section 3, and describe an example in Example 1. For a formal definition of general FR storage codes, we refer to [29] (Section 3.1.1).

1.3. Effectiveness of a Storage Code

Key considerations for measuring the effectiveness of a storage code are the *storage overhead* and the *efficiency of the repair process*. The storage overhead is determined by the fraction of *redundancy* employed by the code, and is measured by the *rate* of the code. Efficient repair, first of all, requires an easily implementable repair algorithm. Other important factors are the amount of data that needs to be transferred during repair, referred to as the *repair bandwidth*, and the amount of *disk I/O*, the number of times that a symbol is accessed on disk. In addition, it is desirable to limit the number of nodes that participate in the repair process, known as the *repair degree* [6] or *repair locality* [34,35].

In general, the data that is transferred by a helper node during repair may be *computed* from the available data symbols stored in that node. If each of the helper nodes simply transfers a *subset* of the symbols stored in that node, then we speak of *help by transfer (HBT)* [26,29]; if, in addition, no computations are done either at the newcomer node then we speak of *repair by transfer (RPT)* [36,37]. We say that a storage code is an *optimal-access* code if the number of symbols read at a helper node equals the number of symbols transferred by that node [26,29,38].

1.4. Regenerating Codes and Locally Repairable Codes

Research into storage codes has diverged into two main directions. Regenerating codes (RGCs) investigate the possible trade-off between the storage capacity per node and the repair bandwidth (the total amount of data download during repair), which is determined by the cut-set bound [6]. On the other hand, Locally Repairable Codes (LRCs) study the influence of the *repair degree*, the number of helper nodes that may be contacted during node repair [34,35,39]. A good overview of the different lines of research on codes for distributed storage and the obtained results can be found in [40].

We first discuss an often-used model for storage codes, see, i.e., [6,26,27,29]. A *regenerating code* (RGC) with parameters $\{m,(n,k),(r,\alpha,\beta)\}_q$ is a code that allows for the storage of m information symbols from some finite field $\mathbb{F}_q$, in encoded form, onto n storage nodes, each of which being capable of holding α data symbols from $\mathbb{F}_q$. We will refer to α as the *storage capacity* or the *subpacketization* of a storage node. The parameter k indicates that at all times, the original stored information can be recovered from the data stored on *any* set of k nodes. It is assumed that k is the smallest integer with this property; since any set of r nodes can repair all the remaining nodes, we then have $k \leq r$. Note that the *rate* of the code is the fraction $m/(n\alpha)$ of information per stored symbol. The resilience of the code is described in terms of a parameter r, referred to as the *repair degree*, and a parameter β, referred to as as the *transport capacity* of the code. If a node fails, then a *replacement node* is introduced into the system, which is then allowed to contact an *arbitrary* subset of size r of the remaining nodes, referred to as the set of *helper nodes*. Each of the helper nodes is allowed to compute β data symbols, which are then sent to the new node, which uses this data to compute a *replacement block*, again of size α. Therefore, the repair bandwidth γ of a RGC satisfies $\gamma = r\beta$. It has been shown [6] that the parameters of an RGC satisfy the *cut-set bound*

$$m \leq \sum_{i=0}^{k-1} \min(\alpha,(r-i)\beta). \tag{1}$$

Remarkably, the cut-set bound is independent of n (but n does influence the required field size q for code construction). For fixed m, k, and r, the equality case in (1) takes the form of a piece-wise linear curve that represents the possible trade-off between the storage capacity α and the transport capacity β. Note that we have $\alpha \geq m/k$ (since k nodes can recover the data) and $\beta \geq \alpha/r$ (since r nodes can repair); the points on the curve where $\alpha = m/k$ with minimal β (so with $\beta = \alpha/(r-k+1)$) and $\beta = \alpha/r$ with minimal α (so with $\alpha = rm/(rk-(k^2-k)/2)$) are referred to as the Minimum Storage Regenerating (MSR) and Minimum Bandwidth Regenerating (MBR) points, respectively. It is easily verified that the achievable region determined by (1) is convex and has precisely k extreme points (also referred to as *corner points*), see Figure 1. We review the cut-set bound in detail in Section 4.

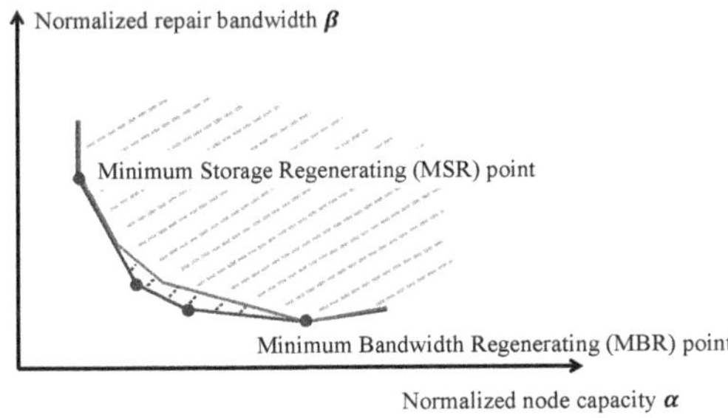

Figure 1. The typical achievable region for functional repair and for exact repair when $k = 4$, with fixed m and r.

An *optimal* RGC is an RGC with parameters that attain the cut-set bound (1). It has been shown [41] (Theorem 7) that the MSR and MBR points are the only corner points that can be achieved by exact-repair RGCs; indeed, the only points on the cut-set bound between the MSR and MBR points that can be achieved by ER RGCs are the MSR and MSB points, with the possible addition of a small line segment starting at the MSR point and not including the next corner point. In fact, it is conjectured that the achievable region for ER RGCs is described by the (identical) parameter sets of Cascade codes [42] and Moulin codes [43]. Conversely, it has been shown [44] that every point on the cut-set bound is achievable by functional-repair RGCs; however, these codes are not (or not really) explicit, require a very large field size, and do not come with a repair algorithm. As far as we know, the only known explicit optimal FR RGCs are the partial exact-repair MSR codes with $m = 2k$ from [37], the explicit $k = n - 2$ HBT "FMSR" codes in [45] (see also the "random" NCCloud HBT codes in [46] and the non-explicit $k = 2$ MSR codes in [47]), and the two explicit optimal FR RGCs from [48] and from [49,50]. Therefore, it is of great interest to construct "simple" FR RGCs with a small field size, in corner points different from the MSR and MBR points.

A *Locally Repairable Code (LRC)* also has parameters $\{m, (n,k), (r, \alpha, \beta)\}_q$, where m, n, k, α, and β have the same meaning as for RGCs, but now we just require that repair of a failed node is always possible if we employ a *specific* set of r helper nodes (i.e., we are allowed to *choose* the r helpers). In [51,52] the maximal *rate* of such codes (without any constraint on k) was investigated, and in [52], it was conjectured that for the case where $r + 1 \mid n$, the optimal rate is achieved by partitioning the n storage nodes into *repair groups* of size $r + 1$ and, within each repair group, using an $\{m, (n,r), (r, \alpha, \beta)\}_q$ *optimal* RGC, so with m attaining equality in (1). This partly explains our interest in RGCs with these parameters in this paper. It is an interesting problem to investigate optimal codes for the case where $r + 1 \nmid n$.

1.5. Our Contribution

Many existing storage codes employ MDS codes or, essentially, *arcs* in projective geometry, in their construction. Some examples are the MBR exact-repair codes obtained by the matrix-product code construction in [53], the MSR functional-repair codes in [37] and in [47], and the exact-repair Moulin codes in [43]. In this paper, we use MDS codes to construct *explicit* optimal linear RGCs with $n - 1 = r = k$, $\beta = 1$, and with α an integer with $1 \leq \alpha \leq r$, so with $m = (2r - \alpha + 1)\alpha/2$, which we refer to as (r, α)*-regular codes*. In fact, we show that the existence of (r, α)-regular storage codes is *equivalent* to the existence of an $[r, \alpha, r - \alpha + 1]_q$ MDS code, so they can be realized over finite fields $\mathbb{F}_q$ with $q \geq r - 1$, and even as binary codes if $r - \alpha \leq 1$. These codes come with a relatively simple repair method, and we show that, if desired, they allow for help-by-transfer (HBT) repair. The parameters of these codes achieve the r extremal points of the achievable cut-set region for varying α. Note that by employing the obvious *space-sharing technique* [37], we can use the two storage codes in consecutive extremal points on the cut-set bound (1) to also achieve the points between these extremal points. Our construction is based on what we call (r, α)-regular configurations, collections of $r+1$ subspaces of dimension α in an ambient space of dimension m with restricted sub-span dimensions (such configurations where called $(r, \alpha-1)$-good in [48] and [49], see also [51] (Example 3.3)).

The contents of this paper are organized as follows. In Section 2, we introduce some notation and we recall various notions from coding theory, and in Section 3, we review linear storage codes. We revisit the cut-set bound in Section 4, where we also show that in optimal RGCs with $k > 1$, no two nodes store identical information; in addition, we show that if s an integer such that $(s-1)\beta \leq \alpha \leq s\beta$, then any $r-s+1$ nodes carry *independent* information, that is, together they carry an amount of information equal to $(r-s+1)\alpha$. In addition, in the case where $r = k$, we derive an inequality that motivates our definition of (k, r, s, β)-regular configurations in Section 5, where we also construct such configurations for all relevant parameters. The (k, r, s, β)-regular configurations with $k = r$, $\beta = 1$, and $\alpha = s$ are called (r, α)-*regular*. In Section 6, we investigate the structure of such configurations. Section 7 contains our main results. Here, we show that the repair of a lost node in an (r, α)-regular coding state necessarily involves an MDS code, thus providing a lower bound for the size of the finite field for which an (r, α)-regular storage code can be constructed. Theorems 3 and 4 together demonstrate existence of (r, α)-regular codes for all feasible pairs (r, α), and include precise and simple repair instructions for the corresponding codes. In Section 8, we describe how to obtain smaller (r, α)-regular storage codes with extra symmetry, involving only (r, α)-regular configurations of a more restricted type. Finally, in Section 9, we present some conclusions.

2. Notation and Preliminaries

For a positive integer n, we define $[n] := \{1, \ldots, n\}$. We write $\mathbb{F}_q$ to denote the (unique) finite field of size q. For two vectors $\boldsymbol{a} = (a_1, \ldots, a_m)$ and $\boldsymbol{b} = (b_1, \ldots, b_m)$ in some vector space $V \cong \mathbb{F}_q^m$, and for a $k \times m$ matrix $\boldsymbol{M} = (M_{i,j})$ with entries in $\mathbb{F}_q$, define the *dot product* $\boldsymbol{a} \cdot \boldsymbol{b} := a_1 b_1 + \cdots + a_m b_m$; define $M \cdot \boldsymbol{a} := (\boldsymbol{M}(1) \cdot \boldsymbol{a}, \ldots, \boldsymbol{M}(k) \cdot \boldsymbol{a})$, where $\boldsymbol{M}(i)$ denotes the i-th row of $\boldsymbol{M}$; and define $\boldsymbol{a} \cdot \boldsymbol{M} = (\boldsymbol{a} \cdot \boldsymbol{M}_1, \ldots, \boldsymbol{a} \cdot \boldsymbol{M}_k)$, where $\boldsymbol{M}_j$ denotes the j-th column of $\boldsymbol{M}$.

We define the *span* $\langle U_1, \ldots, U_n \rangle$ of subspaces $U_1, \ldots, U_n$ of an ambient vector space V as the collection of all sums $\boldsymbol{u}_1 + \cdots + \boldsymbol{u}_n$ with $\boldsymbol{u}_i \in U_i$ for $i \in [n]$. (In other works, the span is sometimes denoted as $U_1 + \cdots + U_n$.) We simply denote the span $\langle \langle \boldsymbol{u}_1 \rangle, \ldots, \langle \boldsymbol{u}_n \rangle \rangle$ of the vectors $\boldsymbol{u}_1, \ldots, \boldsymbol{u}_n$ in V by $\langle \boldsymbol{u}_1, \ldots, \boldsymbol{u}_n \rangle$. We say that subspaces $U_1, \ldots, U_n$ of a vector space V are *independent* if $\dim\langle U_1, \ldots, U_n \rangle = \dim U_1 + \cdots + \dim U_n$, where $\dim V$ denotes the *dimension* of a vector space V.

We repeatedly use *Grassmann's identity*, which states that for vector spaces U, V we have

$$\dim U \cap V + \dim\langle U, V \rangle = \dim U + \dim V.$$

We need various notions from coding theory. For reference, see, e.g., [54].

The *support* $\text{supp}(\boldsymbol{v})$ of a vector $\boldsymbol{v} \in \mathbb{F}_q^n$ is the collection of positions $i \in \{1, \ldots, n\}$ for which $v_i \neq 0$; the *(Hamming) weight* $w(\boldsymbol{v})$ of $\boldsymbol{v}$ is the number of positions $i \in \{1, \ldots, n\}$ for which $v_i \neq 0$, that is, $w(\boldsymbol{v}) = |\text{supp}(\boldsymbol{v})|$. The *(Hamming) distance* $d(\boldsymbol{v}, \boldsymbol{w})$ between $\boldsymbol{v}, \boldsymbol{w} \in \mathbb{F}_q^n$ is the number of positions $i \in \{1, \ldots, n\}$ for which $v_i \neq w_i$. Note that $d(\boldsymbol{v}, \boldsymbol{w}) = w(\boldsymbol{v} - \boldsymbol{w})$.

A *code* C of length n over $\mathbb{F}_q$ is just a subset of $\mathbb{F}_q^n$; the code C is called *linear* if C is a *subspace* of $\mathbb{F}_q^n$. We often refer to the vectors contained in a code as *codewords*. The *minimum weight* $w(C)$ of a code C is the smallest weight of a nonzero codeword from C, and the *minimum distance* $d(C)$ of C is the smallest distance between two distinct codewords from C. Note that if the code C is linear, then $d(C) = w(C)$. We often refer to a linear code C of length n, dimension k, and minimum distance d over $\mathbb{F}_q$ as an $[n,k]_q$ code or as an $[n,k,d]_q$ code; we simply write $[n,k]$ or $[n,k,d]$ if the intended field is clear from the context.

A *generator matrix* for an $[n,k]_q$ code C is a $k \times n$ matrix $\boldsymbol{G}$ over $\mathbb{F}_q$ with rank k and with its rowspace equal to C, that is, C consists of the vectors $\boldsymbol{a} \cdot \boldsymbol{G}$ with $\boldsymbol{a} \in \mathbb{F}_q^k$. An $(n-k) \times n$ matrix $\boldsymbol{H}$ is a *parity-check matrix* for C if $\boldsymbol{H}$ has rank $n-k$ and $\boldsymbol{c} \in C$ if and only if $\boldsymbol{H} \cdot \boldsymbol{c} = \boldsymbol{0}$. The *dual* code $C^\perp$ of C is the collection of all vectors $\boldsymbol{x}$ for which $\boldsymbol{x} \cdot \boldsymbol{c} = 0$ for all $\boldsymbol{c} \in C$. It is not difficult to see that $C^\perp$ is an $[n, n-k]$-code, and has generator matrix $\boldsymbol{H}$ and parity-check matrix $\boldsymbol{G}$, see also [54] (Chapter 11).

Finally, we need some notions related to MDS codes. As a general reference for this material, see [54] (Chapter 11). The *Singleton bound* states that an $[n,k,d]_q$ code satisfies $d \le n-k+1$. For a proof, see, e.g., [54] (Chapter 1, Theorem 11), or see [55] (Theorem 4.1) for a generalization for non-linear codes. An $[n,k,n-k+1]_q$ code, that is, a linear code that attains the Singleton bound, is called an *MDS code*. A related notion is that of an *arc*, a collection of nonzero vectors in $\mathbb{F}_q^k$ with the property that any k of them are independent. (Usually, an arc is defined *projectively*, that is, as a set of points in $\mathrm{PG}(k-1,q)$, but for our purposes, this will do.) We say that a $k \times n$ matrix $\boldsymbol{M}$ represents an n-arc if the columns of $\boldsymbol{M}$ constitute an n-arc (i.e., an arc of size n) in $\mathbb{F}_q^k$; alternatively, we refer to such a matrix as an *MDS-generator*. (The term *MDS matrix* comes from cryptography and is commonly reserved for a matrix M for which $[IM]$ is an MDS-generator.) Consider an $[n,k]_q$ code C, with generator matrix $\boldsymbol{G}$ and parity-check matrix $\boldsymbol{H}$. Obviously, if $\boldsymbol{H}$ has $n-k$ columns that are dependent, then C has a nonzero codeword of weight at most $n-k$. Therefore, C is MDS if and only if the columns of $\boldsymbol{H}$ form an n-arc. Moreover, if $\boldsymbol{G}$ has k columns that are dependent, then there exists $\boldsymbol{a} \in \mathbb{F}_q^k$ with $\boldsymbol{a} \neq \boldsymbol{0}$ such that the codeword $\boldsymbol{c} = \boldsymbol{G}^\top \boldsymbol{a}$ is nonzero but has a 0 in the corresponding positions, so that $0 < w(c) \le n-k$ and C is not MDS. Hence, C is MDS if and only if $\boldsymbol{G}$ is an n-arc, that is, if and only if its generator matrix (or parity-check matrix) is an MDS-generator. In particular, C is MDS if and only if $C^\perp$ is MDS [56] and [57] (Lemma 6.7, p. 245).

Note that $\mathbb{F}_q^k$ itself, the repetition codes with parameters $[n,1,n]_q$ and their duals, the codes with parameters $[n,n-1,2]_q$ (called even-weight codes when $q=2$), are all MDS codes. For $k \ge 2$, let $m(k,q)$ denote the largest n for which an $[n,k,n-k+1]_q$ MDS code exists. The famous MDS conjecture, proven by Simeon Ball for the case where q is prime in [58], claims that

$$m(k,q) = \begin{cases} q+1, & \text{for } 2 \le k < q; \\ k+1, & \text{for } k \ge q, \end{cases} \tag{2}$$

except that when q is even,

$$m(3,q) = m(q-1,q) = q+2. \tag{3}$$

For $k \ge q$, it was shown in [59] that $m(k,q) = k+1$, and that an $[k+1,k]_q$ MDS code is equivalent to the dual of the repetition code, see also [54] (Corollary 7). It is well known that $m(k,q)$ is at least equal to the stated values in (2) and (3). Indeed, we already mentioned that

$$\begin{pmatrix} 1 & 0 & \cdots & 0 & -1 \\ 0 & 1 & \cdots & 0 & -1 \\ \vdots & \vdots & & \vdots & \vdots \\ 0 & 0 & \cdots & 1 & -1 \end{pmatrix} \tag{4}$$

is an MDS-generator for all k; the corresponding linear code for $q = 2$ is called the *even-weight code*. Furthermore, let $\alpha_1, \ldots, \alpha_{q-1}$ be the non-zero elements of $\mathbb{F}_q$. If $k \leq q-1$, then

$$\begin{pmatrix} 1 & \cdots & 1 & 1 & 0 \\ \alpha_1 & \cdots & \alpha_{q-1} & 0 & 0 \\ \vdots & \cdots & \vdots & \vdots & \vdots \\ \alpha_1^{k-2} & \cdots & \alpha_{q-1}^{k-2} & 0 & 0 \\ \alpha_1^{k-1} & \cdots & \alpha_{q-1}^{k-1} & 0 & 1 \end{pmatrix} \tag{5}$$

is a $k \times (q+1)$ MDS-generator; moreover, if q is even, then

$$\begin{pmatrix} 1 & \cdots & 1 & 1 & 0 & 0 \\ \alpha_1 & \cdots & \alpha_{q-1} & 0 & 1 & 0 \\ \alpha_1^2 & \cdots & \alpha_{q-1}^2 & 0 & 0 & 1 \end{pmatrix} \tag{6}$$

is a $3 \times (q+2)$ MDS-generator. The corresponding codes are referred to as *(Generalized) Reed–Solomon codes*. In fact, for any k, $1 \leq k \leq q+1$, such that q is even or k is odd, there exists a $[q+1, k, q-k+2]$ cyclic MDS code over $\mathbb{F}_q$ [60] (this corrects an erroneous claim in [54]). For a reference for the above claims, see, e.g., [54] (Chapter 11, Sections 5–7).

3. Linear Storage Codes

In this paper, we adhere to the *vector space view* ([33,41,48,51,53,61–63]) on linear storage codes. Informally, a storage code with symbol alphabet $\mathbb{F}_q$ is called *linear* if the four processes of data storage, data recovery, the generation of repair data from the helper nodes, and the generation of the replacement data from the repair data, are all linear operations over $\mathbb{F}_q$ [29]. It turns out that in that case, the storage code can be described in terms of subspaces of an ambient vector space over $\mathbb{F}_q$ referred to as the *message space*. In the description below, we will follow a similar approach as in [49,50]. We first need a few definitions.

Definition 1. *We say that the subspaces $U_1, \ldots, U_k$ of a vector space V form a* recovery set *for V if $V = \langle U_1, \ldots, U_k \rangle$.*

Definition 2. *We say that a subspace U_0 of a vector space V can be obtained from subspaces $U_1, \ldots, U_r$ of V by β-*repair, *written as*

$$U_1, \ldots, U_r \xrightarrow{\beta} U_0,$$

if there are β-dimensional helper *subspaces $H_j \subseteq U_j$ ($j \in [r]$) such that $U_0 \subseteq \langle H_j \mid j \in [r] \rangle$.*

We can now present a formal definition of a Linear Regenerating Code (LRGC) in terms of vector spaces, which can be seen as a "basis-free" representation of a linear storage code. To understand the definition, think of the data that is stored by the storage code as being represented by a vector $\boldsymbol{x}$ in the ambient vector space $V \cong \mathbb{F}_q^m$, referred to as the *message space* of the code. Then for every subspace W of V that occurs in the definition, choose a fixed basis $\boldsymbol{w}_1, \ldots, \boldsymbol{w}_t$, and think of W as representing the t data symbols $\boldsymbol{x} \cdot \boldsymbol{w}_1, \ldots, \boldsymbol{x} \cdot \boldsymbol{w}_t$.

Definition 3. *Let $m, n, k, r, \alpha, \beta$ be integers for which $1 < k \leq r < n$ and $\beta \leq \alpha \leq r\beta$. A linear storage code with parameters $\{m, (n,k), (r, \alpha, \beta)\}_q$ consists of an ambient m-dimensional vector space V over $\mathbb{F}_q$ together with a collection $\mathcal{S}$ of sequences $\sigma = U_1, \ldots, U_n$ of α-dimensional subspaces $U_1, \ldots, U_n$ of V, referred to as* coding states *of the storage code, with the following properties.*

(i) (Data recovery) Every k subspaces in a coding state $\sigma \in \mathcal{S}$ constitute a recovery set for V. Moreover, we will assume that k is minimal with respect to this property.
(ii) (Repair) For every $i \in [n]$ and for every $J \subseteq [n] \setminus \{i\}$ with $|J| = r$, there is a subspace U_i' of V such that $(U_j)_{j\in J} \xrightarrow{\beta} U_i'$ for which $\sigma' := U_1, \ldots, U_{i-1}, U_i', U_{i+1}, \ldots, U_n$ is again a coding state in $\mathcal{S}$.

For future use, we introduce some additional terminology.

Definition 4. *We refer to the collection of all the α-dimensional subspaces of V that occur in some coding state in $\mathcal{S}$ as the* coding spaces *of the linear storage code $\mathcal{S}$.*

A subsequence $\pi = U_1, \ldots, U_{i-1}, U_{i+1}, \ldots, U_n$ $(i \in [n])$ of a state $\sigma = U_1, \ldots, U_n \in \mathcal{S}$ will be referred to as a protostate *of the storage code $\mathcal{S}$.*

So to actually employ the collection $\mathcal{S}$ as in Definition 3 as a storage code, think of the stored data as a vector $\boldsymbol{x} \in V$ (or as a *linear functional*, that is, as an element of the *dual* $V^\vee$ of V mapping $\boldsymbol{a} \in V$ to $\boldsymbol{x} \cdot \boldsymbol{a} \in \mathbb{F}_q$ as in [64]). Then, for every coding space U involved in $\mathcal{S}$, choose a *fixed* $m \times \alpha$ matrix $\boldsymbol{U} = \boldsymbol{U}(U)$ with columnspace equal to U; now, if U is the coding space associated with a particular storage node, then we let this node store the α symbols of the vector $\boldsymbol{c}(U, \boldsymbol{x}) := \boldsymbol{x} \cdot \boldsymbol{U}$. Note that if $\boldsymbol{u}$ is any vector in U, with $\boldsymbol{u} = \boldsymbol{U}\boldsymbol{a} \in U$, say, then $\boldsymbol{x} \cdot \boldsymbol{u} = (\boldsymbol{x} \cdot \boldsymbol{U}) \cdot \boldsymbol{a}$, so for every $\boldsymbol{u} \in U$, we can compute $\boldsymbol{x} \cdot \boldsymbol{u}$ from the stored vector $\boldsymbol{x} \cdot \boldsymbol{U}$. Similarly, for a repair subspace H contained in a helper node with associated coding space U during repair, we choose a fixed $m \times \beta$ matrix $\boldsymbol{H} = \boldsymbol{H}(H)$ with columnspace equal to H, and let this (helper) node contribute the β symbols $\boldsymbol{x} \cdot \boldsymbol{H}$. The *code* associated with a coding state $\sigma = U_1, \ldots, U_n$ is the collection C_σ of all words $\boldsymbol{c}(\boldsymbol{x})$ in $\mathbb{F}_q^{n\alpha}$ obtained as the concatenation of the words $\boldsymbol{c}(U_i, \boldsymbol{x})$ for $i \in [n]$ when $\boldsymbol{x}$ ranges over V. Note that C_σ is an $[n\alpha, m]_q$ code with $m \times n\alpha$ generator matrix

$$G(\sigma) = [\boldsymbol{U}_1 \cdots \boldsymbol{U}_n],$$

where $\boldsymbol{U}_i$ is a matrix with columnspace U_i, for all i. It is not difficult to verify that the family of codes C_σ associated with states σ from a storage code $\mathcal{S}$ as in Definition 3 indeed has the desired repair properties when used in this way to store data. Note that the resulting functional-repair (FR) storage code is exact-repair precisely when the code consists of a *single* coding state. In the case where the storage code is FR, at any time every storage node must "know" its associated coding space. The extra overhead that this entails can be relatively small if the code is used to store a *large number* of data vectors *simultaneously*. For further details, we refer to [49,50]. The next example illustrates the above.

Example 1 (See also [48] (Example 2.2), [49] (Example 2.6), and [50] (Example 2.7)). *We will construct a binary linear functional-repair storage code $\mathcal{S}$ with parameters $\{m, (n, k), (r, \alpha, \beta)\}_q = \{5, (4, 3), (3, 2, 1)\}_2$ (representing the smallest non-MSR/MBR extreme point of the achievable cut-set region). So let V be a 5-dimensional vector space over $\mathbb{F}_2$. A set of three 2-dimensional subspaces $\{U_1, U_2, U_3\}$ of V is said to be* (3,2)-regular *if any two of them are independent and $\langle U_1, U_2, U_3\rangle = V$ (this was called* (3,1)-good *in the cited papers). It is easily verified that if $\{U_1, U_2, U_3\}$ is (3,2)-regular, then there are nonzero vectors $\boldsymbol{a}_i \in U_i$ $(i = 1, 2, 3)$ such that $\boldsymbol{a}_1 + \boldsymbol{a}_2 + \boldsymbol{a}_3 = \boldsymbol{0}$; as a consequence, there is a basis $\boldsymbol{e}_1, \boldsymbol{e}_2, \boldsymbol{e}_3, \boldsymbol{a}_1, \boldsymbol{a}_2$ for V such that $U_i = \langle \boldsymbol{e}_i, \boldsymbol{a}_i\rangle$ $(i = 1, 2, 3)$. It is easily checked that with $U_4 := \langle \boldsymbol{e}_1 + \boldsymbol{e}_2, \boldsymbol{e}_1 + \boldsymbol{e}_3\rangle$, any subset of $\{U_1, U_2, U_3, U_4\}$ of size 3 is (3,2)-regular. As a consequence, the collection of all states $\sigma = U_1, U_2, U_3, U_4$ for which any set of three of the spaces form a (3,2)-regular collection is a linear storage code with the parameters as specified. Note that there are coding states that are* unreachable, *that is, not obtainable by repair from a protostate; for example, states of the form $\sigma = U_1, U_2, U_3, U_4$ with*

$U_i = \langle \mathbf{e}_i, \mathbf{a}_i \rangle$ $(i = 1,2,3)$ *and with* $U_4 = \langle \mathbf{e}_1 + \mathbf{e}_2, \mathbf{e}_1 + \mathbf{e}_3 + \mathbf{a}_1 \rangle$; *obviously, such states can be freely deleted from the code.*

4. The Cut-Set Bound Revisited

Suppose that the DSS employs an $\{m, (n,k), (r, \alpha, \beta)\}$ storage code. Since k is assumed to be minimal and any r nodes can regenerate the stored information, we have $n - 1 \geq r \geq k$. (Indeed, to see this, choose an arbitrary set of r helper nodes, and one by one destroy and repair all the other nodes, employing these helper nodes for each repair. Then the information contained in the system is just the information that is contained in these r helper nodes.) Note also that, obviously, $m/k \leq \alpha$ (since any k nodes regenerate the stored information), and $\alpha \leq r\beta$ (since r helper nodes, each contributing an amount β of information, can create a replacement node), and $\beta \leq \alpha$ (since α is the maximum amount that can be contributed by a helper node). Finally, let s be an integer such that $(s-1)\beta \leq \alpha \leq s\beta$, or such that $\beta \leq \alpha \leq s\beta$ if $s = r - k + 1$; therefore, we may assume that $r - k + 1 \leq s \leq r$. We let $\overline{\alpha} := \alpha/m$ and $\overline{\beta} := \beta/m$ denote the *normalized* storage capacity and transport capacity, respectively. Our aim is to provide a quick and informal derivation of the cut-set bound for RGCs and to establish a few simple properties of optimal codes that seem to have gone unobserved. First, we show the following.

Lemma 1 (Cut-set bound). *Let m, n, k, r be positive integers with $n - 1 \geq r \geq k$, and let α, β be positive real numbers with $\beta \leq \alpha \leq r\beta$. Let s be an integer such that $(s-1)\beta \leq \alpha \leq s\beta$ if $s = r - k + 2, \ldots, r$ or such that $\beta \leq \alpha \leq (r - k + 1)\beta$ if $s = r - k + 1$. A storage code with parameters $\{m, (n,k), (r, \alpha, \beta)\}$ satisfies*

$$m \leq \sum_{i=0}^{k-1} \min(\alpha, (r-i)\beta) = (r - s + 1)\alpha + ((s-1) + \cdots + (r - k + 1))\beta. \tag{7}$$

Moreover, in the case of equality in (7), we have the following.

- *Any $r - s + 1$ nodes, together, contain an amount of information $(r - s + 1)\alpha$, that is, these nodes carry independent information.*
- *Any two nodes carry an amount of information of at least 2α if $s < r$ or $\alpha + (k-1)\beta$ if $s = r$. Therefore, if $k = 1$, then every node carries the stored information, so the code is essentially a repetition code, but if $k \geq 2$, then no two nodes carry identical information .*
- *If, in addition, we have $r = k$, then for any $J \subseteq [n]$ with size $|J| \leq k$, the information $I(N_j \mid j \in J)$ contained in any collection of storage nodes N_j with $j \in J$ satisfies*

$$I(N_j \mid j \in J) = |J|\alpha \tag{8}$$

if $|J| \leq r - s + 1$, and

$$I(N_j \mid j \in J) \geq (r - s + 1)\alpha + ((s-1) + \cdots + (s-t))\beta. \tag{9}$$

if $|J| = r - s + 1 + t$ with $1 \leq t \leq k - r + s - 1$.

Proof. Assume that nodes $N_1, \ldots, N_n$ store the file, and that each k nodes regenerate the stored file, with every node storing α symbols. Consider nodes $N_1, \ldots, N_{r+1}$. Pretend that nodes $N_{r-s+2}, \ldots, N_k$ fail in turn, and are replaced by newcomer nodes $N'_{r-s+2}, \ldots, N'_k$, with none of the nodes $N_{r+2}, \ldots, N_n$ ever participating in a repair. Assume that for $i = 1, \ldots, k - r + s - 1$, the lost node $N_{r-s+1+i}$ is replaced by newcomer node $N'_{r-s+1+i}$, which receives an amount of β information from each node contained in the set of r helper nodes consisting of the old nodes $N_1, \ldots, N_{r-s+1}$, the new nodes $N'_{r-s+2}, \ldots, N'_{r-s+i}$, and the old nodes $N_{r-s+2+i}, \ldots, N_{r+1}$. Now consider the sequence $\mathcal{K}$ of k nodes defined by $\mathcal{K} := N_1, \ldots, N_{r-s+1}, N'_{r-s+2}, \ldots, N'_k$. The first $r-s+1$ nodes $N_1, \ldots, N_{r-s+1}$ in $\mathcal{K}$ contain an amount of information that is at most equal to $(r-s+1)\alpha$. And for $i = 1, \ldots, k-r+s-1$, the information in $N'_{r-s+1+i}$ that is not already contained in the preceding nodes $N_1, \ldots, N_{r-s+1}, N'_{r-s+2}, \ldots, N'_{r-s+i}$ in $\mathcal{K}$ is the information obtained from $N_{r-s+2+i}, \ldots, N_{r+1}$, so is at most equal to $(s-i)\beta$. As a consequence, the amount of information contained in $\mathcal{K}$ is at most equal to $(r-s+1)\alpha + (1+2+\cdots+(r-k+1))\beta$, and since any k nodes should be able to regenerate the stored information, we conclude that (7) holds. Moreover, we conclude that if the bound (7) holds with equality, then the nodes $N_1, \ldots, N_{r-s+1}$ in $\mathcal{K}$, together, contain an amount of $(r-s+1)\alpha$ of information, and, in addition, a node $N_{r-s+2+i}$ contributes a further amount $i\beta$ of information that is independent of the information already present in preceding nodes in $\mathcal{K}$.

By keeping track which of the nodes among $N_{r-s+2}, \ldots, N_{r+1}$ contributed the various pieces of information during the above repair process, we see that node $N_{r-s+2+i}$ for $i = 1, \ldots, k-r+s-2$ contributes an independent amount of information $i\beta$, and the nodes $N_{k+1}, \ldots, N_{r+1}$ each contribute an independent amount $(k-r+s-1)\beta$. Also note that the sequence of nodes $N_1, \ldots, N_k$, as well as their order, is arbitrary, and nodes N_1 and N_{r+1} form an arbitrary pair of nodes. Now, if $s < r$, then $r-s+1 \geq 2$ and we already showed that any $r-s+1$ nodes, together, contain at least an amount of 2α of information; and if $s = r$ then nodes N_1 and N_{r+1}, together, contain at least an amount of $\alpha + (k-r+s-1)\beta = \alpha + (k-1)\beta$ of information. Obviously, in the case where $k = 1$, every node carries the same information, so the code is essentially a repetition code. Finally, in the case where $r = k$, by considering the sequence of nodes $N_1, \ldots, N_{r-s+1}, N_{r+1}, \ldots, N_{r-s+3}$, we see that the last claim in the lemma holds. □

Definition 5. *We say that a Regenerating Code (RGC) with parameters $\{m, (n,k), (r,\alpha,\beta)\}$ is* optimal *if the bound (1) is attained with equality, and if, moreover, lowering α or β results in violation of this bound.*

Note that if $\alpha \leq (r-k+1)\beta$, then (7) reads as $m \leq k\alpha$. In that case, if the code is optimal, then according to Definition 5, we must have $\alpha = m/k$ and $\beta = \alpha/(r-k+1)$.

It is not difficult to see that in terms of the normalized parameters $\overline{\alpha} := \alpha/m$ and $\overline{\beta} := \beta/m$, we have the following. For $s \in \{r-k+1, \ldots, r\}$, define

$$m_{k,r,s} := (r-s+1)s + (s-1) + \cdots + (r-k+1) = (r-s+1)s + \binom{s}{2} - \binom{r-k+1}{2}, \quad (10)$$

and set

$$\overline{\alpha}_s := s/m_{k,r,s}, \quad \overline{\beta}_s := 1/m_{k,r,s}. \quad (11)$$

Then the *feasible cut-set region*, the region of all pairs $(\overline{\alpha}, \overline{\beta})$ that can be realized by tuples (m,k,r,α,β) for which $m \leq k\alpha$, $\beta \leq \alpha \leq r\beta$, and for which (7) holds with s as defined above, has extreme points $(\overline{\alpha}_s, \overline{\beta}_s)$ for $s = r-k+1, \ldots, r$, and is further bounded by the half-lines $\overline{\alpha} = 1/k = \overline{\alpha}_{r-k+1}, \overline{\beta} \geq \overline{\alpha}/(r-k+1) = \overline{\beta}_{r-k+1}$ and $r\overline{\beta} = \overline{\alpha} \geq 2/(2rk-k^2+k)$, see Figure 1 in Section 1.

We sometimes refer to the extreme points $(\overline{\alpha}_s, \overline{\beta}_s)$ $(s = r-k+1, \ldots, r)$ as the *corner points* of the achievable region. The corner points $(\overline{\alpha}_{r-k+1}, \overline{\beta}_{r-k+1})$ and $(\overline{\alpha}_r, \overline{\beta}_r)$ are known as the *MSR point* and the *MBR point*, respectively (note that these points are equal if and only if $k = 1$).

Definition 6. *We say that an RGC with parameters $\{m, (n,k), (r,\alpha,\beta\}_q$* attains a corner point *of the achievable cut-set region if the pair $(\alpha/m, \beta/m)$ equals one of the pairs $(\overline{\alpha}_s, \overline{\beta}_s)$ with $s \in$*

$\{r-k+1,\ldots,r\}$. *An RGC that attains the MSR point or the MBR point is referred to as an* MSR code *or an* MBR code, *respectively.*

Remark 1. *The result in (9) may well hold also for optimal storage codes where $r > k$, but we have no proof and no counterexample.*

Remark 2. *There are cases of optimal codes where (9) is not satisfied with equality. Consider an MBR code with $\alpha = r = k = 3$, $n = 4$, and $m = 3+2+1 = 6$. The "standard" code has coding spaces $U_i = \langle e_{\{i,j\}} \mid j \in [4], j \neq i\rangle$, where the $C(4,2) = 6$ vectors $\boldsymbol{e}_{\{i,j\}}$ with $1 \leq i < j \leq 4$ form a basis. This code satisfies (8) and (9) with equality.*

Now, let $U_1 = \langle e_1, e_2, e_3\rangle$, $U_2 = \langle e_4, e_5, e_6\rangle$, $U_3 = \langle e_1 + e_4, e_2, e_6\rangle$, and $U_4 = \langle e_2 + e_6, e_3, e_5\rangle$. Note that U_4 can be obtained by repair from U_1 (use e_3), U_2 (use e_5), and U_3 (use $e_2 + e_6$). Now any two coding spaces span at least a 5-space, and any three span a 6-space, but U_1, U_2 are independent.

This example shows that in a coding state, (9) is not necessarily satisfied with equality. But note that this example can only represent an unreachable *state in a storage code with these parameters, since once we have a protostate with no two spaces disjoint, then the new space has a repair vector in common with each of the other coding spaces.*

5. (k,r,s,β)-Regular Configurations

In this section, let n, k, r be integers with $n-1 \geq r \geq k \geq 1$, let s be an integer with $r-k+1 \leq s \leq r$, and let $m_{k,r,s}$ be as defined in (10). Moreover, let β be a positive integer and let $\alpha := s\beta$. Motivated by the results from the previous section—notably, by (8) and (9)—and by the form of the "small" storage codes from [48,49]) (see also [50]), we introduce and investigate the following notion.

Definition 7. *Let V be a vector space with $\dim V = m_{k,r,s}\beta$, and let $U_1, \ldots, U_n$ be α-dimensional subspaces of V. We say that the collection $\{U_1, \ldots, U_n\}$ is (k,r,s,β)-regular in V if $\alpha = s\beta$ and, for every integer t with $0 \leq t \leq k-(r-s+1)$ and for every $J \subseteq [n]$ with $|J| = r-s+1+t$, we have $\dim\langle U_j \mid j \in J\rangle = d_t\beta$, where*

$$d_t := d_t^{r,s} := (r-s+1)s + \sum_{i=1}^{t}(s-i) = (r-s+1)s + (s-1) + \cdots + (s-t). \tag{12}$$

In addition, we say that $\{U_1, \ldots, U_n\}$ is (k,r,s)-regular if it is (k,r,s,β)-regular with $\beta = 1$, and (r,s)-regular if it is (k,r,s)-regular with $k = r$. We will write

$$m_{r,s} := m_{r,r,s} = (r-s+1)s + (s-1) + \cdots + 1 \tag{13}$$

to denote the dimension of the ambient space of an (r,s)-regular collection.

Note that Definition 7 requires, in particular, that any $r-s+1$ of the vector spaces in a (k,r,s,β)-regular collection are independent, and that any k of the vector spaces span V. Our aim in the remainder of this section is to study the properties of the numbers $m_{k,r,s}$ defined in (10), and to describe a construction of (k,r,s)-regular collections (and, hence, of (k,r,s,β)-regular configurations for all integers β). To that end, we need the following.

Lemma 2. *For $i \in [s]$, define $m_i := \min(r-s+i, k)$. Then $r-s+1 = m_1 \leq \cdots \leq m_s = k$. Let t be an integer with $0 \leq t \leq k-(r-s+1)$, and set $u := (r-s+1)+t$. Then $r-s+1 \leq u \leq k$ and*

$$d_t = (r-s+1)s + (s-1) + \cdots + (s-t) = \sum_{i=1}^{s} \min(m_i, u).$$

In particular, for $m_{k,r,s}$ as defined in (10), we have

$$m_{k,r,s} = d_{s-(r-k+1)} = m_1 + m_2 + \cdots + m_s.$$

Proof. Since $r-k+1 \leq s$, we have $r-s+1 \leq k$, hence $m_1 = r-s+1$. Also, $m_s = \min(r,k) = k$. Obviously, $m_i \leq m_j$ if $i < j$. Therefore, the first claim follows immediately. Since $u = (r-s+1)+t \leq k$, we have $\min(m_i,u) = \min(r-s+i,u)$, so we have

$$\begin{aligned} \textstyle\sum_{i=1}^{s} \min(m_i,u) &= (r-s+1)+\cdots+(r-s+t)+(s-t)u \\ &= (r-s+1)t+0+1+\cdots+(t-1)+(s-t)(r-s+1)+(s-t)t \\ &= (r-s+1)s+0+1+2+\cdots+(t-1)+t(s-t) \\ &= (r-s+1)s+(s-t)+\cdots+(s-1) = d_t. \end{aligned}$$

Taking $t = k-(r-s+1)$, we have $u = k \geq m_i$ for all i, and we find that $m_{k,r,s} = d_{k-(r-s+1)} = \sum_{i=1}^{s} \min(m_i,k) = \sum_{i=1}^{s} m_i$. □

Now, to construct a (k,r,s)-regular configuration of size $n \geq r+1$, we proceed as follows. For $i \in [s]$, let M_i be a $m_i \times r$ MDS-generator over a sufficiently large field $\mathbb{F}_q$, and let $M := \mathrm{diag}(M_1,\ldots,M_s)$. Now let $U_j := \langle M_1(j), M_2(j), \ldots, M_s(j)\rangle$, where $M_i(j)$ denotes the j-th column of M_i. Also, write $V_i' = \mathbb{F}_q^{m_i}$ and let $V := V_1 \oplus \cdots \oplus V_s = \langle V_1,\ldots,V_s\rangle$, where we identify V_i' with the subspace $V_i := \{\mathbf{0}\} \oplus \cdots \oplus \{\mathbf{0}\} \oplus V_i' \oplus \{\mathbf{0}\} \oplus \cdots \oplus \{\mathbf{0}\}$ of V. Note that $\dim U_j = s$ ($j \in [n]$), and, by Lemma 2, we have that $\dim V = m_{k,r,s}$.

Theorem 1. *Given the above definitions, $\sigma := \{U_1,\ldots,U_n\}$ is (k,r,s)-regular, and σ can be constructed from a generator matrix of an $[r,k,r-k+1]_q$ MDS code (that is, from a $k \times r$ MDS-generator).*

Proof. We begin by remarking that since $m_i \leq k \leq r$ and $m_s = k$, the matrices M_i can indeed be constructed if the field size q is large enough. Indeed, the matrices $M_1,\ldots,M_{s-1}$ can be constructed from a matrix M_s by deleting some columns, and since $m_s = k$, such a matrix exists if and only if there exists an $[r,k,r-k+1]_q$ MDS code. Note that for $i \in [s]$, the columns of M_i are in V_i'; hence, the corresponding columns in M are in V_i. Next, consider the span of a collection U_i for $i \in I$, where $|I| = u$. Since this span contains u vectors from V_i, which correspond to u columns from M_i, the MDS property of M_i implies that the dimension of their span is equal to $\min(m_i,u)$. Therefore, with $u := (r-s+1)+t$, according to Lemma 2, the span in V is equal to $\sum_{i=1}^{s} \min(m_i,u) = d_t$, as required. In particular, for $t := k-(r-s+1)$, we have $m := \dim V = d_t = m_{k,r,s}$. □

The above suggests investigating storage codes with parameters $\{m_{k,r,s},(n,k),(r,s,1)\}$ and with coding states that are (k,r,s)-regular. This is the subject of Sections 7 and 8 for the case where $k = r$. We note that not every such coding state is reachable by repair, see Example 2 below.

Example 2. *Let $U_1 := \langle \mathbf{a}_1, \mathbf{b}_1\rangle$. $U_2 := \langle \mathbf{a}_2, \mathbf{b}_2\rangle$, $U_3 := \langle \mathbf{a}_3, \mathbf{b}_1+\mathbf{b}_2\rangle$, and $U_4 := \langle -\mathbf{a}_1-\mathbf{a}_2-\mathbf{a}_3, \mathbf{b}_1-\mathbf{b}_2\rangle$, where $V := \langle \mathbf{a}_1,\mathbf{a}_2,\mathbf{a}_3,\mathbf{b}_1,\mathbf{b}_2\rangle$ has dimension 5. Then $\sigma := \{U_1,U_2,U_3,U_4\}$ is $(3,2)$-regular, but no subspace U_i can be obtained from the other three subspaces U_j with $j \neq i$ by 1-repair. Therefore, σ cannot be a reachable coding state in a $\{5,(4,3),(3,2,1)\}$ storage code. Replacing U_4 by $U_4' := \langle \mathbf{a}_1-\mathbf{a}_2, \mathbf{a}_1-\mathbf{a}_3\rangle$ yields a $(3,2)$-regular configuration that could be a reachable state in a storage code with these parameters.*

In Section 8, we shall describe an alternative construction of an (r,s)-regular configuration. Here, we state a useful property of the numbers $m_{k,r,s}$ that is needed in that construction.

Lemma 3. *We have*

$$\begin{aligned} m_{k,r,s} &= (r-s+1)s+(s-1)+\cdots+(r-k+1) \\ &= \begin{cases} r+m_{k-1,r-1,s-1}, & \text{if } s>r-k+1); \\ ks, & \text{if } s=r-k+1, \end{cases} \end{aligned}$$

and hence

$$m_{k,r,s} = r+(r-1)+\cdots+(2r-s-k+2)+(r-s+1)(r-k+1). \tag{14}$$

Proof. If $r-k+1<s$, then with $r' := r-1, k' := k-1, s' := s-1$, we have

$$\begin{aligned} m_{k,r,s} &= (r-s+1)s+(s-1)+\cdots+(r-k+1) \\ &= (r'-\alpha'+1)s'+(r-s')+s'+(s'-1)+(r'-k'+1) \\ &= r+m_{k',r',s'}. \end{aligned}$$

The last claim follows immediately from this claim by induction. □

6. The Structure of an (r,r,s,β)-Regular Configuration

In this section, we consider the case where $r=k$. We begin with a result that is fundamental for what follows.

Lemma 4. *Let $U_1,\ldots,U_r$ be subspaces of a vector space V. Define*

$$\overline{U}_i := \langle U_j \mid j\in[r], j\neq i\rangle. \tag{15}$$

Suppose that H_i is a subspace of U_i with $H_i\cap\overline{U}_i=\{0\}$ for all $i\in[r]$. Then, with $H:=\langle H_i \mid i\in[r]\rangle$, we have $\dim H=\sum\dim H_i$, and for every $J\subseteq[r]$, we have $\langle U_j \mid j\in J\rangle\cap H=\langle H_j\mid j\in J\rangle$.

Proof. Let j and t be integers with $0\le j<t\le r$. Since $U_1,\ldots,U_j,H_1,\ldots,H_{t-1}\subseteq\overline{U}_t$ and $H_t\cap\overline{U}_t=\{0\}$, we have $\dim\langle U_1,\ldots,U_j,H_1,\ldots,H_t\rangle=\dim\langle U_1,\ldots,U_j,H_1,\ldots,H_{t-1}\rangle+\dim H_t$. Since $H_1,\ldots,H_j\subseteq\langle U_1,\ldots,U_j,\rangle$, by induction we have that

$$\dim\langle U_1,\ldots,U_j,H_1,\ldots,H_r\rangle=\dim\langle U_1,\ldots,U_j\rangle+\sum_{i=j+1}^{r}\dim H_i. \tag{16}$$

By (16) for $j=0$, we conclude that $\dim H=\sum\dim H_i$, which proves the first part of the lemma. Next, let $J\subseteq[r]$ with $|J|=j$. After renumbering the subspaces if necessary, we may assume that $J=\{1,\ldots,j\}$. By (16) and Grassmann's identity, we have

$$\dim\langle U_1,\ldots,U_j\rangle\cap H=\dim\langle U_1,\ldots,U_j\rangle+\dim H-\dim\langle U_1,\ldots,U_j,H\rangle=\sum_{i=1}^{j}\dim H_j.$$

Since $H_1,\ldots,H_j\subseteq\langle U_1,\ldots,U_j\rangle$ and $\dim\langle H_1,\ldots,H_j\rangle=\sum_{i=1}^{j}\dim H_i$, we conclude that $\langle U_1,\ldots,U_j\rangle\cap H=\langle H_1,\ldots,H_j\rangle$, so the second part of the lemma follows. □

Now assume that r, s, and β are positive integers with $1\le s\le r$ and $r\ge 2$; set $\alpha:=s\beta$; and let V be an m-dimensional vector space over some finite field $\mathbb{F}_q$ with $m=m_{r,s}\beta$, where

$m_{r,s}$ is as defined in (10). Assume that $\pi = \{U_1, \ldots, U_r\}$ is (r, r, s, β)-regular in V. For $i \in [r]$, let H_i be a β-dimensional subspace of U_i with $H_i \cap \overline{U}_i = \{\mathbf{0}\}$, where $\overline{U}_i$ is as defined in (15), and define $H := \langle H_1, \ldots, H_r \rangle$. Below, we will use these assumptions to draw a number of conclusions. First note that since π is (r, r, s, β)-regular, we have

$$\dim \overline{U}_i = m - \beta \tag{17}$$

and

$$\langle \overline{U}_i, U_i \rangle = V \tag{18}$$

for all $i \in [r]$. By Lemma 4, $H_1, \ldots, H_r$ are independent in H, so $\dim H = r\beta$. Next, we note the following.

Lemma 5. *We have that*

$$\dim \overline{U}_1 \cap \overline{U}_2 \cap \cdots \cap \overline{U}_t = m - t\beta$$

for all t; in particular, with

$$V' := \cap_{j=1}^{r} \overline{U}_j, \tag{19}$$

we have $\dim V' = m - r\beta$.

Proof. We use induction on t. By (17), the result certainly holds for $t = 1$. Now, let $t \geq 2$, and suppose the claim holds for smaller values of t. First, we observe that since U_t is contained in $\overline{U}_1, \ldots, \overline{U}_{t-1}$, by (18), we have $\langle \overline{U}_1 \cap \cdots \cap \overline{U}_{t-1}, \overline{U}_t \rangle \supseteq \langle U_t, \overline{U}_t \rangle = V$. Hence

$$\dim \langle \overline{U}_1 \cap \cdots \cap \overline{U}_{t-1}, \overline{U}_t \rangle = m. \tag{20}$$

By the induction hypothesis, $\dim \overline{U}_1 \cap \cdots \cap \overline{U}_{t-1} = m + (t-1)\beta$, so using (17), (20), and Grassmann's identity, we obtain

$$\begin{aligned} \dim \overline{U}_1 \cap \cdots \cap \overline{U}_t &= \dim \overline{U}_1 \cap \cdots \cap \overline{U}_{t-1} + \dim \overline{U}_t - \dim \langle \overline{U}_1 \cap \cdots \cap \overline{U}_{t-1}, \overline{U}_t \rangle \\ &= (m - (t-1)\beta) + (m - \beta) - m = m - t\beta. \end{aligned}$$

The last claim in the lemma follows by letting $t = r$. □

Lemma 6. *We have* $\langle V', H \rangle = V$ *and* $V' \cap H = \{\mathbf{0}\}$. *(We will write this as* $V = V' \oplus H$, *identifying* V' *with* $V' \oplus \{\mathbf{0}\}$ *and* H *with* $\{\mathbf{0}\} \oplus H$.*)*

Proof. We already noted that $\dim H = r\beta$. Moreover, since $r \geq 2$, using Lemma 4 we have

$$H \cap V' \subseteq H \cap \overline{U}_1 \cap \overline{U}_2 = (H \cap \overline{U}_1) \cap (H \cap \overline{U}_2) = H_1 \cap H_2 = \{\mathbf{0}\}.$$

By Lemma 5, we have $\dim V' = m - r\beta$, so $\dim V = \dim V' + \dim H$, and the claimed result follows. □

Next, for $i = 1, \ldots, r$, we define

$$U_i' := U_i \cap V'. \tag{21}$$

Lemma 7. *For all* $i \in [r]$, *we have* $\dim U_i' = (s-1)\beta$ *and* $U_i = U_i' \oplus H_i$.

Proof. Let $i \in [r]$. Since $U_i \subseteq \overline{U}_j$ for $j \neq i$, we have that

$$U_i' = U_i \cap V' = U_i \cap (\cap_{j=1}^{r} \overline{U}_j) = U_i \cap \overline{U}_i.$$

So by (17), (18), and Grassmann's identity, we have

$$\dim U_i' = \dim U_i \cap \overline{U}_i = \dim U_i + \dim \overline{U}_i - \dim\langle U_i, \overline{U}_i\rangle = s\beta + (m-\beta) - m = (s-1)\beta.$$

Since $U_i', H \subseteq U_i$, $U_i' = U_i \cap V'$, and $H \cap U_i = H_i$ by Lemma 4, the claimed results now follow. □

We summarize the above result in the following theorem.

Theorem 2. *Let r, s, and β be positive integers with $2 \leq s \leq r$ and $r \geq 2$; set $\alpha := s\beta$; and let V be a vector space with $m := \dim V = m_{r,s}\beta$, with $m_{r,s}$ as defined in (13).*

(i) Let V' and H be subspaces of V for which $V = \langle V', H\rangle$ and $V' \cap H = \{\mathbf{0}\}$ (so that $V = V' \oplus H$), and let $m' := \dim V' = m - r\beta = m_{r-1,s-1}$ and $\dim H = r\beta$. Furthermore, let $H_1, \ldots, H_r$ be independent in H with $\dim H_i = \beta$ ($i \in [r]$), and let $\sigma' = \{U_1', \ldots, U_r'\}$ be $(r-1, r-1, s-1, \beta)$-regular in V'. Then, with $U_i := \langle U_i', H_i\rangle = U_i' \oplus H_i$ ($i \in [r]$), we have that $\pi = \{U_1, \ldots, U_r\}$ is (r, r, s, β)-regular in V; moreover, V' satisfies (19), $U_i' = U_i \cap V'$, $H_i \subseteq U_i$, and $H_i \cap \overline{U}_i = \{\mathbf{0}\}$, where $\overline{U}_i$ is as defined in (15).

(ii) Conversely, if $\pi = \{U_1, \ldots, U_r\}$ is (r, r, s, β)-regular in V, then π can be put in the form as in (i) by letting V' be as in (19), and, for all $i \in [r]$, letting $U_i' := U_i \cap V$ and choosing $H_i \subseteq U_i$ with $H_i \cap \overline{U}_i = \{\mathbf{0}\}$.

Proof. We first note that $m - r\beta = m_{r-1,s-1}$ by Lemma 3. With $d_t^{r,s}$ as in (12), we have $d_t^{r,s} = d_t^{r-1,s-1} + (r-s+1) + t$ for integers t with $0 \leq t \leq s-2$. Now, if $U_i = U_i' \oplus H_i$ ($i \in [r]$), then with $J \subseteq [r]$ with $|J| = r-s+1+t$ and $0 \leq t \leq s-1$, we have $\dim\langle U_j \mid j \in J\rangle = \dim\langle U_j' \mid j \in J\rangle + \beta|J|$. So for $t < s-1$, we have $\dim\langle U_j \mid j \in J\rangle = d_t^{r,s}\beta$ if and only if $\dim\langle U_j' \mid j \in J\rangle = d_t^{r-1,s-1}\beta$, and, in addition, $\dim\langle U_j \mid j \in [r]\rangle = \dim V$ if and only if $\dim\langle U_j' \mid j \in [r]\rangle = \dim V'$. We conclude that π is (r, r, s, β)-regular in V if and only if σ' is $(r-1, r-1, s-1, \beta)$-regular in V'. This proves part (i); part (ii) follows from Lemmas 5–7. □

The next lemma handles the case where $s = 1$.

Lemma 8. *Let $\sigma = \{U_1, \ldots, U_{r+1}\}$ be $(r, r, 1, \beta)$-regular in a vector space V with $m := \dim V = m_{r,1,\beta}\beta = r\beta$. Then there is a basis $\{\boldsymbol{h}_{i,j} \mid i \in [r], j \in [\beta]\}$ of V such that $U_i = \langle \boldsymbol{h}_{i,j} \mid j \in \beta\rangle$ for $i \in [r]$ and $U_{r+1} = \langle -\boldsymbol{h}_{1,j} - \cdots - \boldsymbol{h}_{r,j} \mid j \in [\beta]\rangle$. In particular, the resulting storage code is linear, exact-repair, and optimal, meeting the cut-set bound in the MSR point.*

Proof. Since σ is $(r, r, 1, \beta)$-regular, $U_1, \ldots, U_r$ are independent in V and every vector $\boldsymbol{u}$ in U_{r+1} is of the form $\boldsymbol{u} = \boldsymbol{u}_1 + \cdots + \boldsymbol{u}_r$ with $\boldsymbol{u}_i \in U_i$ ($i \in [r]$). Now, let $\boldsymbol{h}_1, \ldots, \boldsymbol{h}_\beta$ be a basis for U_{r+1}, and let $\boldsymbol{h}_i = \boldsymbol{h}_{i,1} + \cdots + \boldsymbol{h}_{i,\beta}$ with $\boldsymbol{h}_{i,j} \in U_i$ for $j \in [\beta]$ and $i \in [r]$. Since $\langle U_j \mid j \in [r+1], j \neq i\rangle = V$, we conclude that $U_i = \langle \boldsymbol{h}_{i,j} \mid j \in [\beta]\rangle$ for all $i \in [r]$. Since $U_{r+1} = \langle -\boldsymbol{h}_1, \ldots, -\boldsymbol{h}_r\rangle$, the first claim follows. It is also easily checked that a lost coding space U_i can be exactly repaired from knowledge of all the vectors $\boldsymbol{h}_{t,j}$ ($j \in [\beta]$ for $t \in [r+1]$, $t \neq i$. Since $s = 1$, the resulting code is an ER MSR storage code. □

The case where $s = r$ is more complicated, as is illustrated by the example below.

Example 3. *The standard example is the following. Let $\dim V = \beta(r+1)r/2$, let $H_{\{i,j\}}$ ($1 \leq i < j \leq r+1$ be independent in V with $\dim H_{\{i,j\}} = \beta$, and let $U_i = \langle H_{\{i,j\}} \mid j \in [r+1], j \neq i\rangle$. Then $\sigma = \{U_1, \ldots, U_{r+1}\}$ is (r, r, r, β)-regular in V. But already for $r = 2$ and $\beta = 1$ we have a different example. Indeed, let $\dim V = m_{2,2} = 3$ with $V = \langle \boldsymbol{e}, \boldsymbol{a}_1, \boldsymbol{a}_2\rangle$, and let $U_1 := \langle \boldsymbol{e}, \boldsymbol{a}_1\rangle$, $U_2 := \langle \boldsymbol{e}, \boldsymbol{a}_2\rangle$, and $U_3 := \langle \boldsymbol{e}, \boldsymbol{a}_1 + \boldsymbol{a}_2\rangle$. Then $\sigma = \{U_1, U_2, U_3\}$ is $(2,2)$-regular.*

We leave the determination of (r, r, r, β)-regular configurations as an open problem.

7. Main Results

In this section, we specialize to the case where $\beta = 1$ and, except in Corollary 1, also $k = r$. The following simple result may be of independent interest.

Lemma 9. *Let $U_1, \dots, U_r$ be subspaces in an m-dimensional vector space V over $\mathbb{F}_q$. Let $\boldsymbol{h}_i \in U_i$ ($i \in [r]$), and suppose that U_0 is a subspace of $H := \langle \boldsymbol{h}_1, \dots, \boldsymbol{h}_r \rangle$ with $\dim U_0 = \alpha$. Define $C \subseteq \mathbb{F}_q^r$ to be the collection of all $\boldsymbol{c} \in \mathbb{F}_q^r$ for which $\sum_{i=1}^r c_i \boldsymbol{h}_i \in U_0$. If every collection $\{U_j \mid j \in J \cup \{0\}\}$ with $J \subseteq [r]$ and $|J| = r - \alpha$ is independent, then $\boldsymbol{h}_1, \dots, \boldsymbol{h}_r$ are independent and C is an $[r, \alpha, r - \alpha + 1]_q$ MDS code.*

Proof. Since U_0 is a subspace, the code C is linear over $\mathbb{F}_q$. Suppose that (after renumbering if necessary) $\boldsymbol{h}_1, \dots, \boldsymbol{h}_t$ form a basis of H, for some $t \le r$. Let C_0 be the subcode of C consisting of all $\boldsymbol{c} \in C$ with $\mathrm{supp}(\boldsymbol{c}) \subseteq [t]\}$. Obviously, every $\boldsymbol{u} \in U_0$ can be written as $\boldsymbol{u} = \sum c_i \boldsymbol{h}_i$ for a codeword $\boldsymbol{c} \in C_0$, and since $\boldsymbol{h}_1, \dots, \boldsymbol{h}_t$ are independent, every such expression is unique. As a consequence, $\dim C_0 = \dim U_0 = \alpha$. Moreover, if C_0 contains a nonzero codeword $\boldsymbol{c}$ with $|\mathrm{supp}(\boldsymbol{c})| \le r - \alpha$, then U_0 and the subspaces U_j with $j \in \mathrm{supp}(\boldsymbol{c})$ are not independent, since the word $\boldsymbol{u} \in U_0$ corresponding to the codeword $\boldsymbol{c}$ can be written as a linear combination of the vectors $\boldsymbol{h}_j$ with $j \in \mathrm{supp}(\boldsymbol{c})$. Therefore, C_0 is a linear code of length at most r, of dimension α, and with minimum distance at least $r - \alpha + 1$. By the Singleton bound, we conclude that $t = r$ and C_0 has minimum distance $r - \alpha + 1$. As a consequence, $\boldsymbol{h}_1, \dots, \boldsymbol{h}_r$ are independent and $C_0 = C$; hence C is an $[r, \alpha, r - \alpha + 1]$ MDS code over $\mathbb{F}_q$. □

Remark 3. *We note that a similar result holds if $\beta > 1$ and $\alpha = s\beta$. As before, we can describe U_0 in terms of an $[r\beta, s\beta]_q$ code, with the positions partitioned into r groups of β positions each, but we can now only conclude that a nonzero codeword is nonzero in at least $r - s + 1$ of these groups, and so the code need not be MDS. However, by considering the code an a code of length r over the larger symbol alphabet $\mathbb{F}_{q^\beta}$, we see that the minimum symbol-weight of this $\mathbb{F}_q$-linear but not $\mathbb{F}_{q^\beta}$-linear code of length r and size $(q^\beta)^s$ is at least $r - s + 1$, so the minimum symbol-distance is $r - s + 1$. Therefore, this code meets the Singleton bound for non-linear codes [55] (Theorem 4.1), and is, again, a (non-linear) MDS code (or MDS array code). We leave further details to the interested reader.*

Lemma 9 has an interesting consequence.

Corollary 1. *If there exists an optimal linear FR storage code with parameters $\{m, (n, k), (r, \alpha, 1)\}_q$ in a corner point of the achievable cut-set region (that is, with α integer), then there exists an $[r, \alpha, r - \alpha + 1]_q$ MDS code.*

Proof. Suppose that $\pi = U_1, \dots, U_{n-1}$ is a protostate of such a code. Then we can choose helpers $\boldsymbol{h}_i \in U_i$ for $i \in [r]$ and a subspace $U_0 \subseteq H := \langle \boldsymbol{h}_i \mid i \in [r] \rangle$ with $\dim U = \alpha$ such that $\sigma = U_1, \dots, U_0, \dots, U_{n-1}$ is a coding state of that code. By Lemma 1, any collection of subspaces U_j ($j \in J$) with $|J| = r - \alpha + 1$ is independent. Now the desired conclusion follows from Lemma 9. □

We are now ready to state our main result. This result was announced already in [48] (Theorem 4.1), but, unfortunately, the required extra condition on the helper nodes was inadvertently omitted.

Theorem 3. *Suppose that $\pi = \{U_1, \dots, U_r\}$ is (r, α)-regular in a vector space V of dimension $m = m_{r,\alpha} = \alpha(2r - \alpha + 1)/2$ over a finite field $\mathbb{F}_q$, and let $\boldsymbol{h}_i \in U_i$ for $i \in [r]$. Define $\overline{U}_i$ as* *in (15). Then $U_i \setminus \overline{U}_i$ is nonempty for all $i \in [r]$. Let $C \subseteq \mathbb{F}_q^r$ and let $U_0 := \{c_1 h_1 + \cdots + c_r h_r \mid c = (c_1, \ldots, c_r) \in C\}$. Then $\sigma := \{U_0, U_1, \ldots, U_r\}$ is an (r, α)-regular extension of π if and only if $h_i \in U_i \setminus \overline{U}_i$ for all $i \in [r]$ and C is an $[r, \alpha, r-\alpha+1]$ MDS code over $\mathbb{F}_q$.*

Proof. Note that by our assumption on π, we have $\dim \overline{U}_i = m-1$ and $\dim\langle \overline{U}_i, U_i\rangle = \dim V = m$, hence U_i is not contained in $\overline{U}_i$; so $U_i \setminus \overline{U}_i$ is nonempty.

We begin by showing that the conditions on the vectors h_i ($i \in [r]$) and on C are necessary. So suppose that σ is (r, α)-regular. First, if $h_i \in \overline{U}_i$, then $U_0 \subseteq \overline{U}_i$, hence $\sigma \setminus \{U_i\}$ is contained in the proper subspace $\overline{U}_i$ of V, so it is not an (r, α)-configuration, contradicting our assumption. Hence $h_i \in U_i \setminus \overline{U}_i$ for all i. Then by Lemma 4 with $H_i := \langle h_i\rangle$ ($i \in [r]$), the vectors $h_1, \ldots, h_r$ are independent. Next, let $\overline{C}$ denote the collection of all $c \in \mathbb{F}_q^r$ for which $\sum c_i h_i \in U_0$. Since $h_1, \ldots, h_r$ are independent, we have $\overline{C} = C$ and by Lemma 9, we have that $\overline{C}$, hence also C, is an $[r, \alpha, r-\alpha+1]_q$ MDS code.

Now, we show that the conditions are also sufficient. So assume that $h_i \in U_i \setminus \overline{U}_i$ for all i and that C is $[r, \alpha, r-\alpha+1]$ MDS. By Lemma 4 with $H_i = \langle h_i\rangle$ ($i \in [r]$), the vectors $h_1, \ldots, h_r$ are independent; hence $\dim U_0 = \dim C = \alpha$. Next, let $J \subseteq [r] \cup \{0\}$ with $|J| = r-\alpha+1+t$ for some integer t with $0 \le t \le k-r+s-1$. According to Definition 5, we have to show that $\dim\langle U_j \mid j \in J\rangle = d_t = (r-\alpha+1)\alpha + (\alpha-1) + \cdots + (\alpha-t)$. If $0 \notin J$, this holds since π is (r, α)-regular. So assume that $J = J_0 \cup \{0\}$ with $J_0 \subseteq [r]$ and $|J_0| = r-\alpha+t$. Again using that π is (r, α)-regular, we have $\dim\langle U_j \mid j \in J_0\rangle = d_{t-1}$, so by Grassmann's identity,

$$\dim\langle U_j \mid j \in J\rangle = d_{t-1} + \alpha - \dim\langle U_j \mid j \in J_0\rangle \cap U_0, \tag{22}$$

which is also correct for $t = 0$ if we set $d_{-1} := (r-\alpha)\alpha$. Setting $H := \langle h_1, \ldots, h_r\rangle$, we have $U_0 \subseteq H$; hence, using Lemma 4 and setting $C_0 := \{c \in C \mid \mathrm{supp}(c) \subseteq J_0\}$, we have

$$\langle U_j \mid j \in J_0\rangle \cap U_0 = \langle U_j \mid j \in J_0\rangle \cap H \cap U_0 = \langle h_j \mid j \in J_0\rangle \cap U_0 = \{\textstyle\sum c_j h_j \mid c \in C_0\}. \tag{23}$$

Now C is MDS and $\dim C = \alpha$; hence, $\dim C_0 = \max(0, \alpha - (r - |J_0|)) = \max(0, t) = t$. So combining (22) and (23), we have

$$\dim U_0 \cap \langle U_j \mid j \in J_0\rangle = d_{t-1} + \alpha - t = d_t.$$

Since J_0 is arbitrary, we conclude that σ is (r, α)-regular and of size $r+1$ as claimed. □

This theorem has the following important consequence.

Theorem 4. *Let $\mathbb{F}_q$ be the finite field of size q. Suppose that there exists an $[r, \alpha, r-\alpha+1]$ MDS code C over $\mathbb{F}_q$. Then the family of all (r, α)-configurations of size $r+1$ in a vector space V of dimension $m = m_{r,\alpha} = (r-\alpha+1)\alpha + (\alpha-1) + \cdots + (r-k+1)$ over $\mathbb{F}_q$ forms the collection of coding states of an optimal linear storage code over $\mathbb{F}_q$ with parameters $\{m, (r+1, r), (r, \alpha, 1)\}_q$. The protostates of his code are the (r, α)-regular configurations of size r.*

Proof. In Theorem 1, we showed how to use an $[r, \alpha, r-\alpha+1]_q$ MDS code C to construct an (r, α)-regular configuration of size $r+1$, so the collection of coding states in the theorem is nonempty. And if a coding space is lost, then we are left with a protostate, which is (r, α)-regular of length r, and we can use Theorem 3 and the MDS code C to repair this protostate to another coding state. □

It is usually possible to use a *subset* of the collection of all (r, α)-configurations of length $r+1$ as coding states. A rather obvious restriction is discussed in the remark below.

Remark 4. *In Theorem 4, we can limit the coding states to all (r,α)-regular collections of size $r+1$ in V that can be obtained by repair from a subcollection of size r, since other ones are not reachable. For example, let $V=\mathbb{F}_2^5$, and let $\boldsymbol{a}_1,\boldsymbol{a}_2,\boldsymbol{e}_1,\boldsymbol{e}_2,\boldsymbol{e}_3$ be a basis for V; set $\boldsymbol{a}_3:=\boldsymbol{a}_1+\boldsymbol{a}_2$. For $i\in[3]$, define $U_i:=\langle \boldsymbol{a}_i,\boldsymbol{e}_i\rangle$, define $U_4:=\langle \boldsymbol{e}_1+\boldsymbol{e}_2,\boldsymbol{a}_1+\boldsymbol{e}_1+\boldsymbol{e}_3\rangle$, and define $U_4':=\langle \boldsymbol{e}_1+\boldsymbol{e}_2,\boldsymbol{e}_1+\boldsymbol{e}_3\rangle$. It is easily verified that both $\pi:=\{U_1,U_2,U_3,U_4\}$ and $\pi':=\{U_1,U_2,U_3,U_4'\}$ are $(3,2)$-regular of size 4 (in fact, it can be shown that, up to a linear transformation,* every *$(3,2)$-regular configuration is equal to either π or π'), and, moreover, no subspace U_i ($i\in[4]$) can be obtained by 1-repair from the other three subspaces in π. So there is no need to include configurations such as π as coding states of a $\{5,(4,3),(3,2,1)\}_2$ storage code.*

In view of Theorem 3, Theorem 4, and of Remark 4, we introduce the following.

Definition 8. *Let r and α be integers with $1\le\alpha\le r$. An optimal linear storage code with parameters $\{m_{r,\alpha},(r+1,r),(r,\alpha,1)\}$ is called an* (r,α)-regular storage code *if the code has an ambient space V with $\dim V=m_{r,\alpha}$ and if every coding state is an (r,α)-regular configuration in V.*

In the next section, we will introduce a more interesting family of (r,α)-regular storage codes.

We end this section with two further remarks.

Remark 5. *We show in Theorem 3 that an (r,α)-regular storage code over a finite field $\mathbb{F}_q$ exists if and only if an $[r,\alpha,r-\alpha+1]_q$ MDS code exists. As rightly pointed out by a reviewer, that leaves open the possibility that a storage code with parameters $\{m_{r,\alpha},(r+1,r),(r,\alpha,1)\}_q$ exists while no $[r,\alpha,r-\alpha+1]_q$ MDS code exists. We are not aware of any non-existence results for regenerating codes in terms of the alphabet size (even for MBR codes, this is listed as Open Problem 1 in [29]), so we cannot rule out this possibility. If one could prove that (9) always holds with equality, then we could conclude that every* linear *$\{m_{r,\alpha},(r+1,r),(r,\alpha,1)\}$ storage code is (r,α)-regular, but we do not see how to prove that (if it is true at all, which we doubt). But given the strong relation between construction methods for storage codes and MDS codes, and given our idea that these (r,α)-regular codes are, in a sense, "best-possible", we strongly believe that these codes indeed realize the smallest possible alphabet size for their parameters. We leave this question as an interesting open problem.*

Remark 6. *Interestingly, every storage code as in Theorem 3 can be realized as an* optimal-access *code, and, in fact, as a* help-by-transfer *(HBT) code. Essentially, with notation as in Theorem 3, the reason is that if a coding space U_i is represented by a basis $\boldsymbol{e}_1,\dots,\boldsymbol{e}_\alpha$, then since $U_i\subsetneq\overline{U}_i$, there must be an index $j\in[\alpha]$ such that $\boldsymbol{e}_j\in U_i\setminus\overline{U}_i$. Note that this property need not hold for* every *(r,α)-regular storage code, since it may be required to choose helper vectors outside the given basis in order to repair to an* available *coding state. An example of this is given by the $(r,\alpha)=(3,2)$-regular code from [48], as can be seen from its description in [50]. It is an interesting problem to find the* smallest *$(3,2)$-regular HBT code. We leave further details to the interested reader.*

8. Smaller (r,α)-Regular Storage Codes

Inspired by Theorem 2, we will use Theorem 3 to produce a second (essentially recursive) construction of an (r,α)-regular collection of size $r+1$.

To this end, let V be a vector space over $\mathbb{F}_q$ with $\dim V=m_{r,\alpha}$. For $t=1,\dots,\alpha$, let $C^{(\delta+t)}$ be an $[\delta-1+t,t,\delta]_q$ MDS code, where $\delta=r-\alpha+1$. In what follows, we will consider bases H for V consisting of vectors $\boldsymbol{h}_{i,j}$ for $i=1,\dots,\alpha$ and $j=1,\dots,\delta-1+i$, arranged as in Table 1.

Table 1. The array of basis vectors.

$\boldsymbol{h}_{1,1}$	$\cdots$	$\boldsymbol{h}_{1,\delta}$				
$\vdots$		$\vdots$	$\ddots$			
$\boldsymbol{h}_{t,1}$	$\cdots$	$\boldsymbol{h}_{t,\delta}$	$\cdots$	$\boldsymbol{h}_{t,\delta-1+t}$		
$\vdots$		$\vdots$			$\ddots$	
$\boldsymbol{h}_{\alpha,1}$	$\cdots$	$\boldsymbol{h}_{\alpha,\delta}$	$\cdots$	$\boldsymbol{h}_{\alpha,\delta-1+t}$	$\cdots$	$\boldsymbol{h}_{\alpha,r}$

Recall that by Lemma 3, we have $m_{r,\alpha} = \delta + (\delta+1) + \cdots + r$, so by counting "by row", we see that these bases indeed have the right size. Given such a basis $H = (h_{i,j})$, we can use the given MDS codes to construct a sequence $\sigma = \sigma(H, C^{(\delta+1)}, \ldots, C^{(r+1)}) = U_1, \ldots, U_{r+1}$ as follows. First, for $t = 1, \ldots, \delta$, we let

$$U_t := \langle \boldsymbol{h}_{i,t} \mid i \in [\alpha] \rangle. \tag{24}$$

Then, for $t = 1, \ldots, \alpha$, we define

$$W_{\delta+t} := \{ \sum_{j=1}^{\delta-1+t} c_j \boldsymbol{h}_{t,j} \mid \boldsymbol{c} = (c_1, \ldots, c_{\delta-1+t}) \in C^{(\delta+t)} \} \tag{25}$$

and we let

$$U_{\delta+t} := \langle W_{\delta+t}, \boldsymbol{h}_{t+1,\delta+t} \ldots, \boldsymbol{h}_{\alpha,\delta+t} \rangle. \tag{26}$$

Lemma 10. *With the above notation and assumptions, we have* $\dim W_{\delta+t} = \dim C^{(\delta+t)} = t$ *(*$t \in [\alpha]$*), and the collection* $\sigma := \{U_1, \ldots, U_{r+1}\}$ *is* (r, α)*-regular.*

Proof. First, since $\boldsymbol{h}_{t,1}, \ldots, \boldsymbol{h}_{t,\delta-1+t}$ are independent, it follows that $\dim W_{\delta+t} = \dim C^{(\delta+t)}$; hence $\dim W_{\delta+t} = C^{(\delta+t)} = t$. Then, from (24), we see that $\dim U_t = \alpha$ for $t \in [\alpha]$, and from (26), we see that $\dim U_{\delta+t} = t + (\alpha - (t+1) + 1) = \alpha$, so all the subspaces in σ have the required dimension α. We will use induction to prove the last claim. To establish the base case for the induction, note that the $\delta + 1$ subspaces $U^{(1)} := \langle \boldsymbol{h}_{1,1} \rangle, \ldots, U^{(\delta)} := \langle \boldsymbol{h}_{1,\delta} \rangle, U^{(\delta+1)} := W_{\delta+1}$ form a $(\delta, 1)$-regular configuration (indeed, since $C^{(\delta+1)}$ is MDS with dimension 1, the unique (up to a scalar) nonzero codeword in $C^{(\delta+1)}$ has weight δ, hence is nonzero in every position). Now, suppose that we have constructed a $(\delta - 1 + t, t-1)$-regular configuration $\sigma^{(t)} := \{U_1^{(t-1)}, \ldots, U_{\delta-1+t}^{(t-1)}\}$. Then, we "add an extra layer" by setting $U_j^{(t)} := \langle U_j^{(t-1)}, \boldsymbol{h}_{t,j} \rangle$ ($j \in [\delta - 1 + t]$), we add an extra subspace $U_{\delta+t}^{(t)} := W_{\delta+t}$, and we apply Theorem 2, part (i) to conclude that $\sigma^{(t)} := \{U_1^{(t)}, \ldots, U_{\delta+t}^{(t)}\}$ is $(\delta + t, t)$-regular. Since $\sigma^{(\alpha)} = \sigma$, the claim follows by induction. □

Next, we want to show that by restricting the allowed MDS codes involved, we can construct an (r, α)-regular storage code using only coding states of the type in Lemma 10. In that case, a coding state of this restricted type, when losing a subspace, must be repairable to a new coding state that is again of this restricted type. We will now sketch how this can be achieved.

Let C be a fixed $[r, \alpha, \delta]$ MDS code C. For every permutation $\tau = \tau_1, \ldots, \tau_r$ of $\{1, \ldots, r\}$, we define codes $C^{(\delta+1)}, \ldots, C^{(r+1)}$ by letting

$$C^{(\delta+t)} := \{(c_{\tau_1}, \ldots, c_{\tau_{\delta-1+t}}) \mid \boldsymbol{c} = (c_1, \ldots, c_r) \in C, \mathrm{supp}(\boldsymbol{c}) \subseteq \{\tau_1, \ldots, \tau_{\delta-1+t}\}\}. \tag{27}$$

Note that since C is MDS, the code $C^{(\delta+t)}$ is easily seen to be $[\delta - 1 + t, t, \delta]$ MDS; note also that $C^{(r+1)} = C$. Now, for every basis $H = \{\boldsymbol{h}_{i,j} \mid 1 \le i \le \alpha, 1 \le j \le \delta - 1 + i\}$

for V, we use these codes $C^{(\delta+t)}$ defined above to construct an (r,α)-regular configuration $\sigma = \sigma(H,\tau)$ as explained earlier, that is, we set $\sigma(H,\tau) := \upsilon(H, C^{(\delta+1)}, \ldots, C^{(r+1)})$. Then by Lemma 10, $\sigma(H,\tau)$ is (r,α)-regular. We now have the following.

Theorem 5. *Let r and α be integers with $1 \le \alpha \le r$, let V be a vector space over $\mathbb{F}_q$, with* $\dim V = m_{r,s}$, *and let C be an $[r,\alpha,\delta]_q$ MDS code, so with $\delta = r-\alpha+1$. The collection of all (r,α)-regular configurations of the form $\sigma(H,\tau)$ as defined above, where $H = (\boldsymbol{h}_{i,j} \mid i \in [\alpha], j \in [\delta-1+i])$ is a basis for V and where τ is a permutation of $[r]$, forms an (r,α)-regular storage code.*

Proof. We sketch a proof as follows. Suppose that for each $t \in [\alpha]$, we choose a basis $\boldsymbol{s}_{1,\delta+t}, \ldots, \boldsymbol{s}_{t,\delta+t}$ for $W_{\delta+t}$. Then

$$U_{\delta+t} = \langle \boldsymbol{s}_{1,\delta+t}, \ldots, \boldsymbol{s}_{t,\delta+t}, \boldsymbol{h}_{t+1,\delta+t} \ldots, \boldsymbol{h}_{\alpha,\delta+t} \rangle.$$

Note that every vector $\boldsymbol{s}_{u,\delta+t}$ can be uniquely expressed as a linear combination of the basis vectors $\boldsymbol{h}_{i,j}$ for V; we will say that a vector $\boldsymbol{h}_{i,j}$ *occurs in* $\boldsymbol{s}_{u,\delta+t}$ if $\boldsymbol{h}_{i,j}$ occurs in that linear combination with a *nonzero* coefficient. Later, we will impose additional conditions on these vectors $\boldsymbol{s}_{u,\delta+t}$.

We can now arrange the vectors $\boldsymbol{h}_{i,j}$ and the vectors $\boldsymbol{s}_{i,\delta+j}$ in a rectangular $\alpha \times (r+1)$ array such that the vectors in column j span U_j, see Table 2 below.

Table 2. The array of vectors constructed above.

U_1		U_δ	$U_{\delta+1}$		$U_{\delta-1+t}$	$U_{\delta+t}$	$U_{\delta+t+1}$		U_{r+1}
$\boldsymbol{h}_{1,1}$	$\cdots$	$\boldsymbol{h}_{1,\delta}$	$\boldsymbol{s}_{1,\delta+1}$	$\cdots$	$\boldsymbol{s}_{1,\delta-1+t}$	$\boldsymbol{s}_{1,\delta+t}$	$\boldsymbol{s}_{1,\delta+t+1}$	$\cdots$	$\boldsymbol{s}_{1,r+1}$
$\vdots$		$\vdots$	$\ddots$		$\vdots$	$\vdots$	$\vdots$		$\vdots$
$\boldsymbol{h}_{t,1}$	$\cdots$	$\boldsymbol{h}_{t,\delta}$		$\cdots$	$\boldsymbol{h}_{t,\delta-1+t}$	$\boldsymbol{s}_{t,\delta+t}$	$\boldsymbol{s}_{t,\delta+t+1}$	$\cdots$	$\boldsymbol{s}_{t,r+1}$
$\boldsymbol{h}_{t+1,1}$	$\cdots$	$\boldsymbol{h}_{t+1,\delta}$		$\cdots$	$\boldsymbol{h}_{t+1,\delta-1+t}$	$\boldsymbol{h}_{t+1,\delta+t}$	$\boldsymbol{s}_{t+1,\delta+t+1}$	$\cdots$	$\boldsymbol{s}_{t+1,r+1}$
$\vdots$		$\vdots$			$\vdots$	$\vdots$	$\vdots$		$\vdots$
$\boldsymbol{h}_{\alpha,1}$	$\cdots$	$\boldsymbol{h}_{\alpha,\delta}$	$\boldsymbol{h}_{\alpha,\delta+1}$	$\cdots$	$\boldsymbol{h}_{\alpha,\delta-1+t}$	$\boldsymbol{h}_{\alpha,\delta+t}$	$\boldsymbol{h}_{\alpha,\delta+t+1}$	$\cdots$	$\boldsymbol{s}_{\alpha,r+1}$

This array has the following characteristics.

- A1 Row i of the array contains $\delta-1+i$ of the basis vectors of V.
- A2 The basis vectors in row i occur only in the vectors $\boldsymbol{s}_{1,\delta+i}, \ldots, \boldsymbol{s}_{i,\delta+i}$.
- A3 The vector space $W_{\delta+i} = \langle \boldsymbol{s}_{1,\delta+i}, \ldots, \boldsymbol{s}_{i,\delta+i} \rangle$ is determined by the basis vectors in row i and by an $[\delta-1+i, i, \delta]$ MDS code $C^{(\delta+i)}$ derived from the $[r,\alpha,\delta]$ MDS code C through a fixed permutation τ of $\{1,\ldots,r\}$.

Now consider what happens if we lose a subspace, that is, if we lose a column of the array in Table 2. Our aim will be to arrange the remaining r subspaces into a similar array, but with the last column removed, and then to use the MDS code C to construct the last column from the last row of the new array. Losing any column j with $j \le r$ has the consequence of losing the basis vectors $\boldsymbol{h}_{i,j}$ in the array, and our aim will be to replace these lost basis vectors with the vectors $\boldsymbol{s}_{u,\delta+t}$ (where $u = 1$ if $j \le \delta$ and $u = j-\delta$ if $\delta+1 \le j \le r$), while maintaining the characteristics A1–A3 above. By A1, a row that contains a lost variable should move one row up, and the row that contains the replacement basis vectors should move into the last row. By A2, if $\boldsymbol{s}_{u,\delta+t}$ replaces $h_{i,j}$, then $h_{i,j}$ should occur in $\boldsymbol{s}_{u,\delta+t}$ and should not occur in $\boldsymbol{s}_{s,\delta+t}$ for $s \ne u$. Note that since $C^{(\delta+i)}$ is an MDS code, there is no position where all codewords have a 0; hence we can always choose a basis $\boldsymbol{s}_{1,\delta+i}, \ldots, \boldsymbol{s}_{i,\delta+i}$ for $W_{\delta+i}$ such that a given vector $\boldsymbol{h}_{i,j}$ occurs in one and in only one of the basis vectors. Finally, by A3, there has to be a suitable permutation τ' that can describe the new $[\delta - 1 + t, t, \delta]$ MDS codes. As we saw above, A1 and A2 determine how the new array should be formed; what is left is to find a suitable τ', and then to verify that A3 holds again. Let us now turn to the details.

As remarked before, if we lose U_{r+1}, then we can recover that subspace *exactly*. For the other subspaces, we distinguish two cases.

First, suppose we lose a subspace U_t with $1 \leq t \leq \delta$. Then, in Table 2, we delete column t, and we take out row 1 and place it after the last row, where we want the α vectors $\boldsymbol{s}_{1,\delta+1}, \ldots, \boldsymbol{s}_{1,r+1}$ to replace the lost basis vectors $\boldsymbol{h}_{1,t}, \ldots, \boldsymbol{h}_{\alpha,t}$. Recall that the vectors $\boldsymbol{s}_{1,\delta+i}, \ldots, \boldsymbol{s}_{i,\delta+i}$ span $W_{\delta+i}$ and are each a linear combination of $\boldsymbol{h}_{i,1}, \ldots, \boldsymbol{h}_{i,\delta-1+u}$; now, choose these vectors such that $\boldsymbol{s}_{u,\delta+i}$ contains $\boldsymbol{h}_{i,t}$ if and only if $u = 1$ (as remarked above, it is not difficult to verify that this is possible). Define a new permutation

$$\tau' = \tau_1, \ldots, \tau_{t-1}, \tau_{t+1}, \ldots, \tau_r, \tau_t, \tag{28}$$

and a new basis $H' = (\boldsymbol{h}_{i,j})$, where, for $i = 1, \ldots, \alpha - 1$, $j = 1, \ldots, \delta - 1 + i$, we let

$$\boldsymbol{h}'_{i,j} = \begin{cases} \boldsymbol{h}_{i+1,j}, & \text{if } j < t; \\ \boldsymbol{h}_{i+1,j+1}, & \text{if } j > t \end{cases}$$

and for $j = 1, \ldots, r$, we let

$$\boldsymbol{h}'_{\alpha,j} = \begin{cases} \boldsymbol{h}_{1,j}, & \text{if } j < t; \\ \boldsymbol{h}_{1,j+1}, & \text{if } t < j < \delta; \\ \boldsymbol{s}_{1,j+1}, & \text{if } j \geq \delta. \end{cases}$$

Finally, with

$$U_0 := \{\sum_{s=1}^{r} c_{\tau_s} \boldsymbol{h}'_{\alpha,s} \mid \boldsymbol{c} \in C\}, \tag{29}$$

it is easily verified that $\sigma' := U_1, \ldots, U_{t-1}, U_{t+1}, \ldots, U_{r+1}, U_0$ is precisely the configuration $\sigma(\tau', H')$.

Secondly, suppose that we lose subspace $U_{\delta+t}$ with $1 \leq t \leq \alpha$. In that case, we proceed in a similar way, where in Table 2 we remove column $\delta + t$, take out row t and place that row after the last row in the table, where we now want the $\alpha - t$ vectors $\boldsymbol{s}_{t,\delta+t+1}, \ldots, \boldsymbol{s}_{t,r+1}$ to replace the lost basis vectors $\boldsymbol{h}_{t+1,\delta+t}, \ldots, \boldsymbol{h}_{\alpha,\delta+t}$. This can be achieved by now choosing $\boldsymbol{s}_{u,\delta+i}$ to contain $\boldsymbol{h}_{i,\delta+t}$ if and only if $u = t$. Define a new permutation

$$\tau' = \tau_1, \ldots, \tau_{\delta+t-1}, \tau_{\delta+t+1}, \ldots, \tau_r, \tau_{\delta+t}, \tag{30}$$

and a new basis $H' = (\boldsymbol{h}_{i,j})$, where for $i = 1, \ldots, \alpha - 1$, $j = 1, \ldots, \delta - 1 + i$, we let

$$\boldsymbol{h}'_{i,j} = \begin{cases} \boldsymbol{h}_{i,j}, & \text{if } i < t, j < \delta + t; \\ \boldsymbol{h}_{i,j+1}, & \text{if } i < t, j > \delta + t; \\ \boldsymbol{h}_{i+1,j+1}, & \text{if } i > t, j > \delta + t \end{cases}$$

and

$$\boldsymbol{h}'_{\alpha,j} = \begin{cases} \boldsymbol{h}_{t,j}, & \text{if } j < \delta + t; \\ \boldsymbol{s}_{t,j+1}, & \text{if } \delta + t < j < r. \end{cases}$$

With U_0 as in (29), it is again easily verified that $\sigma' := U_1, \ldots, U_{\delta+t-1}, U_{\delta+t+1}, \ldots, U_{r+1}$, U_0 is precisely the configuration $\sigma(\tau', H')$.

We leave further details to the reader. □

It turns out that with a proper choice for the MDS code C, the (r,α)-regular configurations described in Theorem 5 may possess extra symmetry, even to the point where they are all equal up to a linear transformation, for example, when $q=2$, $r-\alpha=1$, and the MDS code C is the *even weight* $[r,r-1,2]_2$ MDS code. In such cases, we can apply automorphism group techniques to construct "small" (r,α)-regular storage codes that involve only a relatively small number of different coding spaces. Examples of storage codes constructed in this way are the small $(3,2)$-regular code from [48] that involves only 8 different coding spaces, and the small $(4,3)$-regular storage code from [49,50] that involves only 72 different coding spaces. For more details on how such codes can be constructed, using groups of linear transformations fixing a protostate, we refer to [48–50].

9. Conclusions

A regenerating storage code (RGC) with parameters $\{m,(n,k),(r,\alpha,\beta)\}_q$ is designed to store m data symbols from a finite field $\mathbb{F}_q$ in encoded form on n storage nodes, each storing α encoded symbols. If a node is lost, a replacement node may be constructed by obtaining β symbols from each of a collection of r of the surviving nodes, called the *helper nodes*. The name of these codes stems from the requirement that, even after an arbitrary amount of repairs, any k nodes can regenerate the original data. We say that the code employs *exact repair (ER)* if, after each repair, the information on the replacement node is *identical* to the information on the lost node; if not, then we say that the code employs *functional repair (FR)*. An RGC is called *optimal* if its parameters meet an upper bound called the *cut-set bound*.

Linear MDS codes have often been instrumental in the construction of optimal RGC's. In this paper, we first introduce a special type of configurations of vector spaces that we call *(r,α)-regular*. We show that such configurations can be constructed from suitable linear MDS codes. Then we employ linear MDS codes and (r,α)-regular configurations to construct what we call *(r,α)-regular codes*, which are optimal linear RGC's with $n-1=k=r$ and $\beta=1$, over a relatively small finite field $\mathbb{F}_q$ (if $r-\alpha\leq 1$, then any field can be used; if $r-\alpha>1$, then $q\geq r-1$ is required). Along the way, we show that, conversely, the existence of an (r,α)-regular code over a finite field of size q implies the existence of an $[r,\alpha,r-\alpha+1]_q$ MDS code over that field.

Apart from two known examples, these storage codes are the only known explicit optimal RGC's with parameters realizing an extremal point of the achievable cut-set region different from the MSR and MBR points.

Funding: This work is supported in part by the Estonian Research Council grant PRG2531.

Institutional Review Board Statement: Not applicable.

Informed Consent Statement: Not applicable.

Data Availability Statement: No new data were created or analyzed in this study. Data sharing is not applicable to this article.

Acknowledgments: I gratefully acknowledge various discussions with my colleagues Junming Ke, Vitaly Skachek, and Ago-Erik Riet. In addition, I want to thank one of the reviewers for a very careful reading of an earlier version and for some very useful comments that have helped to improve the quality of this paper.

Conflicts of Interest: The author declares to have no conflicts of interest.

Abbreviations

The following abbreviations are used in this manuscript:

MDPI	Multidisciplinary Digital Publishing Institute
DOAJ	Directory of open access journals
TLA	Three letter acronym
LD	Linear dichroism

References

1. Reinsel, D.; Gantz, J.; Rydning, J. *The Digitization of the World From Edge to Core;* An IDC White Paper. 2018. Available online: https://www.seagate.com/files/www-content/our-story/trends/files/idc-seagate-dataage-whitepaper.pdf (accessed on 29 January 2025).
2. Reinsel, D.; Rydning, J.; Gantz, J.F. Worldwide Global DataSphere Forecast, 2021–2025: The World Keeps Creating More Data–Now, What Do We Do with It All? 2021. IDC Report 2021, Doc #US46410421.
3. Bartley, K. 2024. Available online: https://rivery.io/blog/big-data-statistics-how-much-data-is-there-in-the-world/ (accessed on 29 January 2025).
4. Taylor, P. Volume of Data/Information Created, Captured, Copied, and Consumed Worldwide from 2010 to 2020, with Forecasts from 2021 to 2025. Available online: https://www.statista.com/statistics/871513/worldwide-data-created (accessed on 17 January 2025).
5. Ke, J. Codes for Distributed Storage. Ph.D. Thesis, University of Tartu, Tartu, Estonia, 2024. Available online: https://hdl.handle.net/10062/105396 (accessed on 29 January 2025).
6. Dimakis, A.G.; Godfrey, P.B.; Wu, Y.; Wainwright, M.J.; Ramchandran, K. Network Coding for Distributed Storage Systems. *IEEE Trans. Inf. Theory* **2010**, *56*, 4539–4551. [CrossRef]
7. Yin, C.; Xu, Z.; Li, W.; Li, T.; Yuan, S.; Liu, Y. Erasure Codes for Cold Data in Distributed Storage Systems. *Appl. Sci.* **2023**, *13*, 2170. [CrossRef]
8. Amazon S3. 2006. Available online: https://aws.amazon.com/s3/ (accessed on 24 February 2024).
9. Ghemawat, S.; Gobioff, H.; Leung, S.T. The Google file system. *ACM SIGOPS Oper. Syst. Rev.* **2003**, *37*, 29–43. [CrossRef]
10. Corbett, J.C.; Dean, J.; Epstein, M.; Fikes, A.; Frost, C.; Furman, J.; Ghemawat, S.; Gubarev, A.; Heiser, C.; Hochschild, P.; et al. Spanner: Google's Globally Distributed Database. *ACM Trans. Comp. Syst. (TOCS)* **2013**, *31*, 1–22. [CrossRef]
11. Huang, C.; Simitci, H.; Xu, Y.; Ogus, A.; Calder, B.; Gopalan, P.; Li, J.; Yekhanin, S. Erasure Coding in Windows Azure Storage. In Proceedings of the 2012 USENIX Annual Technical Conference (USENIX ATC 12), Boston, MA, USA, 13–15 June 2012; pp. 15–26.
12. Khan, O.; Burns, R.; Plank, J.; Pierce, W.; Huang, C. Rethinking Erasure Codes for Cloud File Systems: Minimizing I/O for Recovery and Degraded Reads. In Proceedings of the 10th USENIX Conference on File and Storage Technologies (FAST 12), San Jose, CA, USA, 14–17 February 2012.
13. Chen, Y.L.; Mu, S.; Li, J.; Huang, C.; Li, J.; Ogus, A.; Phillips, D. Giza: Erasure Coding Objects across Global Data Centers. In Proceedings of the 2017 USENIX Annual Technical Conference (USENIX ATC 17), Santa Clara, CA, USA, 15–17 February 2017; pp. 539–551.
14. Rashmi, K.; Shah, N.B.; Gu, D.; Kuang, H.; Borthakur, D.; Ramchandran, K. A "Hitchhiker's" Guide to Fast and Efficient Data Reconstruction in Erasure-coded Data Centers. *ACM SIGCOMM Comput. Commun. Rev.* **2014**, *44*, 331–342. [CrossRef]
15. Sathiamoorthy, M.; Asteris, M.; Papailiopoulos, D.; Dimakis, A.G.; Vadali, R.; Chen, S.; Borthakur, D. XORing Elephants: Novel Erasure Codes for Big Data. *Proc. VLDB Endow.* **2013**, *6*, 325–336. [CrossRef]
16. Chiniah, A.; Mungur, A. On the Adoption of Erasure Code for Cloud Storage by Major Distributed Storage Systems. In *EAI Endorsed Transactions on Cloud Systems;* EAI: New York, NY, USA, 2021; Volume 7, pp. 1–11. [CrossRef]
17. Darrous, J.; Ibrahim, S. Understanding the Performance of Erasure Codes in Hadoop Distributed File System. In Proceedings of the CHEOPS 22, Rennes, France, 5 April 2022; pp. 24–32.
18. Apache Hadoop. HDFS Erasure Coding. 2017. Available online: https://hadoop.apache.org/docs/r3.0.0/hadoop-project-dist/hadoop-hdfs/HDFSErasureCoding (accessed on 21 March 2025).
19. Kralevska, K.; Gligoroski, D.; Jensen, R.E.; Øverby, H. HashTag Erasure Codes: From Theory to Practice. *IEEE Trans. Big Data* **2018**, *4*, 516–529. [CrossRef]
20. Ramkumar, M.P.; Balaji, N.; Emil Selvan, G.S.R.; Jeya Rohini, R. RAID-6 Code Variants for Recovery of a Failed Disk. In *Soft Computing in Data Analytics, Proceedings of the International Conference on SCDA 2018;* Nayak, J., Abraham, A., Krishna, B.M., Chandra Sekhar, G.T., Das, A.K., Eds.; Springer: Singapore, 2019; pp. 237–245.
21. Huawei, OceanStor Dorado NAS All-Flash Storage. 2024. Available online: https://e.huawei.com/en/solutions/storage/all-flash-storage/nas (accessed on 17 February 2025).
22. Huang, K.; Li, X.; Yuan, M.; Zhang, J.; Shao, Z. Joint Directory, File and IO Trace Feature Extraction and Feature-based Trace Regeneration for Enterprise Storage Systems. In Proceedings of the 2024 IEEE 40th International Conference on Data Engineering (ICDE), Utrecht, The Netherlands, 13–17 May 2024; pp. 4002–4015. [CrossRef]

23. Vajha, M.; Ramkumar, V.; Puranik, B.; Kini, G.; Lobo, E.; Sasidharan, B.; Kumar, P.V.; Barg, A.; Ye, M.; Narayanamurthy, S.; et al. Clay Codes: Moulding MDS Codes to Yield an MSR Code. In Proceedings of the 16th USENIX Conference on File and Storage Technologies (FAST 18), Oakland, CA, USA, 12–15 February 2018; pp. 139–154.
24. IBM Ceph. 2025. Available online: https://www.ibm.com/docs/en/storage-ceph/8.0?topic=overview-erasure-code-profiles (accessed on 17 February 2025).
25. Chen, J.; Li, Z.; Fang, G.; Hou, Y.; Li, X. A Comprehensive Repair Scheme for Distributed Storage Systems. *Comput. Netw.* **2023**, *235*, 109954. [CrossRef]
26. Balaji, S.; Krishnan, M.; Vajha, M.; Ramkumar, V.; Sasidharan, B.; Kumar, P. Erasure Coding for Distributed Storage: An Overview. *Sci. China Inf. Sci.* **2018**, *61*, 100301. [CrossRef]
27. Liu, S.; Oggier, F. An Overview of Coding for Distributed Storage Systems. In *Network Coding and Subspace Designs*; Greferath, M., Pavčević, M.O., Silberstein, N., Vázquez-Castro, M.Á., Eds.; Springer International Publishing: Cham, Switzerland, 2018; pp. 363–383. [CrossRef]
28. Chen, R.; Xu, L. Practical Performance Evaluation of Space Optimal Erasure Codes for High-Speed Data Storage Systems. *SN Comput. Sci.* **2020**, *1*, 54. [CrossRef]
29. Ramkumar, V.; Balaji, S.B.; Sasidharan, B.; Vajha, M.; Krishnan, M.N.; Kumar, P.V. Codes for Distributed Storage. *Found. Trends® Commun. Inf. Theory* **2022**, *19*, 547–813. [CrossRef]
30. Thomasian, A. *Storage Systems: Organization, Performance, Coding, Reliability, and Their Data Processing*, 1st ed.; Morgan Kaufmann: Cambridge, MA, USA, 2021.
31. Mazumdar, S.; Seybold, D.; Kritikos, K.; Verginadis, Y. A Survey on Data Storage and Placement Methodologies for Cloud-Big Data Ecosystem. *J. Big Data* **2019**, *6*, 15. [CrossRef]
32. Wu, Y.; Dimakis, A.G. Reducing Repair Traffic for Erasure Coding-Based Storage via Interference Alignment. In Proceedings of the 2009 IEEE International Symposium on Information Theory (ISIT), Seoul, Republic of Korea, 28 June–3 July 2009; pp. 2276–2280. [CrossRef]
33. Rashmi, K.; Shah, N.; Kumar, P.; Ramchandran, K. Explicit Codes Minimizing Repair Bandwidth for Distributed Storage. In Proceedings of the 47th Annual Allerton Conference on Communication, Control, and Computing (Allerton), Monticello, IL, USA, 1–3 October 2009; pp. 1243–1249.
34. Gopalan, P.; Huang, C.; Simitci, H.; Yekhanin, S. On the Locality of Codeword Symbols. *IEEE Trans. Inf. Theory* **2012**, *58*, 6925–6934. [CrossRef]
35. Papailiopoulos, D.S.; Dimakis, A.G. Locally Repairable Codes. *IEEE Trans. Inf. Theory* **2014**, *60*, 5843–5855. [CrossRef]
36. El Rouayheb, S.; Ramchandran, K. Fractional Repetition Codes for Repair in Distributed Storage Systems. In Proceedings of the 2010 48th Annual Allerton Conference on Communication, Control, and Computing (Allerton), Monticello, IL, USA, 29 September–1 October 2010; pp. 1510–1517. [CrossRef]
37. Shah, N.B.; Rashmi, K.V.; Kumar, P.V.; Ramchandran, K. Distributed Storage Codes with Repair-by-Transfer and Nonachievability of Interior Points on the Storage-Bandwidth Tradeoff. *IEEE Trans. Inf. Theory* **2012**, *58*, 1837–1852. [CrossRef]
38. Wang, Z.; Tamo, I.; Bruck, J. On Codes for Optimal Rebuilding Access. In Proceedings of the 2011 49th Annual Allerton Conference on Communication, Control, and Computing (Allerton), Monticello, IL, USA, 28–30 September 2011; pp. 1374–1381. [CrossRef]
39. Oggier, F.; Datta, A. Self-Repairing Homomorphic Codes for Distributed Storage Systems. In Proceedings of the 2011 Proceedings IEEE INFOCOM, Shanghai, China, 10–15 April 2011; pp. 1215–1223. [CrossRef]
40. Duursma, I.; Wang, H. Multilinear Algebra for Minimum Storage Regenerating Codes: A Generalization of the Product-Matrix Construction. *Appl. Algebra Eng. Commun. Comput.* **2023**, *34*, 717–743. [CrossRef]
41. Shah, N.B.; Rashmi, K.V.; Kumar, P.V.; Ramchandran, K. Explicit Codes Minimizing Repair Bandwidth for Distributed Storage. In Proceedings of the 2010 IEEE Information Theory Workshop on Information Theory (ITW 2010), Cairo, Egypt, 6–8 January 2010; pp. 1–5. [CrossRef]
42. Elyasi, M.; Mohajer, S. Cascade Codes for Distributed Storage Systems. *IEEE Trans. Inf. Theory* **2020**, *66*, 7490–7527. [CrossRef]
43. Duursma, I.; Li, X.; Wang, H.P. Multilinear Algebra for Distributed Storage. *SIAM J. Appl. Algebra Geom.* **2021**, *5*, 552–587. [CrossRef]
44. Wu, Y. Existence and Construction of Capacity-Achieving Network Codes for Distributed Storage. *IEEE J. Sel. Areas Commun.* **2010**, *28*, 277–288. [CrossRef]
45. Hu, Y.; Lee, P.P.C.; Shum, K.W. Analysis and Construction of Functional Regenerating Codes with Uncoded Repair for Distributed Storage Systems. In Proceedings of the 2013 Proceedings IEEE INFOCOM, Turin, Italy, 14–19 April 2013; pp. 2355–2363. [CrossRef]
46. Hu, Y.; Chen, H.; Lee, P.; Tang, Y. NCCloud: Applying Network Coding for the Storage Repair in a Cloud-of-Clouds. In Proceedings of the 10th USENIX Conference on File and Storage Technologies (FAST 12), San Jose, CA, USA, 15–17 February 2012.

47. Shum, K.W.; Hu, Y. Functional-Repair-by-Transfer Regenerating Codes. In Proceedings of the 2012 IEEE International Symposium on Information Theory (ISIT), Cambridge, MA, USA, 1–6 July 2012; pp. 1192–1196. [CrossRef]
48. Hollmann, H.D.; Poh, W. Characterizations and Construction Methods for Linear Functional-Repair Storage Codes. In Proceedings of the 2013 IEEE International Symposium on Information Theory (ISIT), Istanbul, Turkey, 7–12 July 2013; pp. 336–340. [CrossRef]
49. Ke, J.; Hollmann, H.D.; Riet, A.E. A Binary Linear Functional-Repair Regenerating Code on 72 Coding Spaces Related to PG(2, 8). In Proceedings of the 2024 IEEE International Symposium on Information Theory (ISIT), Athens, Greece, 7–12 July 2024; pp. 2335–2340. [CrossRef]
50. Hollmann, H.D.; Ke, J.; Riet, A.E. An Optimal Binary Linear Functional-Repair Storage Code with Efficient Repair Related to PG(2, 8). Submitted to Designs, Codes, and Cryptography.
51. Hollmann, H.D. Storage Codes—Coding Rate and Repair Locality. In Proceedings of the 2013 International Conference on Computing, Networking and Communications (ICNC), San Diego, CA, USA, 28–31 January 2013; pp. 830–834. [CrossRef]
52. Hollmann, H.D. On the Minimum Storage Overhead of Distributed Storage Codes with a Given Repair Locality. In Proceedings of the 2014 IEEE International Symposium on Information Theory (ISIT), Honolulu, HI, USA, 29 June–4 July 2014; pp. 1041–1045. [CrossRef]
53. Rashmi, K.V.; Shah, N.B.; Kumar, P.V. Optimal Exact-Regenerating Codes for Distributed Storage at the MSR and MBR Points via a Product-Matrix Construction. *IEEE Trans. Inf. Theory* **2011**, *57*, 5227–5239. [CrossRef]
54. MacWilliams, F.; Sloane, N. *The Theory of Error-Correcting Codes*, 3rd ed.; Elsevier: North-Holland, The Netherlands, 1981.
55. Roth, R. *Introduction to Coding Theory*; Cambridge University Press: Cambridge, UK, 2006.
56. Singleton, R. Maximum Distance q-Nary Codes. *IEEE Trans. Inf. Theory* **1964**, *10*, 116–118. [CrossRef]
57. Moon, T.K. *Error Correction Coding*; John Wiley & Sons, Ltd.: Hoboken, NJ, USA, 2005.
58. Ball, S. On Sets of Vectors of a Finite Vector Space in Which Every Subset of Basis Size is a Basis. *J. Eur. Math. Soc.* **2012**, *14*, 733–748. [CrossRef]
59. Bush, K. Orthogonal Arrays of Index Unity. *Ann. Math. Statist.* **1952**, *23*, 426–434. [CrossRef]
60. Dahl, C.; Pedersen, J.P. Cyclic and Pseudo-Cyclic MDS Codes of Length q+1. *J. Combin. Theory Ser. A* **1992**, *59*, 130–133. [CrossRef]
61. Zorgui, M.; Wang, Z. Centralized Multi-Node Repair Regenerating Codes. *IEEE Trans. Inf. Theory* **2019**, *65*, 4180–4206. [CrossRef]
62. Ng, S.L.; Paterson, M. Functional Repair Codes: A View from Projective Geometry. *Des. Codes Cryptogr.* **2019**, *87*, 2701–2722. [CrossRef]
63. Mital, N.; Kralevska, K.; Ling, C.; Gündüz, D. Functional Broadcast Repair of Multiple Partial Failures in Wireless Distributed Storage Systems. *IEEE J. Sel. Areas Inf. Theory* **2021**, *2*, 1093–1107. [CrossRef]
64. Duursma, I.; Wang, H. Multilinear Algebra for Minimum Storage Regenerating Codes. *arXiv* **2020**, arXiv:2006.08911v1.

entropy MDPI

Article

Upper Bounds for Chebyshev Permutation Arrays

Sergey Bereg [1,*], Zevi Miller [2] and Ivan Hal Sudborough [1]

[1] Department of Computer Science, University of Texas at Dallas, Box 830688, Richardson, TX 75083, USA; hal@utdallas.edu
[2] Department of Mathematics, Miami University, Oxford, OH 45056, USA; millerz@miamioh.edu
* Correspondence: besp@utdallas.edu

Abstract: We improve on known upper bounds for the size of permutation arrays under the Chebyshev metric, defined as follows. The Chebyshev distance between permutations π and σ on the symbols $\{1,2,\cdots,n\}$, denoted by $d(\pi,\sigma)$, is $\max\{|\pi_i-\sigma_i| \mid 1 \le i \le n\}$. For an array A (set) of such permutations, the Chebyshev distance of A, denoted by $d(A)$, is $\min\{d(\pi,\sigma) \mid \pi,\sigma \in A, \pi \neq \sigma\}$. An array A of such permutations with $d(A)=d$ will be called an (n,d)-PA. Let $P(n,d)$ denote the maximum size of any (n,d)-PA. The function $P(n,d)$ has been the subject of previous research. In this paper, we consider strings on the symbols $\{0,1,2\}$, with the 0's representing low symbols and the 2's high symbols for the function $P(n,d)$. An array A of such strings of length n is *separable* if for any two strings in A, there is a position $1 \le i \le n$ such that the ith symbol in one string is 0 and the ith symbol in the other is a 2. The maximum size of a separable array of strings of length n, with a occurrences of the symbol 0 and b occurrences of the symbol 2, is denoted by $R(n;a,b)$. We show that $R(n;k,k)$ is an upper bound for $P(n,n-k)$ when $k \le \frac{n}{2}$. We derive upper bounds for $R(n;a,b)$ by various recursive and combinatorial methods, from which follow upper bounds for the Chebyshev function $P(n,d)$, which improve upon previous such upper bounds in the literature.

Keywords: permutation arrays; Chebyshev metric; upper bounds

1. Introduction

In refs. [1,2] , studies of permutation arrays under the Chebyshev metric were presented. This complemented many studies of permutation arrays under other metrics, such as the Hamming metric [3–5], Kendall τ metric [6,7], and several others [8]. The use of the Chebyshev metric was motivated by applications of error correcting codes and recharging in flash memories [6].

The flash memory application is based on a rank-modulation scheme [9], which eliminates the need to use absolute values of cell levels in storing information. Instead, relative ranks are used. The data are coded by permutations of a finite number of ranks.

Let $\pi=\pi_1\pi_2\dots\pi_n$ and $\sigma=\sigma_1\sigma_2\dots\sigma_n$ be two permutations on the symbols in $\{1,2,\dots n\}$. The Chebyshev distance between π and σ, denoted by $d(\pi,\sigma)$, is $\max\{|\pi_i-\sigma_i| \mid 1 \le i \le n\}$. For an array (set) of permutations, say, A, the Chebyshev distance of A, denoted by $d(A)$, is $\min\{d(\pi,\sigma) \mid \pi,\sigma \in A, \pi \neq \sigma\}$. An array A of permutations on $\{1,2,\dots n\}$ with $d(A)=d$ will be called an *(n,d)-PA* . Let $P(n,d)$ denote the maximum size of any (n,d)-PA. We shall also define analogously the Chebyshev distance between two strings and the Chebyshev distance of an array of strings. The context will make clear whether the objects are strings or permutations.

Previous work on permutation arrays under the Chebyshev metric gave upper bounds based on a Gilbert–Varshamov inequality [10,11] (see our Theorem 2, or, for a recursive inequality, see our Theorem 3). In [2], it was also shown for fixed $r \geq 1$ that there exist constants c_r and d_r such that $P(d+r,d) = c_r$ for $d \geq d_r$ (see our Theorem 1). Upper bounds on c_r and d_r were given in [2]. We give substantial improvements on these upper bounds.

We consider strings over the alphabet $\{0,1,2\}$. A set A of such strings of length n is *separable* if for any two strings in A, there is a position $1 \leq j \leq n$ such that the jth symbol in one string is 0 and the jth symbol in the other is a 2. We will often view such a set A as a matrix in which the rows are the strings in A (ordered arbitrarily) and the columns are the coordinate positions $1, 2, \cdots, n$ of entries in these strings. So, the (i,j)'th entry of A in this view is the entry (0, 1, or 2) in the j'th position of string i of A. If every string in a separable array A has length n and has a occurrences of the symbol 0 and b occurrences of the symbol 2, then we call A an *(n,a,b)-array*. The maximum number of strings in an (n,a,b)-array is denoted by $R(n;a,b)$. Examples of a $(5,2,2)$ array and a $(7,1,3)$ array are shown in Figure 1.

Such matrices, consisting of the three symbols 0, 1, and 2, are reminiscent of weighing matrices. A *weighing matrix* W of weight w is a square matrix of rank n containing symbols -1, 0, and 1 such that $W \cdot W^T = wI_n$ [12]. A weighing matrix is an extension of Hadamard matrices [13] by adding the symbol 0 (see [14]). A *circulant weighing matrix* is a weighing matrix in which each row is a circular shift of the first row [14]. There are examples of $n \times n$ weighing matrices that can be transformed to an (n,a,b)-array, for appropriate a and b, by transforming the three symbols (-1, 0, 1) to (0, 1, 2), respectively. For example, the circulant weighing matrix with first row (-1 1 0 1 1 0) is transformed into a circulant (6, 1, 3)-array with first row (0 2 1 2 2 1) by the indicated replacement of symbols.

The motivation for our study begins with Lemma 1, given in the next section, showing that any upper bound for $R(n;k,k)$ also serves as an upper bound for the Chebyshev function $P(n, n-k)$. The resulting upper bounds we obtain on the Chebyshev function give improvements over what was previously known in the literature.

$$\textbf{(a)}\ \left|\begin{array}{c} 00122\\ 01220\\ 12200\\ 22001\\ 20012\\ 02012\\ 20120\\ 01202\\ 12020\\ 20201 \end{array}\right| \qquad \textbf{(b)}\ \left|\begin{array}{c} 0111222\\ 1112220\\ 1122201\\ 1222011\\ 2220111\\ 2201112\\ 2011122 \end{array}\right|$$

Figure 1. (**a**) (5,2,2)-array with 10 rows and (**b**) (7,1,3)-array with 7 rows.

Our results are the following.

1. By means of a transformation, we adapt a result of Bollobás from the theory of extremal sets to show that $R(n;s,t) \leq \binom{2s+2t}{s+t}$. From this, we derive $P(d+r,d) \leq \binom{4r}{2r} = \frac{2^{4r}}{\sqrt{2\pi r}}(1+o(1))$ (as r grows). This improves on the previously known upper bound for $P(d+r,d)$ for large r.
2. We develop recursive methods for upper bounding $R(n;s,t)$. For small r, these yield upper bounds for $P(d+r,d)$, which improve on both the previously known upper bounds for $P(d+r,d)$ and on the bound obtained through the transformation of the Bollobás result stated above.

We will need the following notation and terms. For an array A, we let $|A|$ be the number of rows in A. For any row r in an array A, we let $r(i)$ be the entry of r in column i

(which we also call *position i*) of A. Given a set S of rows in A, we say that S is *separated in a set of columns* C if for any two rows $r, s \in S$ there is a column $i \in C$ such that one of $\{r(i), s(i)\}$ is 0 while the other is 2. Given two sets S_1, S_2 of rows in A, we refer to *internal* separations of S_1 and S_2 as that set of columns at which either S_1 is separated or S_2 is separated. We refer to *cross* separations of S_1 and S_2 as that set of columns C such that for any two rows $r \in S_1 \setminus S_2$ and $s \in S_2 \setminus S_1$, there is a column $c \in C$ at which $\{r, s\}$ are separated.

2. Background and Preliminary Results

We begin with a theorem by Klove et al. [2], preceded by a definition.

Definition 1. *If A is a $(d+r, d)$-PA, then the integers $1, 2, \ldots, r$ and $d+1, d+2, \ldots, d+r$ are called potent symbols. Moreover, the integers $1, 2, \ldots r$ are called low potent symbols and the integers $d+1, d+2 \ldots d+r$ are called high potent symbols.*

Their proof of the following upper bound, here omitted, uses the idea of potent symbols.

Theorem 1 (Klove et al. [2])**.** *For fixed $r \geq 1$, there exist constants c_r and d_r such that $P(d+r, d) = c_r$ for $d \geq d_r$. Moreover,*

$$c_r \leq 2^{2r}(2r)! \tag{1}$$

and

$$d_r \leq 1 + (2r-1)c_r - r. \tag{2}$$

Exact values are known for $r = 1$ and $r = 2$, namely, $c_1 = 3$, $d_1 = 2$ [2], $c_2 = 10$, and $d_2 = 3$ [1]. The upper bounds for c_r and d_r given in (1) and (2) turn out to be quite generous. For example, inequality (1) gives the bound $c_2 \leq 384$, but we know that $c_2 = 10$. We will see additional improvements on c_r as given in Equation (1) later in this paper.

The role of potent symbols motivates the idea behind the following lemma, which establishes the connection between the Chebyshev function and $R(n; k, k)$. Consider an $(n, n-k)$-PA, which we call A, and any row π of A. The idea is to put the symbols $1, 2, \cdots, n$ of π into three groups. Those that are high (resp. low) potent symbols, namely, $n-k+1, n-k+2, \cdots, n$ (resp. $1, 2, \cdots, k$), are relabeled 2 (resp. 0), while all other symbols are relabeled 1. Repeating this replacement over all rows of A, independently in any two rows, will yield an (n, k, k)-array, as we will see below. On the other hand, given an (n, k, k) array B, we perform the inverse replacement independently in each row of B to obtain an $(n, n-2k+1)$-PA. We obtain bounds linking the R function with the Chebyshev function in the lemma following.

Lemma 1. $P(n, n-k) \leq R(n; k, k) \leq P(n, n-2k+1)$ *when* $k \leq \frac{n}{2}$.

Proof. We begin with the first inequality. Let A be an $(n, n-k)$-PA, where $k \leq \frac{n}{2}$. Create an (n, k, k)-array A' as follows. For each row $\pi \in A$, create a row $\pi' \in A'$ by

$$\pi'(i) = \begin{cases} 0 & \text{if } \pi(i) \in \{1, \ldots, k\}, \\ 2 & \text{if } \pi(i) \in \{n-k+1, \ldots, n\}, \text{ and} \\ 1 & \text{otherwise.} \end{cases}$$

Then, A' is an array over the symbols $\{0, 1, 2\}$, having k many 0's and k many 2's in each row. Since $d(A) \geq n-k$, then for any two rows π and σ of A, there is a position i such that $|\pi(i) - \sigma(i)| \geq n - k$. So, one of $\pi(i)$ or $\sigma(i)$ is $\geq n - k + 1$ and the other must be $\leq k$. Consequently, one of $\pi(i)$ or $\sigma(i)$ is transformed into a 2 and the other into a 0. So the rows π' and σ' are separated in A'. Furthermore, as any two rows of A' are separated, any two such rows must be distinct. Therefore A' is an (n,k,k)-array and $R(n;k,k) \geq |A'| = |A|$, so the inequality follows.

Consider now the second inequality. Let B be an (n,k,k)-array with the maximum possible number $R(n;k,k)$ of rows. Let B' be the permutation array obtained from B by arbitrarily replacing, in any row of B, the k many 2's by the high potent symbols $n-k+1, n-k+2, \cdots, n$, the k many 0's by the low potent symbols $1, 2, \cdots, k$, and the 1 symbols by the symbols $k+1, \cdots, n-k$. (It is, of course, required that the replacements create a permutation). The replacements performed on any two rows of B are performed independently of each other. Since B is separable, given any two rows r and s of B', there is a column c in B' for which one of $r(c), s(c)$ is a high potent symbol while the other is a low potent symbol. So, we have $|r(c) - s(c)| \geq n - 2k + 1$. Since rows r and s were arbitrary, this shows that $d(B') \geq n - 2k + 1$. So, by monotonicity in d of $P(n,d)$, we obtain $P(n, n-2k+1) \geq |B'| = |B| = R(n,k,k)$. □

The following Corollary of Lemma 1 shows that $R(n;k,k)$ reaches a maximum that depends only on k.

Corollary 1. *There are constants n_k and m_k (depending only on k) such that for all $n \geq n_k$, we have $R(n;k,k) \leq m_k$. Moreover, we can take $m_k = c_{2k-1}$ and $n_k = 2k + d_{2k-1} - 1$. Here, c_{2k-1} and d_{2k-1} are the constants from Theorem 1.*

Proof. By the second inequality of Lemma 1, we have $R(n;k,k) \leq P(n, n-2k+1) = P(n-2k+1+(2k-1), n-2k+1)$. So, by Theorem 1, $P(n, n-2k+1) \leq c_{2k-1}$ for $n - 2k + 1 \geq d_{2k-1}$; that is, $R(n;k,k) \leq c_{2k-1}$ for $n \geq 2k + d_{2k-1} - 1$. □

We note that a transformation of an (n,k,k)-array with N rows into an $(n, n-k)$-PA with N rows is not known to be always possible.

We will see later that the existence of the constants n_k and m_k follows from one of our theorems (Theorem 6), together with an improvement on the bounds given in Theorem 1 for the constants c_r and d_r. Still, we mention Corollary 1 here to show that the existence of n_k and m_k is already implied by Theorem 1 combined with the argument in that Corollary.

There are a few other theorems in the literature that give upper bounds on the Chebyshev function. Let $V(n,d)$ be the number of permutations on $\{1, 2, \ldots, n\}$ within Chebyshev distance d of the identity permutation.

Theorem 2 (Theorem 11 [2]). *For even d and $2d \geq n \geq d \geq 2$, $P(n,d) \leq \frac{(n+1)!}{V(n+1, d/2)}$.*

Theorem 3 (Theorem 12 [1]). *For $1 \leq k \leq d < n$,*

$$P(n,d) \leq P(n-k,d) \cdot \binom{n}{k}.$$

Corollary 2. *For $s \leq t$ and $1 \leq k \leq s$,*

$$R(n;s,t) \leq R(n-k; s-k, t) \cdot \binom{n}{k}.$$

Proof. Consider any (n,s,t)-array A, which we can take to be of maximum possible size $R(n;s,t)$. Create subsets of the rows of A, determined by the positions of their k many 0's. That is, two rows are in the same subset if they both have k many 0's occurring in the same k positions. There are $\binom{n}{k}$ such sets. Any two rows in such a set must be separated somewhere in the remaining $n-k$ positions, using $s-k$ many 0's and t many 2's in those $n-k$ positions. Hence, any such set of rows must have the size at most $R(n-k;s-k,t)$. It follows that $|R(n;s,t)| = |A| \le R(n-k;s-k,t)\cdot\binom{n}{k}$. □

Corollary 3. *For all* $2 \le t \le n-2$, $R(n;2,t) \le \binom{n}{2}$.

Proof. Setting $s=k=2$ in Corollary 2, we have $R(n-2,s-k,t) = R(n-2;0,t) = 1$ since $R(m,0,t) = 1$ for all m. □

We will see later (Theorem 9) a bound on $R(2,t)$ that depends only on t once n is big enough. But, the bound in Corollary 3 is still the best for n that is small enough relative to t, as we will see.

Some of the best previous upper bounds for small n were given using Theorem 3. For example, from Theorem 3, $P(n,n-3) \le \min\{\binom{n}{3}, 3\binom{n}{2}, 10\binom{n}{1}\}$, choosing $k=3,2,1$, respectively. To see this, consider the following. Since $P(r,r)=1$ for any r, taking $k=3$, we obtain $P(n-3,n-3)=1$. As mentioned previously after Theorem 1, $c_1=3$, so, taking $k=2$, we obtain $P(n-2,n-3)=3$. Again, recalling $c_2=10$, we take $k=1$ to obtain $P(n-3,n-1)=10$. Since $\min\{\binom{n}{3}, 3\binom{n}{2}, 10\binom{n}{1}\} = 10n$ for all $n \ge 10$, Theorem 3 gives the upper bound $P(n,n-3) \le 10n$. In an application of our recursive upper bounds, we will see later in Corollary 7 that $R(n;3,3) \le 169$, yielded by Lemma 1. $P(n,n-3) \le R(n;3,3) \le 169$. Thus, Theorem 3 gave the best upper bound for $P(n,n-3) \le 10n$ for $n \le 16$, while our new recursive results give an improved bound for $P(n,n-3) \le 169$ when $n \ge 17$.

Similarly, from Theorem 3, $P(n,n-4) \le \min\ U$, where $U = \{\binom{n}{4}, 3\binom{n}{3}, 10\binom{n}{2}, P(n,n-3)\binom{n}{1}\}$, choosing $k=4,3,2,1$, respectively. The previous paragraph shows that $P(n,n-3) \le 169$ for all $n \ge 17$. Calculating, $\min U = 10\binom{n}{2}$ for $14 \le n \le 34$ and $= 169n$ for all $n \ge 35$. In Corollary 8, which we will see later, we obtain $R(n;4,4) \le 3087$. Calculating, one observes that $3087 \le \min\ U$ for all $n \ge 19$. So, we obtain the improved upper bound: $P(n,n-4) \le R(n;4,4) \le 3087$ for all $n \ge 19$.

We observe that $R(n;a,b)$ is symmetric and monotone; that is,

$$R(n;a,b) = R(n;b,a), \tag{3}$$

$$R(n;a,b) \ge R(m;a,b) \text{ if } n \ge m. \tag{4}$$

Later in this paper, it will be useful to consider separable arrays on $\{0,1,2\}$ in which the number of 0's and 2's in each row is not constant for all rows. The following definition and the lemma which follows treat this case.

Definition 2. *For* $a,b \ge 2$, *an* $(n,\le a,\le b)$*-array is a separable array of length n strings over* $\{0,1,2\}$ *such that each string in A has at most a many 0's and at most b many 2's. Let* $R(n;\le a,\le b)$ *be the maximum size of any* $(n,\le a,\le b)$*-array.*

Lemma 2. *If* $s,t \ge 1$ *and* $n \ge s+t$, *then*

$$R(n;\le s,\le t) \le R(n;s,t). \tag{5}$$

Proof. Let A be an $(n,\le s,\le t)$-array with entries from $\{0,1,2\}$, realizing $R(n;\le s,\le t)$. Consider any string π in A having $s' \le s$ many 0's and $t' \le t$ many 2's. Since $n-s-t \ge 0$, we have $n-s'-t' \ge s-s'+t-t'$, so A must have at least $s-s'+t-t'$ many 1's in its row corresponding to π. We transform π into a string π' with s many 0's and t many 2's as follows. We convert any $s-s'$ of the 1's in π to 0's and any $t-t'$ of the remaining 1's to 2's and let π' be the resulting string. Let A' be the array obtained from A by replacing each $\pi \in A$ by π'.

It suffices to show that A' is separable. It would then follow that no two strings $\pi', \sigma' \in A'$ are the same, since they would not be separated, and since the number of rows in A' is at most $R(n;s,t)$, then, also, $R(n;s',t') \leq R(n;s,t)$. So, let π, σ be two arbitrary strings of A and let π', σ' be the respective transformed strings in A'. There is a column c of A where $\{\pi(c), \sigma(c)\} = \{0,2\}$ (in either order). Since the transformation affects no symbols in π or σ that are either 0 or 2, it follows that $\pi'(c) = \pi(c)$ and $\sigma'(c) = \sigma(c)$ and, hence, π' and σ' are separated. Thus, A' is separable. □

The following theorem will lead to the exact value $R(n;2,2) = 10$ for $n \geq 5$.

Theorem 4. *Suppose that $R(n_0;k,k) \leq m$ such that*

$$2k(m+1) < (n_0+1)(1+\lfloor n_0/(2k-1)\rfloor). \tag{6}$$

Then, $R(n;k,k) \leq m$ for all $n \geq n_0$.

Proof. Suppose to the contrary that $R(n;k,k) \geq m+1$ for some $n > n_0$. Let n be the smallest such number. Let $A = \{\pi_1, \pi_2, \ldots, \pi_{m+1}\}$ be an (n,k,k)-array. Let k_i denote the number of 0 and 2 symbols in position i, taken over all rows of A. Let $z = 1 + \lfloor n_0/(2k-1)\rfloor$, so that $n_0 \geq (z-1)(2k-1)$. We show that $k_i \geq z$ for all i. Suppose, by symmetry of argument, that $k_1 \leq z-1$ and (by rearranging the order) only π_i, $1 \leq i \leq k_1$, have 0 or 2 symbols in the first position. By our assumption, all of the first k_1 rows, and only the first k_1 rows, have a 0 or 2 symbol in position 1. So, if there are $z-1$ rows, each adding $2k-1$ 0 or 2 symbols to some position $j > 1$, the total number of 0 or 2 symbols (other than the one in position 1) is $(2k-1)(z-1)$. Since the number of positions, namely, $n > n_0$, is greater than $(2k-1)(z-1)$, by the pigeonhole principle, there is a position $j > 1$ where no π_i, $1 \leq i \leq k_1$ do not has any 0 or 2 symbols. Now, do the following:

- For each row π_i, $1 \leq i \leq k_1$, exchange the 0 or 2 symbol in position 1 with the symbol in position j.
- Delete the symbol in position 1 in all rows.

The result is a separable array of $\geq m+1$ rows, where each row is a string of length $n-1$. This contradicts our choice of n being the smallest. So, we have $k_i \geq z$ for all i.

Note that the total number of 0 and 2 symbols in the (n,k,k)-array A is $\geq 2k(m+1)$. As $k_i \geq z$, for all i, we have $2k(m+1) \geq nz \geq (n_0+1)(1+\lfloor n_0/(2k-1)\rfloor)$, which contradicts inequality (6). So, the (n,k,k)-array A with $\geq m+1$ rows does not exist. □

Theorem 15 was used in [1] to prove that $P(n,n-2) = 10$ for all $n \geq 5$. A similar proof shows that $R(n;2,2) = 10$ for all $n \geq 5$.

Corollary 4. *For all $n \geq 5$, R(n;2,2) = 10.*

Proof. $R(n;2,2) \geq 10$ for all $5 \leq n \leq 11$, by computation. In Theorem 4, set $n_0 = 11, k = 2$, and $m = 10$. Then, $z = 1 + \lfloor n_0/(2k-1)\rfloor = 4$ and $2k(m+1) = 44 < 48 = (n_0+1)z$. So, $R(n;2,2)) \leq 10$ for all $n \geq 11$, following Theorem 4.

Therefore, $R(n;2,2) = 10$ for all $n \geq 5$. □

An example of a $(5,2,2)$-array with 10 rows realizing $R(5;2,2)$ is given in Figure 1a .

3. Applying a Result of Bollobás

We begin with the following result of Bollobás from the theory of extremal sets. It is actually a reformulation, given in [15], of a theorem on saturated hypergraphs originally appearing in [16]. The proof can be found in [15].

Theorem 5. *For two nonnegative integers a and b, write* $w(a,b) = \binom{a+b}{a}^{-1}$*. Let* $\{(A_i, B_i : i \in I\}$ *be a finite collection of finite sets such that* $A_i \cap B_j = \emptyset$ *if* $i = j$*. For* $i \in I$*, set* $a_i = |A_i|$*,* $b_i = |B_i|$*. Then,* $\sum_{i \in I} w(a_i, b_i) \leq 1$ *with equality if there is a set Y and integers a, b such that* $0 \leq a \leq a + b \leq |Y|$*, and* $\{(A_i, B_i) : i \in I\}$ *is the collection of all ordered pairs of subsets of Y with* $|A_i| = a_i$ *and* $|B_i| = b_i$*.*

In particular, if $a_i = a$ *and* $b_i = b$ *for all* $i \in I$*, then* $|I| \leq \binom{a+b}{a}$*.*

We obtain an upper bound for $R(n; s, t)$ by reducing to the above theorem.

Theorem 6. $R(n; s, t) \leq \binom{2s+2t}{s+t}$.

Proof. Let M be a an (n, s, t)-array realizing $R(n; s, t)$, and set $p = R(n; s, t)$. For any $1 \leq i \leq p$, let $S_i = \{a_{i1} < a_{i2} < \cdots < a_{is}\}$ be the set of column indices at which row i of M has 0 entries and $T_i = \{b_{i1} < b_{i2} < \cdots < b_{it}\}$ the set of column indices at which row i of M has 2 entries.

Now, construct a $p \times 2n$ array Q whose first n columns are the same as in M and whose subarray M' consisting of the last n columns is obtained by interchanging 0 and 2 entries in M, leaving the 1 entries unchanged. That is, M' is obtained from M by flipping each 2 entry of M to a 0 entry in M', flipping each 0 entry in M to a 2 entry in M' and leaving each 1 in M unchanged as a 1 entry in M'. Let $S'_i = \{a'_{ij} : 1 \leq j \leq s\}$ (resp. $T'_i = \{b'_{ij} : 1 \leq j \leq t\}$) be the column indices in M' corresponding to the column indices of S_i (resp. T_i) by a translation of n. That is, we have $a'_{ij} = a_{ij} + n$ and $b'_{ij} = b_{ij} + n$. Now, for each i, $1 \leq i \leq p$, define two sets of column indices, Q_i and Q'_i, of Q by $Q_i = S_i \cup T'_i$ and $Q'_i = S'_i \cup T_i$. Observe that Q_i (resp. Q'_i) is the set of column indices at which row i of Q has 0 (resp. 2) entries.

We now show that for $1 \leq i \leq p$, the sets Q_i, Q'_i can play the roles of A_i and B_i (respectively) in the statement of Theorem 5 with $p = |I|$. Trivially, we have $Q_i \cap Q'_i = \emptyset$ for each i since $S_i \cap T_i = \emptyset$. Now, take $j \neq i$, $1 \leq j \leq p$. We must show that $Q_i \cap Q'_j \neq \emptyset$ and $Q'_i \cap Q_j \neq \emptyset$. Since M is separable, we have $S_i \cap T_j \neq \emptyset$ or $S_j \cap T_i \neq \emptyset$, so assume by symmetry that $S_i \cap T_j \neq \emptyset$. Then, immediately, we have $Q_i \cap Q'_j \neq \emptyset$ since $S_i \subset Q_i$ and $T_j \subset Q'_j$. Also, it follows from $S_i \cap T_j \neq \emptyset$ and the interchange of 0's and 2's that $S'_i \cap T'_j \neq \emptyset$. Therefore, $Q'_i \cap Q_j \neq \emptyset$ since $S'_i \subset Q'_i$ and $T'_j \subset Q_j$. Thus, the conditions of Theorem 5 are satisfied. Since $|Q_i| = |Q'_i| = s + t$ for all i, we obtain $p = |I| \leq \binom{2s+2t}{s+t}$. □

The preceding theorem implies Corollary 1 with the considerably improved value $m_k = \binom{4k}{2k}$ over that obtained by combining that corollary and Theorem 1.

Corollary 5. $P(d + r, d) \leq \binom{4r}{2r} = \dfrac{2^{4r}}{\sqrt{2\pi r}}(1 + o(1))$ *(as r grows).*

Proof. By Lemma 1 and Theorem 6, we have $P(d + r, d) \leq R(d + r; r, r) \leq \binom{4r}{2r}$. The final equality follows from the Stirling approximation applied to $\binom{4r}{2r}$. □

We note that the preceding corollary implies that $c_r \leq \dfrac{2^{4r}}{\sqrt{2\pi r}}(1 + o(1))$, where c_r is the constant in Theorem 1. This is an improvement on the upper bound for c_r given in that theorem.

4. Recursive Techniques

4.1. The Positions Method

In this subsection, we introduce a technique, called *positions*, to recursively obtain an upper bound for $R(n;a,b)$. The strategy involves considering a fixed row π of a (n,a,b)-array A, with a occurrences of the symbol 0 in positions $p_1, p_2, \ldots, p_a$ and b occurrences of the symbol 2 in positions $q_1, q_2, \ldots, q_b$. By separability, every row in A other than π must either have a symbol 2 in at least one of the positions $p_1, p_2, \ldots, p_a$ or a symbol 0 in at least one of the positions $q_1, q_2, \ldots, q_b$. Let $S(p_i)$ (respectively, $S(q_i)$) be the set of rows in A with the symbol 2 (respectively, symbol 0) in position p_i (resp., q_i). Each $S(p_i)$ (resp. $S(q_i)$ must be a separable subarray of A, with separations occurring at positions other than p_i (respectively, q_i). As one 2 (one 0) is used in position p_i (resp., q_i), there are at most a many 0's and at most $b-1$ many 2's (resp., $a-1$ many 0's and b many 2's) that can be used to separate $S(p_i)$ (resp. $S(q_i)$). This method gives the following recursive bound on $R(n;a,b)$.

Theorem 7. *For all $a, b \geq 1$ and $n \geq a+b$, $R(n;a,b) \leq 1 + aR(n-1;a,b-1) + bR(n-1;a-1,b)$.*

Proof. Let A be an (n,a,b)-array of size $R(n;a,b)$. Let π be a permutation in A. Suppose that in π, the 0's are at positions $p_1, \ldots, p_a$ and the 2's are at positions $q_1, \ldots, q_b$. Every permutation $\sigma \in A - \pi$ has a symbol 2 in at least one of the positions $p_i, 1 \leq i \leq a$ or a symbol 0 in at least one of the positions $q_j, 1 \leq j \leq b$. For every position p_i, there are at most $R(n-1;a,b-1)$ strings $\sigma \in A - \pi$ with $\sigma(p_i) = 2$ and, hence, a total of at most $aR(n-1;a,b-1)$ such strings over all p_i. For every position q_j, there are at most $R(n-1;a-1,b)$ strings in $\sigma \in A - \pi$ with $\sigma(q_j) = 0$ and, hence, a total of at most $bR(n-1;a-1,b)$ such strings over all q_i. The bound follows. □

We can obtain an exact formula for $R(n;1,k)$ in the next lemma and the theorem that follows.

Lemma 3. *For all $k \geq 1$ and $n \geq k+1$,* $R(n;1,k) \geq \begin{cases} n & \text{if } k+1 \leq n \leq 2k, \\ 2k+1 & \text{if } n \geq 2k+1. \end{cases}$

Proof. Suppose $k+1 \leq n \leq 2k+1$. Let π_0 be the permutation

$$\pi_0 = (0, \underbrace{1,1,\ldots,1}_{k \text{ times}}, \underbrace{2,2,\ldots,2}_{n-k-1 \text{ times}}).$$

Consider permutations $\pi_0, \pi_1, \ldots, \pi_{n-1}$ defined by $\pi_i(j) = \pi_0(j-i) \pmod{n}$, that is, π_i is obtained from π_0 by shifting elements rightward by i with wraparound.

First, we observe that the array A with rows $\pi_0, \pi_1, \cdots, \pi_{n-1}$, appearing in A in order of their index, is separated. It suffices to show that row π_0 is separated from any row π_i, $i \geq 1$. The 0 in position 1 of π_0 separates π_0 from the 2 in column 1 of π_i for $1 \leq i \leq k$. The 2's in columns $k+2$ through n of π_0 each separate from the 0 in the same columns for π_i, $k+1 \leq i \leq n-1$. Therefore, the permutations $\pi_i, 0 \leq i < n$ are pairwise separable and $R(n;1,k) \geq n$.

If $n \geq 2k+1$, then $R(n;1,k) \geq R(2k+1;1,k) \geq 2k+1$, the first inequality by monotonicity of $R(n;1,k)$ for a fixed k (see Equation (4)) and the second by the same circular shift construction just given. □

Theorem 8. *(a)* *For all $k \geq 1$ and $n \geq k+1$, $R(n;1,k) = \begin{cases} n & \text{if } k+1 \leq n \leq 2k, \\ 2k+1 & \text{if } n \geq 2k+1. \end{cases}$*

(b) *Suppose a separated array A has at most one 0 and at most k many 2's in each row. If A has $2k+1$ rows, then A must have exactly one zero and k many 2's in each row.*

(c) *Suppose A is an $(n,1,k)$-array. If A has $2k+1$ rows, then A is a $(2k+1) \times (2k+1)$ array also with one 0 and k many 2's in each column.*

Proof. Consider first (a). In view of the lower bound in Lemma 3, it remains only to prove the corresponding upper bounds.

The upper bound $R(n;1,k) \leq n$ follows from the fact that any two rows do not have 0 in the same position. Suppose $n \geq 2k+1$.

Take an $(n,1,k)$-array with p rows. There are $\binom{p}{2} = (p-1)p/2$ pairs of rows that have to be separated. Let Q be the total number of unordered pairs $\{0,2\}$ with both the 0 and the 2 lying in the same column of A. Then, $\binom{p}{2} \leq Q$.

But, Q $\leq$ {the number of 2's that are members of such a pair (since there is only one 0 per column)} $\leq$ {the total number of 2's in the array} $= pk$.

So, we obtain $\binom{p}{2} \leq pk$. Solving for p, we obtain $p \leq 2k+1$.

Consider now (b). Recall that no two 0's of A can be in the same column, since, otherwise, the two rows containing those 0's cannot be separated. For any column i containing a 0, let s_i be the number of of 2's in column i. Since A is separated, the number of pairwise row separations in A is at least $\binom{2k+1}{2} = k(2k+1)$. Since there is at most one 0 in each column, we have $\sum_i s_i \geq k(2k+1)$.

Assume to the contrary that claim b) is false, so that either some row contains no 0 or some row has fewer than k many 0's. Suppose first that some row contains no 0. Then, since it has at most k many 2's, this row can be separated from most k other rows since its separation from other rows can only occur at columns containing its 2's, and each column has at most one 0. This contradicts A being separated, which requires each row to be separated from $2k$ other rows.

So we may suppose that A has $2k+1$ many 0's, but that some row has at most $k-1$ many 2's. Then, by the assumption in b), the total number of 2's in A is less than $(2k+1)k$ but is also equal to $\sum_i s_i$. Then, we have $(2k+1)k \leq \sum_i s_i < (2k+1)k$, a contradiction.

Consider now (c). Since no two 0's of A can be in the same column, it follows that each column has exactly one 0. It also follows that A must be a $(2k+1) \times (2k+1)$ array.

Suppose to the contrary that some column c of A has at most $k-1$ many 2's. Consider the row r passing through the 0 in column c. Row r must be separated from each of the $2k$ other rows of A. There are $k-1$ separation pairs involving row r that use the 0 in column c. The remaining $k+1$ separation pairs involving row r must use the k many 2's in row r. But each such 2 participates in only a single separation, that being with the unique 0 in its column. Hence, we cannot find $k+1$ separations involving these 2's, a contradiction. □

An example of a $(7,1,3)$-array realizing $R(n;1,3) = 7$ is given in Figure 1b.

In the next lemma and theorem that follow, we use the positions technique to obtain an upper bound on $R(n:2,k)$.

As a notation, for any subarray B of an array A, let $col(B)$ (resp, $row(B)$) be the set of columns (resp. rows) of B. Further, let B^r (resp. B^c) be the set of rows (resp. columns) of A containing entries of B. For a particular column c, $1 \leq c \leq n$, in some array A of n columns, we refer to it just by its index c. For example, for a subarray B of A, we write $c \cap B$ or $B \setminus c$ for $column(c) \cap B$ or $B \setminus column(c)$, respectively.

Now, let A be an $(n,2,k)$-array and let c be some column of A. Let B be the subarray consisting of all rows of A with a 0 in column c. Then, $B \setminus c$ has one 0 and k many 2's in each row. Assume now that B has exactly $2k+1$ rows. We then let $\underline{sep(B)}$ be that $(n,1,k)$-array in B (guaranteed to exist by Theorem 8), which has dimensions $(2k+1) \times (2k+1)$.

Lemma 4. *Let A be an $(n,2,k)$-array and let c_1, c_2 be two distinct columns of A. Let S_1 (resp. S_2) be the subarray of A whose rows have a 0 entry in column c_1 (resp. c_2). If $|S_1| = |S_2| = 2k+1$, then $|S_1^r \cap S_2^r)| = 1$.*

Proof. Since each row of $S_1 \setminus c_1$ and $S_2 \setminus c_2$ has one 0 and k many 2's, we have $|S_i| \leq R(1,k) = 2k+1$ by Theorem 8. By our assumption and the same theorem, we then see that $sep(S_i), i = 1,2$, is a $(2k+1,1,k)$-array with dimensions $(2k+1) \times (2k+1)$ and one 0 and k many 2's in each row and in each column. Note also that if $|S_1^r \cap S_2^r| \geq 2$, then any two rows in this intersection have both 0's in the same two coordinates c_1 and c_2 and, hence, cannot be separated, a contradiction to A being separated.

We are thus reduced to showing that $|S_1^r \cap S_2^r| = 0$ leads to a contradiction. Slightly abusing previous notation, in what follows, we use the term *potent symbol* to refer to either a 0 symbol or a 2 symbol in A.

Assume that $|S_1^r \cap S_2^r| = 0$. It follows that every entry in $c_1 \cap S_2$ is nonzero. So, $c_1 \cap S_2 \notin col(sep(S_2))$ since every column of $sep(S_2)$ has a 0. Since each row of $sep(S_2)$ contains one 0 and k many 2's, and since every entry of $c_2 \cap S_2$ is 0 by definition, it follows that every potent symbol in S_2 lies in $(c_2 \cap S_2) \cup sep(S_2)$. So, there remain no potent symbols of S_2 that can appear in $c_1 \cap S_2$. So, every entry in $c_1 \cap S_2$ is 1. By a symmetric argument, we also have that every potent symbol in S_1 lies in $(c_1 \cap S_1) \cup sep(S_1)$ and that every entry of $c_2 \cap S_1$ is 1. It follows that all $S_1 - S_2$ cross separations must occur in the columns contained in $sep(S_1)^c \cap sep(S_2))^c$.

The number of $S_1 - S_2$ cross separations must be at least $(2k+1)^2$, since every row of S_1 must be separated from every row of S_2. Now, in each column $c \in sep(S_1)^c \cap sep(S_2)^c$, there are $2k$ many $S_1 - S_2$ cross separations, obtained by pairing the 0 in $c \cap sep(S_1)$ with each of the k many 2's in $c \cap sep(S_2)$, and the same with S_1 and S_2 interchanged. Since $|sep(S_1)^c \cap sep(S_2)^c| \leq 2k+1$, the total number of $S_1 - S_2$ cross separations is at most $2k(2k+1) < (2k+1)^2$, a contradiction. □

In the theorem that follows, we abbreviate the symbols $R(n;2,k)$, $R(n-1;2,k-1)$, and so on by $R(2,k)$ or $R(2,k-1)$; that is, we drop the first coordinate in the R function. We take n large enough so that $R(n;2,k)$ depends only on k (see Corollary 1). By monotonicity, the upper bound we then obtain for $R(n,2,k)$ holds also for $R(n',2,k)$, where $n' < n$.

Theorem 9. $R(2,k) \leq \dfrac{k(k+4)(2k+1)}{3} - 10.$

Proof. Let A be be an $(n,2,k)$ array achieving the maximum possible number of rows $R(2,k)$ for such arrays. Let π be a fixed row of A, with its two 0's in columns p_1 and p_2 and its k many 2's in columns $q_1, q_2, \cdots, q_k$. Every row of $A \setminus \pi$, being separable from π, must have a 2 in at least one of the columns p_1 and p_2 or a 0 in at least one of the columns $q_1, q_2, \cdots, q_k$.

Let T_1 (resp. T_2) be the subarray of $A \setminus \pi$ consisting of the rows of A with a 2 in column p_1 (resp. p_2). Note that any row of $T_1 \cup T_2$ has at most $k-1$ many 2's outside the columns p_1, p_2.

First, we give an upper bound for $|T_1 \cup T_2|$ as follows. Let B_1 be the set of rows in $T_1 \cup T_2$ with no 0 entry in columns p_1, p_2. Then, $|B_1| \leq R(2, \leq k-1) \leq R(2,k-1)$ by Lemma 2. Let B_2 be the set of rows in $T_1 \cup T_2$ with exactly one 0 in one of the columns p_1 or p_2. Then, by Lemma 4 and Theorem 8, we have $|B_2| \leq 2R(1,k-1) - 1 = 4k-3$. Finally, no row of $T_1 \cup T_2$ can have both its 0's in columns p_1, p_2 since such a row would not be separated from π. Therefore, we have $|T_1 \cup T_2| \le |B_1| + |B_2| \le R(2, k-1) + 4k - 3$.

Let $S_i, 1 \le i \le k$, be the subarray of A consisting of the rows of A with a 0 in column $q_i, 1 \le i \le k$. Note that $|S_i| \le R(1, \le k) \le R(1, k) = 2k + 1$.

We now give an upper bound for $|\cup_{i=1}^{k} S_i^r|$. First note that for any triple of indices $1 \le i < j < t \le k$, we have $|S_i^r \cap S_j^r \cap S_t^r| = 0$, since any row of A contained in this triple intersection has three 0 entries, contradicting A being an $(n, 2, k)$-array. Applying inclusion–exclusion, we thus obtain

$$|\cup_{i=1}^{k} S_i^r| = \sum_{1 \le i \le k} |S_i^r| - \sum_{1 \le i < j \le k} |S_i^r \cap S_j^r|. \tag{7}$$

Also note that $|S_i^r \cap S_j^r| = 0$ or 1 since any two rows of A contained in $S_i^r \cap S_j^r$ have both of their 0 entries in the same two columns q_i, q_j and, hence, cannot be separated.

We now maximize the right side of (7) over all possible collections of subarrays $S_i, 1 \le i \le k$ of A as defined above. Let $|S_i^r| = 2k + 1$ for $1 \le i \le t$, while $|S_i^r| \le 2k$ for $t + 1 \le i \le k$. By Lemma 4, we have $|S_i^r \cap S_j^r| = 1$ for $1 \le i < j \le t$. Therefore, we obtain

$$|\cup_{i=1}^{k} S_i^r| \le (2k+1)t + (k-t)2k - \binom{t}{2} = g(t).$$

To maximize $g(t)$ on the domain $1 \le r \le k$, we differentiate to obtain $g'(t) = \frac{3}{2} - t$, so $t = \frac{3}{2}$ is the only critical point, and, also, $g'(1) > 0$, while $g'(2) < 0$. So, the maximum of $g(t)$ at integer values $1 \le t \le k$ is $\max\{g(1), g(2)\} = 2k^2 + 1$. So, we have $|\cup_{i=1}^{k} S_i| \le 2k^2 + 1$.

Finally, for $k \ge 3$, we obtain the following recurrence, where the first summand "1" accounts for the fixed permutation π.

$$R(2, k) \le 1 + |T_1 \cup T_2| + |\cup_{i=1}^{k} S_i^r| \le R(2, k-1) + 2k^2 + 4k - 1.$$

We can unravel this recurrence to obtain

$$\begin{aligned}
R(2,k) &\le R(2,2) + 2\sum_{i=3}^{k} i^2 + 4\sum_{i=3}^{k} i - (k-2) \\
&= 10 + 2\left(\frac{k(k+1)(2k+1)}{6} - 1^2 - 2^2\right) + 4\left(\frac{k(k+1)}{2} - 1 - 2\right) - (k-2) \\
&= \frac{k(k+4)(2k+1)}{3} - 10.
\end{aligned}$$

□

We note that the upper bound on $R(n; 2, k)$ from Theorem 9, being independent of n once n is big enough, is better than the bound $R(n; 2, k) \le \binom{n}{2}$ from Corollary 3 for n that is large relative to k, but the latter bound is stronger when $n \le Ck^{3/2}$ for a suitable constant C. Also, the bound from Theorem 9 is stronger than the bound $R(n; 2, k) \le \binom{2k+4}{k+2}$ from Theorem 6 for all but small k.

As examples to be used later, we mention the following.

Corollary 6. *$R(2,3) \le 39$ and $R(2,4) \le 86$.*

4.2. The Partition Method

In this subsection, we develop a recursive method, which we call the *partition method*, which, in some sense, generalizes the positions method of the previous subsection. In the partition method, we consider subarrays of a separable array A over $\{0, 1, 2\}$ defined by restrictions of rows of A to a certain set of coordinates in A. In the preceding positions method, the subarrays were defined by their restriction to a single coordinate.

Let A be an (n, s, t)-array with, say, $s \leq t$. Choose a row $\pi \in A$ with s occurrences of the symbol 0 in positions $p_1, \ldots, p_s$ and t occurrences of the symbol 2 in positions $q_1, \ldots, q_t$. For separation, all rows in A other than π must have either a symbol 2 in one of the positions $p_1, \ldots, p_s$ or a symbol 0 in one of the positions $q_1, \ldots, q_t$. Let S be the set of strings in A with at least one 2 in the positions $\{p_1, p_2, \cdots, p_s\}$ and let T be the set of strings in A with at least one 0 in the positions $\{q_1, q_2, \cdots, q_t\}$. Since every string in A is separated from π, we have $A = \{\pi\} \cup S \cup T$, so $|A| \leq 1 + |S| + |T|$. In this section, we upper bound $|S|$ (and similarly $|T|$) by partitioning S into certain collections of strings, and then upper bound the sizes of each of these collections. The collections come in two types as follows. For any string $\sigma \in S$, let σ_P be the length s restriction of σ to the positions $\{p_1, p_2, \cdots, p_s\}$; that is, $\sigma_P = \sigma_{p_1}\sigma_{p_2}\cdots\sigma_{p_s}$. Also, let $\tau(\sigma_P)$ be the set of positions among $\{p_1, p_2, \cdots, p_s\}$ at which σ_P has a 2 symbol. The two types of collections are the following.

(1) $S_0 = \{\sigma \in S : \sigma_P \text{ has no 0 symbols}\}$.
(2) For each nonempty subset $D \subseteq \{p_1, p_2, \cdots, p_s\}$ satisfying $|D| \leq s - 1$, let $S_D = \{\sigma \in S : \sigma_P \text{ contain at least one 0 and } \tau(\sigma_P) = D\}$.

Clearly, $S = S_0 \cup \left(\bigcup_D S_D\right)$ is a partition of S, so $|S| = |S_0| + \sum_D |S_D|$. We upper bound the sizes of these sets of rows in the following lemma.

Lemma 5. *The sets S_0, S_D satisfy the following.*

(a) *No two strings in S_0 and no two string in S_D are separable in any of the coordinates $\{p_i, 1 \leq i \leq s\}$. So, all internal separations in S_0 and in S_D occur outside the coordinates $p_i, 1 \leq i \leq s$.*
(b) $|S_0| \leq R(n-s, s, \leq t-1) \leq R(n-s, s, t-1)$.
(c) $|S_D| \leq R(n-s, \leq s-1, t-|D|) \leq R(n-s, s-1, t-|D|)$.

Proof. For (a), no two strings in S_0 are separable in one of the coordinates $\{p_i, 1 \leq i \leq s\}$, since neither has a 0 in those coordinates. Similarly, no two strings σ, γ in any S_D are separable in a coordinate $c \in \{p_i, 1 \leq i \leq s\}$ since we have $\sigma_c = 2$ if and only if $\gamma_c = 2$. Thus, all internal separations in S_0 or in any S_D occur in columns outside $p_1, p_2, \cdots, p_s$. We then define the subarrays S'_0 and S'_D of A by

$$S'_0 = \{\sigma \setminus \sigma_P : \sigma \in S_0\} \text{ and } S'_D = \{\sigma \setminus \sigma_P : \sigma \in S_D\}.$$

So, S'_0 (resp. S'_D) is the set of length $n - s$ strings obtained by deleting the substring σ_P from each string $\sigma \in S_0$ (resp. $\sigma \in S_D$). Note that $|S_0| = |S'_0|$ since for any two strings $\sigma, \gamma \in S_0$, we have $\sigma \setminus \sigma_P \neq \gamma \setminus \gamma_P$ because, for some coordinate c outside $p_1, p_2, \cdots, p_s$, we must have $\sigma_c = 2$ and $\gamma_c = 0$. This is because all internal separation in S_0 occurs outside the p_i coordinates, as observed above. Similarly, $|S_D| = |S'_D|$ for any nonempty subset $D \subseteq \{p_1, p_2, \cdots, p_s\}$.

Consider now part (b). Since any $\sigma \in S_0$ has no 0's in positions $p_i, 1 \leq i \leq s$, then $\sigma \setminus \sigma_P$ is a length $n - s$ string containing s many 0's and at most $t - 1$ many 2's. Hence, $|S_0| = |S'_0| \leq R(n-s, s, \leq t-1)$. The second inequality then follows Lemma 2.

For part (c), note that by definition for any $\gamma \in S_D$, γ_P contains at least one 0 and $|D|$ many 2's. So, $\gamma \setminus \gamma_P$ is a length $n - s$ string that has at most $s - 1$ many 0's and at most $t - |D|$ many 2's. So, we obtain $|S_D| = |S_{D'}| \leq R(n-s, \leq s-1, t-|D|)$. Again, the second inequality follows Lemma 2. □

We mention the analogue of Lemma 5 for subsets of T that correspond to S_0 and the sets S_D. For any string $\sigma \in T$, let σ_Q be the length t restriction of σ to the positions $\{q_1, q_2, \cdots, q_t\}$; that is, $\sigma_Q = \sigma_{q_1}\sigma_{q_2}\cdots\sigma_{q_t}$. Also, let $\tau'(\sigma_Q)$ be the set of positions among

$\{q_1, q_2, \cdots, q_t\}$ at which v_Q has a 0 symbol. In a similar way, one can define sets of rows T_0 and T_E within T as follows.

(1) $T_2 = \{\sigma \in T : \sigma_Q$ has no 2 symbols$\}$.
(2) For each nonempty subset $E \subseteq \{q_1, q_2, \cdots, q_t\}$, $|E| \leq s$, let $T_E = \{\sigma \in T : \sigma_Q$ contain at least one 2 and $\tau'(\sigma_Q) = E\}$. The restriction $|E| \leq s$ is necessary since each row in A has at most s many 0's.

Again, we have $T = T_2 \cup \left(\bigcup_E T_E\right)$ as a partition of T, so $|T| = |T_2| + \sum_E |T_E|$. The corresponding upper bounds for $|T_2|$ and $|T_E|$ are given in the following lemma. We omit the proof as it is entirely analogous to the proof of Lemma 5.

Lemma 6. *The sets T_2 and T_E satisfy the following.*

(a) No two strings in T_0 and no two strings in T_E are separable in the coordinates $q_i, 1 \leq i \leq s$. So, all internal separations in T_0 and in T_E occur outside the coordinates $q_i, 1 \leq i \leq t$.
(b) $|T_2| \leq R(n-t, \leq s-1, t) \leq R(n-t, s-1, t)$
(c) $|T_E| \leq R(n-t, \leq s-|E|, \leq t-1) \leq R(n-t, s-|E|, t-1)$.

We illustrate the use of the partition method for upper bounding $R(n;3,3)$ in the following corollary.

Corollary 7. $R(n;3,3) \leq 169$.

Proof. Consider an $(n,3,3)$ array A achieving $R(n;3,3)$. We find the sets S_0, S_D (with a symmetric procedure for finding the sets T_2, T_E). Then, we use Lemma 5 and other theorems to upper bound $|S_0|$ and $|S_D|$ for each $D \subset \{p_1, p_2, p_3\}$, $|D| \leq 2$. From this, we obtain a bound for S and, using Lemma 6, a symmetric bound on T. Finally, using $|A| \leq 1 + |S| + |T|$, we obtain our bound for $R(n;3,3)$.

Again, we take π to a row of an $(n,3,3)$ array A, with its three 0's in coordinates $p_1 < p_2 < p_3$ and its three 2's in coordinates $q_1 < q_2 < q_3$. We describe the sets of rows in S_0 or S_D by specifying for each row σ in such a set its length 3 restriction σ_P to p_1, p_2, p_3. Then, we upper bound S_0 and S_D using the preceding lemmas and additional results already given. The justification for these bounds are given after the list of sets S_0 and S_D.

1. $S_0 = \{\sigma \in S : \sigma_P \in \{222, 221, 212, 122, 211, 121, 112\}\}$, $|S_0| \leq R(n-3, 3, \leq 2) \leq 39$.
2. $D_1 = \{p_1, p_2\}$, $S_{D_1} = \{\sigma \in S : \sigma_P = \{220\}\}$, $|S_{D_1}| \leq R(n-3, 2, 1) \leq 5$.
3. $D_2 = \{p_1, p_3\}$, $S_{D_2} = \{\sigma \in S : \sigma_P = \{202\}\}$, $|S_{D_2}| \leq R(n-3, 2, 1) \leq 5$.
4. $D_3 = \{p_2, p_3\}$, $S_{D_3} = \{\sigma \in S : \sigma_P = \{022\}\}$, $|S_{D_3}| \leq R(n-3, 2, 1) \leq 5$.
5. $D_4 = \{p_1\}$, $S_{D_4} = \{\sigma \in S : \sigma_P = \{201, 210, 200\}\}$, $|S_{D_4}| \leq R(n-3, 2, 2) \leq 10$.
6. $D_5 = \{p_2\}$, $S_{D_5} = \{\sigma \in S : \sigma_P = \{021, 120, 020\}\}$, $|S_{D_5}| \leq R(n-3, 2, 2) \leq 10$.
7. $D_6 = \{p_3\}$, $S_{D_6} = \{\sigma \in S : \sigma_P = \{012, 102, 002\}\}$, $|S_{D_6}| \leq R(n-3, 2, 2) \leq 10$.

The bound for S_0 in item 1 comes from Theorem 9, for S_{D_i} in items 2–4 from Theorem 8, and in items 5–7 from Corollary 4. We obtain $|S| = |S_0| + \sum_D |S_D| = 84$ by symmetry $|T| = 84$ using sets T_2 and T_E, as in Lemma 6. Finally, we have $R(n;3,3) = |A| \leq 1 + |S| + |T| \leq 169$. □

Note that from Lemma 1, we then have $P(d+3, d) \leq 169$, an improvement over the previous bound $P(d+3, d) \leq 2^6(6!) = 46{,}080$, cited in Theorem 1. This bound is also an improvement on the bound $P(d+3, d) \leq \binom{12}{6} = 924$ in Corollary 5 derived from the theorem of Bollobás.

The partition technique shown in the above example is generalized in the next two theorems.

Theorem 10. *For all $k \geq 3$, $R(n;k,k) \leq 1 + 2\sum_{i=0}^{k-1}\binom{k}{i} \cdot R(n-k;k-1,k-i)$.*

Proof. Let A be an (n,k,k) array realizing $R(n;k,k)$ and let π be a row of A. As usual, we take π to have 0's in positions $p_1, p_2, \ldots, p_k$ and 2's in positions $q_1, q_2, \ldots, q_k$. We continue with the notation S, T, S_0, S_D, T_0, T_E from the two lemmas preceding this theorem and we take $s = t = k$ in those lemmas. In particular, we have $|A| = 1 + |S| + |T|$, and we now proceed to estimate $|S|$, the estimate for $|T|$ being identical by symmetry.

By Lemma 5, we have $S_0 \leq R(n-k;k,k-1)$.

For each subset $D \subseteq \{p_1, p_2, \cdots, p_k\}$, we have by Lemma 5 that $|S_D| \leq R(n-k,k-1,k-|D|)$. If $|D| = i$, there are $\binom{k}{i}$ such D's. Since $|S| = |S_0| + \sum_D |S_D|$, we obtain

$$|S| \leq R(n-k;k,k-1) + \sum_{i=1}^{k-1}\binom{k}{i} \cdot R(n-k;\leq k-1,k-i), so \tag{8}$$

$$|S| \leq \sum_{i=0}^{k-1}\binom{k}{i} \cdot R(n-k;\leq k-1,k-i), \tag{9}$$

We have the same bound for T based on Lemma 6 and $|T| = |T_0| + \sum_E |T_E|$. Since $|A| = 1 + |S| + |T|$, we then obtain

$$R(n;k,k) \leq 1 + 2\sum_{i=0}^{k-1}\binom{k}{i} \cdot R(n-k;\leq k-1,k-i). \tag{10}$$

By Lemma 2 and Equation (4), the theorem follows. □

Theorem 11. *For all $t > s \geq 2$,*
$R(n;s,t) \leq 1 + R(n-s;s,t-1) + R(n-t;s-1,t) + \sum_{i=1}^{s-1}\binom{s}{i} \cdot R(n-s;s-1,t-i) + \sum_{i=1}^{s}\binom{t}{i} \cdot R(n-t;s-i,t-1)$.

Proof. We continue with the notation of Theorem 10 and the Lemmas that precede it.

Using exactly the same reasoning as in Theorem 10, we obtain

$$|S| \leq R(n-s;s,t-1) + \textstyle\sum_{i=1}^{s-1}\binom{s}{i} \cdot R(n-s;s-1,t-i).$$

The estimate for T is very similar, except for a restriction on the sizes of sets E defining the sets T_E.

By Lemma 6, we have $T_2 \leq R(n-t,s-1,t)$. By the same lemma, we have that for any $E \subset \{q_1, q_2, \cdots, q_t\}$ with the size restriction $|E| \leq s$, we have $|T_E| \leq R(n-t,s-|E|,t-1)$. Since there are $\binom{t}{i}$, $1 \leq i \leq s$ choices for the set E, we obtain

$$|T| \leq R(n-t;s-1,t) + \sum_{i=1}^{s}\binom{t}{i} \cdot R(n-t;s-i,t-1). \tag{11}$$

Finally, the theorem follows from Equations (11) and the preceding bound for $|S|$. □

We now calculate some values from the above recurrences.

Corollary 8. $R(n;3,4) \leq 605, R(n;4,4) \leq 3087, R(n;3,5) \leq 1,669, R(n;4,5) \leq 12,327,$ *and* $R(n;5,5) \leq 69,435$.

Proof. We denote $R(n;s,t)$ by $R(s,t)$ for short (using monotonicity of $R(n;s,t)$ in n). Then, the bounds in Theorems 10 and 11 can be written as

$$R(k,k) \leq 1+2\sum_{i=0}^{k-1}\binom{k}{i}\cdot R(k-1,k-i)$$

$$R(s,t) \leq 1+\sum_{i=0}^{s-1}\binom{s}{i}\cdot R(s-1,t-i)+\sum_{i=0}^{s}\binom{t}{i}\cdot R(s-i,t-1)$$

$$= 1+(s+t)R(s-1,t-1)+\sum_{1\neq i=0}^{s-1}\binom{s}{i}\cdot R(s-1,t-i)+\sum_{1\neq i=0}^{s}\binom{t}{i}\cdot R(s-i,t-1).$$

For starting values in these recurrences, we use Theorem 9 for $R(2,3) \leq 39$ and $R(2,4) \leq 86$, Corollary 7 for $R(3,3) \leq 169$, Theorem 8 for $R(3,1) = 7$, Corollary 4 for $R(2,2) = 10$, and $R(0,k) = 1$ for all k. Now, applying the recurrences, we obtain the following values.

1. $R(3,4) \leq 1+7R(2,3)+R(2,4)+3R(2,2)+R(3,3)+6R(1,3)+4R(0,3)$ $\leq 1+7\cdot 39+86+3\cdot 10+169+6\cdot 7+4\cdot 1 = 605$.
2. $R(4,4) \leq 1+2(R(3,4)+4R(3,3)+6R(3,2)+4R(3,1)) \leq 1+2(605+4\cdot 169+6\cdot 39+4\cdot 7) = 3087$.
3. $R(3,5) \leq 1+8R(2,4)+R(2,5)+3R(2,3)+R(3,4)+10R(1,4)+10R(0,4)$ $\leq 1+8\cdot 86+158+3\cdot 39+605+10\cdot 9+10 = 1669$.
4. $R(4,5) \leq 1+9R(3,4)+(R(3,5)+6R(3,3)+4R(3,2))+(R(4,4)+10R(2,4)+10R(1,4)+5R(0,4)) \leq 1+9\cdot 605+1669+6\cdot 169+4\cdot 39+3087+10\cdot 86+10\cdot 9+5$ = 12,327.
5. $R(5,5) \leq 1+2(R(4,5)+5R(4,4)+10R(4,3)+10R(4,2)+5R(4,1)) \leq 1+2(12327+5\cdot 3087+10\cdot 605+10\cdot 86+5\cdot 9)$ = 69,435.

□

By Lemma 1, we have $P(n,n-4) \leq 3087$, so in the notation of Theorem 1, we have $c_4 \leq 3087$. This is an improvement over that given in inequality (1), namely, $c_4 \leq 2^8(8!) = 10,321,920$. It is also an improvement on the bound $P(n,n-4) \leq \binom{16}{8} = 12,870$ derived from Corollary 5 based on the reduction from the theorem of Bollobás. The latter bound is still best though for large r.

Similarly, from the bound $R(5,5) \leq$ 69,435, we obtain $c_5 \leq$ 69,435. This improves considerably the bound $c_5 \leq 2^{10}(10!)$, which is roughly 3.6×10^9.

A rough upper bound for $R(k,k)$ obtained by applying the positions technique is $R(k,k) \leq k^{k-1}\left(\frac{e}{2}\right)^k$. Since $c_k \leq R(k,k)$ (for n large enough), this is also a considerable improvement on the bound for c_k from inequality (1). The positions and partition techniques give good bounds for $R(k,k)$ (and, hence, c_k) for moderately large k, but, still, the best such bounds so far for large k come from Corollary 5.

Author Contributions: Conceptualization, S.B., Z.M. and I.H.S.; methodology, S.B., Z.M. and I.H.S.; validation, S.B., Z.M. and I.H.S.; formal analysis, S.B., Z.M. and I.H.S.; investigation, S.B., Z.M. and I.H.S.; resources, S.B., Z.M. and I.H.S.; writing—original draft preparation, S.B., Z.M. and I.H.S.; writing—review and editing, S.B., Z.M. and I.H.S.; visualization, S.B., Z.M. and I.H.S. Each author contributed equally. All authors have read and agreed to the published version of the manuscript.

Funding: This research received no external funding.

Institutional Review Board Statement: Not applicable.

Data Availability Statement: The original contributions presented in this study are included in the article. Further inquiries can be directed to the corresponding author.

Conflicts of Interest: The authors declare no conflicts of interest.

References

1. Bereg, S.; Haghpanah, M.; Malouf, B.; Sudborough, I.H. Improved bounds for permutation arrays under Chebyshev distance *Des. Codes Cryptogr.* **2024**, *92*, 1023–1039. [CrossRef]
2. Kløve, T.; Lin, T.-T.; Tsai, S.-C.; Tzeng, W.-G. Permutation arrays under the Chebyshev distance. *IEEE Trans. Inform. Theory* **2010**, *56*, 2611–2617. [CrossRef]
3. Bereg, S.; Levy, A.; Sudborough, I.H. Constructing permutation arrays from groups. *Des. Codes Cryptogr.* **2018**, *86*, 1095–1111. [CrossRef]
4. Bereg, S.; Miller, Z.; Mojica, L.G.; Morales, L.; Sudborough, I.H. New lower bounds for permutation arrays using contraction. *Des. Codes Cryptogr.* **2019**, *87*, 2105–2128. [CrossRef]
5. Chu, W.; Colbourn, C.J.; Dukes, P. Constructions for permutation codes in powerline communications. *Des. Codes Cryptogr.* **2004**, *32*, 51–64. [CrossRef]
6. Jiang, A.; Schwartz, M.; Bruck, J. Correcting charge-constrained errors in the rank-modulation scheme. *IEEE Trans. Inform. Theory* **2010**, *56*, 2112–2120. [CrossRef]
7. Buzaglo, S.; Etzion, T. Bounds on the size of permutation codes with the Kendall τ-metric. *IEEE Trans. Inform. Theory* **2015**, *61*, 3241–3250. [CrossRef]
8. Deza, M. M.; Huang, T. Metrics on permutations, a survey. *J. Comb. Inf. Syst. Sci.* **1998**, *23*, 173–185.
9. Jiang, A.; Mateescu, R.; Schwartz, M.; Bruck, J. Rank modulation for flash memories. *IEEE Trans. Inf. Theory* **2009**, *55*, 2659–2673. [CrossRef]
10. Gilbert, E.N. A comparison of signalling alphabets. *Bell Labs Tech. J.* **1952**, *31*, 504–522. [CrossRef]
11. Varshamov, R.R. Estimate of the number of signals in error correcting codes. *Dokl. Akad. Nauk SSSR* **1957**, *117*, 739–741.
12. Arasu, K.T.; Hollon, J.R. Group developed weighing matrices. *Aust. J. Comb.* **2013**, *14*, 205–233.
13. Horadam, K. *Hadamard Matrices and Their Applications*; Princeton University Press: Princeton, NJ, USA, 2007.
14. Arasu, K.T.; Ma S.L. Some new results on circulant weighing matrices. *J. Algebr. Comb.* **2001**, *14*, 91–101. [CrossRef]
15. Bollobás, B. *Combinatorics: Set Systems, Hypergraphs, Families of Vectors and Combinatorial Probability*; Cambridge University Press: Cambridge, UK, 1986.
16. Bollobás, B. On generalized graphs. *Acta Math. Acad. Sci. Hungar.* **1965**, *16*, 447–452. [CrossRef]

MDPI AG
Grosspeteranlage 5
4052 Basel
Switzerland
Tel.: +41 61 683 77 34

Entropy Editorial Office
E-mail: entropy@mdpi.com
www.mdpi.com/journal/entropy

www.ingramcontent.com/pod-product-compliance
Lightning Source LLC
Chambersburg PA
CBHW061444210926
51850CB00008B/1605
9783725862160